FASHION AND EROTICISM

FASHION AND EROTICISM

Ideals of Feminine Beauty from the
Victorian Era to the Jazz Age

VALERIE STEELE

New York   Oxford
OXFORD UNIVERSITY PRESS
1985

Oxford University Press

Oxford   London   New York   Toronto
Delhi   Bombay   Calcutta   Madras   Karachi
Kuala Lumpur   Singapore   Hong Kong   Tokyo
Nairobi   Dar es Salaam   Cape Town
Melbourne   Auckland

and associated companies in
Beirut   Berlin   Ibadan   Mexico City   Nicosia

Copyright © 1985 Oxford University Press, Inc.
Published by Oxford University Press, Inc.,
200 Madison Avenue
New York, New York 10016

Library of Congress Cataloging in Publication Data

Steele, Valerie.
Fashion and eroticism.

Bibliography: p.
Includes index.
1. Fashion—Europe—History.   2. Fashion—United
States—History.   3. Fashion—Psychological aspects.
4. Fashion—Social aspects.   5. Sex symbolism.
I. Title.
GT720.S67   1985   391'.2'09034   84-10512
ISBN 0-19-503530-5

Printing (last digit):   9 8 7 6 5 4 3 2 1

Printed in the United States of America

for John

Acknowledgments

I am greatly indebted to many people who have generously shared their knowledge and time, and offered thoughtful and stimulating insights into the meanings of fashion. This work owes much to the influence and inspiration of my teachers at Yale, especially my thesis advisor, Professor Peter Gay, who has read hundreds of pages on "Fashion and Eroticism" since 1979. I would also like to thank Professors Jules Prown, Robert Herbert, and Nancy Cott; as well as Professor John Brewer (now at Harvard), and Dr. Robert Harding. Judy Coffin offered the original inspiration for my subject when she gave a presentation at Yale on the possible significance of the Victorian corset. Two years later, she provided the pleasantest possible introduction to historical research in Paris. Mark Micale read and commented on several chapters; Anne Higonnet, Anne Schirmeister, and Mary Lee Townsend also offered bibliographical information, assistance, and encouragement. Although this work has benefited greatly from their knowledge of Victorian sexuality, psychoanalysis, women's history, and the analysis of material culture and visual imagery, none of them are responsible for my conclusions (some of which they may not agree with), or for any errors I might have made.

Writing is painful, but the research that accompanied it was almost invariably a delight, not least because it enabled me to make the acquaintance of so many interesting and charming individuals in the United States, Great Britain, France, and the Far East. Moving in geographical and roughly chronological order, I would like to begin by thanking the staff of The Costume Institute at The Metropolitan Museum of Art, especially Stella Blum (then Curator), Jean Druesedow, Assistant Curator, and Gordon Stone, Librarian. The late Herbert Callister, of The Wadsworth Atheneum, also showed me some of my first Victorian dresses, which he patiently explained. The staff of the Fashion Institute of Technology—and especially the librarians—smoothed my path at every turn.

My grateful thanks to Laura Sinderbrand, Director of the Edward C. Blum Design Laboratory, and Harold Koda, Associate Curator, for arranging for me to see Poiret dresses and Edwardian tea-gowns. Many thanks to Lillian Clagett of the Cooper-Hewitt Museum, and to the staffs of The Brooklyn Museum Art Reference Library, The New York City Public Library, and The Library of Congress. Also to many individuals in The Costume Society of America, among them Elizabeth Ann Coleman of The Brooklyn Museum and Margaret Spicer of Dartmouth College. Michael Ermarth read the first part of the manuscript, vastly improving it. Dr. Peter Whybrow of the Dartmouth Medical School loaned me a rare copy of *The Family Doctor.* I would also like to express my appreciation to Mrs. Gail Patten for typing part of the text and most of the bibliography. I am profoundly indebted to Helene Roberts for stimulating me to think seriously about clothes, even when we sometimes disagreed in our interpretations.

In Great Britain, I would especially like to thank Jane Tozer, Keeper, and Miss Sarah Levitt at The Gallery of English Costume, Platt Hall, who made every visit to Manchester as pleasant as it was informative, with discussions of fashion theory interspersed with viewing tea-gowns, corsets, and lingerie. Anthea Jarvis, Assistant Keeper of Decorative Arts of the Merseyside County Museums, showed me dozens of rare early twentieth-century dresses. Penelope Byrde, Keeper of Costume, The Museum of Costume, Bath, and her associates there and at The Costume and Fashion Research Centre, arranged for me to see many items of dress and material in the Library. Annette Carruthers, Assistant Keeper of Decorative Arts of The Leicestershire Museum and Art Gallery, took the trouble to show me hundreds of items of corset literature, and provided a valuable service to all fashion historians with her exhibition of period corsetry. Many thanks also to Jacqueline Bailey, Librarian of The Liverpool Polytechnic Art Library, and the librarians of The British Library (including The Colindale Newspaper Library), The National Art Library of The Victoria and Albert Museum, and The Cambridge University Library—especially everyone in the West Room. Grateful acknowledgments to David Doughan, Assistant at The Fawcett Library (women's history); Murial Ross, Chief Librarian at The London College of Fashion; and Susanna van Langenberg, Library and Syndication Manager at The National Magazine Company Limited, all of whom provided valuable assistance.

Special thanks are due to Mr. Peter Farrer of Liverpool, for generously sharing his extensive bibliographic knowledge and private library. Thanks also to Miss Cleo Witt, Mrs. Judy Tregidden, Mrs. Doris Langley Moore, and many other members of The Costume Society for their encouragement and excellent suggestions, and for inviting me to give a paper at The Costume Society's 1984 Symposium on "The Meaning of Dress," thus allowing me to test some of my ideas in front of a very knowledgeable audience. Mr. John Gibson permitted me to see and photograph his collection of fashion and corset memorabilia. Friends at Cambridge University offered intelligent criticism and ideas about medical history. Thanks especially to Dr. Toril Moi for obtaining information for me at The Bodleian Library, Oxford. Thanks also to the President and members of Clare Hall for their hospitality that made our year in residence at Cambridge so pleasant. Three individuals in particular offered unique personal insights into the fashions of the early twentieth century. My deepest thanks to Mrs. D., Mrs. I., and Lady Naomi Mitchison, for consenting to be interviewed.

In France, I would especially like to thank Madame Fabienne Falluel, Conservateur of the Musée de la Mode et du Costume, for her many kindnesses, and for arranging for me to visit the offices of *Le Corset de France*. My thanks there to Madame Bonhomme. Although the Bibliothèque Nationale has an intimidating reputation, I found only cordial assistance there. I also enjoyed working at the delightful Library of the Musée des Arts Décoratifs and at the Bibliothèque Forney. Although I was never able to gain admittance to the Centre d'Enseignement et de Documentation du Costume (Union Française des Arts du Costume), I would like to thank Lord and Lady V., for trying to help me do so.

In Japan, I would like to thank Mr. Koichi Tsukamoto, President of The Kyoto Costume Institute, and the Director, Atsuo Ohtomo, for permitting me to see the collection on short notice. My thanks also to Miss Atsuko Miyoshi, who took the trouble to show me virtually everything, from hats and corsets to Poiret and Fortuny dresses. To Midori Ogawa and her family, a special thanks for their hospitality, and for helping me learn to tie an obi. Thanks to friends and acquaintances in The People's Republic of China, Indonesia, India, Yemen, Bahrain, and Morocco, for sharing their knowledge of their own costume traditions, without which this study of western fashion would have been immeasurably impoverished.

Returning to America, I would like to thank my friends and colleagues at The Smithsonian Institution, especially those associated with the Division of Costume: Claudia Kidwell, Fath Ruffins, Carol Kregloh, Shelly Foote, Barbara Dickstein, Karen Harris, Laurice Stewart, and Brenda Moore. Mrs. Kregloh and I debated the "leg" versus "limb" question; and Mrs. Kidwell's analysis of men's clothing influenced my interpretation of fashion and gender roles. Thanks also to Dr. Laurence Angel, for a provocative discussion about corsets and bone disease.

Thanks to my family for all of their support, from baby-sitting to photocopying several entire books at The Library of Congress. And thanks to all of my fashionable friends, especially Jane Barry, Suzie Cahill, Jo Covey, Mary Doering, Susan Hewitt, Mary Scattergood, and Hallie Gay Walden.

I would like to thank my editors at Oxford University Press, Nancy Lane and Rosemary Wellner, for their encouragement and meticulous work on the manuscript. Victoria Wong's design was also everything an author could hope for.

Most of all, I would like to thank my husband, John Major, to whom this book is dedicated. He took hundreds of photographs, read and discussed all of the text in each of its successive incarnations, and typed most of it onto the computer. Although I might have been able to finish the book without his help, it would certainly not have been done so soon, so well, or with so little pain and so many happy moments.

Grateful acknowledgments for permission to reproduce photographs are made to the Louvre; The Tate Gallery; The National Gallery, London; The Art Institute of Chicago; The Gallery of English Costume; The Liverpool Polytechnic Art Library; The Kyoto Costume Institute; The Metropolitan Museum of Art; the Philadelphia Civic Center Museum; Dover Publications; Condé Nast Publications; The Victoria and Albert Museum; the Musée des Arts Décoratifs; the Hamburger Kunsthalle; and The Sterling and Francine Clark Art Institute.

New York   V. S.
November 1984

Contents

Illustrations and Their Sources

Grateful acknowledgments for permission to reproduce illustrations are made to the museums and other institutions listed below. In cases where a source is not given, the illustration is privately owned.

FASHION AND EROTICISM

Introduction

The image of the Victorian woman has long been that of a person both sexually repressed and socially oppressed. Her clothing has been interpreted as an outward manifestation of her ambivalent psychology and subordinate position in society. Indeed, fashion is thought to have played an active and invidious part in defining the female role. The notorious corset controversy in *The Englishwoman's Domestic Magazine* continues to be quoted as evidence that the Victorian woman suffered torture to look beautiful and respectable. She was strait-laced and dressed to kill—squeezed into an enticingly tight corset, veiled in a prudishly long skirt, and covered with a wealth of irrational ornaments. Even recent reassessments of the Victorian period have tended to leave these cliches unexamined. Similarly, the eventual disappearance of Victorian fashion has been attributed to the late nineteenth-century movement for women's rights, or alternatively to the social and sexual dislocations caused by the First World War. But the evidence does not support these conclusions.

The conventional understanding of Victorian fashion needs to be radically revised. Not only does the meaning of fashion come into question, but the sartorial evidence has implications far beyond the study of fashion per se. Victorian fashion revolved around an ideal of feminine beauty in which eroticism played an important part. In this respect, there is more continuity than contrast between the nineteenth and twentieth centuries. *Eros* was present in the most "respectable" Victorian conventions of dress, although the sartorial expression of female sexuality was relatively more acceptable in certain contexts. For example, dress appropriate for a private social gathering of one's peers was more overtly erotic than that worn on the street. This interpretation of fashion and eroticism in the Victorian era should contribute to our increasingly complicated and subtle picture of Victorian sexuality. If, as I believe, the Victorians were far

Ball Dress and Walking Dress. Fashion plate (ca. 1830) for *Cotton's Athenaeum.*

less "prudish" or anti-sexual than we had thought, then the significance of erotic dress for Victorian women also needs to be reconsidered.

Victorian fashion expressed neither the social and sexual repression of women nor male perceptions of them as primarily sexual beings. Victorian women themselves sought to appear attractive—even sexually attractive—within the changing limits of the socially acceptable. I believe that this emulation of an ideal of beauty should be seen more as a personal choice or an aspect of women's self-development than as a part of their oppression as "sex objects." Obviously, to some extent, the desire to look "beautiful" was a product of the Victorian woman's socialization, and she had relatively little choice other than to make a "profession" of being pleasing and attractive to men. Yet the current trends in women's history have increasingly and, I think, accurately, emphasized women's relative independence and their interaction with the wider society, rather than their passivity. Certainly the nineteenth-century literature indicates that men tended to be more or less *opposed* to (instead of initiating or encouraging) women's "egotistical" interest in fashion and "artificial" beauty.

The so-called "revolt against fashion" also needs to be reevaluated. Most historians have tacitly accepted the dress reformers' line—that orthodox Victorian fashion was unnatural and unhealthy, and that women's emancipation went hand-in-hand with the progressive reform of women's dress. Yet neither statement is accurate. The women's movement in the nineteenth and early twentieth centuries was often hostile to sexual expression. Many modern feminists have also perceived erotic dress and the pursuit of beauty as antithetical to women's rights. Consequently, liberal historians have remained oblivious to the prejudices, exaggerations, and contradictions inherent in the dress reform literature, which is not so much "feminist" (indeed it is often antifeminist) as it is an expression of puritanism, and specifically of the movement for "social purity." While recognizing the biases behind the medical diatribes against masturbation, alcohol, and the dangers of female education and exercise, historians have been predisposed to accept unquestioningly even the most confused pseudo-medical theories about the disease and debility caused by women's dress. Furthermore, they have had to distort the actual history of women's fashion by introducing a fictitious teleology. Dress reform was *not* an important influence on fashion, and indeed fashion did not *ever* develop in the direction of "rational" dress or "natural" beauty, but rather toward new versions of sexually attractive clothing.

There remains the problem of explaining when and why fashions and ideals of beauty changed: Why do women today no longer wear corsets, crinolines, and long skirts? Why do they model themselves after a very different physical ideal? The standard sociohistorical explanations are inadequate (and often inaccurate in their particulars), but the specific causes of this evolution remain somewhat opaque. All my research has led me to believe that the concept of beauty is sexual in origin, and the changing ideal of beauty apparently reflects shifting attitudes toward sexual expression. At the deepest level, the meaning of clothing in general and fashion in particular is also erotic. Symbiotic with changing ideals of erotic beauty, the evolution of fashion has an internal dynamic of its own that is only very gradually and tangentially affected by social change within the wider culture. I realize that it remains somewhat unsatisfactory to say that "fashion did it," but I am reluctant to engage in extended speculation about the reasons for the relative autonomy of fashion. Fashion is not a power unto itself, but the principal dynamic of fashion is an internal one. World historical events and subsequent changes in popular attitudes might appear to precipitate dramatic changes in fashion—such as the emergence of the Empire style and the Twenties style—but closer investigation will reveal that the roots of the change in fashion *precede* the great event—be it the French Revolution or the First World War. Wars and revolutions might help to explain the wider and more rapid acceptance of new fashions, but they do not usually engender them.

It is clear, however, that the "modern" style of feminine dress appeared in the years between 1907 and 1913—that is, the crucial period of fashion change occurred *before* the First World War. Furthermore, the new style of dress (and related body type) evolved from *within* the world of high fashion. Although the new look was closely associated with the French designer Paul Poiret, it was neither an ideological nor a one-man rebellion against earlier Victorian styles. Rather, by 1903 the world of haute couture showed a definite trend toward an "empire" style. The pre-World War I emergence of the "New Look" indicates how the *erotic* element in the Victorian ideal of beauty developed and changed.

We can, to some extent, identify successive types of ideal beauty: the pretty and sylph-like Early Victorian woman, the voluptuous Mid-Victorian woman, the statuesque "Gibson Girl" type, and the slender Poiret "flapper." Why the erotic ideal underwent these transformations is difficult to determine; but it is naive and culture-bound to assume that women were progressing toward a "natural" ideal. Rather, there was an increasing affirmation of the differences between the sexes, followed (in the early twentieth century) by a relative decrease in emphasis on the relationship between female beauty and maternity.

The time span covered in this book is roughly 1820 through the 1920s, with the focus on the period between about 1860 to the First World War. It witnesses a gradual evolution of attitudes toward eroticism in dress and the image of the ideal feminine beauty. Initially, I studied the period from 1868 to 1888—the so-called High Victorian period, which was characterized by back-fullness of dress.[1] I discovered that attitudes toward dress were far less "Victorian" than historians have believed. It is possible that the Early to Mid-Victorian period was more "prudish" than the High to Late Victorian periods, but on moving backward in time, I found little evidence of this. The years from about 1890 on saw the gradual development of attitudes into those popularly regarded as "Edwardian." This period was itself evolving into something else between about 1902 and 1908. I could have stopped any time between 1908 and 1914, when the new, modern style of dress and appearance came into being; but I wanted to explore, if only briefly, the fashions of the war years and the Twenties, since historians have consistently misinterpreted their significance. The year 1928 is the closing date, only because the fashion took a somewhat different direction in 1929, more characteristic of the Thirties.

The countries studied are primarily England and France, to a lesser extent the United States, and, occasionally, Germany. This was a deliberate choice, since most of the work done on women's history and sexuality has focused on Anglo-American developments, but women's fashion was really set in Paris. A particular new fashion cannot logically be said to "reflect" developments within English society (such as the movement for women's rights) or particularly English social attitudes, if, in fact,

English women copied it from a French model. The term "Victorian," which originally applied to England between 1837 and 1901, has been extended to France and the United States, on the grounds that, for all their differences, they shared similar general experiences and formed a loose trans-Atlantic community. Naturally there were important differences between the lives of Boston ladies, Lancashire mill-girls, and Parisian *bourgeoises*, and I have tried to point out differences in attitudes (with respect both to time and place) toward dress and beauty.

French dominance in women's fashion dates from the seventeenth century, when France was the most powerful European state and the French court the most prestigious. The early and continuous development of an institutional structure for the creation and dissemination of new modes meant that even after France was no longer pre-eminent politically, it continued to be the fashion capital of the western world at least into the 1960s. The importance of the fashion industry for the French economy probably also contributed to the more positive attitude in France toward fashion. The sense of *chic* in France (acknowledged by everyone, and evident today in costume collections) probably also stemmed from widespread familiarity with the vocabulary of fashion. Conversely, English hostility toward things French may have played a role in their greater reservations about new fashion—designed, as the English were fond of saying, by Frenchmen for the Parisian demi-monde. Americans also tended to be nationalistic in their discussions of dress.

For although the French, English, and Americans wore essentially the same fashions, the French looked more fashionable. Furthermore, they differed (at least in degree) in the attitudes they held about novelty and conformity, sartorial eroticism, and the morality of artificial adjuncts to beauty. Yet, considering the differences between art, architecture, music, and literature in France, England, and America, their relative homogeneity with regard to fashion is surprising. Indeed, the absence of national boundaries in fashion is evident in the existence of the German periodical, *Die Modenwelt*, which published a dozen different national editions—using the same fashion plates.[2]

Because fashion is primarily an urban and an upper- and middle-class phenomenon, I have only touched on the question of working-class dress and have ignored the separate issue of rural costume. All the evidence indicates that fashion was set by aristocratic and upper-class women and by expensive courtesans; it was followed by middle- and even working-class women, to the extent that they could afford to. The degree of eroticism in fashion was not closely correlated to the class of the wearer. Historical accounts of the relationship between class status and sexual attitudes have often tended to rely on old clichés, or else to reflect the historians' own class biases. I have found no evidence to support the recent assertion that the nineteenth-century trend toward greater "opulence" of figure represented a "lower-class model of beauty" and sexual "emancipation" that filtered upward from a "vanguard" of "working-class women." Nor did the rise of the upper-class Gibson Girl ideal represent either a reaction against "voluptuousness" (and its "retreat ... to the lower-class subculture"), or a "positive ideal of the new woman ... who had previously appeared among the working classes."[3] Significantly, this analysis largely ignores the middle-class woman; yet it was middle-class women who ratified new styles of appearance set by the upper classes.

Fashion—or the prevailing mode of dress—has been studied in terms of its relationship to culture, the socioeconomic development of society, group behavior, and individual psychology, particularly female sexual psychology. The "why of fashion" is complex and overdetermined. I have tried both to look more *on the surface*, and to look *deeper* than most previous historians of fashion. That is, my approach has been to look carefully at the clothes themselves, and at the changing ideal of beauty in fashion. At the same time, I have tried to develop an interpretive framework for an understanding of the *meaning* of clothing, both generally and within particular historical contexts. I have found the psychoanalytic theory of human sexuality to be particularly helpful in this regard.

How is the historian to "read" a dress, a hat, or a fashion plate? Although research into material culture is still in an embryonic phase, the methodology of stylistic analysis has been shown to be useful, since it deals both with the formal properties of a single artifact and with the relationships among objects.[4] The dressmaker works within a world of craft with its own traditions and possibilities for change. Whether or not a particular innovation is accepted or rejected depends on a number of factors, such as the history of dress within a given culture, the situational context, and the social institutions through which new ideas and styles may spread. In practice, formal analysis must be supplemented by documentary information. Who wears what, when, and where? But to interpret what the object is "saying" remains problematical. Clothing has often been used to send out false messages, and the messages may be read differently by different observers. According to most semioticians, the equations drawn between signs and their meanings are essentially inexplicable or arbitrary. How is it then that styles or elements of dress become associated with certain concepts or acquire particular connotations? Philippe Perrot has concluded that *differences* produce meaning—for example, the differences between the sexes, classes, occasions, and periods of time. Yet the meanings associated with sartorial signs are probably not entirely divorced from their historical context.[5]

Dress (clothing) is common to most cultures, some form of bodily adornment (ornament) apparently to all; but fashion is generally considered to be a specific historical and geographical phenomenon that first appeared in Europe in about the fourteenth century. Fashion is defined as a distinct sub-category of dress that differs from the traditional *costumes* of non-western and pre-modern cultures and from European folk costumes in that it is characterized by a sequence of relatively rapid changes in style. The expressions "in fashion" and "outmoded" indicate the association of fashion with a regular pattern of style change.[6]

Fashion-oriented behavior seems to be almost universal, but the appearance of fashion (as opposed to costume) is almost certainly related to the development of a modern class society. This distinction between costume and fashion is basically valid, although historians of the great cultures of the Orient and of ancient and early-medieval Europe have demonstrated that costumes were by no means static in appearance. Nevertheless, changes tended to be either relatively subtle variations or else incorporations of aspects of other costumes, and not part of a pattern of changes in form. Elite costume tended to be characterized by richness, rather than novelty (although other aspects of appearance, such as hair styles and color combinations, sometimes fluctuated in a way that we would define as "fashionable"). In addition, to the extent that something approaching fashion existed, it was restricted to narrow and sophisticated circles, often associated with court culture.[7] Initially, European fashion was also part of a pattern of competition and emulation within the feudal elite.

The subsequent evolution and expansion of fashion reflected the social and economic development of European society, and particularly nineteenth-century bourgeois society. A fairly advanced stage of capitalism was a prerequisite for the development of haute couture and ready-made clothing. But fashion is not only a class-related phenomenon. It became associated primarily with women, since, in the course of the eighteenth and nineteenth centuries, men seemed to have renounced fashion in favor of a drab uniform, while women's fashion seemed to change more rapidly and dramatically, and to be adopted by increasing numbers of women of all classes. Partly because of the striking nature of this phenomenon, the dominant theories of fashion have focused on women's fashions of the Victorian period, ignoring earlier, flamboyant male fashions.

Ideally, however, a theory of dress should be flexible enough to be valid as an explanation of clothing for men as well as women, in non-western and traditional cultures as well as in the modern European world, without being so general as to be unhelpful in the study of specific cases. In Chapter 1, "The Fig Leaf," I review the most important theories of dress and fashion, and try to determine to what extent they contain valid observations and reasoning (or are, at least, unintentionally revealing), and to what extent they are facile, illogical, and misleading. Although I am not trying to "debunk" anyone, I do think that the history of fashion has been seriously hampered by faulty methodology and the lack of a coherent theoretical framework.

Because clothing is so intimately associated with the physical body, at the deepest level all clothing is erotic. Obviously this insight can be applied reductively, and most earlier attempts to use psychoanalysis to interpret the meaning of dress have been unsatisfactory. The idea that fashion is essentially sexual is not new, and I am not in the camp of the

Sex Appeal theorists, many of whose ideas strike me as being crude, inaccurate, and biased in their focus on female sartorial eroticism and female sexual psychology. Nevertheless, and contrary to popular belief, I think that orthodox Freudian theory is not necessarily anti-feminist, and it has undeniably revolutionized our understanding of human sexuality and the unconscious. Chapter 2, "Fashion and Eroticism," deals with psychoanalytic interpretations of fashion. Chapter 3, my proposal for a new theory of fashion, has been heavily influenced by psychoanalysis. However, such concepts as "pathological exhibitionism," to say nothing of "female narcissism," are of far less importance than the attraction of concealment and the erotic origin of the concept of "beauty." I conclude the first part, "The Why of Fashion," by making an argument about the meaning of fashion itself.

With the second part, "Fashion and Erotic Beauty in the Victorian Period," I turn from the strictly theoretical to the main body of historical analysis. Chapter 4, "Victorian Fashion," is a description of the articles of clothing and basic trends in nineteenth-century fashion. Chapter 5, "Victorian Sexuality," reviews and criticizes the current interpretations of Victorian fashion—interpretations that are based on questionable assumptions about Victorian women and about sexuality in the Victorian period. In Chapter 6, "The Victorian Ideal of Feminine Beauty," and Chapter 7, "Artificial Beauty," I construct a new interpretation by investigating what the Victorians themselves thought about beauty and fashion. Although there existed a range of attitudes toward sartorial sexual expression, by and large, women did want to project an attractive image. Chapter 8, "The Revolt Against Fashion," stresses that dress reform was not successful, in large part because women perceived it as sexually unattractive.

The third part deals with what are literally "The Foundations of Fashion," and probably the main focus of eroticism in fashion. Chapter 9, "The Corset Controversy," analyzes the single most notorious item of Victorian dress. Chapter 10, "The Attractions of Underclothes," surveys why people found clothing such as petticoats, nightgowns, and underpants erotic.

The forth part, "Into the Twentieth Century," covers the changing ideal of feminine beauty from about 1900 to 1928. In terms of body type, the "superb" and often Junoesque physical proportions of the Edwardian matron gave way to the slender and youthful "Poiret figure"—the predecessor of the Twenties' flapper. Edwardian fashion, while clearly deriving from Victorian dress, was epitomized by "The Cult of Chiffon," and the "new religion" of dedication to erotic beauty. It was from within this milieu, with its acceptance of artifice and sexual attractiveness, that modern fashion and the modern beauty industry developed. The "Conclusion" emphasizes that the seeds of more recent "sexy" beauty and fashions were present in the Victorian period, and it touches on the continuing controversy about the relationship between fashion, feminism, and femininity. What does fashion say about women's changing roles, and why do so many people remain hostile to the very idea of "fashion"?

The Why of Fashion

1

The Fig Leaf: Explanations of Clothing and Fashion

Sexual Modesty

The image of the fig leaf immediately conjures up one explanation for clothes—sexual modesty. When Adam and Eve ate the fruit of the tree of knowledge of good and evil, "the eyes of both were opened, and they knew that they were naked; and they sewed fig leaves together and made themselves aprons." Then, before driving them from the Garden of Eden, "the Lord God made for Adam and for his wife garments, and clothed them." Having sinned and lost their innocence, it was necessary that they be clothed.

Saint Augustine explained that once they had experienced lust (or at least Adam had, the Saint was unsure about Eve), they became ashamed of their previously innocent nakedness, and especially ashamed of their genitals. The naked body was suddenly a sexual body. Hence arose the "lust-shame theory" of the origin and purpose of clothing, more innocuously known as the "modesty" or "decency theory," which was widely accepted for centuries in the West.[1]

Other cultures had very different myths describing the origin of dress, sometimes involving the idea that the gods themselves were clothed, or that the gods gave mankind the essential elements of culture— including the ability to make clothing. [2] Despite this evidence of a different attitude toward clothing, there also developed in these cultures definite standards of modesty in dress.

Christian doctrine, however, viewed clothing not as a desirable attribute of culture, but as a necessary evil in light of humanity's fallen state. It often equated nakedness with shame and sin, but it also stressed the potentially sensual and worldly aspects of dress and adornment. The prophet Isaiah warned that the Lord would "take away the finery" of the daughters of Zion to punish them for their pride and wantonness—"and

The Fig Leaf. Illustration by Bertall from *La Comédie de notre temps* (Paris: E. Plon et cie., 1874).

instead of a rich robe, a girding of sackcloth; instead of beauty, shame." The New Testament also admonished the religious to dress with modesty and simplicity—and here, too, the focus tended to be on the dress of women. In the first letter of Paul to Timothy, the apostle maintained that "women should adorn themselves modestly and sensibly in seemly attire, not with braided hair or gold or pearls or costly attire but by good deeds." Tertullian also argued that women ought to content themselves with "the silk of honesty, the fine linen of righteousness, and the purple of chastity."[3]

In a culture that seemed to make women embody sex (and sin), it was not surprising that women's dress and adornment were most frequently attacked as immodest and immoral. This was true even during periods when men's clothing was at least as extravagant and revealing as women's dress. Early Christian writers, such as Tertullian and Clement of Alexandria, thought that the sight of women's bodies or faces posed a temptation to sin, and that they should be concealed as much as possible. It

would be oversimplistic, however, to place all responsibility for this attitude on the Judeo-Christian (and Islamic) tradition.

Much of the emphasis on female modesty of dress was probably related
to the social value placed on female chastity—which was characteristic of
Greco-Roman and other cultures as well. The importance of female chastity may, in turn, have been related to woman's position as the "property"
of fathers or husbands. If a woman were clothed, this at least gave the
illusion that she was "pure," clothing providing not only a "defense
against strange eyes," but by extension an obstacle (albeit perhaps mostly
a symbolic one) to illegitimate possession. Yet whatever influence "male
jealousy" and female "propriety" may have had on "the custom of shroud-
ing and veiling women," they are inadequate as explanations of the origins
of female clothing, to say nothing of male clothing.[4]

Furthermore, it was recognized very early that concealment and modesty could function to arouse sexual passion; as Casanova observed, a
totally naked woman seemed without charm or mystery. Yet the theory
that dress was primarily intended to preserve modesty was cited throughout the nineteenth and early twentieth centuries. In 1854, for example,
Mrs. Merrifield defined the objects of dress as "decency and warmth." As
late as 1906, G. W. Rhead argued in *Chats on Costume* that "decency"
was the "first use of dress," followed by "comfort and protection" and
"beauty and adornment." He stressed that the importance of decency was
"sufficiently clearly established if we may accept the Mosaic account,"
and went on to quote from Genesis.[5] The implication was certainly that
adornment and beautification need not—and should not—contradict the
primary purpose of dress: the preservation of modesty and decency.

Sexual Attraction

Then, in the 1880s and 1890s, anthropologists began to suggest that their
studies of "primitive" tribes indicated that "ornament and clothing were,
in the first place, intended, not to conceal or even protect the body, but,
in large part, to render it sexually attractive . . . to accentuate, rather than
to conceal." Like body paint, tattooing, and jewelry, clothing was used to
decorate the body and draw attention to sexual characteristics. The sociologist William Graham Sumner stated flatly, "The connection of dress
with warmth and modesty is derived and remote." The ethnologist E. A.
Westermarck listed dress under the heading of "Primitive Means of
Attraction," and left no doubt that the attraction was erotic.[6]

Thus what has been called the "attraction" or "immodesty theory" of
dress began to influence interpretations of contemporary fashions. In
addition, the "protection theory" of dress was complicated by the possibility that the protection afforded by clothing was less physical than psychological, or, in terms of the cultures studied, magical.[7]

With the gradual growth of a secular world view and the development
of modern anthropology, the attraction theory of the origin and functions

The Fig Leaf. Caricature from *Courrier Français* (1888), Paris, reproduced in
Friedrich Wendel, *Weib und Mode* (Dresden: Paul Aretz Verlag, 1928).

of dress gained increasing numbers of adherents. It represented, of course,
a complete reversal of the Biblical hypothesis. Was this simply a paradox
or a difference of opinion? Not according to psychoanalysis. Apparently,
such antithetical interpretations and irreconcilable value judgments indicate an intense social interest. What appears to be a debate about the
origin and functions of clothes is really an argument about sexuality. As
Freud says, "At the root of every taboo, there must be a desire." When
desires are repressed, people feel ambivalent. What could be a more
ambivalent symbol than the fig leaf, calling attention to that which it
ostensibly hides?[8]

Clothing almost invariably consists of more than a genital covering,
however. In traditional cultures, there may be distinctions in dress
between male and female, married and unmarried, young and old, noble
and commoner, but the appearance of the clothed body remains apparently static. Fashion, on the other hand, is characterized not only by dress
distinctions, but by a recognizable pattern of style change. "Most theoretical analysis of fashion centers on the major question of what is respon-

sible for the operation of fashion."[9] What *causes* the phenomenon of fashion change? And what, if anything, do the *forms* that fashion takes mean?

The Earthly Goddess and the Follies of Fashion

For centuries people perceived the changing form of fashion as essentially inexplicable. Fashion was often personified as a deity, who periodically issued yet another capricious decree. The metaphors used to describe fashion focused on images of power and nonrationality—force, tyranny, royalty, and divinity, or "folly" and "fickleness," mystery, and deviousness. The acceptance of new modes was interpreted as the result of human nature. Critics attacked "Fashion's Slaves," but most people accepted with greater or lesser equanimity that attempts to be fashionable were "actuated by the delight in novelty and the passion for display."[10] The forms that fashion took seemed arbitrary and basically meaningless.

In the course of the nineteenth century, perceptions of fashion began to alter. The most significant contributing factor to the new perspective was the emergence of an austere and relatively static form of male dress— a kind of uniform. Since male behavior was regarded as the norm, people did not ask why men had renounced fashion, but rather why women had not. Indeed, increasing numbers of women followed fashion. The dominion of the goddess now seemed to extend over only the feminine half of humanity. The apparent feminization of fashion had important implications for the later development of theories purporting to explain both the phenomenon of fashion change and the forms of fashion. In the short run, though, disquisitions on human nature tended to become critiques of the feminine mind.

The Man-Milliner and the Parisian Demi-Monde

Another hypothesis, still popularly held, was that changes in fashion resulted from the machinations of a cabal of Parisian designers. Only women, it was implied, would be foolish enough to submit blindly to every bizarre style invented by fashion's dictators. This belief in an economic conspiracy ignores the fact that fashions changed centuries before the organizational and propagandizing institutions existed that later disseminated fashion information. Furthermore, the ability to influence consumer demand through sales promotion is limited when it goes against the prevailing trends of fashion.[11] It is not surprising, however, that this simplistic causal explanation, focusing on obvious economic motives, should gain wide credence.

Nor is the more sophisticated explanation—the primacy of economic structures—sufficient, although the gradual emergence of bourgeois-capitalist society was a precondition for the appearance and spread of fashion. In feudal Europe, sumptuary laws attempted to restrict fashion to aristocratic circles, with, however, only limited success. With the rise—over centuries—of the bourgeoisie, fashions became more widely adopted. Wealth, leisure, a particular philosophy of life, methods of production, and commercial promotion were among the factors that affected the development and spread of fashion. The institutions that constitute the fashion industry largely developed in the course of the nineteenth century, a period that also witnessed the emergence of internationally known fashion designers. The rise of the department store and the proliferation of fashion journals would have been obvious to any observer. It is also true that fashion can be manipulated, and that the fashion industry has a vested economic interest in promoting variations of style. The German economist Werner Sombart was not alone in perceiving fashion as "capitalism's favorite child."[12]

Fashion is obviously to some extent an economic issue. As the historian Fernand Braudel points out, "Costume is linked to the possibilities of the material situation. . . . The history of costume . . . touches on every issue—raw materials, production processes, manufacturing costs, cultural stability, fashion, and social hierarchy." Available technology influences clothing design and manufacture; industrialization provided the "means for producing new fashions quickly and inexpensively"; class structure affects the extent to which fashions are diffused through that society.[13] Nevertheless, even a sophisticated economic interpretation of fashion is inadequate for an understanding of why fashion changed *as it did*—why one particular style succeeded another. The majority of nineteenth-century observers, however, offered only the most naive versions of an economic interpretation of fashion.

A corollary of the conspiracy theory focused on the personal influence of certain famous or infamous women. Thus the Empress Eugenie was widely credited with the invention of the crinoline, while responsibility for every new and immodest style was attributed to Parisian courtesans. Fashion dictators supposedly instituted changes that were either senseless (except in terms of the profit motive) or deliberately immodest (to appeal to the most immoral among their clientele). Fashion was a "hoax" perpetuated by people seeking financial profit or personal notoriety. Historians today generally agree that the role of individuals in the development of fashion was relatively insignificant. Worth was more influential than the Empress Eugenie, but he was much less a dictator than a sensitive barometer of fashion trends.[14]

These explanations contain elements of truth, however. Advocates of the idea of capricious fashion change recognized that some people do enjoy novelty for its own sake, and that many people try to use clothing as a means of social and sexual display. Similarly, the emphasis on personal influence indicates (albeit in a distorted form) the importance of trend-setters in the adoption of new styles.

Sociological Explanations of Fashion

Herbert Spencer is little read today, but in his own time he was the most celebrated and popular of philosophers. Like many Victorians, he interpreted fashion primarily in terms of reverential imitation and assertive competition. Fashion in a class society reflected competition for status and the desire to demonstrate affluence and personal distinction. Thorstein Veblen also argued that competition in the demonstration of socioeconomic status was the primary moving force behind the vicissitudes of fashion. In *The Theory of the Leisure Class*, he suggested that in the transition from feudal aristocratic society to bourgeois capitalist society, the function of dress as a symbol of status underwent an important change.[15]

Whereas aristocratic male dress had been characterized by features designed to express Conspicuous Consumption and Conspicuous Leisure, this became increasingly less true of bourgeois male dress. The woman of the "leisure class," however, became the instrument of a kind of Vicarious Consumption so extreme as to verge on Conspicuous Waste—hence the elaborateness of fashionable female dress, as well as its emphasis on novelty. Her clothing also expressed an enforced Conspicuous Leisure—hence the persistence of long skirts, long hair, high heels, and corsets.

Veblen was correct in pointing out the importance of socioeconomic development and the different social roles of men and women, but he almost entirely ignored the sexual aspects of clothing. Thus he argued that the "substantial reason for our tenacious attachment to the skirt" is that it "is expensive and it hampers the wearer at every turn and incapacitates her for all useful exertion." This was also true of the "custom of wearing the hair excessively long," while the corseted waist (like the bound foot) were "mutilations of unquestioned repulsiveness" that came to be regarded as beautiful only because they showed that the woman was "useless and expensive." The "purpose" of corsetry was to render its wearer "obviously unfit for work." It impaired her "personal attractions," but increased her "reputability."[16]

The idea that infirmity was the purpose (as opposed to a possible effect) of the corset and foot-binding ignores the wealth of evidence that the most important motive behind these forms of body transformation was sexual. Furthermore, since almost all working-class and peasant women in Europe wore skirts (among the few exceptions were women who worked in mines) and upper class men wore some form of trousers, it cannot convincingly be argued that the persistence of gender-distinctive clothing was simply a reflection of the greater "functionalism" of trousers. (Veblen also ignored the fact that in other cultures women wore trousers and men wore long, flowing robes.) Similarly, long hair was not necessarily an obstacle to productive labor, but—like the skirt—it did have definite connotations of feminine sexual beauty.

Later there emerged a division between those theorists who interpret fashion (or at least women's fashion) primarily in terms of sexual psychology and those who interpret it in terms of the social and economic development of society. To a considerable extent it is valid to interpret fashion in terms of conflict and emulation within class society,[17] but it is a false dichotomy to argue that fashion is *either* a product of social forces *or* of sexual and psychological motivations. Both psychological and sociological factors play a role in the development of fashion. Nor, of course, can society be described solely in terms of class.

The German philosopher and sociologist Georg Simmel attempted to analyze fashion both in terms of social structures and individual psychology. He argued that clothing functions as a guide to identity—both identification of the other (a necessity if social intercourse is to take place) and identification with the other. Fashion fulfills both the desire for conformity (identification with and membership in a group) and differentiation (the assertion of one's own identity and the act of distinguishing oneself from those "lower" on the social ladder). He traced change in fashion to the desire of those in the upper classes to distinguish themselves from those "below" them who persisted in imitating them to the extent that they could afford it.[18]

Simmel's view of fashion was a sophisticated presentation of the idea that "fashion is basically an emulation of prestige groups." Yet even this version of the "trickle-down theory" of the adoption and diffusion of new fashions is inadequate. Apart from the fact that fashions can also trickle across or even, occasionally, up, his theory fails to deal with the question of why fashion leaders choose particular styles from the range of limited alternatives.[19]

Simmel's recognition that fashion and adornment function at the crossroads where personal (even egotistic) and social concerns meet is surely worthy of further investigation. If a person clothes herself as if for a role, what is the relationship between actress and audience? Adopting the modern metaphor of radioactivity, Simmel suggested that adornment "intensifies and enlarges the impression of the personality by operating as a sort of radiation emanating from it ... and everybody else ... is immersed in this sphere."[20] In order to understand how fashion assists in the establishment of identity and the intensification of personality, it is necessary , however, to place fashion firmly within a social context. Unfortunately, after offering these suggestive remarks, Simmel moved on to other subjects.

The *Zeitgeist* Theory of Fashion

The sociological and "functional" approach to the study of fashion had little immediate influence. Instead, explanations of fashion that focused on arbitrary change (and human nature) or economic conspiracy (and personal influence) gave way, in the later nineteenth century, to the plausible idea that fashion was a reflection of the prevailing "spirit of the time." What we may call the *Zeitgeist* theory explained both the phenomenon of fashion change and the forms taken by fashion in terms of social evolution and the corresponding development of cultural attitudes, including attitudes toward sexuality.

The late-nineteenth-century French writer Louis Octave Uzanne concluded that "Nothing . . . so conjures up a people or a special period, nothing so closely tallies with their character, and mental . . . state, as the dominant note of their costume. . . . Dress and adornment . . . are a very evident clue to the ruling ideas of any special period." The early-twentieth-century German fashion historian Max von Boehn echoed this proposition in his appropriately titled work, *Modespiegel*, in which he argued that fashion was "a visible manifestation of the *Zeitgeist*."[21]

If fashion reflects and reinforces aspects of a culture, nevertheless the relationship between fashion and culture is neither direct nor obvious. Although the various manifestations of a particular period may appear to share certain stylistic traits, no modern culture is a monolithic unity. The nineteenth century in particular was the scene of a multiplicity of competing and often contradictory world views, and it would be a misleading simplification to try to identify a single attitude and announce that this represented the *Zeitgeist*.

Attempts by fashion historians to match specific modes with contemporary psychological attitudes or social role playing are frequently provocative and even plausible, but they are based on a process of circular reasoning. It is as if the historians looked back at women's fashion and maintained that it was inevitable that women should have dressed that way then. Therefore the style of dress reflects the culture of the time—as it is perceived by the historian in question. In one of his later works, von Boehn betrayed an awareness of this problem:

> We naturally ask ourselves why they chose a particular dress at some particular period instead of any other? . . . It has become the habit to explain the fashions of a period by the spirit of the time and to declare that they could not therefore have been other than they were. There can, I think, be no doubt of the connection between the two, but no one has been able to explain their influence upon each other.[22]

A most unfortunate result of the *Zeitgeist* theory of fashion change has been its pernicious effect on research into fashion history. Many reputable modern fashion historians (most notably James Laver) apparently felt that it absolved them from the need to search for evidence of direct connections between fashion and contemporary behavior and beliefs:

> The aristocratic stiffness of the old *régime* in France is completely mirrored in the brocaded gowns of the eighteenth century. The Republican yet licentious notions of the Directoire find their echo in the plain transparent dresses of the time. Victorian modesty expressed itself in the multiplicity of petticoats; the emancipation of the post-War flapper in short hair and

short skirts. We touch here something very mysterious, as if the Time Spirit were a reality, clothing itself ever in the most suitable garments and rejecting all others. One is almost driven back on the mystical conception of a *Zeitgeist*, who determines for us every detail of our lives . . . . [23]

But such an argument is a tautology: "Fashion is what it is because the *Zeitgeist* makes it so."[24] Furthermore, in hindsight historians can easily create "reasons" why fashion looked as it did—reasons that may reflect their own prejudices or ignorance. There is, however, no clear correlation between fashion and the religious, ethical, political, or aesthetic ideas of the people who wore particular modes. Yet the *Zeitgeist* theory remains so popular today that it seems necessary to demonstrate the weakness of its theoretical foundations and to suggest an alternative approach.

The Hegelian concept of a "spirit of the age" is an essentially mystical idea. In G. W. F. Hegel's romantic mythology of history, the past was peopled with the "spirits" of nations, races, and ages; and any philosophy, work of art, or artifact of a particular culture somehow "expressed" the "collective spirit or group mind" of that culture. In other words, this "spirit" was the "key cause" or ordering principle that determined the various concrete manifestations of a culture, such as art, morality, and dress—all of which were (theoretically) connected.

It is true that there appear to be connections among the artifacts of a particular culture. This is why we can speak of "period styles." But do formal properties automatically reveal a special "mentality" that is "symptomatic of everything else . . . in society"? Do changing styles really indicate "profound psychological changes"? A critic of the Hegelian approach to cultural history, Sir Ernst Gombrich, argues that "The fact that we cannot assume such automatic connections makes it more interesting to find out if and when they may have existed." He echoes Karl Popper's suggestion that it would be more productive to focus on a "detailed analysis of the *logic of situations*," together with an "analysis of social movements . . . [and] social institutions through which ideas may spread and captivate individuals."[25]

In other words, rather than assuming that the *Zeitgeist* dictated that "Victorian" women should be sexually prudish and should wear a "multiplicity of petticoats," the historian should look for more convincing reasons for the existence of a particular style. She should begin by examining the process by which fashion changed from the lightweight, high-waisted Empire style to the corseted style with an increasingly full and bell-shaped skirt. How, exactly, did particular fashions develop?

Fashion, like art, has its own history—and changes in style are related not only to changes in the larger culture, but are also reactions to previous fashions. Styles in clothing should be viewed partly "in terms of the inner logic of their evolution."[26] The conscientious art historian would not analyze an artist's work simply in terms of that individual's psychology (or the psychology of his audience). Nor would he relate it primarily to larger cultural concerns—social, economic, or political. He would also have to take account of the artistic tradition within which the artist worked. Similarly, the fashion designer and the dressmaker worked within a "world of craft" with its own traditions.[27] Whatever connections they might have with the wider culture and with social change, styles of dress are clearly and more directly related to earlier styles and to the internal process of fashion change.

Some understanding of the traditions and possibilities for change within the "world of craft" are essential for any coherent explanation of developments in fashion. To begin with, fashion change was (and continues to be) characterized by both annual (and seasonal) variations and long-term trends. These annual trends give the impression that fashion change is rapid. When viewed over a relatively long period of time, however, the various annual fashions fall into fairly clear categories.

Cycles of Fashion

To a certain extent, the gradual evolution from one dominant silhouette to another (to say nothing of evolution and variation within each cycle) develops "naturally" from within the "world of craft." Agnes Brooks Young makes the most extreme claim, in her work *Recurring Cycles of Fashion*, wherein she argues that fashion change is essentially cyclical, and "independent of historical events, epochs of thought, ideals, artistic periods." Fashion is "subject to laws of growth, duration, and decline," and the major impetus for fashion change is "inherent in fashion itself." Thus, Young draws no conclusions about the wider culture on the basis of the nineteenth-century evolution of fashion from the "tubular" (Empire) silhouette to the "bell-shaped" skirt of the mid-nineteenth-century to the "back-fullness" bustle style, and finally to the early-twentieth-century "tubular" silhouette.[28]

It is undoubtedly true that developments in fashion are characterized by a "continuous, slow process of modification," yet this theory fails to explain why, for example, skirts did not gradually rise over the course of the century. Even if fashion design evolves according to internal "laws" or "tendencies," these are subject to constraint, so that, to some extent, the resulting forms of fashion probably do reflect cultural attitudes toward, say, the body. Furthermore, style is related to the total effect of a costume, not merely to single elements, such as the shape or length of the skirt. There is rarely, if ever, the total repetition of an earlier style. It is also misleading to divorce fashion totally from its social and psychological context, since the various forms, colors, and other "expressive elements" of fashion tend to have different connotations in different times and places.[29] The "tubular" style of 1910 looked different and was perceived differently from the "tubular" style of 1810. Nevertheless, although Young carries the theory of organic growth to untenable extremes, when employed with more caution it can provide a useful corrective to some of the more over-explanatory theories of fashion change.

2

Fashion and Eroticism:
The Psychoanalytic Approach

Sigmund Freud's theories of human sexuality and the unconscious have revolutionized our understanding of the way the mind works, and it is not surprising that fashion historians and psychologists should attempt to apply his ideas to the study of dress. Unfortunately, many of them have tended to use psychoanalytic concepts in an imprecise and reductionist manner.

The psychologist Edmund Bergler, for example, suggested in *Fashion and the Unconscious* that a repressed, masochistic fear and hatred of the female body lay behind both "the masculine invention of women's clothes" and the "dress absurdities" designed by the homosexual "czars of fashion creation." Yet there is no evidence that men "invented" women's clothes; indeed, in most cultures weaving is a female occupation. Both sexes wear clothes, and male fashions have been easily as "absurd" as women's—does this mean that men fear and hate their own bodies, too? Bergler's theory shows clearly how fashion can arouse anxieties about sexuality. Lawrence Langner's *The Importance of Wearing Clothes*, on the other hand, shows how a writer can avoid discussing sexuality. It is based on Alfred Adler's ideas about inferiority and superiority, which are inadequate for understanding either human psychology or fashion.[1]

Two other writers have made systematic attempts to apply orthodox Freudian psychoanalytic theory to the study of fashion: J. C. Flügel, author of *The Psychology of Clothes* and of "Clothes Symbolism and Clothes Ambivalence," and René König, author of *A La Mode: On the Social Psychology of Fashion*.[2]

Since Freud wrote relatively little about clothing, per se, Flügel and König have sometimes elaborated on ideas that Freud mentioned in passing (such as the idea that clothing permits a socially acceptable form of passive exhibitionism), and at other times they constructed theories that derive, perhaps more distantly, from Freud's ideas (such as Flügel's extension of Freud's "erotogenic zones" to a theory that fashion change is linked to the "shifting erogenous zone"). Although I do not always agree with their conclusions (particularly some of Flügel's), their work demonstrates the importance of psychoanalytic theory for the attainment of a deeper understanding of fashion. Yet König has had little influence on recent fashion history, while Flügel's more questionable theories have become highly influential. In popularized form they appear in every work propounding some variant of the "sex appeal" theory of fashion.

The Sexual Symbolism of Clothing

Everyone knows about Freud's interpretation of the sexual symbolism of various articles of clothing. In *The Interpretation of Dreams* (1900) and in his article on "Fetishism" (1927), he argued that fur can symbolize the pubic hair, lingerie the moment of undressing, and silk the softness of the skin, while the coat, the hat, and, of course, the necktie can symbolize the phallus. Flügel continued Freud's analysis: among the articles of clothing that he identified as phallic symbols were the hat, the tie, the coat, the collar, the button, trousers, the heel and toe of the shoe and sometimes the entire shoe—although this could also symbolize the vagina into which the phallic foot was slipped. (Presumably, the glove would fulfil a similar symbolic function.) Garments that represented the female genitals included the veil, the girdle, the garter, the bracelet, and jewelry in general. Protective clothing might symbolize the womb.[3]

Yet according to Flügel, not only may certain articles of clothing symbolize the sexual organs, but the symbolism of clothing as a whole is sexual. The key words here are "displacement" and "ambivalence." Originally, both the desire to display oneself and the reaction formation of modesty or shame were related to the naked body. The unconscious conflict between exhibitionism and modesty is displaced—shifted away—from the naked body onto clothing, which then functions as a "compromise," since it both covers the body and attracts attention to it. Ostensibly used to "frustrate" exhibitionistic tendencies, clothing actually provides a means of gratifying them "with far less opposition from modesty."[4]

But there is still some opposition. The ambiguity of public opinion—the strong feelings "for and against" fashion—are themselves "a result of displacement." They actually express ambivalent feelings about sexuality.[5]

Clothes are also both erotic and moral, because they differentiate between the sexes. Truly "unisex" clothing is very rare. To a Japanese, for example, a man's kimono looks very different from a woman's kimono. Gender distinction in dress is not primarily based on limited functional grounds, nor is it a recent or western phenomenon. Anthropologists have found that in preindustrial societies, "the great bifurcation of dress is sexual." Havelock Ellis believed that "The extreme importance of clothes

Carolus-Duran, *Lady with a Glove* (1869). Courtesy of the Louvre, Paris.

would disappear at once if the two sexes were to dress alike."[6] Clothes make the man (or the woman).

The Bible states, flatly, "A woman shall not wear that which pertaineth unto a man, neither shall a man put on a woman's garment; for whosoever doeth these things is an abomination unto Jehovah, thy God." Similarly, Philip Stubbs's sixteenth-century work, *The Anatomy of Abuses*, maintained that

> our apparell was given as a signe distinctive to discerne betwixt sexe and sexe; and therefore one to weare the apparell of another sexe is to participate with the same, and to adulterate the veritie of his own kinde.[7]

The urgent tone of these texts indicates that a fear of homosexuality or bisexuality lay behind the injunctions against transvestism. (Taboos and desires again.) Sex specific clothing is a sign indicating who are acceptable as potential sexual partners. Conversely, cross-dressing can be highly erotic, in part because of its forbidden character.

Although theories about the sexual symbolism of specific articles of clothing seem to be of limited significance, Flügel's idea that clothing as a whole is sexually symbolic represents an important insight into sartorial eroticism that explains the ambivalent image of the fig leaf. The complexity of human sexuality and its potential polymorphous perversity are both controlled and expressed through clothes.

The Libido for Looking

According to Freud, "one of the original components" of the sex drive is the "libido for looking." This "desire to see the organs peculiar to each sex exposed" exists in everyone (male and female), in both an "active and passive" form, and may be derived from the libido for touching. In terms of the perversions, scoptophilia—voyeurism or sexual gazing—is thus closely associated with exhibitionism—or self-display. In common with other manifestations of the sex drive, the libido for looking is generally subject to considerable repression and sublimation.

The focus on the genitals shifts to an interest in the naked body as a whole. Beyond this, one or the other form of libido dominates in any given ("normal") individual. Men tend to repress their exhibitionism and are characterized by a "high degree" of the active form of the libido for looking. Partly because of their role in society, women have tended to turn the instinct "round upon the subject," taking on the "passive aim" of wanting "to be looked at."[8]

> In women, the inclination to passive exhibitionism is almost invariably buried under the imposing reactive function of sexual modesty, but not without a loophole being left for it in relation to clothes.[9]

Social conventions and circumstances then dictated the permissible amount and type of physical and sartorial exhibitionism. In practice, these potentially very useful ideas have tended to degenerate into disquisitions on "female exhibitionism."

Exhibitionism and Narcissism

Women's fashion (at least in recent centuries) has tended to be simultaneously "more modest and more exhibitionistic" than men's clothing. According to Flügel, its greater modesty derived from the "fact" that, while phallic symbolism results in display, vaginal and uterine symbols form "the unconscious foundations of the conscious motives of modesty and protection."[10] However, it seems more reasonable to assume that modesty is a reaction formation to exhibitionism (as Freud indicated), and that the desire to display the self applies not only to the phallus or

The Secret Out At Last—Why Mrs. Brown Has Such a Perfect Figure. American trade card (ca. 1882) for the Adjustable Duplex Corset.

phallic symbols, but also to the female genitals and body. The cultural emphasis on female chastity is closely related to the emphasis on female modesty, while the female role as "sexual object" undoubtedly contributes to the relatively greater sexual display of women's clothing. These historical facts seem to explain adequately why women's dress was (and is) both more modest and more erotic than men's clothing.

Flügel, however, offered two other related explanations for the greater eroticism of women's fashion—that the lack of a penis resulted in the female body being characterized by a "diffused eroticism," and that women are more "narcissistic" than men. According to Flügel, the libido in men is "concentrated on the genitals." Since women lack a penis, they "compensate" by displaying other parts of the body. He concluded that, in women, "the castration complex may lead to general exhibitionistic tendencies with regard to the whole body." The concentrated male libido, on the other hand, "can more easily find, in various ornaments or garments, a symbolic substitute" for the penis; the rest of the male body could remain relatively neglected.[11]

Without going into the contested issue of the "castration complex," it is still possible to offer a few historical objections to Flügel's hypothesis. Portions of the male anatomy other than the penis *have* been singled out for erotic emphasis by past fashions. That men's fashions have generally become less erotically expressive (while women's have become more so) over the past two and a half centuries is undeniable, but this can be explained in cultural-historical terms.

Flügel's other argument—that the greater eroticism of women's fashion is largely the result of women's greater narcissism—also seems unconvincing. According to Flügel, the narcissistic woman remains stuck at the stage of self-love and thus, he argues, she has an excessive interest in her own appearance—and not even, especially, her physical body, but rather her clothes. Flügel presents the situation as a vicious circle: women's greater narcissism and exhibitionism is largely displaced onto their dress, while the existence of "distinctive and decorative" female fashion in turn "fosters" women's "relatively greater narcissism."[12] The psychoanalytic theory of narcissism is highly complex, and Flügel does not do justice to it. Although many psychoanalysts have emphasized the existence of "feminine narcissism," which is supposedly a reaction to penis envy, they admit that men can also be narcissistic.

Vanity has traditionally (although not theologically) been seen as primarily a feminine trait. To the idea of vanity as a moral flaw, Flügel has added the idea of narcissism as a lack of psychological maturity. In the process, he repeats the accusations of earlier moralists, that women adorn themselves from "sexual jealousy" and social envy and competition. Unlike women, who *failed* to advance, in Flügel's view men have largely *outgrown* their narcissistic tendencies. Indeed, they might have gone a little too far in their renunciation of masculine beauty: The cultural repression of phallicism has made the male body seem ugly. Flügel suggests that they could increase their beauty consciousness a little—provided they avoided the twin dangers of homosexuality and narcissism. Such a step might also help relieve women from the "enormous temptations in the direction of an exaggerated indulgence in Narcissism."[13]

To speak of "an exaggerated indulgence in Narcissism" is to misuse the term, and to give a spurious scientific gloss to an old idea. Narcissism is a serious personality disorder, involving an erotic focus on the self and an inability to establish an emotional relationship with another person. It is not equivalent to vanity or an interest in dress. Flügel's interpretation of fashion is clearly colored by his prejudice against it, which is apparent in his rosy but unconvincing picture of the egalitarian fraternity expressed by male dress. It is true that women were (and are) permitted, even encouraged, to show more of an interest in their appearance than men are—but this in itself is not evidence of abnormal "narcissism" or "exhibitionism."

Fetishism

Psychoanalysis deals with extreme attitudes and behavior in part on the view that these offer important clues to "normal" behavior. It would be a serious mistake to assume that psychoanalysis is only useful for the study of deviance; yet it is also an error to blur the distinction between pathology and "normal" sexuality. Fashion historians who have been influenced by psychoanalysis often imply that fetishism is very closely connected to the "normal" erotic appeal of fashion, and that the changing form of fashion reflected cultural (rather than purely personal) obsessions with certain parts of the anatomy and certain articles of clothing. Fashion exploits the erotic appeal of those physical characteristics—such as the small waist—that attract "normal" individuals as well as fetishists. As James Laver put it, "Fashion is the comparative of which fetishism is the superlative."[14]

There are problems with this interpretation, however, since its adherents oversimplify and overapply the psychoanalytic concept of fetishism. Fetishism is a perversion or variation of the sexual instinct, involving a desire for only a part of the body or even an article of clothing that functions as a substitute for the loved person. Writers such as Laver who describe late Victorian and Edwardian fashion in terms of "frou frou and fetishism" imply that the average woman was a proto-fetishist—but this is a a serious distortion of the concept of "fetishism."

The popularly accepted idea of cultural quasi-fetishism involves the conflation of the distinctions between individual perversions (such as foot and shoe fetishism) and widespread erotic interest in, say, feet and shoes. Thus, many fashion historians argue that the long skirts of the nineteenth century contributed to the development of a cultural obsession with female feet, since concealment theoretically invested these appendages with greater erotic appeal. These historians then jump to the conclusion that this indicated that the incidence of foot and shoe fetishism was significantly higher in the nineteenth century than in earlier or later periods—an hypothesis that the available evidence does not necessarily support.[15]

Recently, David Kunzle, author of *Fashion and Fetishism*, has suggested that fetishism was almost entirely distinct from fashion. Yet some important if limited connections between ordinary erotic symbolism and fetishism do merit investigation. In other respects also, Kunzle's approach appears to be inadequate for an understanding of either fetishism as such or of the erotic aspects of ordinary fashion. Kunzle deliberately eschews any attempt to analyze the possible unconscious significance of fetishism, presumably because such an analysis might make tight-lacing appear to be a sexual perversion, rather than an unorthodox but legitimate and sexually liberated form of behavior. Indeed, he argues that psychoanalytical and sexological research into fetishism (from Krafft-Ebing, Stekel, and Freud to Kinsey) is necessarily reductionist and repressive, and interprets fetishism in "pathological" terms. He prefers an empirical approach that relies on describing the feelings and experiences (real or fantasied) of tight-lacers. It is probably not unfair to characterize his work as a *defense* of fetishism.[16]

The psychological analysis of fetishism was first made in the later nineteenth century, as part of a more general expansion of theoretical writing on sexuality. The older categories of morality and disease were expanded and supplemented in the new "sexology" by medical and psychological categories, such as "degeneracy."[17] Thus, in *Psychopathia Sexualis* (first published in 1886), Richard von Krafft-Ebing, the celebrated German physician, neurologist, and professor of psychiatry, maintained that "Adornment, ornament and dress" played a role of "great importance . . . in the normal *vita sexualis* of man." This normal "erotic fetichism" was, however, significantly different from "pathological erotic fetichism," which he defined as "The Association of Lust with the Idea of Certain Portions of the Female Person, or with Certain Articles of Female Attire." In pathological cases, the fetish itself (rather than the person associated with it) became the exclusive object of sexual desire, while "instead of coitus, strange manipulations of the fetich" became the sexual aim. According to Krafft-Ebing, among the object chosen as fetishes were parts of the female body (feet, hair, skin) or physical characteristics (lameness), articles of female attire (dress-fetishism in general or the fetishism of particular garments, such as shoes, petticoats, corsets), and special materials (fur, velvet, silk, white starched linen, leather). The fetishes of women remained somewhat conjectural. Women seemed to be attracted, however, to beards, "the emblem of virility"; and "It is a well-known fact that the female heart has predominant weakness for military uniforms." Significantly, though, Krafft-Ebing admitted that he had "thus far not succeeded in obtaining facts with regard to pathological fetichism in women."[18] There appeared to be only *male* fetishists.

Krafft-Ebing was concerned with fetishism, both as a psychological abnormality and as a matter of criminal behavior—theft or assault. At the same time, however, there developed, particularly in the work of the English psychologist Havelock Ellis, "an almost mystical idealisation of sexuality" that encompassed a variety of unorthodox sexual practices. Havelock Ellis expounded an analysis of fetishism that was in many respects similar to that of Krafft-Ebing, but he tended to emphasize the basic normality and ubiquitousness of "erotic fetichism." He also denied Krafft-Ebing's suggestion that fetishism might be associated with masochism.[19]

Another early sexologist, Doctor Wilhelm Stekel, on the other hand, largely ignored the issue of "normal fetishes" to focus on "the psychopathology of fetishism"—its connection to homosexuality, "psycho-sexual infantilism," onanism, religion, and "compulsion neurosis," together with its "invariable criminal component." He remained confused about the cause(s) and psychological significance of this "sexual aberration." For example, in various cases he associated silk, satin, and fur fetishism with frigidity or impotence; petticoat, chemise, and dress fetishism with "incestuous strivings"; corset fetishism with "the sadistic fantasies of an ascetic"; foot fetishism with masochism; button fetishism with "the repression of a fellatio phantasy"; and uniform fetishism with "infantilism," "criminal instincts," and homosexuality.[20]

Although Krafft-Ebing, Havelock Ellis, and Stekel (among others) made certain possibly valid observations, they failed to develop a comprehensive theory of fetishism. Over a period of time, Freud did develop such a theory, which appears to be the most coherent explanation of the phenomenon. Freud first discussed fetishism and "unsuitable substitutes for the sexual object" in *Three Essays on the Theory of Sexuality* (1905), in which he observed that there existed cases in which

> the normal sexual object is replaced by . . . some part of the body (such as the foot or hair) which is in general very inappropriate for sexual purposes, or some inanimate object which bears an assignable relation to the person whom it replaces and preferably to that person's sexuality (e.g., a piece of clothing or underlinen).

Like his predecessors, Freud noted that in transitional cases, the individual might only require that the sexual object "fulfil a fetishistic condition—such as the possession of some particular hair-colouring or clothing . . . — if the sexual aim is to be obtained." He concluded that:

> A certain degree of fetishism is thus habitually present in normal love . . . The situation only becomes pathological when the longing for the fetish passes beyond the point of being merely a necessary condition attached to the sexual object and actually *takes the place* of the normal aim, and . . . the fetish becomes . . . the *sole* sexual object.[21]

At this stage in his work, Freud was still uncertain about the causes of fetishism and the choice of particular objects as fetishes. He suggested tentatively that fetishists might have an intrinsically weaker than average drive toward genital union, and that their choice of a fetish might have been a consequence of a childhood sexual impression. Two decades later, however, in his article of 1927, "Fetishism," Freud offered an explanation of the genesis of fetishism and the significance of the fetish, together with possible causes for the choice of particular fetishes.

Freud argued that "The fetish is a substitute for the woman's (the mother's) penis that the little boy once believed in and . . . does not want to give up . . . for if a woman had been castrated, then his own possession of a penis was in danger." The fetish represented an unconscious "compromise" between the "unwelcome perception" that the mother has no penis and the wish and earlier belief that she does. The ego defends itself by disavowing or repressing an unpleasant perception. "Yes, in his mind the woman *has* got a penis ... but this penis is no longer the same. .... Something else has taken its place." The fetish thus serves to assuage his fear of castration, at the same time "transfer[ring] the importance of the penis to another part of the female body" or to some article of clothing. It remained unclear why the "fear of castration caused by the sight of the female genitals" made some men become fetishists and others homosexuals, while the majority "surmount" this fear.[22]

The objects chosen as "substitutes for the absent female phallus" were not necessarily those that appeared elsewhere as symbols of the penis; but they were perhaps related to "the last moment in which the woman could still be regarded as phallic." Thus, for example, "pieces of underclothing, which are so often chosen as a fetish, crystallize the moment of undressing." Fur or velvet was associated with the pubic hair that should have revealed a penis. The appeal of shoes is related to the association of the foot and penis: "The foot represents a woman's penis, the absence of which is deeply felt." The fetishist was often ambivalent about his fetish. For example, the type of hair fetishist who cuts off women's hair feels "the need to carry out the castration which he disavows. ... His action contains in itself the two mutually incompatible assertions: 'The woman has still got a penis' and 'My father has castrated the woman'." Obviously this type of equation is unconscious.[23]

If fetishism functions as a defense against castration fears, then this would support Kinsey's conclusion that "fetishism is an almost exclusively male phenomenon."[24] Since women very rarely have fears of castration, it is doubtful whether one can even speak of female fetishists. This is an important issue if we want to understand the appeal *for women* of certain articles of clothing that men often choose as fetishes, such as lingerie, high heeled shoes, and corsets. Furthermore, only a very small minority of men are real fetishists. Consequently, it is unlikely that pathological fetishism plays a very significant role in fashion.

Rather, it appears that the fashion historian should distinguish between this relatively uncommon perversion, on the one hand, and a more widespread erotic symbolism, on the other. Fetishism should be studied, since it so clearly emphasizes the appeal of phallic symbolism in dress, and thus draws attention to some of the attractions felt by many "normal" individuals for certain parts of the body and articles of clothing, but it is hardly typical. Furthermore, erotic symbolism may well extend beyond fetishism, in ways that would appeal to both men and women.

Thus, for example, in *The Sex Life of the Foot and Shoe*, William A. Rossi suggested that foot and shoe eroticism derived in part from the intrinsic sensitivity of the feet (especially the soles and toes) to tactile stimulation, as well as from the phallic symbolism of the foot and the ambivalent symbolism of the shoe. The erotic appeal of the foot led simultaneously to the desire to ornament it and to cover it. Furthermore, many of the characteristics commonly associated with feminine sexual attractiveness are accentuated by high heeled shoes, which affect the wearer's gait and posture. By putting the lower part of the body in a state of tension, the movement of the hips and buttocks is emphasized and the back arched, thrusting the bosom forward. High heels also change the apparent contour of the legs, ankles, and feet.[25] Thus, much of the sexual appeal of the foot and shoe is potentially experienced by nonfetishists as well.

This is not to deny Freud's analysis of fetishism, but only to point out that there are additional reasons for the erotic appeal of objects often chosen as fetishes. It might be more productive for the fashion historian to explore these, rather than to rely so heavily on "fetishism" as an explanation for sartorial eroticism. When certain phenomena appear to be genuinely fetishistic, these can be compared with other forms of erotic symbolism. We will return to this issue later, when we consider the subject of corset and tight-lacing fetishism.

Sex Appeal and the Shifting Erogenous Zone

Today, the single most influential explanation of fashion is the "sex appeal" theory, also known as the "theory of the shifting erogenous zone." Its proponents argue that the primary purpose of women's fashion—and the driving force behind fashion change—is the desire to attract the opposite sex. According to James Laver, women's fashion is governed by the "Attraction" or "Seduction Principle." Not so with men's clothing, which is governed by the "Hierarchical Principle," emphasizing socioeconomic status rather than sexual beauty.[26]

Women's fashion is said to attract by means of the selective exposure, concealment, and emphasis on the various erotic "zones" of the female body. These can be the secondary sexual characteristics (such as the breasts, hips, and derriere), or parts of the body that acquire sexual connotations (such as the legs, feet, back, waist, shoulders, and so on). According to this theory, male sexual interest in these portions of the anatomy fluctuates, "and it is the business of fashion to pursue [the shifting erogenous zone], without actually catching it up." The fashionable exposure or emphasis must be extreme enough to be exciting, but not so overt as to be widely considered obscene. According to Laver, "If we accept the theory of the shifting erogenous zone, we must admit that nearly all women's clothes are an exploitation of immodesty."[27]

The sex appeal interpretation of fashion sometimes appears as a variant of the *Zeitgeist* theory. The ordering principle of the "spirit of the time" or the "mentality of the age" is, to some extent, replaced by the idea of the dominant psychology. Thus, in *Feminine Attitudes in the Nineteenth Century*, C. Willett Cunnington matched changes in female fashion with decade-by-decade changes in feminine psychology, with particular regard to feminine attitudes toward sex. According to Cunnington, the nineteenth century was divided into: The Vertical Epoch (although his perception of its morality might have made The Horizontal Epoch a better title), The Dawn of Romance, The Romantic '30s, The Sentimental '40s, The Perfect Lady of the '50s, The Revolting '60s, The Ornamental '70s, The Symbolic '80s, and The Prude's Progress in the '90s.[28]

In *The Perfect Lady*, he modifies these divisions somewhat, so that, for example, he characterizes women's dress from 1866 to 1880 as "essentially sensual" with "fascinating undulations," whereas dress from 1881 to 1887 expressed both "sex appeal and a grim prudery." He portrays the Victorian woman as having been "the perfect lady," a being who was sexually repressed, but who "unconsciously" strove to increase her sexual attractiveness. Since men were also repressed (although to a lesser degree), they found the sometimes "grotesque undulations" of Victorian fashion "peculiarly fascinating."[29]

To a considerable extent, the sex appeal theory is based on a stereotype of Victorian sexuality that is probably false, and on a highly questionable interpretation of *feminine* psychology in the nineteenth century. Related to this is the problem of a one-sided and possibly misleading emphasis on the eroticism of *female* dress. In the past, men wore clothing that was at least as erotic and extravagant as women's clothing. In most pre-industrial cultures, men paid more attention than women to dress and adornment. When a pattern of fashion change developed in Europe in the Middle Ages, men adopted each new style with enthusiasm. They dressed to kill, using clothing to emphasize the legs, shoulders, chest, buttocks, even the penis itself. It was only after about 1760 that men began to adopt a kind of anti-fashion uniform. Yet no one has suggested that changes in men's fashions reflected the vagaries of masculine psychology or shifting sexual interests on the part of women. Meanwhile, in other civilizations, the clothing of both sexes changed only slowly and did not seem to emphasize first one and then another "erogenous zone." Thus the theory largely fails to apply to male dress and to other cultures.

It is certainly true that one of the most obvious functions of dress is to differentiate between the sexes. Women's fashion has frequently created artificial ideals of feminine beauty, many of which might be considered a "caricature" of the female body. It is possible that, in a general sense, the changes in women's fashion were based on differences between the sexes. Nevertheless, fashion cannot be reduced to a shifting emphasis on parts of the anatomy, or to a series of sexual invitations.

Advocates of the theory of the shifting erogenous zone read too much into the formal elements of fashion. It is possible to put these into perspective, by looking at the internal patterns of change in the development of fashion. Fashion often tends gradually to exaggerate one feature, almost to the point of parody, and then to reverse direction. "A fashion which seems most daring and fantastic, full of purposeful invention and curious meaning, may in reality be the almost haphazard outcome of going as far as one can go in a direction which circumstances may have rendered inevitable."[30]

The internalist interpretation of change in fashion—sleeves became full because they had been tight—may seem to *explain* nothing, but it is more accurate than the overexplanatory approach. Thus, instead of interpreting the very large sleeves of the 1890s as "breast symbols," it is more likely that they had little or no sexual or psychological significance. When the very tight sleeves of the 1880s began to puff up, they had the appeal of novelty and the desirable side effect of making the waist look smaller. Widespread imitation led to further exaggeration, which was bolstered by historical references to the "romantic" sleeves of the 1830s. Concurrently, the skirt lost its bustle and much of its decoration (these features had been worked to death over the past two decades). In a sense, it was "time" for the focus to shift to the bodice.

The idea of the "erogenous zones" is probably an extension of Freud's concept of the "erotogenic zones." But there is no direct and obvious connection between the idea of "erotogenic zones," as characterized by Freud, and Flügel's theory that the sexual interest of a culture shifts from one "erogenous" part of the female anatomy to another, and that these shifts are reflected in the changing form of fashion.[31] Fashionable emphasis on the buttocks (greatly enlarged by the bustle) might, conceivably, indicate regression to the anal stage of sexual development, although I would be most reluctant to interpret this style primarily in these terms. Would the "erogenous zone" of the bosom be related to the "erotogenic zone" of the mouth and the oral personality type? Conceivably, the legs could be interpreted as the avenue to the genitals, but could they be independent erotogenic zones? In any case, an individual's sexual and psychological development is not necessarily paralleled by the attitudes widely held in that person's society.

It is perfectly plausible that different fashions could emphasize different parts of the body—the crinoline the hips, the bustle the derriere, the Edwardian blouse the bosom, the Twenties frock the legs, the Thirties evening gown the back, and so on. What is more dubious is the suggestion that these changes reflected society's shifting sexual interest in these various parts of the body. Whether or not *fashion* emphasized a particular feature has more to do with the "natural" development of styles of dress and with the constraints of modesty (as interpreted at the time) than it does with the perceived sexual attractiveness of the feature itself.

In only a few cases does there seem to be a correlation between the part of the body currently perceived as extremely erotic and that part emphasized by fashion. The torpedo-shaped brassieres of the later 1940s and 1950s seem to be related to the contemporary male "fixation" on the mammary glands, while the corsets of about 1820 to 1905 "reflect" the erotic significance of a slender, tapering waist. The bosom, however, was always a popular feature of the female anatomy—even during the 1920s, when the ideal bosom was smaller and fashion deemphasized the breasts. The Victorians thought that plump legs were sexually attractive— although legs were generally hidden by long skirts.

The theory of the shifting erogenous zone is not entirely incorrect, but it grossly oversimplifies the *real* erotic appeal of concealment and display, and it confuses changes in the form of fashion with a shifting sexual interest in parts of the anatomy. Moreover, it is highly questionable whether "sex appeal" is the primary purpose and motive force behind fashion, and whether dress is an obvious indicator of "feminine psychology."

Nevertheless, versions of the sex appeal theory continue to influence popular histories of dress, such as Alison Lurie's *The Language of Clothes* and Prudence Glynn's *Skin to Skin. Eroticism in Dress*. Lurie and Glynn are frequently amusing (especially when they describe attitudes toward contemporary dress), but they also tend to be highly subjective and unanalytical. (Glynn actually argues that objectivity and documentation would be boring and masculine.)[32] Thus, although neither can be said to have developed a real *theory* of sartorial eroticism, their books are worth considering briefly here, for the light that they shed on popular perceptions of the eroticism and psychology of dress.

Glynn devotes considerable attention to the female erogenous zones— the waist (which, she suggests, "symbolises virginity," because a woman who has had a child loses her figure); the foot (she cites Chinese foot-binding and the supposed historical prevalence of foot fetishism); the breasts (less "threatening" than the vagina, and especially favored by bottle-fed Americans); the legs ("It took two wars of global proportions to reveal the legs of the women of the world"); the bottom ("Buttock-lovers ... frequently ... prefer sexual penetration from the back"); the hair and the head (hair is an erogenous zone because it is associated with "virility, and because of its creepy ability to grow, like toe-nails, after death"); the neck, shoulders, arms, and hands; and the stomach, thighs, and "pudenda." Men, she argues, "have fewer erogenous zones than women"—and they "seem to be very badly informed" as to which ones women are actually interested in.[33] These enthusiastic overstatements not only contain factual inaccuracies, they also, ironically, limit the ways in which fashion emphasizes the eroticism of the human body, while stressing a few perverse or repressed reactions to the body.

Both writers emphasize the sexual motivations supposedly revealed by the wearer's dress, but they go about it in a rather chaotic fashion. Lurie, for example, argues that "As well as telling us whether people are male or female, clothes can tell us whether or not they are interested in sex, and if so what sort of sex they are interested in." In support of this hypothesis, she jumbles together a variety of "sexy" styles and attitudes toward sex: black leather has sado-masochistic associations, and fur allegedly "turn[s] its wearer into an animal symbolically." The "old hand-bag" reveals its owner to be an "old bag" ("bag also being a symbol of the vagina"), while the "shabby, small or—worst of all—ill-functioning umbrella is a source of shame that often seems excessive unless some erotic meaning is presumed." A woman who wears ecru lingerie is elegant, a woman who wears pink is romantic, and a person who wears rubber or edible underpants is one of those with "minority sexual interests."[34] Well, yes, but not every "Venus in Furs" has a masochistic lover. This is reductionism with a vengeance.

Some of this confusion is understandable, since the erotic aspects of dress and adornment are so varied and the individual's psychological motivations so complex. The issue has also been clouded by prurience, and Glynn opens her book with the warning that it "is not a book about 'dirty' clothes, nor is it a 'dirty' book about clothes." It is, though, a book dedicated to the "conviction" that Richard Burton "was right" to argue that "the greatest provocations of our lust are from our apparel." Glynn (even more than Lurie) is in the camp of the sex appeal theorists, when she argues that "everything can be boiled down to sexy dressing" intended to "provoke the crucial clash of two parties to produce a third."[35] Just as she is reluctant to admit that the "pudenda" constitute the primary erotic zone of the body, so also does she shy away from the very idea of bisexual or homosexual attraction.

Yet psychoanalysis *can* be an extremely useful methodology for the study of fashion. It is not merely that the sex appeal theorists "strain the sexual motive to the breaking point and [tend to] ... greatly underrate other motives" involved in fashion, but that they focus on only a very limited range of ways in which fashion emphasizes the erotic.[36] Clothing, though—all clothing—is intrinsically erotic, and its appeal is far wider and more complex than the sex appeal theorists dream.

3

A New Theory of Fashion: Sexual Beauty and the Ideal Self

As you read this, chances are that you are wearing clothes—and not just any clothes, but your clothes. Although people frequently argue that their clothing is primarily "functional," in fact this "second skin" does far more than cover the body. A blanket would do that. Clothes have a real significance and appeal, because they are a guide to identity and an important element of personal appearance. "Fashion . . . enables a person to express what he or she either is or would like to be in terms which other people living in the same society will immediately recognize and understand."[1] Yet many people are not conscious of making clothing choices that communicate information and create a particular image. Nor is it always easy to "read" other people's clothing. To decode this vestimentary language, it is necessary to realize that layers of meaning are woven into every article of dress. And, although it is unlikely that your clothing "says" anything very specific about your sexual attitudes and behavior, at the deepest level the message is sexual.

Because clothing is so intimately connected to the physical self, it automatically carries an erotic charge. The child candidly says, "You show me your's and I'll show you mine." As the individual grows up, however, the libido for looking (and touching) is partially repressed and sublimated. This tension between sexual modesty and sexual display is the fundamental fact in the psychology of clothes. It would be reductionist, though, to interpret the history of either sex or dress as "a long warfare between the dangerous and powerful drives and the systems of taboos and inhibitions which man has erected to control them."[2] Furthermore, this concept of sex as an autonomous biological force may be misleading because it ignores the ways in which sexuality is a social construct.

The Sexual Origin of Beauty

According to psychoanalysis, the concept of "beauty" ultimately derives from the sphere of sexual sensations. "Beauty" and "charm" are attributes of the sexual object. To some extent, physical beauty is perceived as an *exaggeration* of the sexual characteristics. The curving shape of the female torso is a universal symbol of femininity, and a Viennese cartoon of 1887, "Man's Ideal of Beauty," showed a woman who was all derriere and legs. Freud, as usual, looked more deeply into the question:

> There is to my mind no doubt that the concept of "beautiful" has its origins in sexual excitation and that its original meaning was "sexually stimulating."[3]

Yet (he added), "the love of beauty seems a perfect example of an impulse inhibited in its aim." The *origin* of beauty is sexual, but beauty is not the same as sexual stimulation, since the aim of sexual pleasure is inhibited.

Almost without exception, the *primary* sexual characteristics—the penis and vagina—have not been utilized by fashion for the purpose of sexual allurement. Some "primitive" tribes did deliberately draw attention to the genitals, but in modern European history, the one striking example of this was the codpiece: not only its shape, but also its color and decoration made the penis the central focus of male dress. Yet clothing may have developed originally in part to call attention to the genitals. How and why did this change?

Man's Ideal of Beauty. Caricature from *Karikaturen-Album* (1887), Vienna, reproduced in Friedrich Wendel, *Weib und Mode.*

Freud maintained that, while "genital-worship" had existed in the past, "In the course of cultural development so much of the divine and sacred was ultimately extracted from sexuality that the exhausted remnant fell into contempt." Even if Freud's historical analysis is flawed, in terms of individual psychological development it is true that, eventually, the genitals became "the *'pudenda'*, objects of shame, and even (as a result of further sexual repression) of disgust." Although this conclusion may later be consciously rejected, the residual sense of shame results in an altered perception of the genitals. Thus, while the sight of the genitals "is always exciting," they "are nevertheless hardly ever judged to be beautiful; the quality of beauty seems, instead, to attach to certain secondary sexual characters."[4]

Although it seems clear that the cultural conception of beauty contains a very significant sexual element, beauty is not reducible to sexual attraction. If it were merely a question of sexual characteristics, the ideal of physical beauty would not change so much over time and in different places. To a considerable extent, beauty is not even a physical given, but an artificial construct that varies from culture to culture. Nor is the overwhelming emphasis on female beauty an historical constant. (In antiquity the male body was regarded as at least as beautiful.) Yet because of the connection between beauty and sexuality and because of the greater power of men, the issue of female beauty has been more problematical and ambiguous. The celebration of female beauty tends to reduce woman to her body, to being an instrument of pleasure; its denigration reflects the masculine fear of female sexual power. Meanwhile, women have tended to remain relatively silent about male beauty. Yet for both sexes, beauty incorporates, but goes beyond, physical attractions and sexual stimulation. The genitals are exciting in a direct sense, but a beautiful face attracts, as Stendal said, because it is a promise of happiness. Beauty is eroticism deflected from the goal of immediate sexual pleasure; it is like the civilized erotic attraction between friends, who may or may not ever make love.

The idea of "beauty" is particularly important for an understanding of the role that eroticism plays in dress. When fashion historians ignore the differences between beauty and sexual stimulation, they can grossly oversimplify the sexual element in fashion, and exaggerate the element of conscious and deliberate "immodesty." As König points out, the "play of eroticism in fashion" often involves the "displacement . . . of the erotic effects to dimensions that are not primarily sexual."[5] A woman dresses to be beautiful, perhaps even to attract sexual admiration, but only occasionally with the aim of actually seducing the viewer.

There are myriad ways in which fashion can emphasize the erotic. For example, since the libido for looking is derived from the desire to touch and be touched, the skin and the eye are primary erogenous zones for everyone. Consider, for example, "Upon Julia's Clothes," Robert Herrick's seventeenth-century tribute to the tactile and visual appeal of fabrics:

"Whenas in silks my Julia goes/ Then, then (methinks) how sweetly flowes/ The liquifaction of her clothes." In "Delight in Disorder" he explores how the way in which clothes are worn can also be erotic: "A sweet disorder in the dress/ Kindles in clothes a wantonness/ . . . Do more bewitch me than when art/ Is too precise in every part."[6] The desire for the body can be partially transferred onto clothes, which then provide an additional erotic charge of their own. But ultimately it is the wearer who is "sweet" and "wanton," More work needs to be done on such specific types of sartorial eroticism.

The Attraction of Concealment

In *Three Essays on the Theory of Sexuality*, in the context of an analysis of looking and touching, Freud suggested that "The progressive concealment of the body which goes along with civilization keeps sexual curiosity awake." Clothing is erotic because it arouses curiosity about the "hidden parts" (the genitals), and by a process of sublimation, curiosity about "the body as a whole."[7]

The attraction of concealment has been accepted as real by many people. A nineteenth-century cartoon, "The New Temptation of Saint Anthony," portrayed the saint as immune to the charms of a totally naked woman, but sexually excited when she redonned her underwear. Why should this be so? Psychoanalysts believe that inquisitive behavior, per se, has an "erotic root." Originally the desire to know meant the desire to know about sex. By concealing the body, clothes excite sexual curiosity and create in the viewer the desire to remove them, "to reach the source of erotic attraction." In addition," as König points out, "this stimulus of curiosity continuously strives to alter the system and means of concealment and display, so that their appeal never weakens."[8]

In general, when anything is constantly exposed to view, it leaves nothing to the imagination, tends to be perceived as ordinary, and, eventually, is hardly noticed at all. The eye becomes jaded; habitual nudity is notably unerotic. This is true not only for the body as a whole, but also for parts of the body. To some extent, therefore, Flügel's admirer, Laver, was correct to argue that whenever the female body is "habitually covered up, the exposure of any part focuses the erotic attention" there.[9] Fashion (and adornment) maintain erotic interest in the body by ensuring that interesting variations cause the viewer to *see* the body with renewed interest and awareness.

But the erotic appeal of concealment and display operates more generally than the idea of the shifting erogenous zone indicates. It entails far more than a fluctuating emphasis on bosom, hips, legs, and so on; and it is not a product of male boredom with one part of the anatomy resulting in fashion's new stress on another part. The cartoon, "Man's Ideal of Beauty" for example, dates from a period when the derriere was emphasized by the bustle, while the legs were concealed under long skirts, but

The New Temptation of St. Anthony. Caricature from *Le Rire* (1895), Paris, reproduced in Friedrich Wendel, *Weib und Mode.*

both parts of the body were perceived as sexually attractive. (They are both highlighted in a different way by late twentieth-century advertisements for blue-jeans—for men and women.) Furthermore, the changes in women's fashion need not focus directly on sexual attributes (or erogenous zones) at all to produce feelings of curiosity and "fascination" for the male viewer. The erotic element can even remain unconscious. Novelty of any sort—variations of color, silhouette, decoration, etc.—plays a role in the appeal of the changing form of fashion.

It has become a cliché that the concealment characteristic of nine-teenth-century dress reflected the extreme sexual repression of the Vic-torians, while the short skirts of the Twenties supposedly heralded the appearance of widespread sexual promiscuity. Yet any such connection between dress and morality is far less direct and obvious than this equa-tion might indicate. We have seen that Freud implied that the progress of civilization was accompanied by the "progressive concealment of the body"—that is, that the body was becoming ever more hidden. Since he was writing in 1905, this was not an unreasonable conclusion—although, in fact, neither the nineteenth century nor "civilization" witnessed a sim-ple, progressive advance of modesty and concealment.

Rather, with the passage of (historical) time, there developed an increasing sensitivity (initially among the upper classes) to the physical aspects of human life. More of the body was hidden, for example, and greater privacy was sought for sexual relations. According to König, there was a "progressive advance of the 'threshold of embarassment' and the 'limit of modesty'." Sexual display in dress

> assumed progressively more indirect, sublimated, and symbolic forms ...
> Because the taboos modesty imposes have become more and more powerful,
> the overt decoration and representation of the male and female sex organs
> becomes less and less prominent; but this development is accompanied by
> a host of symbolic representations of sex characteristics.[10]

At the same time, he suggests that certain forms of display such as deeper décolletage for women's dress, were "no longer felt as a direct provocation, but only as aesthetically tamed eroticism."

Furthermore, although Freud thought that modern civilization seemed to demand an increasingly strict sexual morality, he apparently did not interpret contemporary fashion as a reflection of this demand, since he specifically associated concealment with the *renewal* of sexual interest, not with its repression. Some contemporaries agreed with Freud, among them the psychoanalytically minded Austrian writer, Robert Musil.

In his novel, *The Man Without Qualities*, Musil denied that the body-concealing character of pre-war dress was the result of people's feelings of shame about the naked body:

> In those days women wore clothes that encased them from throat to ankles
> ... The water-clear candour of exhibiting oneself naked would then have
> been regarded, even by a person ... not hampered by any feelings of shame
> in his appreciation of the undraped body, as a relapse in the animal state,
> not because of the nakedness but because of the renunciation of the civilised
> erotic stimulus afforded by clothes ... Human beings at that time still had
> many skins ... dress ... forming a many-petalled, almost impenetrable
> chalice loaded with an erotic charge and concealing at its core the slim
> white animal that made itself fearfully desirable, letting itself be searched
> for ... [11]

The clothes themselves provided a "civilised erotic stimulus" or "erotic charge." Indeed, Musil explained a large part of the appeal of these fashions in terms of the "over-refined transference of the desire from the body to the clothes, from the embrace to the obstacles, or in short, from the goal to the approach." The eroticism of fashion may not even be primarily intended to lead to sexual union.

Clothing conceals not only the genitals and the sexual body, but also "the commonness of nakedness." Dress is so closely associated with the wearer's personal self-image and his or her social being that it produces a "quality of individuality."[12] If the sexual appeal of the naked body is eternal, the charm of fashion lies partly in the way its changing beauties reveal facets of the wearer, who remakes nature by means of art. As Marcel Proust wrote, each of the Duchess de Guermantes's dresses was "like the projection of a particular aspect of her soul."[13] It may initially appear strange that a person could seem more human and more individual clothed than naked, but this perception derives not from a sense of shame about the body, but from the belief that a person is *more* than his or her body.

The Ideal Self

The myth of the fig leaf emphasizes the relationship between clothing and the sexual body. But there exists another clothing myth that associates the development of clothing with the process of becoming fully human. According to the Balinese, "The first human beings were extremely imperfect creatures. They walked around naked, had no permanent dwellings and slept together like animals." Disturbed, the gods decided to send some of their number to earth "to teach men manners and customs." Thus, the "goddess Angga Ratih and her retinue of heavenly nymphs brought the women cotton and weaving tools and showed them how to weave plain cloth." But people still lacked ceremonial (religious) dress. "Dewi Ratih had taught mankind how to weave simple, one-coloured cloths and to dress as well as possible with them. But the situation changed when the soul of Bhagawan Nraweya, who was known for his self-discipline and virtue, was allowed to visit the divine heaven and see how the gods dressed. And Bhagawan Nraweya taught mankind to dress as the gods do."[14] Rather than living "like animals," people consciously emulated the deities; both men and women, male and female deities participated in this civilizing process.

Recent anthropological studies also suggest that clothing and adornment function to "improve on nature," to make the body more beautiful and, in some way, more human. Clothes are thus associated not only with sexual matters and with questions of status, but can also "symbolize" an entire "social order," with all that this entails concerning behavior and belief.[15]

But, above all, clothing and adornment are significant because of their intimate connection with the self. Clothing expresses a particular image of the physical body, the individual's self-awareness, and his or her social being. I have used the expression "the ideal self," because the individual (whether consciously or not) chooses the style of dress that he or she feels presents the "best" image of the self— within, of course, the limits of contemporary possibilities and personal resources.

One difference between modern fashion and traditional costume is the degree of choice permissible. Prior to the development and spread of fashion, a person's clothing was, to a far greater extent, determined in advance by his or her position in the social hierarchy. An analogy with uniforms is perhaps not inappropriate: A Sargeant might feel that the uniform of a Colonel is more attractive (and certainly more prestigious) than his own, but he cannot simply decide to wear it. On the other hand, by the nineteenth century, his wife could wear exactly the same dress as the Colonel's wife, if she so chose. The change from the old the new vestimentary regime represents a shift from legal restrictions (only partially enforced) to normative ones. Yet the theory of the ideal self may, I think, be applied to traditional costume as well as to modern fashion, to men's clothing as well as to women's.

Why do we look the way we do at any given point in time? According to my theory of the ideal self, our appearance is a form of self-presentation, a look that has meaning, involving a compromise between who we are and who we would like to be, our personal self image and a "self-for-others." Fashion is an overdetermined phenomenon that expresses more than the sum of its parts: an "autonomous" evolution, the "mirror" of society, and personal "expression." The individual is not always entirely aware of his or her motivations, such as the desires to have a new appearance, to attract attention, to be sexually attractive, and to manifest membership in a socially prestigious group. No matter how apparently "natural" or "functional," clothing is always a social attribute.

In his analysis of the language of fashion, Philip Thody argues persuasively that "Clothes express our freely elected vision of ourselves." Our appearance is neither the "spontananeous emanation from inner character" nor "the inevitable consequence of what society requires"—although we may often resist admitting that it is we who have chosen and assembled a particular collection of visual signs.[16] Similarly, in her study of the dandy, Domna Stanton argues that, "If dress is language, then the specific way we dress is speech."[17]Of course, we do not have absolute freedom to dress and look any way we please, but this does not mean that fashion is "tyrannical." Compared with traditional costume and revolutionary anti-fashion (such as the "Mao uniform"), modern fashion offers a wealth of "bourgeois individualist" freedom of choice. It is not (if I may extend the political metaphor) a situation of "anarchy," in which every individual invents his or her "own" look, without any reference to a common style. It is actually difficult to imagine such a situation, which would be comparable to inventing personal (and mutually unintelligible) languages. In reality, the situation is one in which there is a common language that allows individuals to develop a personal style of "speech" (such as dandyism or old-fogeyism) or to use the slang of a particular subculture (such as Aesthetic Dress or Punk).

Just as language has a grammar and syntax, so also must the arrangement of clothing-signs be consistent in order to be comprehensible: the top hat goes with the white tie, which goes with the champagne and the Rolls Royce. In other words, to quote Stanton: "The relationship between signifiers (beads, gray flannel suit) and the signified (hippy, businessman), although ostensibly arbitrary, will appear less so once rationalized and legitimized by the contextual culture. The choice of signs in each category of dress or ornamentation and their intercategoric combination constitute sartorial speech." Indeed, the body itself may become a "signifying surface."[18] A very important aspect of identity that is expressed through the language of dress is gender identity, but what it means to be a man or a woman is tremendously complex and variable.

Furthermore, appearance (a style of dress and adornment, a body and a mode of self-presentation) is more than a series of *statements* about social and psychological phenomena. Clothing is also significant on another level, because it helps create a total visual image—a *look*. Fashion changes gradually but regularly, and every new style is presented as a question: "Wouldn't you like to look like this?" The art historian Anne Hollander has argued that clothes should be viewed "not primarily as cultural by-products or personal expressions but as connecting links in a creative tradition of image-making." Changes in fashion, she suggests, are caused far less by practical, accidental, or ideological considerations than by the visual need for a new image.[19] So far, so good; but who feels this need? And why does it manifest itself in particular ways?

Fashions evolve by means of a symbiotic relationship between developments within the world of craft (the clothing tradition itself more than the tradition of picture-making, as Hollander suggests) and the more gradual evolution of cultural ideals of beauty. The concept of "beauty," however, is complex, since although beauty is sexual and implicitly emphasizes sexual characteristics and gender distinction, these vary in degree and type and interact with other social ideals and aesthetic tastes. Among the social ideals are conceptions of appropriate gender-linked behavior. Cultural influences such as the role of women and the position of the young, as well as aesthetic tastes in the fine and decorative arts, also influence conceptions of personal beauty. It is often asserted that as beliefs and behavior change, so also does appearance. There is evidence, though, that appearance may change *in advance of* widespread changes in belief systems and behavior. The visual need for a new image is a constant, which emphasizes an opposition to whatever the *old* look was: If the old look was full, the new look will become slim. In this way, sexual curiosity will be renewed. The need for a new image only becomes a serious issue within society when it is interpreted as a challenge to social conventions that are beginning to be contested in other ways as well.

One important factor in the development of new looks is the existence of specific settings for fashion-oriented behavior. What a person does and where affects the style of self-presentation, which encompasses such variables as posture, movement, and expression, as well as dress. The individual is always posing on some stage, and his or her appearance needs to be congruent with the physical setting. Costume links the "natural" body to its cultural surroundings and decor. Furthermore, although the significance attached to clothing may be symbolic or merely conventional, it does seem clear that various looks are perceived as having meaning. A style creates the image of a particular *type* of person, with all that this entails of personal expression and social role playing. The ideal self represents not only who a person *is*, but also who he or she would like to be.

Along with the eroticism of fashion, its essential artificiality has aroused the greatest resistance. Yet the popular belief that fashion has progressed or should progress towards greater naturalness is antithetical to the phenomenon. Fashion is never "natural." It is not that "fashion" has failed to "accept" the human body, but that people use fashion to create images of themselves. Just as the individual cannot be conceived of apart from society, so also is the body itself a product of "The glass of fashion and the mould of form."

Fashion and Erotic Beauty
in the Victorian Period

4

Victorian Fashion

What Is Victorian Fashion?

What we think of as "Victorian" or "nineteenth-century" fashion lasted just under a century—from about 1820 (almost two decades before Victoria was crowned Queen of England) to about 1910. The period encompassed is thus synonymous neither with the nineteenth century nor with the reign of Queen Victoria. Rather, Victorian fashion begins with the transition away from the immediately preceding—and very different— female fashion known today as the "Empire" or "Regency" style. Victorian fashion ends with the appearance of a "Neo-Empire" look.

During the first Empire period (circa 1795–1815), the fashion was referred to as the "Greek" or "Classical" mode; and the primary garment was the "chemise dress," which closely resembled the traditional undergarment of that name. Consequently, it has been said that "the eighteenth and nineteenth centuries met in the middle of a decade of undress." In fact, however, the Empire dress was worn with undergarments, while the corset was only to some extent abandoned; an American textbook of 1806 exaggerated slightly when it taught the student of French how to say, "The women no longer wear stays."[1]

The Empire mode was characterized by a high waistline (sometimes just below the bust) and a straight skirt with a hemline that rose to ankle height. The vertical silhouette emphasized the bosom and deemphasized the waist, making the corset a much less crucial structuring garment. In addition, the relative narrowness of the skirt and lightness of material (usually muslin or lawn) and color (usually white) indicated—although it did not reveal—the legs.

By the early 1820s, the waistline gradually dropped to its "normal" position and became more pronounced; simultaneously, the skirt became fuller, longer, and heavier. Despite all subsequent changes in the shape of the skirt and sleeves, the basic lines of Victorian fashion were set: The typical female silhouette was essentially formed by two cones—the long,

full, structured skirt and the tailored, boned bodice—intersecting at a
narrow and constricted waist.

If women's fashions of the mid-eighteenth and mid-nineteenth centuries were not dissimilar in general form, the same could not be said of
men's fashions. The Empire style was only a brief interlude in the continuum of female fashion, but male clothing changed permanently. In the
mid-eighteenth century, both men and women of the elite wore clothing
of similar ornamentation and novelty, and with a parallel emphasis on the
sexual body. By the mid-nineteenth century, vivid colors, luxurious fabrics, decoration, and changeability were essentially restricted to women's
dress, and most men wore some version of the plain, dark, uniform three-
piece suit. Knee-breeches and silk hose gave way to long, loose trousers.
The only vestiges of men's earlier elaborate costumes remained in military
uniforms and very formal evening dress.

Contrary to popular belief, simpler, darker male clothing did not orig-
inate with the revolutionary bourgeoisie in France, but instead appeared
several decades earlier in England; and it was not a crude expression of
one socioeconomic class supplanting another. It developed in part from
the clothing of the mercantile classes, but also from the country and sporting clothes of the English landed aristocracy. (Long trousers, however,
seem to have been revolutionary in origin.) As early as the 1760s, plainer
male dress had begun to be associated in England with liberty, patriotism,
virtue, enterprise, and manliness, while elaborate and modish male dress

Charles H. Gibbs-Smith, illustration from *The Fashionable Lady in the Nineteenth-Century* (London: Her Majesty's Stationery Office, 1960). Courtesy of
The Victoria and Albert Museum.

carried connotations of tyranny, political and moral corruption, and a "degenerate exotic effeminacy." After about 1790, these ideas spread throughout Anglo-American and French society, and the plainer suit was increasingly widely adopted.[2]

By the mid-nineteenth century, men of the upper and middle classes and even urban working-class men, all wore a plain and somber coat and waistcoat, trousers, a shirt, underclothes, and some kind of hat or cap. At the same time, the luxury and modishness hitherto associated primarily with the clothing of the aristocracy became characteristic of the dress of middle-class women as well. The clear sartorial distinction between men and women is a primary characteristic of Victorian fashion. Class distinctions, while very important, were nonetheless secondary. At least in towns, the dress of women of all classes was more-or-less fashionable, worn over a corset and a variety of undergarments. Within this general framework, "Victorian dress was a sequence of many different styles," each of which evolved gradually from its predecessor.[3]

Dress and Undress (A Satin Corset). Fashion plate from *Modes de Paris. Petit Courrier des Dames* (1837).

Male and Female Day Dress. Fashion plate from *Costumes Parisiens* (1827).

Undergarments determined the line of the outer dress. Most important was the corset—a foundation garment made of cloth and whalebone (or some substitute for it, such as cording or steel) that defined or constricted the waist and supported the bust. The corset had existed for centuries, but its contours changed over time. During the eighteenth century, the corset formed a heavily boned V-shape. When the Empire mode dominated in France, the corset became lighter and shorter, evolving into something more akin to a linen bust-support (although in England the corset sometimes instead became long and straight). After about 1806, the corset was again boned and fitted with a busk, flattening the stomach and

LES MODES PARISIENNES

A. Varin, *Male and Female Evening Dress*. Fashion plate from *Les Modes Parisiennes* (ca. 1845).

hips. With the development of Victorian fashion, the corset again constricted the waist, but the shape was now closer to that of an hourglass.

The shape of the skirt and sleeves and the general character of the dress also changed over time. The period from about 1815 to 1825 was transitional, becoming less Classical and more Romantic, often harkening back to Renaissance styles. The ethereal images of butterflies, fairies, and ballerinas had some influence as well. There was more ornamentation. Gores were introduced into both the skirt and the cut of the bodice. Then the waistline began to drop and the sleeves to swell up into the famous *gigot* (leg-of-mutton) and imbecile sleeves. The female fashions of the 1820s and early 1830s had wide shoulders, full, puffed sleeves, and flared, bell-shaped skirts. Hair, cut short *à la Titus* or in Grecian bands during the Empire period, was in exuberant loops and piles of curls, *à la giraffe*, during the 1820s and 1830s; large, flamboyant hats were popular. Fashion plates from the first three decades of the century show small, young, and sprightly figures; by the 1840s and 1850s they tend to look more subdued.

In the late 1830s, 1840s, and 1850s, the emphasis shifted to a sloping, narrow shoulderline, tight sleeves set into the dress just below the shoulder making it difficult to raise the arms. The waist became increasingly long, low, and slender-looking, while layers of petticoats gave a dome-shape to the skirt. The design of the dress was intended to give the illusion of a little waist through the use of converging lines, coming to a point over the stomach. Bonnets replaced hats. Hair was either smoothly pulled back or in ringlets. Colors began to soften. In short, a rather jaunty look was replaced by a more lady-like style.

Anais Toudouze, *Theatre Dresses*. Fashion plate from *Le Conseiller des Dames et des Demoiselles* (1857), also published in *Le Follet*.

Yet it is not entirely accurate for costume historians to characterize this as a "sentimental," "gothic," or "prudish" mode. Evening décolletage was very low and straight, and exposed the shoulders. The curves of the bosom and hips were also indicated, sartorially, both by way of contrast with the slender pointed waist, and through the fullness of the skirt at the hips. It was at this time that Theophile Gautier described the charm of the full skirt as deriving in part from its role as the pedestal from which the woman's head and torso stood out becomingly.[4]

Furthermore, the rather insipid simplicity of 1840s styles gave way in the 1850s to a revived worldliness, as the somewhat drooping silhouette became more ample and brilliant again. Thus, although the faces in fashion plates are of a candy-box prettiness, the flounced skirts, elaborate sleeves and bodices, and wealth of lace on dresses in bright green, magenta, periwinkle blue, and violet present a more overtly alluring image of femininity. Although outdoor dresses were more subdued, indoor and evening dresses certainly presented a picture that was far from the Quakeresque modesty commonly associated with the Mid-Victorian woman. Even the style of high-class prostitutes changed, as romantic courtesans like Marie Duplesis gave way to flamboyant grande cocottes like Cora Pearl.

As late as the 1830s and 1840s, men's fashion still emphasized the wearer's physical attractions. Indeed, there are fashion plates in which the male looks sexier than his female companion—in long, very tight trousers or pantaloons and a short tight tail-coat, cut high in front, nipped in at the waist and with broad shoulders. During the first half of the nineteenth century, there were three types of male legwear. Breeches were worn as full evening wear until mid-century, and for sport throughout the century. Pantaloons, often with a strap under the instep, were worn from the late eighteenth century until about 1850. Trousers, initially unfashionable, became fashionable after about 1810, and were even acceptable as evening dress after the 1830s. They were still close-fitting, but did not outline the shape of the leg as clearly as pantaloons did. Jane Carlyle disapprovingly described the Count d'Orsay's pantaloons as "skin coloured and fitting like a glove."[5]

Conversely, Queen Victoria described in her diary how "excessively handsome" the youthful Albert was—with his "beautiful" eyes, "exquisite nose," "such a pretty mouth with delicate mustachios," and "a beautiful figure, broad in the shoulders and a fine waist."[6] A decade or two later he would have had to be in uniform to show off his figure. Some men such as the dandified D'Orsay and the young Disraeli struggled against the trend toward the disappearance of color, line, and decoration in male clothing. But eventually even they abandoned their all too conspicuous dress.

The ordinary man's suit of the second half of the century tended to conceal any possible physical attractions or evidence of physical strength, other than sheer size and bulk. Broad shoulders were interpreted as evi-

François Courboin, *The Picture Exhibition at the Salon: Looking at Manet's "Olympia"*. Illustration from Octave Uzanne, *Fashion in Paris in the Nineteenth Century* (London: William Heineman, 1901).

dence of male strength, and were admired, but they were not clearly delineated or padded by clothing. By the 1860s, coat, trousers, and waistcoat were all of looser fit and solid, boxy shape. The hallmark frock-coat began to replace the tail-coat as day wear after about 1820. Other even less formal coats included various sporting or lounging "jackets." By the 1880s, the dinner jacket (known in America as the "Tuxedo") was accepted for informal evening wear. Although the legs were indicated, their form was hidden by what dress reformers described as "ugly and shapeless" trousers. Increasingly, clothes were made of the same materials and in the same colors. Even that last male bastion of color and pattern—the waistcoat—became generally dull. The drab and slightly baggy three-piece suit might have been somewhat more functional than previous aristocratic styles or the anachronistic military uniform, but, intended to hide both paunches and muscles, it was hardly an obvious "expression" of the active, strong, aggressive male. It was only toward the end of the century that the waist and shoulders began to become somewhat more clearly delineated.[7]

Meanwhile, in the late 1850s, women's dress was altered by the invention of the *cage-crinoline*—a dome-shaped structure of graduated hoops (of whalebone, steel, or watch-spring) that supported the skirt. Hitherto, an ever-increasing number of petticoats had given the skirt its bell-shape; now these could be dispensed with, and the wearer have an even fuller skirt. The swinging of the crinoline imparted a new, flirtatious aspect to women's dress, although it was the size that attracted most attention—most of it unfavorable. Through the normal fashion process of competitive inflation, the crinoline continued to grow throughout the first half of the 1860s. Contemporary cartoons attest to male views of the crinoline as being ridiculously oversized. Some historians have uncritically accepted caricatures as facts. Yet Victorian women's fashion far from immobilized its wearers. Crinolines might have been "incommodious incumbrances," but they were lighter than multiple petticoats, and were worn by intrepid Englishwomen in Africa and even by many peasant women in Europe.

After about 1860, the crinoline flattened gradually in front, and became larger behind. The full skirts were no longer marked by rows of flounces, but rather by complex arrangements of over-draperies, such as the apron over-skirt, which was designed in part to be modest, as the flatter front might otherwise have shown the outlines of the legs. The new back-fullness is also indicated by decorations. As the style became increasingly overloaded, a simple walking costume with a shorter skirt appeared, and by the 1880s evolved into the tailored suit or *trotteur*. Fashionable hairstyles—a combination of the full, high chignon and curls—were more elaborate and "artificial" than their immediate predecessors, although less so than the hairstyles of the 1820s and early 1830s; they matched the style of the dress by echoing the silhouette of crinolette, bustle, and train. The modest indoor cap was now a vestigial piece of lace and ribbon covering the front of the hair.

Meanwhile, color combinations became more garish. In 1898, the fashion historian Georgianna Hill observed that "The mixtures were sometimes rather startling—or we should think so now."[8] One fashion plate from 1869 shows a woman wearing a light green overdress above a striped yellow and black silk, showing at the hem and cuffs, and at the false décolletage of the bosom (see next page). Other popular shades included peacock blue, canary, pink coral, and mandarine (orange). Followers of the Aesthetic movement criticized these colors as vulgar, and promoted the use of neutral and faded colors.

The beautiful hand painting of fashion plates and the careful use of shading and cross-hatching to give a sense of texture and weave was nec-

Jules David, *Day Dresses Worn Over Crinolettes*. Fashion plate from *The Englishwoman's Domestic Magazine* (1869), reproduced from *Le Moniteur de la Mode*.

essary, since by the 1860s dresses were frequently made of more than one material and color:

> Velvet over brocade. . . . Brocade over satin. Silk over silk of a different colour. Very few dresses are of only one material, or of one colour. If two colours are not worn, two shades become imperative.

And the bright shades were simply regarded as appropriately gay: "Fashion . . . shows us the way to dress coquettishly at every age. . . . We are to look young, bright and happy in youth's bright gladdening hues."[9] The complex construction, bright colors, and elaboration were intended to produce a rich and opulent yet feminine and coquettish effect. It is questionable, however, whether contemporaries and historians were correct in interpreting these sartorial changes as evidence of either a new feminine self-assertion or even an imitation of the more overtly erotic styles of the demi-monde. Yet the overall look of fashion plate figures *is* more self-assured and less coyly demure, a style of self-presentation that may well reflect women's widening sphere. The figures are also physically more substantial and solid. Indeed, the English fashion historian Sarah Levitt has suggested that over the course of the nineteenth century, the figures in

Il est vrai que jamais une femme ne consentait à avouer le supplice qu'elle subissait.

Et quand on disait à une femme qui semblait à la torture dans son appareil de coutil, de fer et d'acier : « Prenez garde, vous êtes trop serrée ! » elle avait immédiatement à sa disposition une réponse qui consistait à soulever d'une certaine façon le bas du corset : « Vous voyez, disait-elle invariablement, je ne suis pas serrée du tout, on y passerait la main. »

Quitte à se trouver mal une demi-heure après; de telle sorte qu'on était immédiatement contraint

Getting Dressed. Illustration by Bertall from *La Comédie de notre temps* (1874).

James Jacques Tissot, *The Ball on Shipboard* (ca. 1874). Courtesy of the Trustees of The Tate Gallery, London.

fashion plates "grow up," becoming increasingly adult and capable-looking.[10]

The 1860s have been stigmatized as a period of extreme corsetry, but fashion plates from even the notorious *Englishwoman's Domestic Magazine* give no evidence whatsoever of tight-lacing. Most prints, of course, were imported from France; yet more important, the fashions have waistlines so high that the focus of sartorial interest is more on the bulk of the crinolette. Almost any waist would look small in comparison with such a full skirt. But corsets and fashions changed in the next decade. The corset of the 1860s was short, emphasizing rather abrupt curves. New techniques of cutting and seaming in the later 1870s and 1880s allowed the corset to be fitted more precisely. The fashionable waist lengthened, and the new *corset-cuirasse* "moulded" more of the torso. The ideal figure was in the process of becoming longer in the waist, with hips that were slightly slimmer and perhaps a more opulent bosom. Advertisements proliferated for Bust Improvers and corsets with laced "regulators" inside the bust gores.

The fashions of the 1870s are extremely body-revealing, featuring an increasingly long sheath-like cuirasse-bodice, and a skirt that was tied back with concealed tapes, to give a straighter and noticeably tighter fit in front. "Ladies . . . must be encased in a sheath. . . . The cuirasse-corsage now moulds not only the waist, but encloses the whole figure." Or as another journalist wrote, "Bodies are made to fit like wax." In the early 1870s, the half-crinoline or crinolette evolved into the bustle—a half-cage or puff behind, filled with horsehair or stiffened gauze and net. It was by no means a new invention—bustles appear in numerous eighteenth-century caricatures, where they are openly referred to as "false bums." The fashion historian, Doris Langley Moore, argues convincingly that "The discomforts of a bustle dress are more apparent than real, as the *tournure* is partly collapsible and easily moves to one side when the wearer sits down." Modified bustles were even used for children's dresses, and Rosamund Napier recalled when she was five: "I don't suppose I have ever been more happy than walking up to the church through the sunny fields, before a slow stream of villagers, conscious of my bustle."[11]

Then from about 1876 to 1880, the fullness of the skirt was pushed down from the upper half of the back to the lower half. The arrangement

Anais Toudouze, *Evening Dress with Cuirasse Bodice, and Princess Dress.* Fashion plate from *La Mode Illustrée* (1877).

of drapery formed a cascading train or tail behind. A fashion plate from 1877 (shown on page 63) shows the elaborate draping and trimming in great detail, which the viewer would have needed to see, since

> It is now quite impossible to describe dresses with exactitude; the skirts are draped so mysteriously, the arrangement of trimmings is usually one-sided and the fastenings are so curiously contrived that after studying any particular toilette for even quarter of an hour the task of writing down how it is made remains hopeless.[12]

The figure on the left wears a pale yellow dress with a trim of cherries on a pleated and asymmetrical band. There is a bow on her derriere and other bows caught up in a train. Her companion wears a slim pink "princess" dress, another style popular during the "vertical" years between the two bustle periods. The princess dress has no waist seams, and the all-in-one-piece style emphasized an elongated line. The illustration is typical in showing side and back views of the dresses.

How might these styles be read? The bow on the derriere obviously serves to call attention to that part of the anatomy, and was a common feature on evening dress of the period. The bows running up the front of the pink dress look like fastenings (though they are not), and call to mind the image of the dress opening down the front. It is unlikely that the bows are icons for knots and thus symbols of bondage. The lacing up the back of the yellow dress, however, clearly recalls corset laces and would have obvious connotations of undress. Cherries probably had some of the erotic connotations then that they have now. Students of visual perception believe that diagonal lines give an impression of greater movement or action than vertical or horizontal lines. Decorative diagonal bands could be signs that signify movement, as could tassels which were also popular in the 1870s and 1880s. On the other hand, since Oriental art was something of a vogue in Paris at this time, the use of asymmetrical decoration could reflect an awareness of Japanese design. This is only speculation, but what is clear is that this fashion plate does not exaggerate the relatively close fit of many 1870s fashions, which was especially noticeable after the bulk of the bell-shaped skirt.

By the 1870s, the outdoor bonnet of earlier decades had largely given way to the small and fancy hat and hat-like bonnet, decorated with feathers, lace, and flowers, and worn tilted coquettishly forward or back. As Charles Blanc observed, "The bonnet is a protection from stolen glances," but "as austerity diminishes, the front of the bonnet diminishes likewise" and "extreme coquetry of the head-dress" becomes fashionable. "A bonnet is simply an excuse for a feather, a pretext for a spray of flowers. . . . A fashionable young lady. . . . has discovered how to wear a bonnet without its covering her head, and who, far from concealing her her hair draws it back, puffs it, crimps it, displays it, and even adds to it an artificial abundance." Whether the style worn was the full dress hat, the morning hat, or the country hat, the intended effect was "charming."[13]

Another popular accessory that reinforced the image of graceful, coquettish beauty was the fan, which appears in many fashion plates and paintings of the period. The well-known French fashion historian, Octave Uzanne, asked, rhetorically, "Is there any toy more coquettish than this Fan? any plaything more charming? any ornament more expressive?" Other fashion writers agreed that "Fans were in universal request." A "language" of fan gestures existed throughout the eighteenth and nineteenth centuries, although a gesture that might have been merely flirtatious when used in one situation could carry a quite specific meaning in another.[14]

The style of an ensemble of the 1870s and 1880s could be either predominantly "pretty" and "frivolous" or "smart" and "dignified." One classic High Victorian look, for example, consisted of a dress in an "eighteenth-century" pink floral print like those worn by "the sentimental shepardesses represented upon . . . Watteau fans."[15] A flower-trimmed crimson hat was worn tilted to the side, while its wearer shielded herself with a small parasol. Various contemporary fashion writers insisted that "Parasols are now quite indispensable" as a "complement of the toilette for the promenade"—and not only for "protection from the sun," but because they could be a "gracious adjunct of feminine costume" that permitted the sight of "a rosy head with dishevelled hair, on the transparent ground of a Japanese sunshade."[16]

Yet tailor-mades also became extremely popular in the 1880s. Many women chose to wear austere-looking dark wool "suits"—with crisp white cuffs and collars, a jacket-bodice, and sometimes a matching waistcoat. But even for the woman who actually worked, the skirt was worn over a bustle, and the torso was corseted. For other women, the semi-masculine mode was simply a fashionable style, and did not necessarily indicate either advanced views or the need for "practical" clothes. A very elaborate dinner dress illustrated in *Harper's Bazar*, for example, had a bodice that echoed the shape of a man's waistcoat, but this was an affectation. Furthermore, although dark colors were popular for tailor-made suits, "light and vivid shades" were popular for other dresses—and, indeed, for some suits as well. In the mid–1880s, "pink and pale blue had perhaps their greatest vogue in the history of fashion."[17]

Eighties fashions, then, were rather more severe than the styles of the Seventies, although the relatively stark lines were usually relieved by more overtly feminine details. In general, the bodice was simple and snug-fitting with tight sleeves, while the skirt was the focus of interest. With the return of the bustle (1882–1889), it grew larger than ever, was placed higher, and jutted out more sharply. The new, shorter skirt now hung straight, no longer pulled back by hidden ties. Initially, there was often a draped apron over-skirt in front, and bunches of puffs behind. Gradually, pleats replaced drapery. Meanwhile, the hair was dressed closer to the head, sometimes with a fringe in front. (Queen Victoria complained that it made women look like "poodles.") The new high-crowned toques and vaguely military hats certainly looked less obviously flirtatious than the elaborate hairstyles and revealing little hats of the 1870s.

One of the most significant developments in fashion was the increasing luxury of underwear. The basic garment was the "chemise"—the precursor of the slip, made of white linen or cotton, low-necked, sleeveless, and calf-length. By the 1880s, it was increasingly trimmed with lace and ribbons. Over this came knee-length "drawers" (knickers or underpants), "with the chemise pulled through the back opening to provide extra support for the back of the dress, in lieu of the bustle."[18] Or in addition to the bustle. Some women replaced the chemise and knickers with a type of union suit, called "combinations." The corset came next; it was laced up the back and fastened with hooks in front. Contrary to popular belief, most women got in and out of their corsets by themselves; they did not need to clutch a bedpost while their maids laced them up. At this time, usually two petticoats were worn—one just below knee-length, and then a longer, fuller one to give the skirt the proper line. Silk petticoats were fashionable, and they were sometimes colored. More common, however, were calico and strong linsey petticoats, with muslin for best. Corsets were often made of colored silk or satin. Red was especially popular. Stockings could be either silk or cotton, black, white, striped, or colored to match the dress. They frequently had decorative designs on the front.

The shoes of the early Victorian period were narrow and heelless, in black or white satin. In the 1850s and 1860s, the foot was allowed to be slightly broader; leather and cloth, as well as satin, were used; and heels appeared—an inch or less in height. Ankle-length laced or buttoned boots were also popular. From the 1870s to the turn of the century, heels grew higher (one or two inches) and toes more pointed. Low-cut pumps were worn for evening.

By the 1890s, fashion interest shifted from the skirt to the bodice; the bustle and skirt drapery largely disappeared, although the skirt was still usually supported at the waist by a small pad. The sleeves began to puff up. From about 1890 to 1897, skirts fitted tightly over the hips and curved out below the knee; they usually remained long and were held up for walking. Sleeves became very full, and bodice decoration was often extravagant. The tall, statuesque figure was the ideal—clad either in traditional formal dress or in a somewhat more youthful and "modern" style. An excellent example of the fine woman in an evening gown from Worth is shown in a fashion plate by the brilliant fashion illustrator A. Sandoz. The fashionable woman is presented as a figure with full curves and a slim waist clothed in haute couture luxury (here a sky-blue satin trimmed with black fur and bead embroidery), carrying an oversize black lace fan, and with a coiffure from Lentheric of Paris. The woman's facial features are much bolder than the ideal of the Early- to Mid-Victorian period, which by now was widely regarded as insipid.

An alternative was the stylish suit, consisting, for example, of a grey cloth jacket and skirt worn with a high-necked white surah blouse and

A. Sandoz, Evening Gown by Worth. Fashion plate from *Harper's Bazar* (1894), probably reproduced from *The Queen,* and again reproduced in Stella Blum, ed., *Victorian Costumes and Fashions from Harper's Bazar* (New York: Dover Publications, 1974). Courtesy of Dover Publications.

grey satin belt, a lacy white hat, and a white parasol. A related and very popular style was the skirt and blouse, which were immortalized somewhat later in countless Gibson Girl drawings. The corset and long skirt remained as essential in the 1890s as in the 1850s, yet the overall appearance of the Late Victorian woman was very different from that of her counterpart at mid-century.

Around the turn of the century, the fashion line altered again, when the corset became straight in front, throwing the sloping line of the bosom forward and creating an S-shaped silhouette. In illustrations, the bosom is often stylized to appear as a monolithic expanse in the shape of a sine-curve—the notorious "monobosom" of fashion history. In real fashion terms, the pouched fabric at the front of the bodice and the forward tilting posture encouraged by the corset did emphasize the bosom. Fashion photographs show how the monobosom was often an illusion created by a hanging triangle of lace—a trim that was both delicate and filmy and potentially very expensive. The popularity of fashion models with frankly voluptuous figures and rather heavy faces indicates that the Junoesque figure was the ideal. Nor was it considered necessary or desirable to paint out part of the waist and hips, as was sometimes done with earlier photographs to give the impression of a smaller waist.

Fashions became increasingly *froufrou*, particularly for evening wear and (semi) private occasions. Soft, clinging fabrics, pale colors, and delicate, expensive trimmings were typical. In general, a "seductive," "delicate," "adorable," and "airy-fairy" effect was aimed for. If the 1890s were magnificent, the early twentieth century was both splendid and ultrafeminine.[19]

Yet day dress continued to be characterized by the increasing popularity of the fashionable tailored suit. According to *Les Modes* of 1901, the suit was revolutionary:

> The great 89 of feminine costume has been the tailored suit. it has triumphantly remedied the abuses of the old regime [such as vulgar over-decoration]. . . . Only this 89 has found its Dix-huit-Brumaire, that has put it back a step. Gentlemen have not fully appreciated the tailored costume. They have found it too closely resembling their own.[20]

It seemed to make a "pretty woman" look like a "pretty boy!" Despite a few anxieties about creeping *habitudes garconnières*, the suit was both chic and popular. As with men's clothing, quality depended on cut, material, and accessories, rather than trim, which had been devalued in fashion terms by widespread imitation.

A 1907 fashion illustration from *Revue de la Mode* shows a perfectly fitting dark blue striped wool suit, appropriate for walking in the city. It is shown being worn in central Paris by a self-assured woman with the fashionable S-shaped silhouette and an expensive and very large feathered hat. In place of a parasol, she carries a dandified cane, a tiny reticule, and what could be either a letter or business papers. Bust emphasis is limited to the position of a large soft green bow. The throat itself is covered completely by a high collar—a development of the 1890s that shows how standards of modesty in dress do not merely give way over time, but may also become more stringent. The skirt also is longer than that of the 1860s or 1880s. This woman looks so chic that it is immediately clear that she could easily have afforded obvious opulence of dress, but that she has rather chosen this more severely and discreetly elegant style. Meanwhile, men's costume changed only in details. In general, the three-piece business suit was worn for all but rather formal occasions.

Rousseau, *Tailored Suit*. Fashion plate from *Revue de la Mode* (1907).

Between about 1902 and 1907, the fashionable female silhouette continued to evolve, and the line of the corset became gradually straighter and
longer. The exuberant, flared Edwardian petticoat shrank. By 1910, the
S-shaped line had disappeared, and the narrow "hobble skirt" was worn
with a long, straight corset, creating a rigorously vertical line. Tailored
suits continued to be popular for daytime, but the new style was little
more "practical" than the tailored suits of the bustle period, some twenty-
five years earlier. For evening and private wear, however, the trend was
toward an Empire look. Young, slim women even began to trade in their
corsets for short girdles and brassieres. Contemporaries at first perceived
the new style as a revival of the slim, straight Empire style of a century

A. E. Marty, *Les Reminiscences de la Mode: Cent Ans Après*. Fashion plate from *Femina* (1913).

before, as to some extent it was. A 1913 drawing by A. E. Marty was revealingly, and perhaps reassuringly, titled "Les Reminiscences de la Mode." If the *élégante* of 1813 is shown exposing the top of her breasts, while her counterpart of 1913 does not, nevertheless the connotations of sexual freedom had for so long been closely associated with the Empire mode that this comparison implicitly hints at a more relaxed attitude toward erotic display. As the style evolved, however, it became clear that this was no mere historical revival, but a genuinely new look.

Just as the demise of the first Empire style marked the beginning of the Victorian era in dress, so also did the Neo-Empire style mark the end of that era. For all the fluctuation of fashion between 1908 and 1928—from the hobble skirt and lampshade tunic through the calf-length "war crinoline" to the flat-chested, low-waisted Twenties look—the dominant trend was away from the full hourglass figure with the narrow waist and toward a vertical line and a relatively unconstricted waist. This was such a break with the past that it genuinely deserved the title given to another fashion illustration: "Les Révolutions de la Mode," a picture that compared the S-shaped silhouette of the Edwardian grande dame with the casual, slouching young woman in her modern tiered dress (see next page). This shift, which has been called "the beginning of modern fashion," occurred *before* the First World War. It is my belief that the change had relatively little to do with practical considerations, and a great deal to do with the development of a new image of beauty and chic.

Who Wore It? Who Made It?

Today, it is widely believed that in the nineteenth century only the elite wore fashionable dress. Certainly, the Victorians were able to "place" an individual by his or her clothing. Upper-class people wore different clothes than their middle- or working-class contemporaries did. And yet we are still able to date the majority of old photographs of middle-and working-class people by the clothing that they wear. We are able to do so because specialized class costumes died out over the course of the century as more and more middle- and working-class people imitated current fashions to the extent that they could afford to. The materials they used were cheaper and the designs simpler and sometimes clumsy, but to a considerable extent they wore the style of the day.

The so-called "democratization" of clothing was (and remains) a complex phenomenon. The French Revolution saw the temporary demise of court costume in France and the permanent disappearance of the legal costume of the Third Estate (a black cloak and breeches) and the aristocracy (gold-embroidered cloaks and white-plumed hats). During the Revolution, simplicity of dress had political overtones, but it was partly a question of labels, as, for example, when a Paris dressmaker renamed her shop the "Maison Egalité" and called herself "citizeness." The clothing of the *sans-culottes* (wide trousers, sabots, a red cap, and the short jacket known as the *carmagnole*) was worn by Marat, but not Robespierre—and after the end of the Reign of Terror, proletarian garments fell out of favor. The pseudo-Roman costumes of the Directory were worn briefly (if at all) by members of the government. Napoleon revived court costume, with a heavy emphasis on military uniforms—but for most middle-, upper-, and even working-class men, there was a steady movement toward the "respectable" suit, which did, however, include trousers.

There were, of course, differences in clothing materials. Corduroy, for example, was one working-class fabric; while in the 1840s, Engels observed that working men of the Manchester mills were identified as "fustian jackets and call themselves so in contrast to the gentlemen who wear broadcloth, which latter words are characteristic of the middle classes."[21] Somewhat different styles had different class connotations: Middle-class men

Les Révolutions de la Mode. Unidentified French fashion illustration (1913).
Courtesy of the Musée des Arts Décoratifs, Paris, Maciet Collection.

wore shirts with starched collars, cravats, and stovepipe hats. Working-class men wore caps and shirts with soft collars or no collars; they did not wear cravats. There existed sartorial evidence of class fractions: The shopwalker at a department store wore a black morning coat and striped trousers; the lower apprentices wore a short coat without tails. The neat black suit was the mark of a clerk. Particular garments had specific class associations: Flaubert, the scourge of the bourgeoisie, argued that working men in "overalls" could be quite as bourgeois (that is, idiotic) as the middle-class in "frock coats."

In the 1860s, a journeyman engineer from London distinguished between working dress, on the one hand, and the better quality Sunday suits and Saturday evening suits:

A favorite Saturday evening costume with masses of working men consists of clean moleskin or cord trousers that are to be worn at work during the ensuing week, black coat and waistcoat, a cap of a somewhat sporting character, a muffler somewhat gaudy. . . . [These are] not the evening dress suits of society be it understood but the strong, useful, well-fitting, somewhat sporting looking 'mixed' cloth suits which they don when going on their evening rambles in search of amusement after working hours and which enable them to pass muster in any society they are likely to go into, without causing them to feel that chronic fear of spoiling their clothes which haunts the working man when dressed in his best.[22]

In the 1890s, an English trawlerman in his teens boasted that he could afford "a Sunday rig out"—"a sealskin cap, gansey, pilot cloth trousers and Wellington boots. I went and had my effigy took in my best rig and sent one to Jinny my gal."[23] Good clothes represented pride and self-respect.

By mid-century, even in rural England, the traditional working-class garments, such as the smock (for men) and the bedgown and kirtle (for women), were fast disappearing. This was less true in rural France, where peasant costumes continued to be worn much longer—although more often by women than by men. For example, in photographs of French strikes in 1901 (in Montceau-les-Mines), the men wear modern workers' clothing—trousers and a *chemise* (shirt) and no vest or cravat—but the women still wear local bonnets and capes. And yet, even here, what we regard as "traditional" peasant costumes were basically derived from festival dress and were often influenced by current or out-of-date urban fashions.

Accessories had considerable significance as indicators of class, age, and occupation. Hats (and gloves) were crucial to a "respectable" appearance for both men and women. It was not fear of cold or sunstroke that kept hats on, nor even the longstanding association of uncovered female hair with eroticism. To go bareheaded was simply not proper. The top hat, for example (made of beaver or silk, in black or fawn), was standard formal wear for upper- and middle-class males; it grew lower over the course of the century. The bowler, trilby (one variant of which was the Homburg),

Pierre-Auguste Renoir, *The Umbrellas* (ca. 1884). Courtesy of the Trustees of The National Gallery, London.

and boater were informal hats. Caps were either working-class or sporting. Working women in the industrial towns of northwest England wore shawls long after they had ceased to be fashionable (after 1870); and they wore them pinned under their chins—both for warmth and as a substitute for the necessary hat or bonnet.

Working-class urban women consciously tried to follow the current mode. Courtaulds instructed its workers in 1860:

> The present ugly fashion of Hoops or Crinolines . . . is . . . quite unfitted for the work of our Factories. . . . We now request our hands at all Factories to leave Hoop and Crinoline at Home.

Even that oppressed individual, the servant, wore crinolines, at least on Sundays, and (if *Punch* may be believed) sometimes at work as well. Mrs. Gaskell's 1863 story, "The Cage at Cranford," described the appearance of a mysterious present from Paris. The recipients failed at first to recognize it, but the "little stupid servant maid Fanny" identified it correctly as a crinoline. Servants had sources of fashion information, too. In the American south, slaves at least sometimes also wore stays, and even home-made hoops made out of grape-vines.[24]

Jane Carlyle was typical of the middle class when she complained that working-class people wore inappropriate fashionable dress, and she rejected a photograph of the servant, Mary, on the grounds that "The crinoline quite changes her character and makes her a stranger to me. I would like her if she would get herself done for me as she is on washing mornings in little pink bedgown and blue petticoat."[25] Although Mary wore this eighteenth-century style for working dress, nevertheless for best dress she chose to follow fashion.

The well-known photographs of working-class women collected by A. S. Munby showed Hannah, the maid-of-all-work, in conventional maid's costume—"a loose-fitting, front-fastening print dress" and a small servant's cap. Her underwear consisted only of a chemise and a short petticoat. Factory girls wore similar clothing, as is apparent in Eyre Crowe's painting of millworkers, "Dinner Hour, Wigan" (1874). Milkwomen, however, wore deliberately archaic country dress, as did fisherwomen, who were also known for their short skirts. Collier girls who worked in the mines wore bedgowns and breeches. Munby described working-class women in a variety of mixed costumes, such as cotton frocks and aprons worn with "shabby but once fashionable" bonnets. Others wore soiled and ragged clothes and not even a bonnet. Prostitutes generally wore fashionable clothes. But Munby also had photographs of maids and women workers in very stylish "holiday clothes."[26]

An individual's social status and milieu helped determine the degree of sartorial eroticism, luxury, and novelty considered affordable and appropriate. Contemporary reports and visual evidence indicate that the women of the social elite (still largely aristocratic) and the famous courtesans of the day dressed in much the same style—and set the standards of beauty and chic. Courtesans dressed with great luxury, and to maximize their sexual beauty.

Women of the aristocracy and the haute bourgeoisie, on the other hand, dressed not to attract rich patrons, but rather for an active social life. Their role—at soirées, balls, receptions, the races, the theatre, etc.—was to look beautiful and elegant. As social leaders, they were in a position to set the rules of appropriate dress, as long as they did not drastically break from previous standards. Some (but by no means all) of these women patronized the famous—and very expensive—couturiers of the day, such as Charles Frederick Worth, whose dresses could cost thousands of dollars. Early twentieth-century accounts indicate that "great ladies" might spend several hundred pounds (or tens of thousands of francs) every year on dress.

Women of the upper-middle and middle classes led a more restricted social life, centering around their children, visits to friends, shopping, and so on. Although they, too, were supposed to look beautiful and well dressed, the situations themselves implicitly limited the degree of erotic display that would have been acceptable. Middle-class women were also not in as strong a position to risk public criticism by appearing too avant-garde. In large urban areas, such as London and especially Paris, there was a greater awareness of fashion trends.[27]

These women read fashion journals like *La Mode Illustrée* and *The Queen*, and had their clothes made by less well-known dressmakers, whose names often appeared under the published fashion plates. Or, probably more often, they had the illustrated dresses copied by very inexpensive local dressmakers, or they made them themselves. An upper- and upper-middle class magazine, such as *The Queen*, included not only illustrations of expensive Paris fashions, but also articles (such as this one from 1878) explaining how to dress on an allowance of £100 a year. Although such a sum was beyond most people's means, the ideas were intended to inspire less wealthy readers as well:

Reasonable Dress . . . £100 a year. I have to dress . . . out of that amount, having to be ready for about fifteen balls a season. I calculate it thus—a black silk, velvet, net, and a coloured silk each with low and square-cut bodice, answers for dinners and balls . . . and with lace flounces, shawls, scarves or sashes may be made to look quite different year by year. A black silk (about £17) will serve for two seasons, being turned into dinner, ball, and evening dresses, successively afterwards. Two silk and cashmere (or fashionable material) costumes, each with high and square-cut bodices, are useful for afternoon and evening dresses alternatively; while an Ulster and plain dress, with soft felt hat to match, are suitable for driving tours, picnics, and excursions. . . . My plan is to buy dress patterns at 5s to 8s each, cut out and fit on my dresses, sending them with directions and trimmings, to a woman to complete at 10s the dress. . . . In linen . . . employing poor people who owe me money to work off their debts; or women who would occasionally have to be helped, work at it when unemployed by others.[29]

Fashion journals such as *The Englishwoman's Domestic Magazine (EDM)* and *Le Petit Echo de la Mode* were directed toward less well off middle- and lower-middle-class women. By 1869, *EDM* was praising the convenience and price of ready-made summer dresses. By 1900, *Le Petit Echo* had two million readers, who bought both ready-made and home-made clothing. Home dressmakers were also encouraged with advertised patterns for slightly simpler dresses. Silks and velvets were considered suitable for day (as well as evening) dresses, as were a multiplicity of trimmings. The popularity of the sewing machine made more complicated styles and trims easier to make. An illustration in *Sylvia's Home Journal* (February, 1881)—reproduced in *Harper's Bazar*—shows a dinner dress available from the dressmaker Madame Letellier of Covent Garden, London, for approximately £10 10s (in silk or brocade) or from £7 7s (in silk and cashmere), but for which a pattern cost only 3s 3d. The dress has a square décolletage, gold brocade basque and train, and an apron over-skirt. The wearer is shown holding a powder puff and a fan, while her

Dinner or Evening Dress by Madame Letellier, Covent Garden. Fashion plate from *Sylvia's Home Journal* (1881), also published in *Harper's Bazar.*

maid looks on admiringly. The maid wears a simple dark dress and apron, but she also has earrings and a fashionable fringe.

Perhaps more realistically, a series of articles in *Cornhill Magazine* (1901) described "How to Live On" incomes ranging from 30 shillings a week to £10,000 a year, providing valuable information on clothing budgets, as did the case studies in *Family Budgets* (1896). The worker making 30 shillings a week (£78 a year) would spend approximately 7 for rent, 8 for food, 2 for fuel—and 2 shillings a week for clothes: primarily spent on boots ("an expensive and important item") and repairs, with clothing often made from cast-offs or bought at the "slop shop." Many working-class people relied on the second-hand shop, the street sellers of old apparel, and peddlers for their clothing. Though cheap—3s. for a silk dress—even these were sometimes insufficient. The case study of a poverty-striken London plumber and his wife (a former nursemaid) reported that they were in "urgent needs of clothing: 'Out of doors the man wears an overcoat, which is warm and conceals a deficiency of other clothing. Indoors, or at work, the overcoat is removed, and reveals him in shirt sleeves.' "[29]

Clothing gifts to the poor remained an important part of charity, although frowned on by Benthamites, whose utilitarian philanthropy stressed self-help. Madeleine Ginsberg quoted one rural Englishperson (interviewed in 1913): "If we didn't hae cleas given, we suld hae to black ooursels ower an' go nakt." The average woman worker made only half as much as a man—perhaps £10 to £30 a year. According to *The Girl's Own Paper*, its readers often had £10 or less a year to spend on clothes—still twice as much as the worker with three children, and at least four times as much as the woman worker. After buying new boots, underwear, and so on, a woman might make one dress a year, at a cost of £1.[30]

A lower-middle-class family—a cashier, his wife (a farmer's daughter), and two children—had an income of £150 a year, of which a "very considerable expenditure" had to go for dress, since the breadwinner was "in a very different position from the skilled mechanic who may be earning a like income."

Whether they be salesmen in shops or clerks in banks or offices [they] must be habited in what may be called a decent professional garb. The bank clerk who looks needy or the solicitor's clerk who is out-at-elbows will find that he has little chance of retaining his position. Here he is clearly at a disadvantage compared with the man who works with his hands and who only has to keep a black coat for high days and holidays. Thus the "lower middle" breadwinner is forced into an extravagance in the matter of clothes out of all proportion to his income. Nor is it his own clothes alone that will be a matter of anxiety, for whatever may be said of false pride and suchlike, a man is most properly not content to see his wife and children dressed in a manner unbecoming their station. The wife must of course be her own and her children's dressmaker.[31]

Ultimately, boots might cost £6, a tailor £6, and dress for the wife and children £13. Governesses had similar obligations to dress as well as possible on a very small salary. Books such as *How to Dress on £15 a Year as a Lady* "by a Lady" (1878) advised making dresses in such materials as black washing silk, made with various bodices and over-skirts, so that a dress could be worn for "garden parties," for dinner, and even for evening wear, with only minor adjustments.

The professional man earning £800 a year (which is on the high side) would spend about £40 a year on clothes with another £30 as pocket money, while his wife would get an allowance of £70, of which she would spend about £50 on clothes, the remainder for miscellaneous expenses (such as carfare). A couple with an income of £1800 a year might spend £200 for their clothes, somewhat less if they lived in the country. At this level a lady's maid was thought to "pay for herself by the saving of dressmakers' bills, and turning old things into new. It is fancy things made at home that really pay [i.e. save money], not petticoats and underlinen." The fabulously wealthy couple with £10,000 a year might each spend £450 on clothes.

This sounds as though the working-class or lower-middle-class woman could hardly expect to follow fashion—and yet she did. However cheap and poorly made, her clothing copied fashionable styles. The multi-volume *Life and Labour*, for example, described the London factory girl (with a wage of 7 to 11 shillings a week) out walking:

> She is adorned and decked out, not so much for conquest as for her own personal delight and pleasure ... She wears a gorgeous plush hat with as many large ostrich feathers ... as her funds will run to—bright ruby or scarlet preferred. Like all the working women in the East End, she wears good tidy boots on all occasions, perhaps with high heels. ... The standard of dress among young people [in the East End] is rising fast, clothing, like other things, is cheap ... scent for instance is extensively sold in small bottles at a low price, and girls very generally wear jewelry of some sort.[32]

Historians such as Bruno de Roselle and Philippe Perrot have argued that nineteenth-century fashion expressed an essentially bourgeois worldview, and indeed that fashion itself was a product of nineteenth-century bourgeois society. It supposedly expressed the bourgeois desire to "distinguish themselves from the people" and to "feel assured of their power." (In other words, the middle-class was a new and insecure elite.) The development of haute couture, in particular, allegedly served to "neutralize" the potentially revolutionary dangers of change by "codifying" fashion change. But Roselle admits that bourgeois women were not the primary purchasers of haute couture, nor were they the fashion trend-setters.[33] This interpretation also ignores the fact that fashion apparently existed in Europe since the mid-fourteenth century, when the long, flowing costumes worn by both sexes developed into a variety of more fitted and spectacular styles that were slit, buttoned, and laced. Throughout Western Europe, but especially in France, Italy, and Burgundy, artists like Pisanello and the Limbourg brothers designed new styles, commercial organizations expanded, and silk-weaving was developed. Both courts and towns had an influence, while the Renaissance idealization of the body may also have been important.

Of course, fashion evolved and expanded in the nineteenth century. A capitalist economy—indeed an advanced stage of capitalism—was a prerequisite for the development of both haute couture (known at the time as grande couture) and mass-produced ready-made clothing, but their ideological significance is far more difficult to define. It is generally accepted that couture first appeared in Paris in the mid-nineteenth century, and was inaugurated by the English-born dress designer, Charles Frederick Worth. Unlike his contemporaries Mme. Palmyre and Mme. Vignon, Worth designed a collection of models in advance and presented them to a select clientèle. Whether the client chose a dress or commissioned a design, it was then made up to her measurements. What also distinguished Worth's productions from earlier fashions was that he made dresses not only for private customers, but also for other top dressmakers, foreign buyers, and eventually for manufacturers, who distributed them commercially throughout the world. This was not only exclusive fashion but also big business.

Most couturiers were not very adventurous, and Worth was less a fashion dictator than a designer with an astute sense of what small changes his clients would be willing to accept. Stories of his "inventing" the crinoline, for example, are a misinterpretation of the processes of fashion change. The people who bought couture fashions were the very wealthy— aristocrats, the *haute bourgeoisie*, actresses, and demi-mondaines—for whom luxury and style were most important. In 1871, Worth estimated that a well-dressed Paris lady spent about £60 (about 1500 francs) a year on clothes, but that his clients spent anywhere from £400 to £4000. He sold his creations primarily to French, English, and Russian aristocrats (who tended to be relatively conservative in their tastes), to the stars of the stage and bedroom (who were more avant-garde), and to wealthy Americans. He was especially fond of the last group, who had, he argued, "the faces, the figures, and the francs." At his death in 1894, Paris fashion "had attained a structure recognisably like that of haute couture in more recent years."[34]

Nor is it accurate to argue that "the urban working masses . . . were in the process of creating a new type of clothing—*la mode confection*."[35] Ready-made was worn by many working-class men by the second half of the nineteenth century; it was only slowly accepted by women, although La Belle Jardinière sold women's working clothes. Ready-made clothing was ultimately successful because persons of all classes bought it. As long as cheap clothes looked conspicuously cheap, ready-made had only limited success, especially when so many second-hand clothing shops existed. The mass production of clothing was first applied to Army uniforms, then to men's suits, then to loose-fitting women's and children's clothing, such as mantles and shawls. Only gradually was it adopted for clothing that needed to be fitted and sized more precisely (although corsets were mass-produced).

For a long time, the traditional clothing producers—dressmakers and tailors—continued to produce individual garments that were copies (or copies of copies) of the clothing produced by the couturiers. The custom tailors and dressmakers themselves gradually moved in the direction of mass production, by making and keeping in stock ready-made clothes, in addition to producing custom-made clothes. In general, pattern making and cutting took place inside the premises, while sewing, pressing, and

Mary Cassatt, *The Fitting* (1891). The Mr. and Mrs. Martin A. Ryerson Collection, courtesy of the Art Institute of Chicago.

finishing were contracted out to less skilled workers. Haute couture models inspired dressmakers working for the grande bourgeoisie, who in turn inspired more humble dressmakers.

Along with mass production came mass distribution, new merchandising techniques, and the retailing of ready-made clothing. The small haberdashery shop gave way to "monster" department stores, with a greater diversity of products and fixed, low prices and high turnover that increased sales volume. This "Retail Revolution" took place almost simultaneously at mid-century in France, England, and the United States. Department stores began to make and sell their own lines of ready-made clothing. Or, more accurately, *partially* made clothing, which was begun in the department store workshop and then completed at home or by a small dressmaker. By the 1870s and 1880s, underwear, wrappers, children's clothes, suits, and a few dresses were available from department stores. In the 1890s, the popular and simpler skirts and shirtwaists were also sold. The department stores consistently aimed to attract customers in the upper reaches of the middle class. Revillon even produced "ready-made" furs in conjunction with the new stores.

The development of the department store inaugurated significant commercial changes (recorded in Zola's novel *Au Bonheur des dames*), and vastly expanded the popular pastime of shopping. A Gavarni cartoon from the 1860s shows a peasant staring in astonishment at the lifelike mannequins in crinolined evening dresses standing in a department store window. Other illustrations from the era show women pausing to look at a corset display, or strolling through *salons de confections* that often incorporated various social or theatrical fantasies. Department store catalogues and brochures emphasized the fashionable nature of their goods, and associated commodities with the exciting possibilities of personal transformation.[36]

The nineteenth century saw an enormous expansion of the world of fashion as part of the expansion of national economies and international trade networks: wool came from Normandy, cotton from the United States, silk from Italy and Lyons as well as Japan, lace from England and Belgium. By 1860, there were 10,000 weaving looms in Lyons, which were improved and later mechanically powered; England led in automation of the textile industry with faster shuttles and more spindles and new technologies like the sewing and embroidery machines. The transportation and communications network for passengers, goods, and information expanded, and styles that failed in Paris were shipped by rail to the provinces or abroad and sold there.

Individual units of production might remain small: During the Second Empire, the average Paris dressmaker employed four to forty seamstresses, who made only two or three francs a day. (Worth was unusual in having more than a thousand employees.) But the total production of clothes for women in France in 1864 was estimated to be worth £4 million (or about one hundred million francs). Only one sixth of the clothes were exported. By 1898, the exported clothes for both sexes were worth more than one hundred million francs. The crinoline industry produced about £800,000 worth of crinolines yearly, half of which were exported. Dozens of sub-industries contributed to the mode: There were milliners, lace-makers, ribbon-makers, lingerie-makers, and so on. Paris was the capital of fashion, but other cities throughout western Europe, Britain, and America also produced and distributed more and more clothes of all types, in all price ranges.[37]

Fashion information was transmitted by the fashion press, which dated from the eighteenth century, but which expanded greatly in the course of the nineteenth century. The availability of the sewing machine (by the 1850s) and paper patterns (by the 1870s) meant that the home-dress-maker had practical assistance, as well as information. Ready-made cloth-ing was available, and seamstresses were pathetically inexpensive. If a new dress were still unaffordable, dyes and ready-made trimmings were widely used to renew old dresses. Although clothing rendered the class divisions within society clearly visible, nevertheless those lower on the hierarchy consistently strove to follow fashion. This was true for men as well as women: The clerk's shiny black suit functioned both as a badge of respect-ability and as an involuntary sign of his relatively humble position in the social order. The nineteenth-century man's suit was not a symbol of equality and fraternity; rather, distinctions and pretensions were some-what more subtle than previously. Women's clothing showed social differ-ences more clearly, due to the greater range of materials and trimmings and the more rapid changes in fashion:

> Is not fashion in dress after all the outward distinction between the upper middle and lower grades of society? ... Does not the thought of a new dress made according to the latest modes of fashion induce Sally, the housemaid, and Julia, the cook, to work harder that they may the sooner be able to ape their mistress to such an extent, that visitors are frequently at a loss to know which is the servant and which the mistress? But, cruel fashion soon con-signs Julia and Sally to the chamber and the kitchen, for as soon as the modes they have adopted become common, new ones are propounded and adopted by the mistress.[38]

The historical debate about who actually wore fashion is based in large part on differing definitions of the word "fashion." Those who argue that only a minority wore fashionable dress actually mean that only a minority wore "high fashion." True enough. Nevertheless, as Doris Langley Moore points out, "People in the past ... seldom ... went about looking like fashion plates," but that was "not because the clothes they portray were fictitious" or even minority styles. Rather it was because the fashion plate is not merely reportage, but also a type of "propaganda for the current or coming mode," designed "to create a favorable climate of opinion for it." Furthermore, the (high) "fashions that *set* the fashion tend to be rather more pronounced than those of everyday life." Finally, the fashion illustrations themselves were stylized both to correspond to the viewers' conceptions of fashionable beauty, and to exaggerate the most important features of the current mode.[39]

"Fashion," however, refers not just to high fashion, but more importantly to a regular pattern of style change—the crinoline dress evolves into the bustle dress, and so on. Almost all middle- and most working-class people can therefore be said to have worn the fashion of the day. The very fashionable Victorian lady was "the tip of an iceberg of which the huge base was beginning to be visible and significant as the fashion followers increased."[40]

5

Victorian Sexuality

Because clothing is intimately connected to the physical self and expresses a particular "body image," the study of fashion may offer the historian "a good index to attitudes about the body," and about sexuality.[1] It is also possible that clothing not only "reflects" attitudes, but also plays an active role in defining how the wearer behaves and is perceived. In recent decades, a number of writers have analyzed nineteenth- and early twentieth century fashion in attempts to determine what clothing might reveal about attitudes toward the body (especially the female body), sexuality, and the social roles of men and women. Yet such analysis is almost invariably flawed, because a too-uncritical acceptance of stereotypes apparently determined the stylistic analysis.

The Anatomy of Prudery and
the Cloak of Lasciviousness

The dominant popular interpretation of Victorian fashion emphasizes its "prudery," and, secondarily, its covert and "hypocritical" eroticism. Early Victorian dress especially is described in terms of a flight from corporeality:

> Henceforth, woman was not a two-legged viviparous animal, but an exquisite and unreal being who moved, without any apparent means of locomotion, in a perpetual sighing rustle of silken drapery. At most, a tiny foot might sometimes appear, emerging mousily from beneath the folds of a heavy skirt.

Later and perhaps more obviously erotic styles were portrayed in a way that implied a certain prurient appeal:

> By emphasizing the hips, the bustle imparted a provocative undulation to every stride and, by accentuating the posterior parts of the body, gave a steatopygous charm to the primmest figure.[2]

These descriptions (which are highly exaggerated) convey in a nutshell the apparently contradictory aspects of Victorian fashion: Did it express a denial of female sexuality or an exploitation of it or a combination of both? It is possible that while the earlier styles emphasized demure modesty, over the course of the century there was an increase in sartorial sexual display. If true, this might be evidence for a gradual movement away from a repressive sexual morality. Yet we find the same dual interpretation of *late* Victorian fashion (1870–1900): "The dread of the human body which haunted the Victorian mind was responsible for the efforts made by fashion to obscure as well as cover the lines of that fearful monster, the flesh." However, fashion also "managed to proclaim rich bargains in flesh beneath the copious packing."[3]

The terms used to characterize Victorian dress fit in neatly with the stereotype of Victorian sexual hypocrisy. Notice, for example, the ambiguous association made between the "provocative undulation" and "steatopygous charm" of the bustle and the "primmest" Victorian figure. The dress of Victorian women might superficially be extremely modest and concealing , but it also allegedly functioned surreptitiously to draw attention to the sexual characteristics of the female body—the "rich bargains in flesh." (With this phrase, it is virtually implied that Victorian girls sold themselves into marital prostitution.) Victorian dress supposedly projected an unresolved tension between "puritan prudery" and erotic "enticement."

This picture is not entirely incorrect: Victorian dress did function both to preserve modesty and to accentuate the wearer's sexual beauty. What is misleading and inaccurate about this type of interpretation is its exaggeration of the "dread of the human body" and the denial of sexuality, together with a sometimes lurid stress of the "hypocritical lasciviousness" allegedly revealed by the erotic aspects of Victorian dress.

Two of the most notorious clichés about the subject are frequently juxtaposed—the frigid Victorian woman and her ultra-modest, leg-concealing dress. Victorian wives who "endured" the sexual act "in a sort of coma" also hid their bodies under long, bell-shaped skirts "that concealed everything except the toe." "Who could so much as imagine two female legs within that dome of drab material?" But the same writer later went on to quote from an actual letter of 1862, in which William Hardman cheerfully described how the swinging of the crinoline revealed the female ankles and calves: "The girls of our time like to show their legs . . . it pleases them, and does no harm to us: I speak for married, not single men."[4] This could be read as documentary evidence that at least some Victorians (both male and female) apparently felt a comfortable acceptance and even enthusiasm for the human body, and, specifically, the female legs. Does this not potentially contradict the picture of the Victorian woman as neurotically prudish and anti-sexual? The historian implies that this anecdote shows the sexual hypocrisy of the Victorians, ignoring Hardman's implication that married men could safely enjoy the sight of legs, because they had access to sexual fulfillment within their marriages.

Other popular historians of the Victorian scene frequently quote anecdotes intended to demonstrate the Victorians' fear of the body and sexuality, and then follow these with others illustrating an obsessive and even perverted interest in certain portions of the anatomy or articles of clothing. The veracity of these anecdotes is usually not an issue, but their typicality and the constructions put on them are questionable.

The dress of Victorian women is presented as an instrument of seduction, *masquerading* as extremely modest apparel: "The myth of Victorian purity" was a hypocritical fabrication—a "mask of respectability" placed over a reality of "vice." The "billowing tent" of the crinoline only seemed to be a symbol of "impregnable virtue," but it really exposed an indecent amount of the female body: not only the ankle but also, on occasion the "————." The dresses of the 1870s and 1880s , which fit more closely in front and were worn over a bustle behind, functioned as "a tight-fitting cloak of lasciviousness." "Attention was now solicited for the buttocks." The décolletage of evening dress was a form of "semi-nudity." Underpants that were open down the inside of each leg were even "worn by Queen Victoria"—and that lady's drawers could now be seen at the South Kensington Museum. So much for Victorian modesty![5]

This is obviously one of the more crudely stated versions of Laver's Attraction or Seduction Principle of women's fashion, and of the theme of the "wicked Victorians." But in some form, this picture of Victorian sex and fashion appears in every history of the period. It is argued that many men and most women of the middle classes were neurotically anti-sexual: "The more repressed could see sex in everything." At the same time, some unspecified number of outwardly respectable men led "secret" sexual lives, generally of a perverted nature, and often in the company of prostitutes. Although women were rigidly classified as either Madonnas or Magdalens, both wives and whores wore clothing that was simultaneously concealing and indecent.[6] Through a process of exaggeration and misplaced emphasis, nineteenth-century fashion is set within the familiar outline of a repressed, hypocritical, and perverted sexuality.

The Respectable Sexual Ideology

In recent years, a somewhat more sophisticated and scholarly version of the traditional interpretation of Victorianism has been formulated, in which it is argued that Victorian society was dominated by what Peter Cominos calls the "respectable sexual ideology." According to this theory, a highly restrictive sexual morality was "functionally integrated into the social and economic structure of society." Victorian sexual mores were essentially bourgeois, associated with the capitalist economy, and centered on the ideal of sexual continence (saving) except for the purposes of procreation (spending). Deviations from this restrictive sexual code were theoretically "found only in the very lowest or the very highest strata of society."[7]

There was, of course, an underside to the "official" sexual ideology—the world of pornography and prostitution. But here, too, not only the dominant sexual beliefs and practices, but even the fantasies of the Victorians were supposedly the products of the economic system and reflected the growing power of the capitalist bourgeoisie. There is, however, almost no hard evidence for this theory, which is based on a very few atypical sources.

There is some evidence for the supposed connection between the rise to power of the bourgeoisie and the development of a more restrictive sexual morality. However, the bourgeoisie rose over a period of centuries, and even in the Victorian period, they were not entirely in control in either England or France. (Indeed, it appears that the upper class retained far more power far longer than had earlier been believed.) It is even less convincing to go on to argue that the transition from the Empire style of dress (circa 1795–1815) to the more body-concealing Victorian fashions reflected a significant change in European attitudes toward sexuality and the human body:

> In the early decades of the nineteenth century, European sexual morality shifted decisively from the permissiveness of the previous century to the severely restrictive rules and attitudes that have come to be characterized as Victorianism.[8]

Despite all problems of logic and (lack of) evidence, the theory of the respectable sexual ideology has strongly influenced current interpretations of Victorian fashion. Indeed, it might be said merely to have given a spurious scholarly gloss to old prejudices, for the histories emphasizing fashion's assault on the body bear a close resemblence to the old stories of prudery and hypocrisy.

The Sartorial Assault on the Body

According to the new interpretation, Victorian attitudes toward the body were "a combination of denial, distortion, and fear," while "attitudes regarding sexuality ranged from moral condemnation to disutility." Victorian clothing was an expression of the dominant anti-sexual ideology, which weighed most heavily on women. According to the historian Stephen Kern, "In no other age throughout history was the human body, in particular the female body, so concealed and disfigured by clothing." While men's "drab" and "static" clothing merely hid the body, women's clothing constituted "an attack on the body as much as an effort to conceal it." "Not just the leg[s] but the entire body was covered with a great deal of clothing"— long sleeves, high collars, a hemline that "dropped to the ground and stayed there for a century," gloves, bonnets—amounting to a kind of "mummification." But it "was not enough just to cover the

female body; Victorian clothing also abused it." Shoes and garters were a
problem, but the "major assault on the body was achieved by the corset,"
which not only impeded "any inclination women might have had to exercise or enjoy their bodies," but also (allegedly) damaged the respiratory,
circulatory, digestive, and reproductive systems.[9]

Women wore these uncomfortable, physically restrictive, and probably
unhealthy fashions because they were "caught between the contradictory
demands to be both physically desirable and morally proper." The body
was perceived as "bad"—i.e., sexual—and so it was hidden, disfigured,
and mutilated. At the same time, the instruments of this concealment and
disfigurement generated an "exaggerated eroticism." Thus, the concealment of the lower half of the body (a product of "excessive prudery") supposedly led to a "high incidence" of foot and shoe fetishism; while the
corset emphasized the female sexual characteristics, at the same time that
it contributed to women's "sexual subordination."[10]

This use of clothing to illustrate the allegedly repressive and conflict-
ridden sexuality of the nineteenth century is seriously marred by an
apparent lack of knowledge about the fashions of earlier periods. The
female body was concealed and "disfigured" during the Elizabethan era
(to choose a supposedly sexually lusty period) at least as much as it was
in the nineteenth century—as any picture of a woman in a stiff, elongated
bodice and a farthingale will show. Boned corsets or bodices have been in
existence since the sixteenth century; and criticism of the corset on the
grounds of health and morality existed since the eighteenth century—as
did condemnation of, say, masturbation. Women's legs were covered for
centuries, in the "permissive" eighteenth as well as the "severely restrictive" nineteenth century.

The French fashion historian, Philippe Perrot, for example, although
aware of "the centuries-old seculsion of the legs," nevertheless deliberately uses the language of capitalism to describe the effect of the long skirt
on bourgeois sexual fantasies:

> In the nineteenth century, whereas bosoms and hips were generously
> stressed, the legs were hidden away from view in a radical fashion, thus
> amassing amongst the frothy secrets of lingerie another [type of] erotic cap-
> ital, the high value placed on which [may be] measured by the intensity of
> the cult consecrated to the calves, and by the agitation provoked by their
> fleeting vision.[11]

If nineteenth-century fashion is placed in historical context, it becomes
more difficult to interpret it as evidence that, in the early nineteenth century, the body ceased to be perceived as an "instrument of pleasure" and
became only "an instrument of production"—albeit one invested with
"erotic capital." Only to a limited degree is it legitimate to argue that Victorian women were "buried under ever more complicated, expensive, and
restricting clothing." Is the concealment characteristic of Victorian fashion evidence (as Stephen Kern argues) that men and women in the nine-

teenth century experienced "extraordinary difficulty ... in dealing with their bodies"?[12]

It is true that nineteenth-century technology developed ways of making more elaborate clothes more easily, while the developing socioeconomic structure of society enabled far more women to wear fashionable dress. But even here, the facts complicate the issue of using Victorian fashion as an illustration of negative attitudes toward the body. For example, Victorian technological advances enabled corset manufacturers to make more closely fitting corsets, but the degree of constriction and discomfort they caused varied according to a variety of factors, including the shape of corsets fashionable at any given time.

Men's outerwear today is scarcely less concealing than it was a hundred years ago. A business suit now still consists of long trousers, a jacket, shirt, and (at least sometimes) a vest. Underwear has shrunk, though, from what was equivalent to a union-suit to briefs and a short-sleeved shirt. Nevertheless, this change hardly seems radical enough to serve as evidence for a completely new sexual morality. Women's fashions, of course, have changed much more in the last hundred years. And it is Victorian women's fashion that is interpreted in the most invidious terms.

According to Kern, the Victorian anti-sexual ideology lasted until the First World War, which had, he argues, "a revolutionary impact on European morality," and thus dramatically affected clothing:

> It took the insane destruction of human life in the First World War to transform the demands of [dress] reformers into concrete historical change and bring about the world of fashion's acceptance of the human body.[13]

This statement, however, is completely false.

Woman as "Exquisite Slave"

If it is true that clothing "defined the role of each sex," and influenced "the actions and attitudes of both wearer and viewer," then Victorian women's clothing may be seen as reflecting and reinforcing the feminine role of a submissive, masochistic, and narcissistic being—an "exquisite slave."[14] According to the art and fashion historian Helene Roberts:

> Men were serious (they wore dark colors and little ornamentation), women were frivolous (they wore light pastel colors, ribbons, laces, and bows); men were active (their clothes allowed them movement), women inactive (their clothes inhibited movement); men were strong (their clothes emphasized broad chests and shoulders), women delicate (their clothing accentuated small waists, sloping shoulders, and a softly rounded silhouette); men were aggressive (their clothing had sharp definite lines and a clearly defined silhouette), women were submissive (their silhouette was indefinite, their clothing constricting).[15]

There is some truth to these arguments, but they are highly oversimplified, as is Roberts's stylistic analysis of female dress. Men's clothing in the nineteenth century did facilitate relatively greater ease of movement than women's clothing did. Nevertheless, both the ease and practicality of men's dress and the constriction of women's have been exaggerated.

It would have been highly impractical to do physical labor while wearing the Victorian dresses that I have examined, both because they restricted free movement and because the materials they were made of could be damaged. On the other hand, they are sometimes deliberately designed to look more restrictive than they really were. Furthermore, although the middle-class male may have looked more practical and could stride along easily, he was hardly dressed for manual labor either. If he worked, it was at some form of "white collar" employment. The middle-class woman, dressed for "leisure," *could* have done as much. In general, the signs of leisure remained prestigious, while the signs of practicality and functionalism were only beginning to acquire prestige. In addition, there are different sorts of physical activity. Manual labor was a low status activity, and so it is not surprising that middle-class men and women wore clothing that testified to their exemption from such activity. Sports were socially prestigious, especially those that were expensive and associated with the aristocracy, but men and women usually adopted *specialized* costumes, such as riding habits, for sport.

Did Victorian dress emphasize female delicacy and male strength? The stereotype of the delicate, weak, even ailing, Victorian woman was, perhaps, more or less valid for the early part of the Victorian period, but increasingly inaccurate thereafter. Certainly, by the 1860s and 1870s, most Victorians seem to have favored "healthy," "blooming" girls. Their concept of good health differed, however, from our own: we prize physical strength and a relatively lean physique for both sexes; the Victorians interpreted relative fleshiness as evidence of health—again, for both men and women.

Followers of the Aesthetic Movement were frequently satirized as lean and sickly, and Female Aesthetes especially were compared unfavorably with the cheerful, healthy women whose clothing made the most of their

Eadweard Muybridge, *Woman Jumping over a Stool* (detail of a serial photograph). Courtesy of The Philadelphia Civic Center Museum.

statuesque and fleshly charms. The Victorian woman was not supposed to be "strong" and "aggressive," but the sheer size of her dress and its stylized but definite silhouette might be interpreted as emphasizing the female presence in a way that male clothing singularly failed to do. Indeed, her prized "delicacy" meant less that she was "sickly" than that she was supposed to be "refined."

While it is true that the male physical ideal theoretically involved strength, this was not really reflected in men's clothing after about 1850—with the notable (and anachronistic) exception of officers' uniforms, which continued to draw attention to the chest and shoulders, as well as to the legs and the relatively narrow waist. Military uniforms until some time into the First World War were more restricting and more physically revealing than ordinary suits, and there were even rumors that some officers actually wore corsets.

A cartoon in *Punch* (May 25, 1878), entitled "The New Hussar Hessians and Pants," shows a woman in a tight skirt and a man in tight pants. The caption reads, "See, I've dropped my handkerchief, Captain de Vere!" "I know you have , Miss Constance. I'm very sorry. I can't stoop, either!" Although his uniform emphasizes his physical body, it actually inhibits movement; nevertheless, such uniforms were not yet mere formal wear, but were intended to be worn in action.

What, then, did male clothing signify? The "professional" aspect of male clothing was important, but it is too simple to interpret "the triumph of black" primarily in terms of "bourgeois respectability," let alone of "puritanism," seriousness, or the bourgeois work ethic. In the nineteenth century it was widely thought to be unmanly to devote much time or thought to dress. Carlyle and Thackeray, among others, attacked the "Dandy" as a mere "Clothes-wearing Man." Yet the plain black suit also had romantic and dandiacal associations, and was favored by the young Charles Baudelaire. Increasingly, however, the options narrowed, and it became "caddish" or bohemian for men to wear bright or light colors except in the privacy of their homes. Apparently, the man's dark suit was intended to express both masculinity and the social position of the gentleman.

If men's clothing was generally dark and unornamented, women's clothing tended to be more colorful and decorative. Yet the equation "light pastel colors = frivolity" is both inaccurate and misleading. The popularity of certain colors was often a reaction against earlier shades that had come to seem *démodé*. White was popular for Empire dress, but gave way to first brighter and then paler shades. "Although light and delicate shades of silk still continued to be used all through the 1850s and early 1860s, there was a general increase in richness and depth of colour." Bright colors dominated the 1860s and 1870s. Then aesthetic faded tones, light and vivid colors, and dark, serious colors competed for favor. Dresses in the 1890s were often deep and rich in color; white and pastel shades were typically Edwardian; evening dresses in the pre-war years were often of saturated and "Oriental" colors.

Throughout most of the Victorian period, women also often wore dark or black clothing, and the connotations that this carried depended on other aspects of the dress and on the context within which it was worn. It could mean that she was unable to afford a variety of dresses, and so chose an inconspicuous and easily cleaned color. There was the "respectable" black dress; the elegant black dress, suitable perhaps for the female dandy; mourning clothes; and also the business-like and serious dark tailored-suit.[16]

The ornamentation of women's dress also varied according to the time and circumstances, and was not limited to "ribbons, laces [lace?] and bows" (all of which had previously been worn by men as well), but also more "masculine" trimmings, such as braid and buttons. Nor is it clear that ornamentation "symbolized" frivolity (rather than, say, wealth), although there did develop a feeling that "excessive" ornamentation was both superfluous and superficial.

Some Victorian opponents of conventional female dress did argue that the very changeability of fashion was evidence of female frivolity, while clothing ornamentation seemed to them to be "useless" and "barbaric." Yet the editors of *Punch* would have been no more in favor of granting the vote to women in dark, rational suits than they were to women in tartan crinolines. The dress reformers were also, in their own way, prejudiced in favor of masculine dress. In their view, most *women* were frivolous, and *therefore*, they wore colorful, changeable, decorative dress. In common with most Victorian dress reformers, feminist fashion historians today tend to perceive nineteenth-century men's clothing as vastly superior to women's, and interpret progress in large part in terms of the supposed approach of women's clothes to the "utilitarian" masculine model. One is entitled to ask, though, whether there is anything intrinsically superior about dark colors, unerotic tailoring, and an absence of ornamentation.

Even if we assume, for a moment, that the Victorian woman was supposed to be relatively frivolous, inactive, and delicate, there is still a leap of reasoning in the argument that she was also submissive, masochistic, and narcissistic. Yet Roberts is only one of many historians to imply that the only acceptable form of female sexuality in the nineteenth century was a repressed and "masochistic" one: "The clothing of the Victorian woman clearly projected the message of a willingness to conform to the submissive-masochistic pattern." It seems far more likely that women's dress was intended to convey the impression of *beauty*. The fashion might have been at times uncomfortable or inconvenient, but it diverted attention from possible deficiencies of nature, while drawing attention to attractive features, and ideally making the wearer look and feel pretty and charming. It has been pointed out that "The mind may take pleasure in something which to the body is a pain or at least an inconvenience." This is very different from saying that the mind takes pleasure in something *because* it is painful. A favorable self-image might well be prefered to a greater degree of physical comfort. The popular Victorian writer Mrs. Oliphant for example, criticized the uncomfortable and inconvenient aspects of the dress of her day (and Roberts quotes her), but she also stressed that fashion helped even plain women "look their best," and she believed that most women's hearts "beat with pleasure" at the "exhilarating" sensation of being "well dressed."[17]

Most Victorian women led quite restricted and dependent lives. For the majority, marriage was the most desirable option, and it was thought to be important to dress well to attract a good husband. What is more doubtful is the suggestion that men were attracted to "submissive," "masochistic," and "narcissistic" women, and that women dressed to emphasize these qualities. If women were not expressing submission or courting pain, it does not seem legitimate in this context to speak of "masochism."

Was the corset actually such an uncomfortable and unhealthy garment? Was it both anti-sexual and an agent of the sexual exploitation of women? Did it serve to keep women economically dependent on men, because its use prevented women from working? The Victorian corset is viewed today with undisguised hostility, and has become the subject of a persistent mythology. Whether that view is accurate is another question entirely. Similarly, the fact that women were encouraged to pay attention to their appearance is not, per se, evidence of "narcissism." The casual use of terms with implications of sexual pathology does not seem useful for an understanding of the motivations of conventionally fashionable women.

It is worth pointing out, however, that the antipathy that Kern, for example, feels toward "grossly artificial" styles of dress, together with his assumption that modern dress is "natural," lead him to interpret articles of clothing (such as the corset) as almost necessarily bad. Yet we perceive modern dress as "natural" and as following (rather than distorting or concealing) the lines of the body, primarily because we are used to seeing people look the way they do now. Our perceptions of the body are conditioned by its clothed appearance. (In retrospect, the 1950s brassiere looks as "artificial" as the corset.)

Similarly, his belief that "rationality" and "comfort" are (or should be) the primary determinants of dress leads him to assume that Victorian women would have prefered to wear other types of clothing, had they been permitted to do so. Thus, at one point, he suggests that Victorian men "did not allow" women to wear the "subdued attire" that they "chose" for themselves.[18] He ignores the social constraints placed on both men and women, while the idea that many women might have liked their clothes and thought that they were attractive appears never to have crossed his mind.

Whether or not men and women liked their clothing, to a considerable degree their choice of dress was limited by canons of respectability, suitability, and modesty. Even the most adament dress reformers admitted that "conspicuous" or "peculiar" dress provoked ridicule. A man who wanted to wear a brightly colored and highly decorated suit or a woman who wanted to wear flowing, corsetless robes on the street would have been subject to severe social disapproval. It is at least questionable, however, whether this state of affairs indicated a negative attitude toward the body or the self. Furthermore, there is considerable contemporary evidence that the supposed prudery about the body has been greatly exaggerated.

Recently, still another interpretation has been offered. Bonnie Smith, author of a study of bourgeois Frenchwomen in the nineteenth century, *Ladies of the Leisure Class*, suggests that fashion "symbolized" women's reproductive functions, and thus expressed women's primary social role. "Reproductive contours appeared in the form of ever-widening skirts. Only in pregnancy, when breasts and abdomen swell to reach spherical proportions, is the female figure uniformly round." With the development of the bustle, "the spherical shape receded to the back," while the relatively high waistline of about 1870 "metaphorically accommodated the elongated and impregnated uterus." In the 1890s, "symbolic fullness" shifted to the sleeves. Even the straight-front corset (sometimes called the *sans ventre* corset), while "flattening the stomach" also "created the illusion of breasts swollen with milk."[19] These explanations seem strained. The curves of the female body are not necessarily the result of pregnancy!

Smith is correct, of course, in arguing that maternity was a highly valued female role; and that many Victorians believed that the standard of female beauty was related to woman's reproductive role. The attraction of the secondary sexual characteristics, however, probably derives at least as much from the desire for erotic pleasure as it does from the desire for procreation. Furthermore, fashion also emphasized features such as the slender waist, which seemed to many contemporaries to be the antithesis of the natural and maternal waist. Although beautiful maternity dresses were made, fashion in general definitely did not focus on the creation of a "maternal" and "domestic" look. Instead, Victorian women's fashion emphasized the beautiful-sexual body.

Fashion vs. Progress

But however one might describe and interpret the styles of Victorian dress, eventually fashion evolved into something new and post-Victorian. How did this change come about? What was its significance? According to Roberts, the growing influence of sports, education, the Dress Reform and Aesthetic Movements, and, generally, "progress in women's emancipation" and "greater social and economic opportunities" gradually "led women out of the submissive, masochistic, and narcissistic cul-de-sac of ribbons, bows, and tight laces." She argues that by the 1880s women's clothing was "plainer and more masculine," and that by the 1890s women were well on their way to being "emancipated" from "long skirts and tight-lacing."[20]

Although ideologically pleasing, this picture does not tally well with the actual developments in fashion. Skirts were no higher in 1900 than in 1860 or 1830. The average waist size was apparently no larger; it may even have been smaller. Although the "New Woman" often wore more "serious" clothing, mainstream fashion continued on its path. In short, there was not a direct or linear progression away from ornamentation and corsetry—they only took different forms.

What was the influence of the Dress Reform and feminist movements? Since the women's movement played an important and conspicuous part in nineteenth-century society in the English-speaking world, it is tempting to see changes in fashion in terms of women's emancipation. Yet Paris was the capital of women's fashion, and the women's movement there seems to have been far more of a minority cause. Even in England, many feminists were indifferent to the question of dress reform, or saw it as a minor issue. They tended to wear ordinary fashionable dress as a way of emphasizing their respectability and showing that they were not attempting to blur all distinctions between the sexes. Those in favor of dress reform were often opposed to fashions that increased women's sexual attractiveness, which limited their appeal for many. In general, dress reformers, whether feminist or (as many were) anti-feminist, seem to have had relatively little influence on fashion. The vogue for "healthy" woolen underwear did achieve a substantial following in England (in France it seems to have been inflicted almost exclusively on children), but this affected only hidden garments. Despite the hysteria about tight-lacing, corsets continued to be worn.

The increasing popularity of sports for women probably gradually influenced the ideal of feminine beauty, and this may have had a delayed and indirect effect on fashion. In any immediate sense, however, specialized sporting attire had little effect on ordinary dress. Kern's belief (which Roberts appears to share) that "in the 1890s, the bicycle forced women to abandon bustles" is simply untrue. Fashion evolves gradually, and not in a series of jerky responses to external stimuli. In general, "practical" or "rational" explanations for change in dress are inadequate. Furthermore, as Perrot points out, the practical function of particular clothes is inseparable from their aesthetic, sexual, and social functions. Sports clothes, for example, might or might not be more practical, but they are signs of practicality and sportivité.[21]

Changing fashions in the pre-war period do not appear to have been a direct response to the advocates of dress reform, or to the progress of female emancipation; and we cannot infer from occasional (athletic) dress to daily fashion. Of course in a more general sense women's expanding social and economic opportunities during the second half of the nineteenth and the early twentieth centuries undoubtedly had some effects on fashion. For example, as women spent their time in different ways, they adopted clothing for their various pursuits. The popularity of the tailored suit indicated that women found it suitable for "white-collar" occupations, walking, and (in a country version) sports. One of the verifiable effects of the First World War was that it enabled more women to make more money and to buy more clothes than they could have afforded before. Whether such changes indicated an entirely new attitude toward the self is something else again.

The theory of the respectable sexual ideology conspicuously fails to explain how change came about. Or as one Twenties writer put it: "The author is astonished that this generation is begotten of the Victorian." Cominos argues that changes in the middle-class sexual ideology toward the end of the nineteenth century were part of a general "revolt against authority," including the "movement for female emancipation," which was "as unsettling of patriarchal relations as industrialization." He concludes, rather flamboyantly, that "The Womanly Woman had nothing to lose but her tightly corseted existence, hang-ups, guilt feelings, crucified flesh, innocent mindlessness, and self-absorbing roles of daughter, wife, and mother."[22]

One immediate difficulty with this explanation, however, is that the women's movement in the later nineteenth and early twentieth centuries was by no means a movement for greater sexual freedom, but rather, in part, an attempt to extend and compound a rigid sexual morality to include men. Witness Mrs. Pankhurst's famous slogan, "Votes for Women and Chastity for Men." Sympathetic modern accounts tend to describe feminist hostility toward sexuality in terms of women gaining greater personal freedom and control over the body and its reproductive functions, and with efforts to "keep from being considered or treated as a sex object." Nevertheless, the feminist solution to the problem of inequality between the sexes was often the promotion of extreme standards of sexual purity for both sexes, both inside and outside marriage. Most feminists accepted the "Victorian" ideas that the sex drive in women was weaker than in men, and was directed toward the goal of maternity; they rejected birth control as an "immoral" way of achieving "voluntary motherhood." Instead, they sought to domesticate male sexual desire, and to make marriage a "spiritual relation," rather than the means for male "gratification."[23]

Furthermore, even if the changing sexual ideology were part of a general revolt against authority, those in revolt were presumably often themselves members of the Victorian middle class. Marcus suggests that people were influenced by certain novelists (such as Emile Zola) and by Sigmund Freud, but this is surely incorrect. Why were they not influenced earlier by Balzac and Flaubert? In addition, Freud only became widely read after World War I. Other scholars, indeed, have argued that significant changes in the dominant sexual ideology only occurred after the destruction of the war had brought about the demise of Victorian sexual morality. But it is simply mistaken to believe that the war brought about "the end of tight-lacing." Nor did "shortages of material" lead to shorter dresses. The war did not "inaugurate ... changes in clothing which finally began to *respond to the advocates of reform* who had gone unheeded for the past half century." Women did not finally adopt "rational dress."[24] These statements are not only factually incorrect, they also indicate a profound misunderstanding of the processes of fashion change.

There are, of course, important reasons why the First World War is perceived as having been the dividing line between the Victorian and the post-Victorian eras (or the nineteenth and twentieth centuries). The entire social, economic, and political structure of Europe changed dramatically, as did the intellectual and cultural atmosphere—although the bourgeois-capitalist order survived largely intact. Certainly, contemporaries were convinced that the war had launched a new era of sexual promiscuity and female emancipation. Yet the "liberating" effects of the war have probably been greatly overstated, both in terms of sexual freedom and of economic opportunities. In any case, its effects on fashion do not correspond to the popularly accepted picture.

A New Look at Victorian Fashion and Sexuality

The image of the Victorian era as a period of "harsh and repressive sexual puritanism" allied with "moral hypocrisy" first appeared at the end of the nineteenth century, in the work of writers and sexual reformers such as Grant Allen, Edward Carpenter, and Havelock Ellis. It was a polemical characterization of contemporary sexual life, and may have developed in response to the growth of the "social purity" movement in the last quarter of the nineteenth century. It was only rarely illustrated by reference to dress. After the First World War, however, this image of the Victorian period was used as a way of dismissing the older generation (who were widely blamed for the war) and of ridiculing the past.[25]

In *The Eternal Masquerade* (a satirical history of fashion published in 1922), H. Dennis Bradley described the modern generation as not only the descendants but the "survivors" of that "age of ugliness," when the "false ideals" of "our egregious ancestors" led them to make war instead of making love. The Victorians, he charged, were willing to be "dictators" or "cannon fodder," but they desperately tried to "hide, oh hide, the sinful human form," "concealing not only sex but humanity." "Small wonder," he concluded, "that the Victorian sun set in a welter of hypocritical immorality and humbug."[26]

In the course of time, this interpretation of the Victorian era became increasingly widely accepted, indicating, perhaps, that people experienced a psychological need to feel superior to the Victorians. From being attacked vituperatively, they became the objects of patronizing scorn: "how repressed they were, and how liberated are we." At the same time, what was perceived as the "hypocrisy" of the Victorians was still resented: "they pretended to be moral, but really they weren't; in fact, they were wicked." Several strands of thought combined here, involving not only images of sexuality (prudery and prostitution) but also perceptions of nineteenth-century capitalism and the bourgeoisie as a class (exploitive but also vulgar and philistine). It is rare for popular and scholarly perceptions of the past to be so similar.

The ubiquity of this interpretation is such that the Victorian period is perhaps best known for the supposed sexual repression of the middle classes, and, in particular, of middle-class women. "As every schoolgirl knows, the nineteenth century was afraid of sex, particularly when it manifested itself in women." More specifically, the stereotype of Victorianism includes: "male dominance . . . strict differentiation of sex roles, separate standards of morality for males and females, female coldness in marriage, and general silence about sexual matters, all of it tainted by hypocrisy."[27]

Initially, the "Victorian" phenomenon was thought to be characteristic only of Great Britain and the United States, and perhaps to a lesser extent other largely Protestant countries. Historians considered it highly unlikely that the French bourgeoisie could ever have displayed such egregious prudery. What could be more different from the Court of Queen Victoria than that of Napoleon III? With the development of the field of women's history, however, the focus shifted toward the many ways in which nineteenth-century society restricted and oppressed women. Although most research was done on the English-speaking world, that done on France indicated that there, too, French women were simultaneously idealized and repressed, and the cult of purity was accompanied by widespread prostitution. In France, too, it was argued, women were categorized as either housewives or harlots.[28]

But if the old conception of puritan England and adulterous France is untenable, recent historical research on the nineteenth century also indicates that the traditional view of Victorian culture and the Victorian middle class as sexually repressed and hypocritical may in itself be in need of substantial modification. In addition, new trends in the study of the Victorian woman have focused on possible disparities between the prescriptive ideal of femininity and women's actual lives.[29] So far, however, these new trends in historiography have not affected the study of Victorian fashion, which continues to be dominated by stereotypes.

Whether Victorian fashion is interpreted as a manifestation of the conflict between puritan prudery and covert lasciviousness; as an expression of the "respectable sexual ideology" that allegedly dominated middle-class culture; or as one aspect of women's social and sexual oppression— it has usually been seen in terms of a pre-conceived notion of "Victorianism." Yet the fact that historians are taking a new look at Victorian women and sexuality suggests that a different interpretation of Victorian fashion is necessary.

If we suspend our ingrained belief that nineteenth-century society was uniformly committed to a sexually repressive "ideology," and that Victorian fashion did not accept the human body (especially the female body)—then it is easier to understand how standards of sexual morality and modesty, social roles, and clothing styles evolved gradually over time. It is no longer necessary to explain change as the product of cataclysmic events (such as World War I) or social rebellions "against authority." Changes in attitude and behavior could be seen to develop from within conventional middle-class culture.

The so-called Victorian or respectable sexual ideology did not necessarily reflect the beliefs and behavior of the majority of people, even within the middle class. What we consider "the Victorian conception of women's sexuality" was closer to a *prescriptive* ideal (and possibly a minority ideal) than an accurate description of social reality. Naturally there was some factual basis for this enduring image—deriving from both the early Victorian evangelicals and the late Victorian moral reformers. The evangelical revival in England and America, especially among the middle classes, was accompanied by a tone of increased sexual, social, and sartorial repressiveness. "Nobody is gay now," complained one Englishwoman, "they are so religious." And Thackeray argued that even the evangelicals' guinea-foul looked "Quaker-like." The Bourbon Restoration in France was also accompanied by a militant reestablishment of clerical influence, which weighed most heavily on women.[30]

But neither then nor later were the repressive forces unchallenged. The documentary evidence indicates that there was a wide range of opinion on sexuality, in general, and on the eroticism of fashion, in particular. For every Doctor Acton, who believed that "good" women did not experience any sexual pleasure, there was a Doctor Debay, who thought that they did, or could and should. Similarly, for every Mrs. Linton, who attacked "indecent," "false," and whorish dress, there was a Mrs. Haweis, who argued that a beautiful body and beautiful dress were things to be proud of. And there were all the individual women and girls, who steered their paths between personal desires and social conventions.[31]

The idea that nineteenth-century (male-dominated) society forced women into submissive and masochistic behavior is not really substantiated by the sartorial and documentary evidence. Even though most women were economically dependent on men, and may have needed to conform to male ideals to a certain extent, women's self-images and sexuality were not completely male-defined. More work needs to be done on how nineteenth-century women perceived their clothing, bodies, sexuality, and the many social roles that they played. My own research has indicated that the clothing of the Victorian woman reflected not only the cultural prescriptive ideal of femininity, but also her own aspirations and fantasies.

If we can speak at all of an "official" "middle-class" ideal of femininity, then an analysis of nineteenth-century fashion indicates that that ideal was, in part, an erotic one. The Victorian woman played many often contradictory and ambiguous roles, but she cannot be characterized as a prude, a masochist, or a slave. Her clothing proclaimed that she was a sexually attractive woman, but this had a particular meaning within the context of her culture. In the following chapters, I try to reconstruct a new interpretation of Victorian fashion and sexuality, based on what the Victorians themselves thought about fashion and erotic beauty.

6

The Victorian Ideal of Feminine Beauty

Feminine and Masculine Beauty

The Victorian woman was constantly exhorted to cultivate her personal appearance. She was assured that it was her "first duty to society to be beautiful." Mme. Cavé echoed popular opinion when she argued that, "It is the wife's duty to maintain carefully the charms of her youth and beauty." It was part of her role to use "all her coquetries and all her virtues" to sustain her husband's spirit as he struggled to be successful at his work. Even John Stuart Mill maintained (in a letter to Harriet Taylor) that, "The great occupation of women" should be to "adorn & beautify" the family home "& to diffuse beauty, elegance, & grace everywhere."[1]

It was not only woman's duty, but also her desire and her innate ambition to be beautiful. In the revealingly titled *How to be Pretty though Plain*, Mrs. Humphrey maintained that, "to be pretty is the natural desire of the girlish heart." According to an anonymous male writer for *The Quarterly Review*, "We should doubt . . . whether the woman who is indifferent to her appearance be a woman at all."[2] Both society and her own "nature" demanded that she try to be beautiful.

To a considerable extent, the very idea of "beauty" was associated with femininity. Relatively little attention was devoted to the appearance of the male. Indeed, the writer for *The Quarterly Review* spoke in one breath of "the beautiful person of woman" and "the ugly body of man." Others, such as the French writer Gabriel Prevost, believed that, although male beauty existed, the masculine and feminine ideals of beauty were so different as to be almost antithetical:

Each sex has its definite and particular beauty. The only useful point to establish is that the constituent elements of the beauty of the one would be ugliness with the other, and vice-versa.[3]

Thus, the man should have a powerfully developed chest and shoulders, since "strength . . . is a beauty with him"; but, as "nature" had not created woman for feats of strength, muscular development should be useless and unattractive for her.

To some extent, the traditional idea persisted that feminine beauty compensated for feminine weakness: "strength to men, beauty to women." This was reinforced by the Social Darwinist idea that evolution favored feminine beauty, because males preferred beautiful women. Charles Darwin had showed that, in the animal world, the male was often more beautiful than the female; and he explained this by the process of "sexual selection," or "the accumulated action of the preferences of females." Many of his contemporaries rejected this idea, however, and argued that male beauty was "independent of the preferences of females," and was "consubstantial to virility."[4]

The Goncourt brothers, on the other hand, associated male beauty primarily with intelligence, and female beauty (such as it was) with animality:

> All the physical beauty, all the strength, and all the development of a woman is concentrated in . . . the pelvis, the buttocks, the thighs; the beauty of a man is to be found in the upper, nobler parts, the pectoral muscles, the broad shoulders, the high forehead.[5]

The Goncourts viewed women almost exclusively as sexual objects.

Herbert Spencer focused on woman's maternal function; but he, too, thought that the differences between the sexes were the result of an "earlier arrest of the processes of evolution in women." Men could continue to evolve mentally, but women's "bodies needed strength to reproduce." Reproduction itself was associated with feminine erotic beauty. Nineteenth-century medical and quasi-medical texts often maintained that feminine beauty was a "ruse of nature to attain its ends: a beautiful woman is a woman whose health and freshness promise fecundity." Thus a wide pelvis and full bosom were perceived as beautiful, because the first promised an "easy birth" and the second, "abundant nourishment."[6]

One of the most influential studies of female beauty was Alexander Walker's *Beauty; Illustrated Chiefly by an Analysis and Classification of Beauty in Woman*. Like many Victorians, Walker asserted that "the most perfect models" of feminine beauty were those "created by Grecian art." Unlike the Greeks, he ignored the issue of male beauty entirely. Instead, he divided the Classical ideal into three categories: Locomotive Beauty—"striking and brilliant"—exemplified by the goddess Diana; Vital or Nutritive Beauty—"soft and voluptuous"—exemplified by Venus; and Thinking Beauty—"characterized by intellectuality and grace"—exemplified by Minerva.

Although all three were theoretically examples of ideal beauty, he criticized both the youthful and "actively impassioned" woman and the "intellectual," while favoring the nutritive Beauty: "To this class belong all the more feminine, soft and passively voluptuous women." Walker's association of different personalities with his three physical types is revealing of the non-physical aspects of the ideal woman. The "expanded bosom" and "general plumpness" of the Nutritive Beauty were not merely aesthetically more pleasing than the relative slenderness of the other two. Rather, these characteristics were outward manifestations of woman's proper role. Similarly, the waist of the Nutritive Beauty, "though sufficiently marked, is, as it were, encroached on by that plumpness of all the contiguous parts," while her hips are "greatly expanded for the vital purposes of gestation and parturition." Her "whole figure is soft and voluptuous in the extreme."[7] Her beauty reflects her predominantly erotic and maternal functions. Yet the Victorian ideal of beauty was not merely physical.

The Victorians had inherited all of the earlier Western beliefs about feminine beauty from the Greek myth of Aphrodite, which associated beauty with love (or sexual desire), to the more negative myth of Pandora, in which feminine beauty was evil. In Christian mythology, women were associated with sexuality and sin. Too great a beauty was dangerous. In the Middle Ages, clerics warned that the soul was of infinitely greater importance than the body, and the ideal body was correspondingly ethereal. With the sixteenth-century rise of Neo-Platonism, however, intellectuals began to emphasize that the body was the expression of the soul—and that female beauty was a divine gift. (The corresponding male attributes were intelligence and force.) Both the significance of female beauty and the prefered body type changed, and large, fat, opulent beauties came into vogue. This majestic type became more coquettish, smaller, and younger in the eighteenth century, while the larger, stronger, more obviously maternal type was denigrated as a "peasant" beauty. The ideal beauty was now simultaneously maternal, childlike, and seductive. Yet doctors and moralists had already begun to raise the issue of a healthy, natural, and virtuous beauty. This development was partly moralistic, but also reflected the desire to rationalize and demystify the concept of female beauty.[8]

Spiritual and Physical Beauty

"What is beauty?," asked the author of a Victorian handbook on the subject, "—what are its constituents? —on what does it depend?" He concluded that it was the "happy union of . . . moral excellence, when associated with material beauty." Personal beauty resulted from a combination of moral or spiritual beauty and physical beauty.[9]

Gabriel Prevost took a similar position, when he maintained that the western ideal of physical beauty derived ultimately from the Greeks, while Christianity had introduced the ideal of spiritual beauty—"the beauty of expression or the reflection of the soul in the features."

Alongside, and perhaps beyond, regular, pagan, plastic beauty, Christianity has introduced to humanity the beauty known as that of *expression*. Plastic beauty is the result of proportions; the beauty of expression comes from the concordance of the facial features with the moral qualities.[10]

He believed that this new ideal of beauty had arisen together with a new conception of love: "For the ancients . . . love was symbolized by a goddess whose name meant both *beauty* and *pleasure* [Venus] . . . The body was everything." But Christianity gave woman a soul, a will, a personality.

Religious writers emphasized the overwhelming importance of spiritual beauty, and argued that physical appearance was irrelevant to true beauty. Thus, the anonymous author of *How to be Beautiful* described a girl whose "features were plain in the last degree, her figure and her gait most unlovely," who discovered that "the secret of how to be beautiful" was to "let Christ dwell in your heart by faith."[11] Even while denying the importance of material beauty, the author nevertheless implicitly admitted that standards of physical beauty did exist; at the conclusion of the story, there were hints that inner beauty would, as a side effect as it were, affect the outward appearance: other characters commented on the greatly improved appearance of the Christian heroine.

From a practical point of view, to be as beautiful as possible was important for the Victorian woman, because to a considerable extent it was through her appearance that she won "admiration and affection." "The importance of being 'nice looking' can scarcely be exaggerated from a girl's point of view." Throughout much of the nineteenth century, there were few pleasant alternatives to marriage, since the number of reasonably lucrative professions open to women was limited. "When it is considered that the object of nine-tenths of womankind is that they may marry . . . , it is very natural that they should endeavour to make themselves as captivating as they can."[12] In a sense, woman's profession was to be beautiful, to please, and to marry.

Woman as Our Priestess of Beauty

Beyond this, however, writers produced a flood of hyperbolic prose to the effect that woman's sacred mission was to beautify the world: "God meant women to make the world beautiful, as much as flowers and birds and butterflies." It was not merely that personal beauty was pleasant—for the woman herself and for observers—but rather that the beautiful and the good were, in some sense, inseparable. The "highest" beauty encompassed "spiritual, intellectual, and moral excellence." A "perfect body" reflected a "noble soul." Therefore—and here is the leap of reasoning—"in trying to attain beauty of form and face and clothing, we shall secure other most desirable ends."[13]

In other words, woman's role in society as a moral force was allied to her "mission" as "our Priestess of Beauty." "A woman's natural quality is to attract," and, having done so, exert an influence for good. "Outward ugliness" lessened her power to act as an inspiration to men. Beauty increased both happiness and virtue: "Beauty ... tends to refine and elevate the mind, and to increase the sum of human happiness."[14]

There was perhaps an element of defensiveness or self-justification in the chorus of authors arguing that "Beauty [is] a Great Power," and, therefore, it was not "sinful vanity to think about personal beauty." But "puritanical" strictures on female vanity clearly seemed to be giving way to a glorification of womanly beauty and virtue. Woman was the "most lovely of all created creatures." Furthermore, "Her beauty is an influence which spreads beyond her person, and, like the sunshine, carries brightness and warmth into dark places." This emphasis on woman's beauty and on her high moral influence were clearly related to the doctrine of separate spheres and to the idealization of domesticity. Yet as early as the seventeenth century, Neo-Platonists had reversed the old medieval "identification of woman with evil and female beauty with satanic temptation," arguing instead that physical beauty was associated with ethical superiority, so that a beautiful woman could be "man's guide to salvation."[15]

Men apparently had no such theoretically exalted role. Certainly not in any sartorial sense. Many people, in fact, believed that modern men's clothing was intrinsically ugly, and the appearance of men thus something less than beautiful. Mrs. Aria, then a writer for the rather progressive periodical *The Woman's World*, argued that

> the whole burden of beauty in costume falls nowadays on the shoulders of the fair sex, since the modern garb of the male has settled down to a dead level of unpicturesque broadcloth, and as long as a man looks neat and unobtrusive, that is all that can be expected of him from the point of view of dress ... Why nowadays nobody cares much how men look, unless it be their sweethearts or their wives. It is a very different thing with women. The female form divine ... is a splendid fact to be artistically adorned. The cult of female beauty is more potent than all creeds ... it is ... the sacred duty of all women ... to preserve this cult.[16]

The historians John and Robin Haller argue that "The Victorian woman cultivated beauty" because "her sexuality [was] circumscribed," and so "she turned for relief toward narcissism."[17] If we abandon the concept of "narcissism," and look at the emphasis on female beauty and fashion in social-historical terms, there seems to be an element of what we would call "sexism" in the demand that women should look beautiful, while men are not similarly instructed. Women seem to be reduced to their bodies. Did women have to try to look attractive to please men, or was this (at least in part) their own choice? The enhancement and display of the body can be a means of objectifying the self, or it can be a source of pride and pleasure. Circumstances and the meaning attached to behavior determine its significance. Historically, sartorial self-display was the norm for both sexes, if anything for men more than for women. But, of course, it means something rather different if a warrior in New Guinea wears a head-dress of Bird of Paradise feathers than if a Late Victorian lady wears one. I suspect that, while some elements of beautiful/erotic dress were related to the subordinate and dependent position of the Victorian woman, others were an expression of her own self-image.

It is probable that changing perceptions of the relative beauty of the male and female bodies were related to the diverging paths of male and female dress. Many cultures have regarded the male body as more beautiful. Women's cultural role in modern times as the "decorative" and "beautiful" sex probably played an important role in the increasing eroticism of female dress, and the decreasing eroticism of male clothing. The perception that the male body was "ugly" would necessarily have had a dampening effect on masculine sartorial display.

The clear sartorial distinction between the sexes functioned as an artificial secondary sexual character. Women's beautiful-sexual dress defined femininity, and, perhaps, male clothing was defined in relation to it—that is, as its opposite. The different styles might also have been related to the contemporary emphasis on separate spheres for men and women. A *Punch* cartoon from the crinoline era, for example, showed a man and a woman from behind, with the caption "They might belong to different species."

The Victorians maintained that clothing should be in harmony with the natural beauty of the body, in order to be beautiful and appropriate. Therefore, it should distinguish clearly between the sexes. In fact, the Victorians placed relatively little emphasis on male sexual beauty, as such. They did, however, stress in clothing an image of masculinity which was, almost by definition, the opposite of femininity. To have dressed otherwise would have been to risk looking "effeminate." Therefore, men's clothing might have been plain—even ugly—but it still represented the male ideal self.

Nevertheless, it is also true that clothing is more than a transmitter of particular messages, such as gender-identifying signs. And on closer inspection, it becomes apparent that there are important similarities (as well as differences) between Victorian men's and women's clothing. In the 1830s, for example, the hourglass silhouette and puffed sleeves were as characteristic of men's clothing as of women's. Men's coats were even padded in the chest and hips, and they were distinctly nipped in at the waist. During the Empire period, when women's dresses were high-waisted, so also were men's coats, and so on. Similarities in dress are also related to similarities in ideal figure types, which raises the question: to what extent are fashionable body types a function of the world of craft? Clearly, the look is symbiotic with clothing messages, gender roles, and ideals of beauty.

The idea of a "cult" of female beauty is highly complex, and cannot be reduced either to "vanity" or "narcissism," on the one hand, or to sexual attraction, on the other. In the nineteenth century, women were widely regarded as both "the ornamental sex" and the morally superior sex. They were supposedly drawn "naturally" toward both the beautiful and the good. This idealization of Woman was often associated with the glorification of domesticity and sexual purity. But it was also frequently recognized that female beauty and sexuality were closely related.

The Perfection of Figure:
Amorous Plenitudes and Chaste Slenderness

What were the constituents of female physical beauty? An advertisement in the fashion magazine *The Delineator* (1897) stated flatly: "Woman's beauty depends on the perfection of face and figure."[18] But what type of face and figure were considered "perfect"? And how could the less-than-perfectly-endowed improve their appearance?

According to one observer in 1873, "A well-developed bust, a tapering waist, and large hips are the combination of points recognized as a good figure."[19] The emphasis was on the fullness of the female secondary sexual characteristics—the breasts and hips—and on the slender and highly defined waist. This ideal was, in one sense, only an exaggerated version of the "natural" female figure.

The problem was that, except for the waist (and the hands and feet), the entire body was supposed to be well-padded with flesh. Occasionally a beauty writer would tactfully suggest that excessive fatness was undesirable: "It is very nice to see a woman round and plump, but when the plumpness becomes positive obesity, then it is no longer a beauty." On the whole, though, it was better to err on the side of plumpness: "Extreme thinness is a much more cruel enemy to beauty than extreme stoutness."[20] This emphasis on a desirable plumpness was almost antithetical to the ideal of a slender waist, especially since there was little encouragement to exercise and no mention of exercises specifically designed to slim the waist.

Yet the small waist was apparently the focus of more enthusiasm than any other part of the female body. According to the French beauty writer, Mlle. Pauline Mariette:

> The waist is the most essential and principal part of the woman's body, with respect to the figure ... The bee, the wasp ... those are the beings whose graceful and slender waist is always given as the point of comparison ... The waist gives woman her jauntiness, the pride of her appearance, the delicacy and grandeur of her gait, the unconstraint and delight of her pose.[21]

The artist, George Frederick Watts—an opponent of corsetry—believed that the popularity of the small waist derived from its associations "with ideas of delicacy, lightness, freshness, trimness, brightness. . . . Even that quality which is said to be next to godliness is mixed up with its connection with trimness and neatness." And—since the waist tends to thicken with age—youth. Yet Watts argued that it was an error to think of the waist "as a Thing, *per se*," rather than as a part of a harmonious whole. "[W]hen the shoulders spread above and the hips jut out below, a small waist is nothing but a deformity." To think such a figure was beautiful was "a most depraved taste."[22] It was, in fact, an erotic taste and, as such, it aroused controversy.

A writer for *The Queen* believed that "a slender waist is attractive to persons of the opposite sex." She (or he) argued, though, that it was truly beautiful only when "natural" and "without compression," in which case "the whole figure is slender." But "healthy English girls" tend not to be "spare." Finally the author admitted, "To have a very small waist with a plentiful development of bust is what the tight lacers aim at."[23]

We will study the controversy about the corset and tight-lacing at greater length later, but it is important to touch on it now as well, since it formed such an integral part of the debate on feminine beauty. Opponents of the corseted waist argued that there was an intrinsic antagonism between contemporary fashion and "true" beauty. They maintained that "the waist of beauty" was not the slender and corseted waist, but rather the "Classical," "artistic," or "natural" waist, based on the Greek canons of human proportion. Others, however, tried to reconcile the two ideals, and praised the "naturally small" (pure yet erotic) waist.

The controversy was so widespread that it played a part even in H. Rider Haggard's popular adventure story, *She* (first published in 1886). The fabulous Ayesha displays herself to the hero, saying:

> Now my waist! Perchance thou thinkest it too large, but of a truth it is not so; it is this golden snake that is too large, and doth not bind it as it should. It is a wise snake, and knoweth that it is ill to tie in the waist. But see, give me thy hands—so—now press them round me: There, with but a little force, thy fingers almost touch, O Holly![24]

At this point, Holly falls to his knees and announces that he worships her.

In George Moore's novel, *A Drama in Muslin* (first published in 1886 and set in 1882), the body of the empty-headed young beauty, Olive Barton, was described in terms that associated fleshiness with sensuality and slenderness with chastity: "the arms and bosom were moulded into *amorous plenitudes*, and the extremities flowed into *chaste slenderness*." In fact, both the plump and the petite were regarded as erotic. Thus, the anonymous author of the pornographic "autobiography," *My Secret Life*, maintained that "A small foot, a round, plump leg and thigh, and a fat backside speak to the prick straight." And he added that "Few men . . . will keep long to a bony lady whose skinny buttocks can be held in one hand."[25]

Plenitude and slenderness are very much relative concepts. As Balzac observed in 1847, the ideal was to "manage to possess lovely contours and yet remain slender." For all the emphasis on a pleasing plumpness, fashion journalists also insisted that "Fashion is inflexible on one point, ladies must be slender."[26] The corset seemed essential, not only to compress the waist and to correct "defects"—"Art steps in where Nature fails"—but also to stylize the figure, according to the current fashionable silhouette.

The "round, full, well-developed" bosom was greatly admired and, apparently, increasingly counterfeited. The conservative author of *How to Dress or Etiquette of the Toilette* (1877) admitted that a limited amount of artificial improvement was acceptable:

> Wadding or stuffing should be avoided as much as possible. A little may be judiciously used to round off the more salient points of an angular figure, but when it is used for the purpose of creating an egregiously false impression of superior form, it is simply snobbish.[27]

(At this time, the word "snob" meant a vulgar, ostentatious person with no pretensions to gentility.)

But if such false display was vulgar, nevertheless the Baroness Staffe felt that she had to remind her upwardly mobile readers that "It should not be imagined that one can only go to a ball with naked shoulders, nor that 'it is distinguished' to uncover the bosom excessively."

Although day dress was concealing, ball gowns were almost always décolleté, exposing the upper part of the bosom and the arms and shoulders. Since, traditionally only the upper classes had had occasion to wear low-cut evening gowns, this type of physical display was widely regarded as aristocratic. It was also widely regarded as "naked." Once Munby prevailed on the maid Hannah to try on her mistress's evening dress: "[She] suddenly flung herself into my arms—' . . . Oh, Massa . . . I am naked!'" And before their first ball, the fictional Olive Barton remarked to her sister, "It must be a funny sensation to walk into a room half-undressed, before a lot of men . . . I am quite anxious to see how we shall all look. May's arms are too fat, and Violet's are too thin; I think mine are about the best."[28]

Arms that were too thin were considered to be especially unattractive. Indeed, Mrs. Haweis felt that she had to advise her readers that, contrary to what they might think, *fat* arms were not beautiful.

Moore described the variety of shoulders revealed at Olive's ball:

> Shoulders were there, of all tints and shapes . . . Sweetly turned, adolescent shoulders, blush white, smooth . . . the strong, commonly turned shoulders . . . the drooping white shoulders . . . the pert, the dainty little shoulders, filled with warm pink shadows . . . and . . . the flowery, the voluptuous, the statuesque shoulders of a tall blonde woman of thirty, whose flesh is full of the exquisite peach-like tones of a Mademoiselle Eugène Verdier, blooming in all its pride of summer loveliness.[29]

This admiration for shoulders—and especially the "voluptuous" shoulders of a thirty-year-old woman—was typical of the period. Jean Philippe Worth recalled that in the late 1860s and early 1870s, "The main thing was to have beautiful shoulders and a lovely bust—and show them!"[30]

The ideal derriere tended to be described less often (except in pornography), but women with plump and even massive behinds appear in paint-

J. A. D. Ingres, *Madame Moitessier Seated* (1856). Courtesy of the Trustees of The National Gallery, London.

ings and erotic photographs of the period. In the latter especially, the women often stand with curved spines and projecting buttocks—a reflection both of the favored physical type and of the silhouette created by corsets and bustles.

In the case of clothed women, the bustle greatly exaggerated the derriere. Emile Zola described a department store display of "bustles of horsehair and jaconet, their enormous taut rumps . . . giving them outlines which had the indecency of a caricature." (Caricaturists, of course, made much of the bustle.) The successful writer and businesswoman, Mrs. Peel, recalled that in the late 1880s when she was a girl, trying to look attractive, she "tied the strings of my bustle so tightly that it stuck out aggressively and waggled when I walked."[31] Although it undeniably called attention to that part of the anatomy, both by its size and its movement, the bustle was also worn by little girls, and it did function to support the skirt. Furthermore, "false bums" had existed in previous centuries as well. It would be rash, therefore, to conclude that the bustle, per se, indicated an extreme cultural enthusiasm for the rear end.

One of the most persistent stereotypes of the Victorians involves their prudish attitude toward legs. Yet this alleged prudery has been greatly exaggerated, and the Victorians themselves were critical of the uncommon and "ridiculous form of vulgar gentility" and "pretension to superior refinement" that replaced the word "leg" with "limb":

Walking Dress with a Bustled Skirt (ca. 1884). Photograph from the exhibition catalog, *Rōman Ishō Ten: Evolution of Fashion 1835–1895* (Kyoto, 1980). Courtesy of the Kyoto Costume Institute, and Taishi Hirokawa, photographer.

We have all had our laugh at the American ladies who talk of the "limbs" of their chairs ... If legs are naughty, let us never speak of them; if not naughty, why blush to call them legs? ... If legs be a naughty idea, then no recourse to "limbs" will save you.[32]

Of course, many Victorians on both sides of the Atlantic did use circumlocutions, but this reserve should not be written off as simple prudery or hypocrisy. The story about hiding piano legs is based on a single source, and is either fictitious or described an extraordinarily rare phenomenon. It is undeniably true that the long dresses of the nineteenth century covered the legs. They also often had additional draperies above and at least one petticoat below, further concealing the outlines of the legs. Yet the more closely one looks at the styles of the High Victorian period, the more

Evening Dress and Fancy Dress. Fashion plate from *Petit Courrier des Dames* (1843).

it appears that legs were not so drastically hidden as the stereotype would have it.

Although the cage-crinoline looks inflexible in illustrations, when worn it swung provocatively from side to side, revealing glimpses of ankles and even calves. According to an 1863 article on "Crinoline," the tilting of crinolines allowed "spectators to study the manufacture of the young ladies' balmorals [boots], and the fit of their open-work stockings over their ankles, a word which is now by courtesy applied to some eighteen inches or thereabouts of the leg."[33] Although this account probably involves a degree of satiric exaggeration, other contemporary references indicate that a significant part of the lower leg was not infrequently exposed to view.

As with so much of Victorian sartorial eroticism, the exposure of the lower legs was occasion-specific. Just as the bosom and arms could be partially exposed for private social gatherings restricted to the wearer's social peers, so also could the legs. Although normal evening dress was characterized by very long skirts with trains, the clothing worn for costume balls often featured skirts that rose as high as mid-calf. In such costumes, ladies not only masqueraded as butterflies and fairies, but also as fanciful versions of working-class women, such as milkmaids and fisherwomen. Such skirts were regarded as inappropriate for the street, both for reasons of modesty and because real working-class women did often wear short skirts. Indeed, since the Middle Ages, it had been a general rule that long robes indicated high status and short garments low status. In the nineteenth century, the only other respectable exception to this rule was clothing for certain sports, particularly gymnastics and hunting. The short skirt was, of course, more "functional" for hunting, but it was probably more important that hunting was, by definition, a very high status sport.

An unidentified humorous article (probably from the early 1870s), "How to Choose a Wife by her Legs," described a variety of types of ankles and calves that might be glimpsed under ordinary conditions. The ideal was the "beautifully turned" leg with a "swelling line of beauty in the calf, and an ample development of muscular power—a plumpness that is not a bit flabby." The knees should be "perfectly rounded." "The ankle must be small and round . . . the instep, high and arched. The foot, long and narrow." Legs that were too thin indicated a jealous girl who was "rather too active to make a husband happy." Alternatively, the reader was warned to "avoid podgy feet and ankles as you would the pest"—their owner would spend her time lying "on the sofa and read[ing] 'parlour novels.' "[34]

The emphasis on small, slender hands and small or narrow feet was in some respects comparable to the emphasis on a small waist. Small extremities (like a small waist) were considered more refined, youthful, and aristocratic than large ones. Manual labor deformed and roughened hands, but "a fine hand"—that is "a soft, white hand, small . . . . moderately mus-

Le Francq, *Hunting Dress and Riding Habit.* Fashion plate from *Le Salon de la Mode* (1889).

cular, with slender, straight fingers, and well-formed, transparent nails"— "contributes greatly to the elegance of personal appearance." Conversely, "Wide feet, of the kind uncomplimentarily called 'fleshy' by shoemakers, are decidedly of a plebian cast, though they are often to be seen appended to the ankles of the most aristocratic women in the world when middle age has set in."[35]

Yet when we read of the "fascinations" of a little foot, its size seems to have erotic connotations, to be a mark of femininity as well as class status (and age). An intriguing story, "The Lady with the Little Feet," appearing in the light literary periodical *London Society* (June 1869), testifies to the erotic appeal of the foot. According to the anonymous author, diminutive feet "have gained admiration from a great many persons besides the Chinese"—the reference to the Chinese immediately recalling innumerable contemporary attacks on tight-lacing. The story's protagonist, Roger, has an obsessive interest in small feet. He tells a friend, "I was always fond of feet. . . . I think a woman without a foot—that is to say a good foot, and of course a little foot—is not worth looking at." While staying at a Paris hotel, he sees in the corridor a pair of "beautiful bronze" boots and "the sweetest things you ever saw in shoes," and promptly falls in love, sight unseen, with whoever wears them.[36]

While the feet, ankles, and even sometimes the calves were visible, the upper legs were at least indicated. As the corset became longer and tighter in the late 1870s, so also did the dress become more close fitting in front. "Tight as these dresses are, they are becoming when well worn . . . Handsome figures, indeed, look like animated statues." Since the dress was "tied or made to fall back . . . the contour of the figure has room to assert itself." According to Mrs. Haweis, this style "displays the clear line of the hip" and "indicates those forms of the body which have too long been completely hidden [i.e., the legs] and so far wasted; for beauty implying visibility, a beauty undiscovered is scarcely to be reckoned as a beauty." There were, though, still standards of beauty for thighs—"firm and massive" ones were praised.[37]

White Organdy Reception Dress (ca. 1877). Photograph from the exhibition catalog, *Rōman Ishō Ten: Evolution of Fashion* 1835–1895. Courtesy of the Kyoto Costume Institute, and Taishi Hirakawa, photographer.

James Jacques Tissot, *The Gallery of H.M.S. Calcutta (Portsmouth)* (ca. 1876).
Courtesy of the Trustees of the Tate Gallery, London.

The hips, the outline of the figure, and even the legs were considered
important components of physical beauty that fashion could emphasize.
The vogue for these very tight dresses also indicates that the Victorians
were not nearly so prudish about the female body as is often suggested.
In *A Drama in Muslin*, Olive Barton was described as wearing a ballgown
of "white silk, so tightly drawn back that every line of her supple thighs,
and every plumpness of the superb haunches was seen." Far from being
shocked, the company was filled with admiration for her beauty. Her serious sister, Alice, though, was perturbed by the relative lack of underwear
worn by another girl, the warm-hearted but fast May Gould:

> "And tell me what you think of my legs," [May] said, advancing a pair of
> stately calves. "Violet says they are too large."
>   "They seem to me to be all right; but, May dear, you haven't got a pet-
> ticoat on." "You can't wear petticoats with these tight dresses; one can't
> move one's legs as it is." "But don't you think you'll feel cold—catch cold?"
> "Not a bit of it; no danger of cold when you have shammy-leather
> drawers."[38]

Since her dress, like Olive's, was a ball gown, one may doubt whether May
was as immobilized as she implied.

Tightness is relative and, compared with the crinoline, these skirts were
very tight, but—*Punch* cartoons notwithstanding—they hardly hobbled

their wearers. Nevertheless, it is interesting that they inspired some viewers to fantasize about women in bondage:

> The legs are squeezed together the full length. The skirt is tight. Woman is constrained in her movements. . . . The knees touch. . . . [She] sits sideways; it is all she can do, and this uncomfortable pose is not ungracious. . . . The current fashion . . . obliges Woman . . . to observe herself. Under this sheath, the undulations must be soft and slow, almost imperceptible.[39]

It should be obvious, however, that this is not an accurate description of the actual fashion.

Taken all together, these descriptions of female physical beauty indicate that the Victorians were aware that beauty of form was essentially sexual. If anything, they preferred a more obviously voluptuous figure than is generally admired today. They were also aware that dress could accentuate the erotic appeal of the body.

The Face: Reflection of the Soul

The face was also an important determinant of feminine beauty. Here, the Victorians' belief in women's spiritual beauty is more clearly emphasized. According to the French beauty writer A. Cazenave:

> Real beauty—the beauty which charms and seduces—resides chiefly in the visage. . . . We are never so strongly attracted by any part of the body as by the face.

Cooley, too, argued that, "A perfect face would render its possessor beautiful, even though the rest of the body were devoid of excellence." According to him, "the beauty of the face" depended "chiefly on all its several features being. . . . in proportion."[40]

In actuality, rather delicate facial features seem to have been favored. Fashion plates, for example, show women with oval faces, smooth, pink and rounded cheeks, fairly large eyes, small, straight noses, and little rosebud mouths. Female facial features tend to be somewhat smaller and more delicately structured than is usual for men; the skin is generally of a softer and clearer texture. The Victorians emphasized this sexual dimorphism. Even subtle facial differences carried sexual and cultural connotations.

A "small mouth" was the "general ideal," and was thought to denote "refinement and freedom from strong passions." According to Mrs. Humphry, the mouths portrayed by the Pre-Raphaelite painters "would be called sensual" were they not "accompanied by the large, pure, spiritual eyes." By the turn of the century, the ideal mouth had grown slightly larger than the "infantine" or "niminy-piminy mouth" favored earlier. This seems to have been part of a gradual development away from the ideal of very delicate and ethereal female beauty to one that was more striking or womanly. In one of a series of articles on "The Human Form Divine," *The Englishwoman's Domestic Magazine* maintained that

"Lips were plainly meant to be kissed"—and should be shaped accordingly.[41]

Good eyes were "full, clear, and brilliant," and above all "expressive," with long, silky eyelashes and well-defined, arched brows. If a large mouth seemed overly sensual, large eyes seemed attractive but pure. According to *The Englishwoman's Domestic Magazine*, the eyes were "The most formidable part of feminine artillery," capable of expressing "all the passions of the soul."[42]

A great deal of emphasis was placed on a clear, fine complexion: "Perhaps the chief reason that it appears so important," suggested Mrs. Humphry, "is that it conveys an idea of purity." The ideal complexion was rather pale, but with light pink cheeks. By the 1870s extreme pallor was usually disparaged, on the grounds that it looked unhealthy; on the other hand, the skin was shielded from sunlight, as any kind of tan would have looked ungenteel.[43]

Beautiful hair was regarded as "one of a woman's greatest ornaments," giving "charm . . . even to a plain face." Commentators agreed that hair should be "rich," "luxuriant," "long," "abundant," "soft," "silky," "glossy," "curly," and "wavey." Charles Baudelaire devoted several poems to the associations that the lover's hair conjures up, in which there are occasional intimations that the hair with its "perfume of fur" refers as well to the pubic hair. Symbolically, long hair seemed to represent femininity and short hair masculinity. According to Prevost, "Short hair is virile and perfectly appropriate to the role of man in our epoch. It leaves the head free for struggle, movement, and thought." Long, flowing hair was traditionally associated both with sexual potency and with virginity. One element of its charm derived from associations with feminine sexuality.[44]

The conservative Victorian writer Charlotte Yonge complained that

> The associations of the loose, unkempt locks. . . . are not those of pure and dignified maidens or matrons. . . . Tumble-down hair, falling dishevelled on the shoulders sounds grand in fiction, but it is disgusting in real life. . . . Certain fashions which seem to revel in untidy arrangement . . . scarcely are consistent with the dainty niceness of true womanhood.[45]

Of course, the hair was not worn *loose*, but the vehemence of her reaction together with the traditional and widely understood erotic connotations of loose hair indicate that fashionable hair styles were regarded as overtly sensual. By the later 1860s, the simple chignon (which had also been attacked in its day) had given way to elaborate arrangements that were high on top, with plaits, coils, or rolls of hair behind. Waves, "frizzles," or "fringes" of hair covered the top of the forehead and, especially for evening occasions, long curls and ringlets fell down the neck. Mrs. Elizabeth Lynn Linton thought these styles made women look like "maniacs or negresses."[46]

Much of the controversy about the morality of dress and adornment focused on this type of issue. Women should be beautiful, but elaborate fashions tended to arouse the ire of those who equated simplicity with naturalness and virtue, and artifice with deceit. Another debated issue was the "immodesty" of modern dress, and its supposedly pernicious effects on the moral character of young women. Yet these opinions need not be interpreted as evidence of Victorian prudery. Rather, they represented one response to an ideal of fashionable feminine beauty that clearly emphasized erotic charm.

Face, Form, and Fashion

Personal appearance is the product of the body (however modified), the face, and dress. The relative importance given each of these components varies according to the time, place, and circumstances. In *Beauty and How to Keep It* (1889), "A Professional Beauty" argued that, "A pretty figure is really a much more valuable gift than a pretty face, as it lasts so much longer. With a good figure no woman can possibly be plain." The author of *My Secret Life* was blunter about the immediate sexual appeal of the figure: "Face had for me of course the usual attraction, for beauty of expression always speaks to the soul of man first." But "Form is . . . more enticing . . . than the sweetest face."[47]

More to the point, perhaps, as far as most women were concerned, was the fact that facial beauty was essentially an accidental quality. The face was less amenable to artificial improvement (other than by cultivating a pleasant expression) than was the figure, which could be concealed and altered—in short, made to seem conspicuously more attractive. At least the semblance of a good figure could be obtained with the help of "a good corsetière" and an elegant ensemble. Indeed, A Professional Beauty went so far as to state flatly that "It is dress that makes a woman really pretty." A woman could obtain "the reputation of beauty," without having even "one good feature," if she possessed the "desire to please combined with . . . elegance in dress."[48]

7

Artificial Beauty or The Morality of Dress and Adornment

An Approximation of Beauty

One of the great appeals of fashion has been that it "divert[s] attention from insoluble problems of beauty and provide[s] a way to buy an approximation of beauty." As "A Lady" wrote in 1873, "Dress has much to do with personal loveliness. It can enhance and set off beauties and conceal defects."[1] Although Victorian writers emphasized both functions of dress, the greater part of their advice on improving the personal appearance concerned the concealment of physical "flaws."

This did not necessarily indicate a negative attitude toward the body. "Has the race degenerated?" asked Gabriel Prevost.

> Yes and no. It is certain that one could still find these days some individuals having all the characteristics of perfect beauty; but there is no doubt that the enormous majority would present deformed elements and horribly modified proportions.[2]

"If man were under the obligation to be nude, as in Sparta," he wrote, then "gymnastics and hygiene" would play a crucial role. But modern life exaggerated "sedentary habits," so that people were too often overly fat or thin. "Fortunately we have clothing," which, if it cannot "rectify nature," can at least give "to each individual the highest degree of beauty that he is capable of acquiring."

This belief was held not only by interested parties like the corsetière Madame Roxey Caplin, who thought that ninety-nine women out of a hundred suffered from "deficiencies" in appearance. Even advocates of the natural beauty of the body, like Mrs. Haweis, maintained that "We are not like the Greeks who made the improvement of the body their dearest study; and, not having reduced our superfluous fat, and cultivated our muscles into perfection, we ought to be careful how we expose them."[3]

Neither men nor women were particularly athletic in the nineteenth century, with the partial exception of the English upper class, whose attachment to rural living gave them more opportunities for sports. In urban centers, these were greatly reduced, so, to some extent, middle-class Victorians were simply being realistic about their far from perfect bodies.

Beyond this, every individual has certain features that are more or less attractive according to the standards of the day, and which may be emphasized or minimized. Charles Blanc's example—that vertical stripes increase the short individual's apparent height—is one that has been repeated to the present day. A very different writer, Mrs. Margaret Oliphant, also believed that

> fashion . . . has this one principle of humanity in it, that it is almost always designed to help those who want help, to cover deficiencies of nature, to conceal the evils wrought by time, and to make those look their best to whom no special charms have been given.[4]

If the Victorian ideal of beauty was fairly rigid, nevertheless Victorian clothes concealed physical flaws and signs of age more than modern dress does, and, to that extent, allowed more women to look and feel attractive.

Fashion also served to decorate or "adorn" women, making even a "plain" girl look "ornamental," as well as testifying to her taste and sense of style. Mrs. Haweis argued that "There are some ladies who always look well: they are not necessarily the pretty ones, but they are women gifted with fine natural taste, who instinctively choose right forms, colours, and fabrics."[5] Fashion journalists repeatedly described articles of clothing as "beautiful," "very pretty," and "charming"—with the clear implication that these qualities would be imparted to the woman who wore them. They sometimes went a step further, and seemed to equate beauty with chic. Dresses were described as "elegant," "tasteful," "fashionable," and, especially, "stylish"; with the implication that, by dressing fashionably, one not only achieved an approximation of beauty (and freedom from the accidents and defects of physical endowments), but highly valued intangible qualities as well, such as poise, a desirable social status, an artistic temperament, and a refined sensibility.

Writers stressed, however, that it was ultimately less important that clothing should be in the height of fashion than that it should be becoming to the particular individual. Mrs. Haweis, for example, advised that "A head-dress must be—first, becoming—second, beautiful—and third, useful." The hat should be becoming to the individual in question, since it "has a powerful effect on the face, in either beautifying it or the reverse." Its shape, color, and general style should "draw the eye" to a woman's good features, while minimizing any facial defects. In particular, its color should "enhance" her complexion and the color of her hair. Only later did Mrs. Haweis add that the head-dress should be "a pretty object in itself." She ignored the issue of its putative usefulness entirely.[6]

Edgar Degas, *The Millinery Shop* (1882). The Mr. and Mrs. Lewis L. Coburn Memorial Collection, courtesy of The Art Institute of Chicago.

Conversely, especially among early Victorian evangelicals, fashion was identified with emotional falsehood. Consider the story, "The History of a Hat," printed in America's premier fashion journal, *Godey's Lady's Book*:

> It was certainly the prettiest hat in the world—the most elegant, the most graceful, the most coquettish! It was a hat of lilac gauze, with trimmings of straw round the brim, and a bunch of wild poppies and cornflowers mingled with bows of riband, slightly inclining towards the right, and resting upon the brim!
>
> And it was, also, the frailest and less profound love possible!—a light sentiment of fantasy, with capricious favours and artificial tenderness![7]

It was no accident that a hat was the subject of this moral lesson. Its relative lack of functional character meant that it played an essentially symbolic role.

Artificial Ugliness and True Beauty

Not everyone was wholeheartedly in favor of the artificial "improvement of the appearance." Although some Victorians accepted the idea of possible disparities between being and appearance, others adamently rejected the idea that beauty could—or should—be the product of a lady's toilette, arguing that while beauty of expression and character should be cultivated, "false" and "deceptive" adjuncts to beauty should be avoided. The more conservative believed that to take too great an interest in personal appearance was vain and frivolous and even wicked.

The English novelist Charlotte Mary Yonge, for example, argued that "All attempts to pretend to beauties that we do not possess are clearly falsehood, and therefore wrong." *Godey's Lady's Book* repeatedly offered a moral critique of fashion as hypocrisy and vanity, stressing that "character," "virtue," and "transparent sincerity" alone constituted beauty: "Beauty without virtue is like a painted sepulchre, fair without but full of corruption." The American advice-writer, John Todd, believed that an attractive exterior concealing a wicked heart was like "the beautifulness of the serpent, the more hideous in proportion to their power to charm the victim."[8] It was not merely that a wise person would look at the char-

Hadol, *Être et Paraitre.* Caricature (1869). Courtesy of The Liverpool Polytechnic Art Library.

acter, not the surface. Rather, the more conservative and religious writers sometimes regarded feminine physical beauty as a *trick*. Too much beauty was dangerously attractive to the (usually male) spectator. In part as a defense against the fear of seduction, many writers argued that artifical beauty was really ugly.

The anonymous author of "Artificial Woman-Making" (circa 1869) asked rhetorically:

> When will women learn that, with regard to natural objects, there is no such thing as Artificial Beauty; that the two terms mutually exclude one another ... ? That there is such a thing as Artificial Ugliness, and that it is the invariable result of efforts to create Artificial Beauty.[9]

He (or she) insisted that "all that can be done to improve [the appearance] is to give ... perfect health ... entailing clear skin and bright eyes, and easy, dignified movements; and then add those moral qualities of kindliness, modesty, and self-respect, which shine out through the veil of the body."

Godey's also advocated only "moral cosmetics," such as not staying up late or playing cards. The magazine's editors worried that real cosmetics concealed the evidence of true inner emotions that would normally be expressed by blushing or growing pale. Indeed, the emphasis on "sincerity" and "honesty" was so strong that some Americans professed to prefer daguerreotypes over painted portraits, on the grounds that their rather harsh "realism" did not "flatter" the sitter. To look too good was suspect.

At the opposite end of the spectrum was the outspoken fashion and beauty writer Mrs. Haweis, the daughter of an artist and the wife of a clergyman, whose books *The Art of Beauty* (1878) and *The Art of Dress* (1879) were ten years ahead of their time in their open advocacy of artificial beauty aids and dressing to attract attention. She advised her readers to ignore the "fossilised prejudice" that would stigmatize as "vanity" any attempts to enhance personal beauty; and even advocated the subtle use of rouge and powder, arguing that "the culture of beauty need never interfere with that of goodness and usefulness to others."[10]

The majority took a position somewhere between these extremes, and, while acknowledging the importance of modesty and beauty of character, permitted at least a limited amount of artificial "improvement" of the physical appearance. Fashion was sometimes presented as the great equalizer that made ordinary-looking or even plain girls look as pretty or prettier than girls who were naturally more beautiful. Not surprisingly, this position was strongly held by fashion journalists.

A writer for the young women's fashion magazine *Sylvia's Home Journal* advised her readers:

> We should all try to be as pretty as we can without resorting to deceptions in the form of cosmetics, hair dyes, and pearl powder. The best way to be really pretty, independently of regular features and good complections is to have pleasant thoughts constantly in our minds, always to be doing kind

and good-natured things, and never to listen to anything unkind or bitter about others. If we do this, the eyes will grow clear and bright, the corners of the lips turn up pleasantly and prettily, and the beauty of countenance be fully developed—a far higher beauty than that of feature. But besides this, we should all wear as becoming dresses as we can get without outrunning our allowance or running into debt.

After this initial (and fairly brief) lecture on correct mental attitudes and their good effects, the author went on to describe girls and women whose appearance was drastically improved by attractive dress: "I have seen a really beautiful woman quite outshone by one of very inferior claims to good looks, who was well and gracefully dressed, and possessed, besides, those graces of manner which are to the mind as satin and laces are to the body." Beauty here was a function of both dress and character. As the examples multiplied, however, dress was increasingly emphasized. She described an "American girl" that she knew—"a plain girl. . . . with an angular figure, and *hardly any hair!*" When the girl "fixed herself up," though, "she was really pretty, and all the angularity conjured away from her figure by the charm of a perfectly made dress."[11]

The concepts of truthfulness, naturalness and appropriateness modified the theoretical legitimacy and desirability of trying to be beautiful. To some extent, the purely decorative qualities of dress escaped censure, because they were perceived as being grafted onto the primary function of dress—the preservation of modesty. Other adjuncts to personal beauty were more controversial. For example, Mrs. Yonge thought that a "virtuous woman" would never wear "borrowed plaits," but others believed that false hair might be "excusable," if not fully justifiable, if it concealed a serious deficiency of hair. In fact, the trade in hair was considerable, with the hair often bought from peasant women in Europe who wore traditional head-dresses. Conservatives often maintained that the hair was bought from diseased women and was contaminated—an obvious example of a punitive moralistic threat.[12]

Hair dyes and facial cosmetics often did contain chemicals that were unsafe, but safety was not really the primary issue. The debate about cosmetics and hair dyes was part of a wider controversy about the legitimacy of artifice and the appropriateness of styles of dress and adornment that were overtly erotic.

Opinions varied over time, first permissive, then rigid, then increasingly permissive again. The author of the 1825 book, *The Art of Beauty*, asked, "Ought people to use paint?" and blithely answered, "Why not?" Ten years later, a shift in sentiment had begun that seems to have held on for about three decades. "True" beauty was the product of moral goodness and physical health. "False" and "artificial" beauty could destroy them. Doctors, such as the popular author "Medicus," argued that "health—bounding saucy health—is the fountain from which all true beauty springs." While this was to some extent true, as an argument it also served to devalue the erotic aspects of physical beauty. More commonly, writers emphasized moral self-improvement—"kindliness," "cheerfulness," and "a wholesome frame of mind." According to the authors of one quasi-dress reform text of 1892: "The use of the intellect has a powerful effect upon the moulding and chiselling of the features, removing the marks of sensuality, and replacing them by the fineness of lofty self-control."[13]

As late as the twentieth century, Mrs. Humphry was telling her young readers that the various "attitudes of mind," whether good or bad, write themselves "plainly on the exterior": "In a measure we make our own faces and mould our own figures." Thus,

> Lying late in bed in the morning ruins the complexion! . . . Too much novel-reading is fatal to the temper, and bad temper spoils the expression. The novel-reader who neglects duty and exercise is certain to be irritable and disagreeable and these show in the countenance. Nothing, not even ill-health, has such a deleterious effect upon good looks as the sense of duties left undone.

Ultimately, she implied that too single-minded a concern with beauty was "selfish," and thus self-defeating, as it led to "discontent," a disagreeable expression, and the use of "illegitimate" auxiliaries to beauty—with all the bad effects that that entailed.[14]

Yet beauty books gave recipes for facial cosmetics and hair dyes, and they were fairly widely advertised—although often indirectly: "BEAUTY without PAINT.—a natural colour for the cheeks." Newspapers of the 1860s covered the legal trials of the notorious cosmetician, Madame Rachel, who charged up to twenty guineas for "enameling" a lady's face with products like her Favourite of the Harem's Pearl White.[15] A little artificial improvement was excusable for mature women, who were more in need of assistance, or less in danger of damaging their "moral character."

As well as counterfeiting health and youth, cosmetics seem to simulate the physiological changes that accompany sexual orgasm—the brilliant eye, reddened lips, etc. According to the *Harper's Bazar* "Ugly-Girl Papers," "The painted eye of desire, the burning cheek, and dyed nails, were coeval with the wisdom of Alexandria"—and were certainly "no cause for divorce." The Englishwoman, Gwen Raverat, recalled that such erotic display was popularly associated with "actresses or certain kinds of women." When used with discretion, cosmetics apparently were legitimate for married women "but never young girls."[16]

Charles Baudelaire's defense of *maquillage* was very much the expression of a minority opinion, the more so since he argued that "face-painting" should not attempt to imitate Nature or counterfeit health and youth, but rather that it should be *deliberately artificial*, to give the impression of "a supernatural and excessive life," and to give the wearer a passionate appearance. The very artificiality of fashion was "a symptom of the taste for the ideal." Fashion was "a sublime deformation of Nature, or rather a permanent and repeated attempt at her *reformation*." These

views, of course, were the exact opposite of the widely held belief that
Nature was the ultimate source of standards of morality and beauty. In
one respect, however, Baudelaire appeared to echo contemporary views of
woman's role in life. She had, he argued, "a kind of duty" to appear "magical and supernatural . . . the better to conquer hearts."[17]

The controversy surrounding the cosmetic arts throws into relief some
of the issues involved in the related controversy about the morality of
dress and the position of the modern woman. In England, some of the
most violent attacks on "The Girl of the Period" came from the pen of
Mrs. Eliza Lynn Linton, a journalist and novelist, who emphasized the
pernicious effects of modern dress on moral character. Specifically, she
objected to "paint and powder"; hair dyes; artificial hair; frizzy and/or
loosely flowing hairstyles; small bonnets that did not "shelter . . . the
face"; low décolletage—"charms that were once reserved are now made
the common property of every looker-on"; artificial busts "of rose-col-
oured rubber"; tight skirts—"of those limbs which it is still forbidden to
expose absolutely, the form and contour can at least be put in relief by
insisting on the skirts being gored and straightened to the utmost"—in
sum, all "aids" designed "to give an impression of . . . a more sensuous
development of limb, and a greater abundance of flesh than can be either
natural or true," (and even artificial ears). "These fashions," she insisted,
"do not please or attract men."[18] But that, of course, was precisely the
contested issue.

The Girl of the Period

Much of the outcry in the 1860s about "The Girl of the Period" derived
from fears that respectable young women were imitating the dress, manners, and appearance of "the queens of the demi-monde." Some people
feared that the "lines of respectability were becoming blurred," and that
not only might girls and women be taken for what they were not, but their
actual behavior and character might also degenerate. The girl who wore
cosmetics and "fast" dress might easily lose her modesty and innocence
by imitating those whose appearance, it was argued, accurately reflected
their corrupt morals. "She can not be made to see that modesty of appearance and virtue ought to be inseparable, and that no good girl can afford
to appear bad."[19]

What is the significance of Linton's famous attack on the modern girl?
Was it true that the modern girl had rejected the old domestic and maternal role of "friend and companion," "tender mother," and "industrious
housekeeper," preferring a "fast" life with "plenty of fun and luxury"?
Did "the fashionable woman of the period" really live for "dress, dissipation, and flirting"? Was she "always" in the midst of "some love affair,
more or less platonic, according to her own temperament or the boldness
of the man"?

Mrs. Linton's views to not appear to have been entirely representative of public opinion. *The Saturday Review* seemed to have a policy of printing deliberately provocative articles, often focusing on criticism of the modern girl and woman. In 1870, a writer for *The Tomahawk*, a journal of satire, looked back at "The Girl of the Period":

> People read the article with pleasure. It was very "dreadful" and "improper," but pleasant. . . . However, everybody more or less agreed that the statements in the article savoured of falsehood. "Women were certainly bad, and Miss Dash infamous, but then it was a little too strong." . . . "Girl of the Period" coats, dresses, shirts appeared, and were successful, even a "Girl of the Period" Magazine.[20]

The Girl of the Period. Cover illustration from *The Girl of the Period Miscellany* (1869).

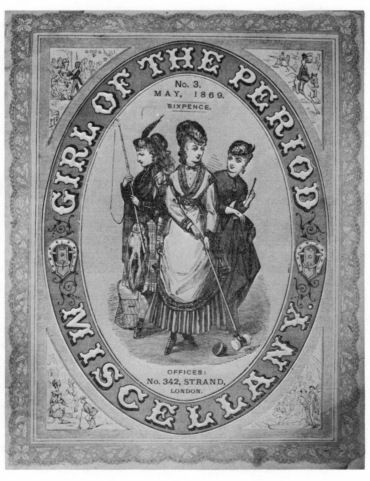

On the other hand, Mrs. Linton's article provided ammunition and a handy slogan for writers opposed to current fashions or engaged in the corset controversy, such as the anonymous authors of articles on "The Waist of the Period," "The Girl of the Period has taken to tight-lacing again," and "The Waste of the Period! or A Plate of Fashions for the British Folly." A cartoon by Howard Del, "A Modern Work of Art—Building up the Girl of the Period," showed a figure being dressed and decorated by tiny men—with a corset, "palpitator" (false bosom), "patent calves," pearl powder and paint, a crinoline, and false hair. The modern girl was attacked as ignorant, vain, pitiable, and unattractive.

These attacks might, to some extent, have reflected a reaction against women's increasing independence. Although Mrs. Linton was a complex, intelligent, and independent person, she was very much opposed both to the movement for women's rights and to the fashionable woman. Was fashion, then, a reflection of women's widening sphere? Sixties fashions do seem generally bolder in effect than their immediate predecessors, and some historians have suggested that there was "almost certainly a connection between this and the nascent efforts towards [women's] social and even political emancipation."[21] To a limited extent, the criticism of fashion was only the projection of deeper anxieties about changing life-styles (including sexual behavior).

Yet the invention of aniline dyes permitted the production of bright and even glaring colors, and does not necessarily reflect a greater feminine audacity (although the popular practice of combining what we should consider grossly clashing colors did, perhaps, indicate a desire to attract attention). Similarly, the normal inflationary aspects of competition in dress contributed to the growth of crinoline size.

Many people in the 1860s perceived contemporary fashions as being conspicuously more elaborate and immodest than earlier styles, but one may doubt whether this was entirely true. Even a casual perusal of the earlier literature indicates that this type of moral criticism was always common. An article, "On Vanity and Love of Dress," from 1843, for example, suggested that vanity was a "selfish" and "essentially . . . female passion," and that it was very difficult to keep "the love of dress . . . within proper bounds, *as the present extravagant mode of dressing will testify.*"[22]

The problem, as a number of Victorians saw it, was that the fashions were set by immoral women. If a woman wanted to look fashionable, she ran the risk of looking immodest. Although women were widely regarded as morally superior to men, they were also regarded, in some sense, as morally feeble; "proper" and "modest" dress provided them with a protective shield. Since Paris was the undisputed capital of women's fashion, English (and American and German) writers frequently blamed Parisian dress designers and demi-mondaines for the "immorality" of contemporary dress. Pernicious fashions were created by "the Man-Milliner" and launched by "the demi-monde fashion-mongers of Paris." [23]

The Queen, for example, printed an article entitled "What are the Sources of Beauty in Dress" by Mrs. Harriet Beecher Stowe, in which she violently attacked the *"outré* unnatural fashion [that] comes from the most dissipated foreign circles." It was "elaborate," "complicated" and "contrary to nature"—and it was not beautiful, because it was not "appropriate" to the character of the good but foolish girls who copied it. On the other hand, it was "perfectly adapted to the kind of life led by dissipated women, whose life is one revel of excitement, and who, never proposing . . . any intellectual employment or any domestic duty, can afford to spend three or four hours every day under the hands of a waiting maid, in alternately tangling and untangling their hair." It reflected all too accurately the character and lifestyle of immoral women:

> A certain class of women in Paris . . . make the fashions. . . . They are women who live only for the senses. . . . They have no family ties; love, in its pure domestic sense, is an impossibility, and their whole intensity of existence, therefore, is concentrated on the question of sensuous enjoyment, and that personal adornment which is necessary to secure it.[24]

Such women, she argued, needed to adorn themselves, however blatantly and deceptively, in order to attract men and hide the ravages caused by a life of dissipation.

Famous courtesans and members of the theatrical profession *were* among the leaders of fashion, in part because it was especially important for them to look attractive, but also because they were much less constrained than most women by the fear of looking immodest or conspicuous. Other women sought to follow fashion closely, but not too closely. But to lag too far behind the fashion was to risk looking dowdy and unattractive. To attempt to flout the fashion was to look "eccentric."

Every new fashion was received with disapproval from at least some quarters. In 1878, F. T. Vischer, the well-known German philosopher and author of *Mode und Zynismus,* described contemporary fashion as *"eine Hurenmode,"* because it revealed the contours of the female body. He had been no happier with the previous fashion of crinolines, however, which he condemned as "impertinent," because they made women appear larger than men. He also maintained that any fashion that deviated so greatly from the natural form of the body was immodest, because it was a distortion that charmed viewers more than the true form would have, and invited curiosity about the body underneath. He denied that he thought that every woman who wore the crinoline had "evil thoughts in her little head." Most were just conforming to the current fashion.[25]

The anonymous author of the pamphlet "Who is to Blame?" blamed men for the spread of this "meritricious style" of "immodest" dress into "good society." He (or she) maintained that girls, "actuated simply by an innocent desire to please—have followed the direction of men's gaze, and have copied that which appears to be attractive." As Mrs. Haweis put it: "Why don't girls marry? Because the press is great, and girls are indistinguishable in the crowd. . . . Men, so to speak, pitch upon the girls they can see."[26]

To a considerable extent, the attack on the girl of the period reflected the unwelcome perception that fashion emphasized female sexual beauty, and that some young women were deliberately trying to attract men.

An Index of the Mind and Character

The morality of dress was an important issue to the Victorians, because they perceived clothing as an "index of the mind" and "character" of the wearer. Dress was

> the second self, a dumb self, yet a most eloquent expositor of the person. . . . Dress bears the same relation to the body as speech does to the brain; and therefore dress may be called the speech of the body.[27]

It was especially true that women were judged on the basis of their appearance. A man's clothing indicated at least his approximate status, but, beyond that, it revealed relatively little about his tastes and character, in large part because men were so constrained in their choice of costume. According to an article in *The Quarterly Review*, "It is all very well for bachelors to be restricted to a costume which expresses nothing . . . since they can be safely trusted for publishing their characters to the world with that forwardness which is their chief element." It was very different for women, who were characterized by "delicacy of mind, and reserve of manner." For women, dress functioned as "a sort of symbolical language . . . the study of which it would be madness to neglect, [since] to a proficient in the science, every woman walks about with a placard on which her leading qualities are advertised."[28]

But which qualities were considered desirable? And which undesirable? How exactly was character expressed by dress? Did everyone "read" a dress in the same way? Roberts argues that a Victorian woman's dress announced her submissive, masochistic, and narcissistic personality, Kern that it expressed an anti-sexual ideology. Most young women, however, wanted to look both sexually attractive and sufficiently "modest" to indicate their good character. Their physical beauty was itself supposed to reflect their inner beauty. An article in *Harper's Bazar* on "Nice Girls" argued that the expression "does not necessarily mean a beautiful girl, or an elegant or an accomplished girl, except to the extent that beauty, elegance, and accomplishments are *essential* to niceness. In a sense, *the nice girl always is, and should be, pretty.*" Apparently, beauty consisted not only of a "sweet mouth" and "kind eyes," but also a perfectly fitting and appropriately decorative dress, gloves, boots, and so on.[29]

Obviously, there were differences of opinion about the degree of sexual display acceptable in dress. According to a writer for *Sylvia's Home Journal:*

Many persons argue that the love of dress is as harmful to the community as the love of drink; and if they see a girl wearing some garment in a specially becoming manner, they stamp her as vain and coquettish, wasteful of time and thought on a worthless object.[30]

Such a girl might well think that her dress and appearance had been grossly misinterpreted, and that her intention was merely to look "pleasant and pretty." Nevertheless, I doubt that these hypothetical disgruntled observers were merely straw men set up by a fashion journalist. It seems probable that many attempts to look attractive and fashionable were perceived negatively by at least some people as "vain," "immodest," or "fast." According to a writer for *London Society*, "the dread of being thought *fast*" prevented many Englishwomen from being well dressed. It was difficult to satisfy everyone.[31]

The boundaries of acceptable dress were fairly narrow, and women were constrained in their choice of costume. Manuals of dress constantly cautioned women against appearing "conspicuous or peculiar." "Fashion is an imperious goddess, and exacts unquestioning submission from her devotees. It is useless to denounce her sway or run counter to her behests. No single person can, with impunity, take an independent position."[32] Even writers for *The Rational Dress Society's Gazette* admitted that

To affect a singularity in attire is to incur a social martyrdom out of all proportion to the relief obtained. . . . It is vain to be comfortably and modestly attired if one is to be made an object of observation or ridicule to every person high and low whom one may chance to meet.[33]

If rational dress was clearly beyond the pale, it was also true that ordinary fashionable dress—neither ultra-modish nor excessive—could still expose a woman to censure.

According to Theodore Zeldin, nineteenth-century treatises on confession in France emphasized that "Women's clothes were a constant source of danger." Yet although fashions could be immodest and an incitement to sin, priests were advised to adopt a relatively tolerant attitude toward the women who wore these styles:

Married ones who dressed to please their husbands, or girls who dressed in order to win husbands should be given some concessions, but not if they sought to please others apart from their husband, or if their aim was not to get married. Those who leave their arms and shoulders naked or only lightly covered were, if they were following the fashion, not guilty, but those who invented the fashions were guilty of mortal sin.[34]

Presumably, most women wanted to look attractive—but as respectable wives or potential wives, not courtesans. The element of gentility or respectability was part of a woman's sexual arsenal. Both her social position and her own self-perception were related to the aspirations and fantasies that she held and that were part of her cultural milieu. Her clothing proclaimed that she was a sexually attractive woman, but this had a particular meaning within the culture of the time.

It is extremely difficult, of course, to determine the nature of the relationship between the prescribed ideal and the historical reality. The idealization of female "purity," the social importance of "respectability," and the shifting definitions of women's social roles must have set the terms within which "female sexuality was expressed." But the rules governing these terms remain somewhat ambiguous. According to the prescriptive ideal of femininity, for example, female sexuality was secondary, and derived from the maternal instinct, but this was not always evident in dress. With regard to modesty and sexual display, the fashion writer, Mrs. Merrifield, merely advised her readers that men tended to be more genuinely attracted to modestly dressed women than to those "who make so profuse a display of their charms."[35]

Yet there does not seem to have been a clear distinction between the clothing of the "pure," "respectable," "maternal," and "domestic" middle-class woman and that worn by her sexual counter-ideal. Middle-class girls and women adopted styles that had initially been launched by courtesans, actresses, and aristocratic ladies; while prostitutes dressed professionally as "ladies." An analysis of fashion indicates that it was not a question of the denial or domestication of female sexuality, but rather that it was only socially acceptable when it manifested itself in certain forms.

It is possible that sexuality was acceptable to the extent that it was seen as an aspect of *the ideal self*, a concept that incorporates both self-image and social perception, and that is not monolithic like the "cultural ideal," but rather focuses on the individual person within a particular environment. For example, if fashionable dress helped "to attract the opposite sex," there was some disagreement about its suitability for unmarried girls, who were, theoretically, supposed to be pre-sexual. (Thus even quite big girls often exposed much of their calves.) Yet in England and America, girls were supposed to attract their own husbands, without, however, overemphasizing their sexual charms. In the absence of arranged marriages, "young ladies" were sometimes even encouraged to wear costumes that were "as effective and coquettish as possible," or advised to dress as well after marriage as they had before.[36]

Although this distinction between France, on the one hand, and England and America, on the other, should not be overdrawn, nevertheless the French did seem to have dressed their daughters more simply. After their parents had married them off, they could safely and legitimately display their charms. In *The Awkward Age*, Henry James compared the European and the English styles of dressing girls. Little Aggie was clothed according to the former style—in "an arrangement of dress exactly in the key of her age, her complexion, her emphasized virginity. She might have been prepared for her visit by a cluster of doting nuns." In *L'Art de la toilette*, Mademoiselle Pauline Mariette advised that "The young girl, like you, my child, renders herself interesting by the qualities of her heart, becomes pleasing by her real and useful talents, touching by her modesty and her virtues."[37] She stressed that every girl should learn how to make her clothes, because fashion was so important to a *woman*.

Just as society showed a greater tolerance for (and indeed acceptance of) marital sexuality than it did for pre-marital sexuality, so also was the dress of married women permitted to be more erotic and more sumptuous than that of unmarried girls. Similarly, many of the rules governing body exposure and sexual display in dress focused on the situation. It was a question less of morals (in the abstract) than of manners. Evening dress was far more revealing than daytime dress, because body exposure was restricted to a circle of one's social equals, who could be expected to understand that this was a form of conventional dress, legitimized by long custom, and not an invitation to "animal lust." It was aesthetically tamed eroticism. Fashion historians who have found it ironic or hypocritical that fashions were more revealing in the *evenings* (traditionally the time of sexual activity) have ignored the importance of the social context.

In 1865, one French writer described the dangers to which a woman would be exposed if she flouted the rules governing situational dress:

> Which among you . . . would dare to appear in the street and to walk under the eyes of the people in the costume for a ball . . .? The most audacious would not take the liberty, . . . for the jeers of the crowd would immediately force her to hide, and the urchins would throw mud and stones at her. Moreover, the police would intervene and probably take her to a safe place, in order to deliver her then to the correctional tribunal, as guilty of an outrage to public morality.[38]

Yet dress that constituted "an outrage to public morality" when worn on the street was not necessarily even remotely *risqué* when worn at a ball. Custom played a vital role in legitimizing sexual display. Evening décolletage was a feature of western women's fashion since the fifteenth century. Short skirts, for example, had no such history of acceptance. Yet rules governing appropriateness could be very strict, even when morality was not an issue: The author of *Etiquette for Women* maintained that "to wear a morning dress in the evening is to commit an outrage on society itself."[39]

In general, the French tended more to accept the essential artificiality and eroticism of dress. The Frenchwoman (and especially the Parisienne) was generally acknowledged to be the best-dressed in the world. She was both "chic" and "charming." The English, however, viewed this with some suspicion—could such a woman be truly "good"? They sometimes argued that the English "girl" was "naturally" more beautiful. The French, on the other hand, often implied that natural beauty was only the beginning. A woman learned to *become* beautiful. As she grew older, she would continue to be admired, since she used dress to express her elegance and personal style. The greater acceptance of fashion in France probably stemmed in part from the recognition that the fashion industry was crucial to the economy. But the fact that the industry had developed in France may also indicate a stronger prior interest in fashion.[40]

Nevertheless, in France too the degree of sartorial eroticism and artificiality permissible in any given case varied according to a number of factors, which are not always easy to determine in retrospect. Until recently, for example, most historians have assumed that John Singer Sargent's portrait of "Madame X" caused a scandal at the 1884 Paris Salon because Mme. Virginie Gautreau is shown wearing a very low-cut black dress. In fact, as Trevor Fairbrother has demonstrated, the original painting was "far more shocking than the work we now know. It had a fallen shoulder strap (long since adjusted by Sargent), emphasizing the brazen aspect of an apparently insolent personality." Mme. Gautreau's black satin evening dress was indeed somewhat daring, particularly since it had no sleeves but only diamond-studded shoulder straps; but the heart-shaped décolleté bodice was not unusually low, and even the straps would have been acceptable—had one strap not slipped completely off her shoulder. As Albert Woolf wrote in *Le Figaro*, "One more struggle and the lady will be free."[41]

What "gave more offense than the perilously décolleté costume," however, was "the paint and powder with which Mr. Sargent plastered the face of this Parisienne belle." Even after Sargent had repainted the shoulder strap, critics continued to complain about the sitter's bluish-white complexion, which indicated a heavy use of "pearl-powder." Apparently, Mme. Gautreau did wear cosmetics: While painting his "Portrait of a Great Beauty," Sargent had described her as one of those "people who are 'fardées' to the extent of being a uniform lavender or blotting paper color." And when Mme. Gautreau and her mother "tearfully" begged Sargent to withdraw the picture, he argued that "He had painted her exactly as she was dressed, that nothing could be said of the canvas worse than had been said in print of her appearance *dans le monde*." Ultimately it was her notorious reputation as a "professional beauty" that permitted "her extraordinary personal displays [which] would have been scandalous on a less sensational woman." It was her reputation (rather than her clothes as such) that caused a scandal when set on canvas.[42]

The Best and Most Becoming Dress

"C. T.," the author of *How to Dress Well*, stressed that "No man is caught by the mere display of fine clothes. A pretty face, or a good figure, may captivate, but fine clothes never. Though it be said that fine feathers make fine birds, yet no man will be caught by a trimming or a flounce." Beauty did captivate, however, and dress did potentially improve the appearance.

> To what end then should attention be given to dress? . . . Because *it is one of beauty's accessories*; because as dress of some kind is absolutely necessary and indispensable, it is better that *people of all classes should dress well* rather than ill. . . . When we may, *why should we not choose the best and the most becoming?* Why are we to mortify ourselves and annoy our

John Singer Sargent, *Madame X (Mme. Gautreau)* (1884). Arthur H. Hearn Fund, 1916, courtesy of The Metropolitan Museum of Art.

friends by choosing something because it is especially hideous? No law, human or divine, enjoins us to disfigure ourselves.[43]

But what kind of clothing was "best and most becoming" for specific people when dress communicated so much information? Since people judged in large part by appearances, rather than by perhaps unknown realities, it was possible to use dress to create a *persona*, to appear to be what one wanted to be. As the duplicitous Madame Merle suggested in Henry James's *The Portrait of a Lady* (1881), "What shall we call our 'self'? I know a large part of myself is in the clothes I choose to wear. . . . Oneself— for other people—is one's expression of of oneself." Isabel Archer disagreed: "Certainly the clothes which, as you say, I choose to wear don't express me. . . . I don't care to be judged by that." She was, she insisted, more than any external measure might indicate.[44]

Many Victorians apparently found the concept of clothes and the self both distressing and tempting for other reasons as well. The controversy about "deceptive" aids to beauty reflected this concern, as did the numerous complaints about people who "dress beyond their means" and "make-believe that they are richer than they really are." The problem was not merely one of economic status, however, but even more one of social "station." Standards of taste and suitability of dress were closely connected to the class hierarchy of nineteenth-century society. The concept of "gentility" played a crucial role in a society bounded at one end by a recognizable upper class and at the other by the laboring class, but which contained between these extremes a number of potentially upwardly mobile groups. Originally, gentility was associated with the established landowning class that sought to distinguish itself from the increasingly wealthy members of the industrial and commercial class. The idea of gentility implied that prestige was essentially divorced from economic status, and was associated instead with certain attributes of birth. The concept was then adopted by the middle classes, whose members used it to reinforce their own position in society: a genteel woman was a "real lady," who knew the rules of etiquette of "good society." The distinguishing characteristic of gentle birth was transformed into the quality of being gentle in manners and (acquired) status; it was an assertion of superior position in society.[45]

The rigid and complex rules governing "appropriate" dress (and rituals of etiquette in general) were intended to distinguish those of genteel birth from the "nouveaux riches" and from quasi-fashionably dressed working-class women. The anonymous "Lady" who wrote *How to Dress on £15 a Year as a Lady* maintained that "A woman is more or less judged by the style of her dress." [46] Her readers (among them a number of governesses) might have been in reduced circumstances, but they wanted to be recognized as ladies. Unfortunately for them, so did a great many other people. And, of course, not everyone agreed that a governess was a lady, or that she should dress as one.

At least since the seventeenth century, even moralists had admitted that women in the "higher circles of society . . . live under a necessity that prescribes propriety . . . and even great splendour of costume." In light of their "position" and wealth, "costly elegance" was in "good taste." By the nineteenth century, the obligation of dressing to indicate high social status fell especially on women, since "men have renounced the gold-laced coats, ruffles, and jewelry of their forefathers." Indeed, it was widely thought that "the devotion of much time or care to dress is unmanly" and foppish. On the other hand, "A married woman has to . . . dress not only to please her husband, but also to reflect credit upon his choice." "Even the most devoted domesticity cannot excuse dowdiness."[47] Veblen, then, was partially correct in his characterization of women and Vicarious Consumption.

There were, however, limits to sartorial splendor. Women should dress well, but only the "nouveaux riches" went in for "showy" clothes. This aesthetic judgment obviously had class connotations. Even in the age of Louis XIV, there were complaints that wealthy bourgeoises dressed more magnificently than some impoverished aristocrats—and, therefore, if this trend could not be stopped, it would be redefined as *un*fashionable. Dress that attracted "observation" was "bad" and "vulgar," as such "gay clothing" would only be admired by "those who are caught by such outward gew-gaws." A woman who would wear an "emerald green" satin dress and a "bonnet with large scarlet flowers" for a summer fête in the country revealed her "vulgarity of mind." Her clothing was too "dressy" for the occasion and too bright and inharmonious in color. "To the educated and refined, glaring tints and discordant combinations are painful and repulsive." Such "violent and stunning effects in costume" resulted in "absurdities," as women "struggle to compel the eye . . . to make the dress or its wearer say, 'Look at me.' "[48]

Those of birth and education learned to discriminate between good taste and "sham finery," and knew the rules governing suitability in dress "in regard to time and place, age and social condition."[49] According to the anonymous author of *Etiquette of Good Society*:

> There is no easier method by which to detect the real lady from the sham one than by noticing her style of dress. Vulgarity is readily distinguished, however costly and fashionable the habiliments may be, by the breach of certain rules of harmony and fitness.

These rules often implicitly reflected distinctions of wealth and status: "The costume for paying calls when on foot differs from that which should be worn for the same purpose when driving in a carriage." The former would be plain, so as not to attract unwanted attention from passers-by. A woman wealthy enough to have a carriage was permitted "much more license" in her dress—"handsome silks, with elaborately trimmed and sweeping skirts, feathery bonnets, and lace parasols, which would look quite out of place when walking."[50]

The rules of dress were sometimes imitated by the "wrong" people, however. Arthur Munby described in his diary a London prostitute who "dressed . . . professionally as a 'lady'," in clothing that was "handsome and good." "She was always well but not gaudily dressed." (Several years later, she bought a coffeehouse with her savings, and dressed "quietly and well, like a respectable upper servant.") Other women also dressed to exaggerate their social status, and literature on fashion is filled with diatribes against "imposture" or "pretension" in dress. It was "hateful," "vulgar," and "offensive" that "persons in [a] humble class of life" would "ape their betters, dressing after them." "Can it be said that this is good taste? Assuredly not. It could not well be worse."[51]

The Victorians were acutely conscious of possible religious objections to fashion, but these tended to be interpreted most rigidly in the case of the least powerful people in society—the poor and, to a lesser extent, the young. According to one vicar, "the sins and evils which are promoted by an excessive care about dress" included "worldly-mindedness," pride, extravagance, selfishness, "grievous waste of time," and immodesty. He argued, though, that good Christians need not, indeed should not, deliberately adopt "any special plainness or any singular coarseness of dress" (which would have a bad effect on industry), but rather they should dress according to "their station, and to the wealth of which God has made them the stewards." The "Christian woman" would not be the first to adopt a new fashion, "but when custom has familiarized the strangeness, she will then draw towards it."[52] Occasionally, even younger, poorer women were told that "everyone ought to make the best of themselves. There is a great deal in the Bible about dress . . . dress with us ought to be symbolical too . . . of beauty, neatness, and purity . . . only undue vanity is rebuked, . . . dress is not of itself sinful."[53] But to be fashionable was, perhaps, less commendable.

Attacks on fashion often focused on its pernicious effects on the women of the working class. Dressing well was an obligation for women of position, and dressing neatly and attractively was a virtue for all women; but that working-class girls and women might aspire to fine dress provoked harsh criticism. Louisa Twining, author of an article on "Dress" in *The Sunday Magazine*, argued that there was a "close connection between the love of dress and sin." She described the room in a London prison where the inmates' clothing was kept, and concluded that the prisoners' "love of . . . tawdry finery . . . had been the first step" to their "degradation and misery":

> Oh that my sisters of the servant class could see the sight and take warning from it! It was impossible to picture . . . those guilty creatures commiting such crimes in modest and womanly attire. Such garments and such wearers were fitting counterparts of each other.[54]

The theme that love of dress led poor girls to ruin appeared in numerous Christian tracts, such as the anonymous *Dress, Drink, and Debt. A Tem-*

perance Tale, which describes how a girl goes into service, where another housemaid encourages her to stop sending her money to her parents. She learns to despise her simple clothes, and desiring to look "smart and fine," she buys a "fine new bonnet trimmed with flowers and a silk dress."[55] She stops going to church, spends her free time walking with men, and ends by going to prison. Perhaps significantly, there was no hint that her mistress erred in setting a bad example; instead another servant was to blame.

In *Our Domestics and Their Mistresses. A Contribution to "The Servant Question,"* the young servant was advised that

> *Finery in dress is a beginning of evil*—a first step in a wrong road ... a love of finery ... arise[s] out of vanity, or a desire to attract attention. Can *that* be right? ... I am far from thinking that a girl should not think about her clothes. ... Let her think how she can be clean and neat, and how she can save her money ... by making for herself and mending. ... Our clothes are for a purpose—for a covering and for warmth. ... But ... don't add to these necessary and suitable garments gay flowers and bead fringes, or tawdry lace. This mode of dressing is a sort of advertisement of a girl's folly, and a challenge for the notice (often improper notice) and disrespect of any young men who may see her. A quiet dress ... and a step that shows you have somewhere to go, and no time to lose—would not this of itself be a protection from impertinent notice? Oh why should a girl deprive herself of so needed and so beautiful a shield?[56]

There was probably an element of sincere protectiveness in this type of advice. But it was accompanied by a strong aversion to the idea that women in service should have *any* form of sexual life, or that they should attempt to blur sartorial class distinctions. It seemed both immoral and presumptuous.

Employers complained that servants wanted "to dress like ladies and get sweethearts ... and they take no interest in the work they have engaged to do." Memoirs indicate that wearing fringes, earrings, stylish hats or decorative dresses could result in instant dismissal. Yet servants resisted the idea that they should be restricted to "sensible," humble, and modest dress: "It is complained against as an infringement upon the liberty of the subject. ... It is very much the fashion for girls to think they may do as they like in this matter; and it cannot be denied that, whatever the station in life, dress is a very strong temptation to most girls."[57]

Everyone seemed to feel that they were entitled to look as beautiful as they could—and fashionable dress appeared almost essential to that end. In Wilkie Collins' novel, *The Moonstone,* Lady Verinder's house-steward believed that "to see [Rachel Verinder] walk was enough to convince any man ... that the graces of her figure (if you will pardon me the expression) were in her flesh and not in her clothes." But the servant and former thief, Rosanna Spearman, jealously insisted that this reputation for beauty was based largely on fine dress:

> Suppose you put Miss Rachel into a servant's dress, and took her ornaments off ... It can't be denied that she had a bad figure; she was too thin ... But

it does stir one up to hear Miss Rachel called pretty, when one knows all the time that it's her dress does it, and her confidence in herself.[58]

Even if dress alone did not create the impression of beauty, it played an important part in setting it off.

Furthermore, attractive dress gave its wearer considerable self-confidence, which contributed to an improved appearance. There are innumerable testimonies to its psychological importance: The Edwardian fashion writer, Mrs. Pritchard, for example, emphasized that "Nothing is so conducive to *sangfroid* as an innate feeling that one is well-dressed." Or, as the American novelist, Mrs. Sherwood, has the character Rose say, "Clothes have a great deal to do with one's happiness."[59]

The Motives Which Determine Dress

The writers for Victorian women's magazines were fond of debating "the motives which determine dress." Did women dress "for their own satisfaction " or "to charm the eyes of their masculine admirers" or "to make other women uncomfortable"? Fashion journalists tended to argue that women dressed to "be beautiful and fascinate." Worth, however, was quoted as saying that women dressed "for the pleasure of making themselves smart, and for the still greater joy of snuffing out the others"—a view that would have seemed cynical to most of his admirers.[60]

If women dressed in part to please men, or to compete with other women, it was nevertheless a tricky business, since men often strongly resisted new fashions. Anthony Trollope's beautiful anti-heroine, Lizzie Eustace, was made to shun all styles that Trollope disapproved of: "There was no get up of flounces, and padding, and paint, and hair, with a dorsal excrescence [i.e. a crinolette or bustle] appended with the object surely of showing in triumph how much absurd ugliness women can force men to endure." Lady Linlithgow apparently expressed the author's views when she argued that

> Girls make monsters of themselves, and I'm told the men like it;—going about with unclear, frowsy structures on their head, enough to make a dog sick. How a man can like to kiss a face with a dirty horse's tail all whizzling about it, is what I can't at all understand. I don't think they do like it, but they have to do it.[61]

Yet women continued to wear new styles despite masculine obstinacy or obliviousness.

And despite possibly unwelcome interpretations. Charles Blanc, for example, approved of all the "coquettish" and erotic aspects of fashion, and he argued that even apparently modest styles were really designed to attract masculine attention: "To hide, yet to display ... are the two objects of the bodice; but it must not be forgotten that often what is concealed is just that which is most wished to be displayed." If a bodice is cut high, it "seems" to express modesty, while if it is cut low, it "attracts the attention to the shape of the neck, to the shoulders, to the outline of the bust"—and so on for pages.[62]

Mrs. Haweis, who was by no means prudish, quite violently attacked Blanc as a "fanatic," arguing that he (and the French in general) had "spoilt and vulgarized the notion of dress as an expression of character" and "an index of the inner self."

> It is almost appalling to think of all we may have implied in our dress without knowing it, for so many years. The mind almost quails before a new fashion, lest it should bear some construction contrary to our feelings.

The various forms, colors, and trimmings of fashion might have "artistic meanings," but she adamantly denied that they had the "moral significance" that Blanc attributed to them. Rather, she maintained that, in enjoining "concealment *pour laisser deviner*," Blanc was "taking the very basest view of the body."[63]

"The body is so beautiful," she wrote, "that it is a pity it can be so little seen." Dress functioned as a means of protection, concealment, and display, but it did not display the female form from any prurient interest. Fashion was "as direct an outcome of the love of beauty as schools of sculpture and painting"—an ideal that could be interpreted both in terms of sublimated sexuality and image-making. Long before the development of the theory of the shifting erogenous zone, Mrs. Haweis explained "The Restlessness of Fashion" by the conflict between "the need of being seen and the need of being covered," "the desire to reveal and the necessity to conceal human Beauty."[64]

> Although we do not like to confess it, . . . the human animal, by nature not a clothed animal but a naked animal, is ever reverting by bits to its original state. Clothed it must be; and yet it is impelled dimly to be at once clothed and unclothed. Now one bit of the body's beauty is displayed, and the rest is sacrificed and covered up. . . . There is no part of the frame which has not been at some time "in fashion." The arm, the bust, the back, the whole outline, has in turn been fully acknowledged.[65]

She admitted that women have "indeed for many generations refused to confess to legs." But it was not inconceivable that fashion might emphasize legs eventually; she observed that, although women still resisted "Turkish" trousers, the styles of the late 1870s clearly indicated the legs.

This description certainly seems to indicate a lack of anxiety about, let alone hatred of, the body. It shows instead a sense of pride and pleasure in the body. Women dressed not only for men or against other women, but also for themselves. Although Mrs. Haweis was not a "typical" Victorian fashion and beauty expert, she seems to have been a well-known and respected one.[66] Ironically, the idea that the Victorians were obsessively prudish developed, in part, precisely because some Victorians were so outspoken in criticizing their contemporaries. As the moderate dress reformer, Helen Ecob, maintained, when standards of modesty evolved, "the prejudice that now exists in the minds of a portion of womankind against such an innovation as liberated legs will vanish."[67] It seems clear that, although a range of opinion existed on the extent to which fashion should emphasize feminine sexual beauty, if we can speak at all of a "Victorian" ideal of femininity, that ideal was, in large part, an erotic one.

8

The Revolt Against Fashion: Dress Reform and Aesthetic Costume

Although fashionable dress was intended to be beautiful and becoming, some people argued that it was ugly and deforming. To a limited extent it was even "considered *bon ton* to criticize the fashions of the day." Perfectly conventional fashion journalists felt free to denounce very tight skirts or an "overload" of trimmings. Such criticisms obviously posed little threat to the dominance of conventional fashion, especially since any apparent defects in the mode tended to be blamed on "its worshippers in the lower walks of life," who had misunderstood and vulgarized an originally "artistic" and "graceful" style.[1]

Others, though, argued that modern dress was intrinsically ugly, and that the concept of fashion as a constantly changing style was antithetical to the creation of truly beautiful clothing. They also emphasized that "health and beauty go hand in hand," and condemned fashionable dress as unhealthy. Yet there were significant divisions within the "rebel camp."[2]

Aesthetes focused on the creation of beautiful dress (whether Classical, Pre-Raphaelite, or "Healthy and Artistic"), whereas Rational Dress Reformers were primarily concerned that clothing should be healthy, modest, and practical. The development of alternatives to fashionable dress and their relationship to alternative ideals of femininity reflects the rather different aims pursued by the various dress reformers.

Rational and Healthy Dress

The first famous advocate of dress reform was an American, Mrs. Amelia Bloomer, who in 1851 popularized a costume consisting of a loose tunic-dress, extending to just below the knee, worn over ankle-length, baggy trousers. An advocate of women's rights, Mrs. Bloomer was primarily concerned with the hygienic and comfortable aspects of "pantaloons."

Although the costume received some support in America, it disappeared quickly, but not without achieving tremendous notoriety. For the next half century, though, "radical" dress reformers continued to advocate some form of trousers or divided skirt for women. According to the American reformer Mary Tillotson, the phrase "to wear the breeches" carried with it "the implied idea that pants are allied to power"; and bloomers were widely regarded as both feminist and masculine. Many men responded with anger and ridicule; according to *The New York Times* (May 27, 1876), the "thirst for trousers" was a "curious nervous disorder," probably "hysteria, attended by . . . mental hallucination."[3]

The feminist dress reformers' critique of fashion emphasized three major points: its unhealthiness, its immodesty and implicit incitement to immorality, and its role in restricting women physically and psychologically. Anti-feminist dress reformers (including many doctors) agreed with the first two points, but, if anything, tended to be in favor of further restricting women's role outside the home. They regarded both the educated woman and the fashionable lady as misfits.

Feminist dress reformers believed that "reformed dress would change the whole position of women" in society. Free from the "thralldom" of male sexual demands and from socially conditioned female vanity, women would "attain health and vigor and compete equally with men in all activities." Anti-feminists believed that reformed dress would make women healthier and more "natural" mothers.[4]

The early dress reform movement in America was related to utopianism and "hygienic perfectionism." The laws of Nature or principles of hygiene (which apparently formed the basis for a new secular morality) were contrasted with the artificial and "aesthetic" laws of fashion. The standard of beauty in dress was the "natural" and the "hygienic"—both terms with clear moral associations. "True health" and "true virtue" were allied. At the same time, for equality of the sexes to be achieved, male sexual passion needed to be curbed, and the sartorial distinctions between the sexes minimized. Thus, at the religious community at Oneida, New York, women wore "trowsers and loose, short gowns, like children's, that thus clad they could regain health and equilibrium of forces adequate to the high influence they must wield in the harmonization of society." Dress reform was but the first step by which women should exert their "ennobling influence" on society.[5]

According to reformers, fashion was a "monster," whose depraved followers were threatened with disease, suffering, and death. Fashion was used by men to stimulate female sexuality, and thus to rule and degrade women.[6]

The form of fashion was designed to incite lust: The swells on the bust and hips, corresponding to that on the lower back-head [i.e. the so-called organ of amativeness], show that the style was not hit upon by accident, but was planned by beings sufficiently depraved to gloat on the spectacle, and must have been devised in the interest of licentiousness ... with the view of bringing the morals of women to the standard of their appearance.

By following fashion women assumed the appearance of "solely sexual creatures," and caused men "to believe them created only to stimulate morbid fancies, [and] minister to excitement." By "foster[ing] depravity in men," women made them "tyrants."[7]

If women would only "discard all prominent devices to distinguish sex," declared one American dress reformer in the 1870s, they would "take one of the most efficient steps toward the emancipation of women." The radical French feminist Madeleine Pelletier argued that women should abandon attractive feminine dress and adopt masculine attire. The American feminist Charlotte Perkins Stetson went beyond advocating asexual clothing and announced in the 1880s that "all clothes were provocative, and that nudity would encourage higher morality." According to Tillotson, the attraction between the sexes should be "first intellectual, then moral and spiritual," and not primarily "sensuous" or "magnetic." The theory was that if women would "show a natural form ... men would lose all excuse to withhold any right."[8]

Although the more radical and utopian aspects of the dress reform movement faded in importance over the second half of the century, dress reform continued to be associated with the sexual purity and temperance movements.

This anti-fashion sentiment was also part of orthodox medical thought. The prestigious English medical journal *The Lancet* frequently attacked not only specific "fashions" such as high heels (anything higher than about half an inch), but also "the sex which worship the idol of fashion." Both doctors and reformers warned that fashionable female dress dangerously overheated parts of the body (especially the reproductive organs), while leaving other parts (such as the bosom) dangerously exposed. The "uncovered body" was "exposed to the prurient eyes of the world, at the risk of life and health." The waist was a "torrid zone," while the legs were "almost bare."[9]

These criticisms of fashion have been taken at face value by most historians, but it is clear that the real issue was the perception that fashion emphasized the erotic aspects of femininity. Perhaps the majority of these attacks were also criticisms of women. Fashion was presented as evidence of feminine vanity, falsehood, extravagance, conformity, ignorance, and stubborn silliness.

Both feminist and anti-feminist dress reformers deplored the fact that most women followed the fashion, but the conclusions that they drew from this differed. Conservatives implied that fashion "proved" women's mental (and perhaps moral) inferiority—after all, intelligent men had told them repeatedly to adopt more sensible clothing. Feminist dress reformers admitted that women were foolish to wear such clothes, but tried to convince them to change and thereby better their prospects for advancement:

Men cannot respect us, or accord us due consideration so long as we behave so foolishly in the matter of our garmenture. . . . If men were to skip about in this style from absurdity to absurdity, dotting themselves over with one irrelevancy after another in the shape of hideous humps, first in one place, then in another, what should we think of them? Could we accord them any respect whatever? . . . They would not long hold the superior position that is now theirs in the political and professional world. They would be on our own level of incapacity and silliness.[10]

Darwin's ideas on evolution and the survival of the fittest were applied to various aspects of the social sphere, including the position of women and the development of feminine fashion. Anthropological studies of "primitive" cultures also played a role in the characterization of women's dress as less "advanced" (or more barbaric) than men's dress. According to the anonymous author of *Dress, Health, and Beauty*, clothing should be utilitarian rather than decorative:

All ornaments worn upon the person should at least pretend to serve some useful purpose. There is no pretence of use in bracelets, ear-rings, necklaces, and such meaningless appendages, which are an inheritance from the barbarous tribes. . . . Men have rid their dress of such unworthy gew-gaws; and since we seem to follow slowly after their styles . . . we shall in time discard heathenish baubles for something less suited to childish tastes.[11]

The ideas associated with Social Darwinism were generally used in support of the status quo; but here it is argued that the processes of evolution continued to advance, and women were developing toward the male standard.

In her book *Rational Dress; or the Dress of Women and Savages*, Mrs. E. M. King, the Honourable Secretary of the Rational Dress Society, argued that "There is no greater proof of the present inferiority of women to men than the way in which women clothe themselves." Women's "barbarous mode of dress" was both "a sign of inferiority" and "a cause of it," as their clothing diminished their "health" and "nerve power." In the course of her argument, however, it emerges that health, per se, was less of a concern than was women's desire "to make themselves 'attractive'."[12]

Unlike the "savage" and the woman, "civilized man" had "worked his way upward, from less and less of personal adornment to more and more of personal comfort, health, convenience, and decency." "Civilized man" expressed his "love of beauty" by, for example, collecting pictures, "rather than attempting to make a picture of himself, to be stared at and admired." That women refused to do the same showed "a lower condition of mind, character, and civilization." Women's "desire to attract to self . . . is both barbarous [and] degrading.[13]

Ultimately, it appears that Mrs. King objected to fashion on the grounds that it made women into sex objects:

But although it is degrading for women alone to seek to make themselves attractive . . . it would not be so if done from other than a personal motive, not merely to attract to self, but to add generally to the brightness and beauty of social life; and by men and women alike. It would be a graceful compliment if each were to seek to become attractive to the other, consistently with honesty, with self-respect, and with purity.[14]

Mrs. King seems to have wanted both men and women to look "attractive," but not, perhaps, *sexually* attractive—but can the two be separated?

Indeed, a certain ambivalence about personal adornment was characteristic of some dress reformers. The author of *Dress, Health, and Beauty*, for example, admitted that while men's clothing was "simple and serviceable," it lacked "picturesque charm." If women should adopt more sensible everyday clothes, then men should, at least for "festive scenes," put on more attractive, if perhaps more uncomfortable, clothing: "let the suffering be equally divided." The "obligation" to make oneself "both useful and beautiful" rests with "the two sexes."[15]

She suggested a less "prosaic" male style that combined elements of European folk dress and earlier aristocratic fashions:

> Our young friend Antinoüs is a joy to behold, even now, with his classic head rising from a cast-iron shirt collar, and his erect and comely form encased in straight, black trousers and a plain frock-coat; but what would he not become in our eyes, could we behold a Tyrolese hat, with a soaring ostrich feather, shading his brow, and his face smiling a welcome over lace shirt frills, and a doublet buttoned with diamonds . . . ?[16]

This description goes far beyond the knee breeches worn by a few male Aesthetes, and sounds similar to the fancy dress occasionally worn by Victorian men at parties, but never adopted as "normal" attire.

The historian William Leach concluded that the dress reformers "believed" they were in favor of individual "independence and variety" in dress, yet at the same time they tried to drive all "superfluous color, ornament and theatre out of dress." They "reinforced the deepening sentiment against expression in male dress" by attacking the "dandy" as a "useless" creature of "ambiguous sex."[17] In England, dress reformers had almost no influence on male dress; and to the limited extent that they influenced women's dress, it was to promote the adoption of "simple and serviceable" styles worn over "healthy" (often woolen) underwear. Despite their protestations to the contrary, the aesthetic element in dress seemed to be of little interest to them.

Nevertheless, feminist dress reformers, like Mrs. King, did make some perceptive observations about contemporary fashion and the way the female body was both hidden and exposed: "women seem to compensate themselves for the complete hiding of the lower part of their bodies, by the undue exposure and display of the upper part." She suggested that this was because "Women always feel themselves in the position of being looked at, rather than looking—the reverse is the case with men." In modern terms, we would say that women were in the position of being sexually "passive" and "exhibitionistic." Mrs. King also recognized that women were encouraged in these feeling of "self-consciousness . . . by those who are constantly assuring women that it is their first duty to society to be beautiful."[18]

Yet socially determined standards of modesty, which had developed over centuries, required that the legs be hidden. According to Mrs. King:

> These naturally strong and powerfully stimulating feelings—passions I might almost call them—are concentrated entirely upon the upper half of her person; what wonder then if they become morbid and diseased? . . . The waist must be squeezed . . . to bring more *en evidence* the bust, shoulders, and arms. For her, from the hips to the head, is, as far as others are concerned, the whole of her body, so she must make the most she can of it. The rest is only so much drapery, so many yards of material, satin, velvet . . . but the top part is emphatically her 'body'. . . . [U]ndue hiding of one part of the body leads to undue exposure and morbid desire for the display of the other.[19]

Unfortunately, she went on to undercut her argument by inaccurate and tendentious references to recent fashion history. Nevertheless, her major point—that so long as the legs were hidden, the focus of erotic interest would be on the curves of the torso—is plausible. Her solution, however, was the adoption by women of clothing that covered the entire body with even layers of cloth. The female body would be subject to neither "undue hiding" nor "morbid" display.

To what extent the adoption of "attractive" but "pure" and "honest" dress would mean the elimination of sartorial sexual display is unclear, but the examples of "rational" clothing exhibited by the Rational Dress Society look like rather plain versions of ordinary fashionable clothing, and were generally perceived at the time as unattractive. On the other hand, the much maligned Bloomer costume bore a striking resemblance to European versions of "Turkish" costume, which was regarded as romantic. In some cases at least, it was not the costume design as such, but rather its associations that determined how it was received.

Classical Dress

Unlike the dress reformers who focused on health and morality, the supporters of the Aesthetic Movement were primarily concerned with the creation of what they regarded as truly beautiful clothing. Since the Victorians had been brought up to admire the Classical ideal of feminine physical beauty (at least in art), one obvious solution to the problem of beautiful dress was a return to Greek clothing. The 1870s and 1880s saw the rise of a new Classical revival, which was reflected in an increased interest in paintings on Classical themes. Visual models for women interested in Greek dress were to be found in the work of Lord Leighton, Alma Tadema, Albert Moore, and others.

A number of fashion periodicals expressed an interest in some form of modified Grecian dress, and praised those "making earnest efforts to revive a pure taste in dress, and to awaken that appreciation of true beauty which seems to be lost among us." Greek dress had the additional advantage that it did "not define the waist like our ordinary dress," so there was "no inducement to tight lacing."[20]

But there were problems with Greek dress. The Empire style of the early nineteenth century had been modeled on Greco-Roman costume, and was still widely perceived as having been "scanty," "loose-fitting," and "indecent." Advocates of the proposed new version of Classical attire had to emphasize how it differed from its predecessor. Only a few years earlier, fashion journalists had mocked those "ladies dressed up as muses or goddesses." "Mrs. Grundy" was still worried that "Grecian drapery . . . displays the form" appreciably more than even the tight skirts of conventional fashion.[21]

Even Mrs. Haweis rejected Greek dress as being too revealing:

The human body uncovered is not necessarily a shocking thing. . . . But what was harmless in the early Greeks would be impossible in nations who have lost to a great extent the simple instinct of natural beauty, whilst they have grown abnormally self-conscious and reflective.

A statue or painted image clothed in "some gauze-like drapery which veiled without concealing" might be acceptable to "the chastest eye," but such clothing was insufficiently modest when worn by a living, moving woman.[22]

Many observers also felt that, except in modified form as a type of at-home or fancy dress, classical dress was impractical. England was too cold (who could imagine a "padded" *chiton?*); and Northern Europe had its own valid traditions of dress. One fashion journalist dismissed the "stir . . . about reviving the greek costume" by pointing out the "insuperable . . . difficulty" of wearing a hat or bonnet with it. A Philistine murmured, "Imagine Athene in a waterproof."[23]

There were attempts to make Classical dress more suitable to the English climate and standards of modesty. Oscar Wilde suggested that "The principles . . . of Greek dress may be perfectly realised, even in a moderately tight gown with sleeves," as long as it was suspended from the shoulders and hung in folds. In modified form, it could be worn "over a substratum of pure wool, thus combining the "healthy" and "artistic" aspects of reformed dress.[24] Fashion plates show some Greek dresses that are fairly closely modeled on the *chiton* and mantle, while others are adapted to the corseted figure and are Greek only in details. But to the extent that they ceased to look "peculiar," and were "wonderfully similar in effect to those now worn," much of their *raison d'être* was lost.[25]

Even on aesthetic grounds, that "most perfect of known costumes" was open to criticism. Few English women had "greek heads and features" or "statuesque" figures; and even journalists for *Woman's World* (a progressive and vaguely Aesthetic magazine) also reminded "admirers of the Greek dress that the greatest perfection of lines and profiles is indispensable for wearing with advantage the clinging draperies of this quaint and graceful attire."[26] Alternatively, Classical dress might blur the lines of admirable figures. An unchanging style also seemed "monotonous," limiting dress to "simple clinging fabrics, which would ensure revolt" from those who prefered "glossy, slippery, and . . . velvety materials."[27] Many women derived pleasure from following fashion, and would have resented being restricted to an unchanging "uniform," no matter how attractive.

Greek dress might be indecent, impractical, unsuitable, unflattering, and monotonous. More generally, the vogue for ancient Greece was controversial. There was perceived to be a tension between the ideals of Christianity and those of Hellenism. In addition, some of the most ardent enthusiasts of Hellenism were also "those with advanced ideas about society, art, and sexual morality."[28]

Just as Rational dress became associated in the public mind with Women's Rights, so also, perhaps, did Classical dress become associated with avant-garde ideas about sexuality. It was conceivable that an actress like Ellen Terry might go hatless and corsetless, in Grecian attire, but it would be less than respectable for ordinary women to follow suit.

Mrs. Oliphant argued, extravagantly, that

> it would be more possible to disestablish the Church, abolish the House of Lords, and cut the sacred vesture of the British Constitution into little pieces, than to translate English garments into Greek.[29]

To adopt "the loose and light garment of an Eastern race" would entail the "entire disruption of all Northern habits and principles"—and for no good reason, since Greek dress was not intrinsically superior to the Northern woman's "close-fitting" dress "with long skirts." Although Greek dress had considerable influence on styles in tea-gowns, particularly later in the century, the attempt to revive Classical dress as a substitute or replacement for conventional fashion soon faded in importance.

Pre-Raphaelite Dress

What became known as Pre-Raphaelite or Aesthetic dress offered another alternative to contemporary fashion. Traditional fashion historians have tended to play down the significance of Aesthetic dress, arguing that it was merely a short-lived attempt to

> revive ancient styles, Oscar Wilde advocating for men the garb of the Cavaliers while William Morris urged women to return to the flowing drapery of the thirteenth century. But women were in no mood to progress thus backwards.[30]

More recently, however, fashion historians have tended to place Aesthetic dress in the larger context of the continuing struggle, over half a century, to develop a "healthy" and "artistic" style of dress. From our perspective, Aesthetic dress is also interesting because it became associated with an alternative ideal of feminine beauty.

Aesthetic dress had its origins in the mid-nineteenth century, when William Morris and the artists of the Pre-Raphaelite Brotherhood rejected what they perceived as the "ugliness" of contemporary society and the decorative arts, and developed a concept of "Beauty" based on medieval forms and craftsmanship and, more generally, on a romanticized vision of "past times" when "the raiment [and] surroundings of life were not ugly but beautiful." For Morris, especially, aesthetic dress was part of a crusade "to reform a philistine age by means of the decorative arts."[31] Pre-Raphaelite dresses varied in appearance, but they tended to be characterized by somewhat loose and "flowing" lines; fabrics were often soft, following Morris's principle that "No dress can be beautiful that is stiff, drapery is essential." Aniline dyes were replaced by vegetable dyes, which produced softer, more subdued colors.[32]

As the work of the Pre-Raphaelite painters became better known in the 1870s, "a large section of English society" adopted at least semi-Aesthetic dress. Or, as Walter Crane wrote bitterly in 1894, "we saw the fashionable world and the stage aping, with more or less grotesque vulgarity, what it was fain to think were the fashions of the inner and most refined artistic cult." An adherent of timeless dress, Crane deplored the "giddy, aimless masquerade of fashion" that assimilated some features of Aesthetic dress in the 1870s and 1880s, only to abandon them later.[33]

True believers might feel that Aesthetic dress was outside fashion, but for several years many fashion journalists and ordinary women thought that aspects of Aesthetic dress could be incorporated into mainstream fashion. And, in fact, to some extent this happened. Fashion journalists referred, knowledgeably, to "delightful arrangements in colour—symphonies is the proper aesthetic word—one tint passing through all its shades," although philistines still sneered at "greenery-yallery" colors. The use of softly draping "art silks" and cashmere as dress fabrics took only a little longer to be accepted. It seemed that Aesthetic dress might be "a lovely and healthy development" of fashion.[34]

But in the late 1870s, the bustle was not fashionable and the straight "princess" line was in style. This temporary convergence between conventional and Aesthetic dress helps explain why the arguments of the Aesthetes received a hearing. When Mrs. Haweis criticized "coarse vulgar curves, unmeaning lumps, superabundant ornament," she was describing "the style that was at the moment on the way out." By the mid–1880s, "lumps" had returned with a vengeance, and the gulf between ordinary fashion and Aesthetic dress widened appreciably.[35]

Furthermore, historical allusions in dress had long been viewed as "picturesque," and those that harked back to "Olde England" carried positive connotations of chivalry and patriotism. The nineteenth century also saw a more general revival of interest in the "Gothic" that extended beyond dress to the other decorative arts and to architecture. French fashion designers, who increasingly perceived themselves as "artists," frequently ransacked the past for costume details.[36]

Full-fledged Aesthetic dress differed significantly from fashionable dress, however picturesque. In 1925 Mrs. J. Comyns Carr recalled "In the days when bustles and skin-tight dresses were the fashion, and a twenty inch waist the aim of every self-respecting woman, my frocks followed the simple straight line as waistless as those of today." This costume, she admitted, had provoked "a certain amount of ridicule."[37]

Although many Aesthetic dresses seem beautiful today, at the time the relative absence of structured underclothing, together with the use of soft, "limp" materials made Aesthetic dress seem both "ill-fitting" and immodestly "clinging." Vernon Lee described an Aesthete in a dress of "crinkled gauze all tied close about her and visibly no underclothing." (This was undoubtedly an exaggeration.) Obviously a hostile witness, she characterized well-to-do Aesthetic visitors to the Royal Academy as "crazy looking creatures" in "shabby and insane dresses." But even the more sanguine observer, F. E. Francillon, recalled meeting "a young woman, dressed, as it seemed to me, in nothing but an old-fashioned bathing gown and an amber necklace."[38]

Healthy and Artistic Dress. Photograph from the exhibition catalog, *Four Hundred Years of Fashion* (London: Victoria and Albert Museum, 1984). Courtesy of The Victoria and Albert Museum.

Some fashion writers speculated that there existed a connection between aesthetic dress and physical unattractiveness. Plain women, having only "charm in character," might be tempted toward "exaggeration" in an effort to look striking and individual. Mrs. Haweis also implied that Aesthetic dress was primarily for "plain" women, although she focused on the ways in which it improved their appearance. "If pretty," she argued, "you can do as you like ... if plain, you cannot ... you must adopt quaintness ... of garb." She described the Pre-Raphaelites as "the plain girl's best friends," and suggested that they had popularized not only a style of dress, but also a particular physical type:

> Morris, Burne-Jones, and others have made certain types of face and figure once literally hated, actually the fashion. Red hair—once, to say a woman had red hair was social assassination—is the rage. A pallid face with a protruding upper lip is highly esteemed. Green eyes, a squint, square eyebrows, whitey-brown complexions are not left out in the cold. In fact, the pink-cheeked dolls are nowhere; they are said to have 'no character'. ... Now is the time for plain women. Only dress after the prae-Raphaelite [sic] style, and you will be astonished to find that so far from being an 'ugly duck' you are a full fledged swan![39]

One reviewer, however, objected to Mrs. Haweis's advice that plain girls should study their "points of attractiveness" and adopt individual dress, on the grounds that this "would make girls very self-conscious, and like the heroine of a novel ... who said of herself, 'I am not pretty in Mary's insignificant way, but my profile is pure Grecian and my pose statuesque.' "[40]

It is, of course, difficult to know how much to believe of these accounts of the appearance, dress, and beliefs of Aesthetic women. Nevertheless, certain characteristics reappeared frequently. Aesthetic women were described as "long and blighted," with "figures all angles" and "faces all chin and cheekbone," "wan," "languid," "sad-eyed," "drooping," and "inclined to melancholy"—in fact, like "Burne-Jones' melancholy beauties."[41] It seems that the adoption of Aesthetic dress was at least sometimes accompanied by an imitation of the melancholy, slenderness, and paleness—the rather ethereal appearance—of some of the Pre-Raphaelite models.

W. Graham Robertson admired many aspects of the Aesthetic Movement, but he was not unaware of its amusing aspects:

> Determined at all hazards to be 'artistic', women arrayed themselves in amazing garments ... their dishevelled hair streamed down their backs, by a projection of their extraordinary imitative gift their faces grew thin and cadaverous. ... All the women at once saw themselves as wan lilies and— well it is not a style becoming to everybody.[42]

Alternatively, they apparently affected a kind of feline sensuality. They "moved ... with a gliding step," reported "A.C.," "when they sat down they assumed poses whose stillness suggested that thus they had sat for a hundred years." When a "Philistine" described one woman as looking like "a panther in a dressing gown," her friends replied, "with indulgent superiority," that her movements, dress, and wild air only deepen "her splendid *sauvage* appearance—if you like, her par ther-like look."[43]

This sounds uncommonly like an imitation of the dolorous "Blessed Damozel" type, with hints of the femme fatale. To the extent that there existed an Aesthetic counter-ideal of feminine beauty, it was an explicit rejection of the "pink-cheeked dolls" in favor of a Romantic image of womanhood that combined the spiritual with a cruel and morbid eroticism. This feminine ideal continued to play a role in Symbolist and Decadent art and in the iconography of Art Nouveau.[44] Although she was a popular fantasy figure in some quarters, such a women struck most people as seeming a little out of place in real life.

We should beware, though, of overemphasizing the intensity (to use a very Aesthetic word) of the correspondence between the artists' image and the self-perception of Aesthetic women, many of whom simply thought that contemporary fashion was ugly and that they could create more graceful and artistic alternatives. In addition, some Aesthetes (such as the novelist E. Nesbit) were socialists and wanted dress to be more egalitarian and less ceremonious.

The existence in English costume museums of a number of Aesthetic dresses—from deluxe Liberty "picturesque" dresses to obviously homemade examples, indicates a widespread (if temporary) affinity for this new look. In *Robert Elsmere* (a very sociological novel), Mrs. Humphry Ward described the character Rose's transformation from Aesthetic girlhood to fashionable (but still artistic) womanhood in terms of an evolving self-image:

> The puffed sleeves, the aesthetic skirts, the naive ornaments of bead and shell, the formless hat, which it pleased her to imagine after Gainsborough, had all disappeared. She was clad in some soft fawn-coloured garment, cut very much in the fashion; her hair was closely rolled and twisted about her lightly-balanced head; everything about her was neat and fresh and tight-fitting. A year ago she had been a damsel from the "Earthly Paradise"; now, so far as an English girl can achieve it, she might have been a model for Tissot.[45]

The Failure of Anti-Fashion

The various alternatives to fashionable dress reflected different ideals of feminine beauty and different conceptions of women's roles. The advocates of Rational and healthy dress thought that woman should be not merely "ornamental"—a "doll, to be decked and draped"—but rather that she should be "useful."[46] Although this was a valid goal and one shared by many women, nevertheless most women rejected anti-fashion clothing. In part, this was because both feminist and anti-feminist dress reformers generally perceived fashion as an outward manifestation of

female sexuality, and they advocated less erotic clothing that was therefore widely perceived as less beautiful.

The issue of clothing choice is significant. But how is choice made? Theories that stress the *Zeitgeist*, cycles of fashion, "bourgeois" society, or
sex appeal largely ignore this question, and are essentially deterministic:
the Time Spirit, the stage in the fashion cycle, "pecuniary standards of
taste," or the individual's unconscious make the decision for her.
Recently, the fashion historians Robert and Jeanette Lauer adopted a
more promising approach when they defined fashion as "a process of collective definition in which a particular alternative in a set of possibilities
is selected as appropriate"; and they argue that the collective definition is
based on an "ideological evaluation." Specifically, fashions may be chosen
if they are "consistent with values and roles" and "useful for reaffirming
or establishing an individual's identity and/or status."[47]

The Lauers, though, have focused on the subject of dress reform—a
clearly ideological style that was probably rejected in large part on ideological grounds. It was too closely associated with both women's rights and
sexual puritanism. Even women who supported many aspects of the wom-
en's movement were reluctant to adopt clothing that shouted out a specific and controversial message. Furthermore, rational dress was not
adopted by fashion trend-setters (such as actresses or aristocrats), so it
was never associated with either physical beauty or status. It received primarily negative publicity (in cartoons and satirical songs) or notoriety (as
when some English barmaids temporarily adopted the Bloomer costume).
Despite articles on the "true" beauty of the "natural" human form, and
praise of the Venus de Milo and the Greek slave, actual illustrations of
beautiful and *clothed* figures tended to adopt conventions of fashionable
beauty. One pamphlet for the Rational Dress Society, for example, complained that the illustrator had still drawn the waists too small, but he or
she was probably only trying to make the figures look attractive in contemporary terms. And, in fact, there was little visual evidence that women
would look more—rather than less—attractive in rational dress.

Dress reform was rejected both on ideological grounds and because
women perceived it (fairly or not) as deliberately sexually unattractive.
Contrary to popular belief, its effects on fashion were minimal, although
a modification of the Bloomer costume was widely adopted as gymnasium
dress. The Aesthetes, on the other hand, seem to have proposed an alternative ideal of feminine beauty that was still erotic and may have played
an important role in widening the conception of feminine beauty to
include many women hitherto dismissed as unattractive. Yet Aesthetic
dress, per se, only really became an important factor in fashion when,
toward the end of the century, there occured the "change from a reformed
dress worn as a mission to the unenlightened, to a dress worn as a badge
that proclaimed the *taste* of the wearer."[48] In short, it was accepted when
it ceased to carry overt ideological connotations, and to remind people of
particular artistic communities or "immoral" neo-Greeks. The fad for

semi-Aesthetic dress in the 1870s was ultimately less significant than the more gradual adoption of artistic dress for private occasions within the wearer's home. The tea-gown, for example, played an important role in the development of new styles of dress. Once an artistic look became fashionable, it was more widely perceived as beautiful.

Thus, the Lauers' theory may be rather less useful as an explanatory framework for conventional fashion. To be fashionable also carries ideological connotations, yet it is not generally regarded in that light. The connection between women's "values and roles" and their clothing is not as direct as fashion historians have thought. As women's lives changed, the logic of situations led to the development of fashions that were regarded as beautiful and appropriate for those situations. Rational dress was rejected, but the popularity of the tailored suit and later the skirt and shirt-waist blouse testifies to their perceived appropriateness for many activities in the wider world. A variety of "artistic" styles were accepted, in both England and France, from the 1890s on—when they were worn as tea-gowns or negligée garments. In the course of the nineteenth century, women's clothing became less "restricted by canons of modesty and decency"— and "really began to 'play'."[49] The acceptance of artifice and sexual display in dress, together with a playing down of the utilitarian aspects of clothing, is antithetical to the functionalist and emancipatory approach to dress. And yet it succeeded—then and now—where anti-fashion failed. The Neo-Empire style of the early twentieth century grew directly out of the world of high fashion. And, significantly, it developed in conjunction with a new ideal of feminine beauty, so that its proponents had the satisfaction of feeling that their appearance reflected the avant-garde of beauty and chic.

The Foundations of Fashion

9

The Corset Controversy

The corset was an integral element of women's fashion because it helped to create the appearance of a well-developed figure with a slender waist, which represented, for most people, the feminine physical ideal. By emphasizing the essentially female characteristics of the body, the corset functioned as a sexualizing device. Yet corset wearing was also widely perceived as *moral*; it was a necessity if a woman were to be decently dressed. To make a play on words, the straitlaced woman was not loose. A woman who went out without a corset was generally thought to show an indecent state of undress, and to lack "tenue" (correct manners, bearing, and deportment). Both the symbolism of the corset and the ideal of femininity were ambiguous, embracing at the same time the erotic and the respectable. It is not so surprising then that the use of the corset and, more particularly, the issue of tight-lacing were the subjects of considerable controversy.

Most historians have perceived the corset as an instrument of women's oppression and a frequent cause of debility and disease. The widespread use of the corset and the alleged frequency of tight-lacing seemed to reflect the Victorian woman's willingness to conform to a restrictive and even "masochistic" ideal of femininity. The dress reform movement was seen as one component of the women's rights movement. Progress in women's emancipation was accompanied by an end to tight corsets.

Recently, the art historian David Kunzle has virtually stood this theory on its head, by arguing that the enemies of the corset were primarily socially conservative and sexually puritanical males, whereas the tight-lacers were primarily sexually assertive women, who rejected the socially prescribed domestic and maternal role. He sees tight-lacing as having been a legitimate form of sexual expression and self-assertion, and, as such, an aspect of female emancipation. In his view, the tight-lacers, not the dress-reformers, were in some sense "progressive." It was an expression of sexual and social rebellion, not male, bourgeois dominance. In class terms, he perceives tight-lacing not as an upper or middle class ("fashionable") phenomenon, but rather as the expression of lower-middle class aspirations. He also argues that, far from being unhealthy and uncomfortable, "the corset gave . . . not merely physical support, but positive physical and erotic pleasure."[1]

Neither interpretation is correct. Both parties allow their respective ideological biases to affect their analysis of the evidence; and both rely very heavily on the more extreme and unreliable sources—particularly the so-called "fetishistic correspondence"—and while the material therein is fascinating and potentially very revealing, it calls for a critical analysis and cannot simply be accepted at face value. Nor is it legitimate to equate extreme and probably atypical attitudes and behavior with the beliefs and practices of the majority. That there was a relationship between the two is probable, but the nature of this relationship needs to be explored with great care, in order to understand the significance of corsetry and tight-lacing in this period.

The nineteenth-century debate was not simply between the opponents and the defenders of the corset. Instead, there existed a spectrum of opinion, encompassing at one extreme those who held that the use of the corset was intrinsically unhealthy, ugly, and immoral; then a much larger middle group, who condoned or actively approved of ordinary corset wearing, but denounced the practice of "tight-lacing" (a term that was variously interpreted by the different segments within this group); to those at the other extreme, who shocked public opinion by openly advocating tight-lacing.

This third party, the self-proclaimed "votaries" of tight-lacing, were very much in the minority, and some of them may have been corset or tight-lacing fetishists. Kunzle maintains that tight-lacing was entirely distinct from ordinary corset wearing. Tight-lacers, he argues, were not following the fashion, but rather responding to inner compulsions. We cannot, however, accept that the term "tight-lacing" referred only to the practices of a sexual minority (although the publication of the pro-tight-lacing position further enraged its opponents). The issue is far more complex. The small waist was fashionable, and for ordinary women tight-lacing was "the extreme of a continuum of corset wearing."[2]

The vast majority of women of all classes wore corsets, and the degree of tightness varied, according to the design of the dress, the social occasion, and the age, personality, and figure of the individual woman. A woman might lace loosely at home, moderately when she visited friends, and tightly for a ball. It was not unreasonable to assume that some women habitually laced more tightly than was usual

But how tightly were these corsets laced? Roberts believes that most women reduced their waists by two or three inches, "causing themselves discomfort, fatigue, and perhaps physical debility," but did not habitually tight-lace, that is (according to her definition of the term), reduce their waists by four or more inches. Kunzle defines tight-lacing as "the point at which a waist attracted attention," yet he also uncritically accepts some highly questionable "statistics" on the incidence of tight-lacing and the degree of constriction attained. Contemporary accounts of tight-lacing refer to waists measuring between twelve and eighteen inches, and occasionally waists as small as nine or ten inches.[3]

A great deal of misunderstanding has arisen because many historians have accepted the most bizarre (and perhaps fetishist) accounts as being not only authentic reports of personal experiences, but actually *typical* of the behavior of the period. The 1860s, in particular, have been stigmatized as a period of tight-lacing, in large part because of the corset correspondence in *The Englishwoman's Domestic Magazine*. Certainly, the popular perception is that Victorian women frequently laced to sixteen or seventeen inches: "Steel-Bound and Whalebone-Lined . . . her corset laced so that she could scarcely breathe," she was "Dressed to Kill, with crinolines and tight lacing." Visitors to costume exhibitions exclaim with horror at the sight of nineteenth-century corsets.[4]

Yet the curators of costume museums tend to believe that most accounts of very small waists represented *fantasies*. Measurements of the many corsets in the collection of the Leicestershire Museum and Art Gallery indicate that one corset (from the 1890s) measured eighteen inches when laced closed. Another eleven (five per cent of the collection) were nineteen inches. The vast majority were twenty to twenty-six inches, with the greatest concentration at twenty-one and twenty-two inches.[5]

TABLE 1. The Waist of Reality. Corset waist measurements from the Symington Collection. (Statistics courtesy of Ms. Annette Carruthers, Assistant Keeper of Decorative Arts, Leicestershire Museum and Art Gallery, Leicester.)

	18"	19"	20"	21"	22"	23"	24"	25"	26"	27"	28"	30"	34"	40"	Average Size	Total Number Measured
1856–1881	0	1	4	9	17	0	2	4	3	0	3	2	1	0	23.2"	46
1881–1900	1	4	9	19	20	2	6	2	0	0	1	1	0	1	22"	66
1900–1910	0	6	26	13	13	5	8	5	7	1	1	0	0	0	21.9"	85

The size alone (usually advertised as eighteen to thirty inches, but occasionally as small as fifteen inches) does not indicate how tightly they might have been laced. According to a booklet on *The Dress Reform Problem*, published in 1886 by E. Ward of Co. of Bradford, which made hygienic corsets and rational dress:

A distinction should be made between *actual* and *corset* measurements, because stays, as ordinarily worn, do not meet at the back. . . . Young girls, especially, derive intense satisfaction from proclaiming the diminutive size of their corset. Many purchase eighteen and nineteen inch stays, who must

TABLE 2. The Waist of Fantasy. Corset Waist measurements from "Does
Tight-Lacing Really Exist?," by Hygeia, from *The Family Doctor*, September
3, 1887, p. 7.

Name	Age	Size of Waist	Reduce to	To Wear Corset
Nelly G.	15	20 inches	16 inches	Night and Day
Helen Vogler	12	21 inches	15 inches	Day
G. Van de M.	14	19 inches	13 inches	Night and Day
V.G.	13	22 inches	12 inches, if possible	Night and Day
Alice M.	17	16 inches	14 inches	Night and Day
Cora S.	16	18 inches	13 inches	Night and Day

leave them open two, three, and four inches. . . . Fifteen, sixteen, and seventeen inch waists are glibly chattered about, as though they were common
enough . . . [yet] we question whether it is a physical possibility for women
to reduce their natural waist measure below seventeen or eighteen inches.[6]

The measurement of existing nineteenth-century dresses would also seem
to indicate either that the corseted waist was not as small as legend has
it, or that tight-lacing was incredibly rare.[7]

Nevertheless, although the incidence and degree of tight-lacing were
less extreme than has been popularly believed, the issue of tight-lacing
aroused widespread condemnation. In order to understand the significance of tight-lacing (both as an idea and as a practice), it is necessary to
consider it in relation to the "ordinary" use of the corset, and within the
context of attitudes toward corsetry.

The Corset: Assassin of the Human Race

One body of opinion held that any use of the corset was detrimental to
health, aesthetics, and morality. Charles Roux, author of *Contre le corset*,
was one of those who argued that "the use of the corset is dangerous. I say
the use. . . . Here the abuse can not be separated from the use; hygiene
proscribes the one and the other." His primary concern was with damage
to the reproductive organs and the ability to nurse one's child, the
"supreme happiness for women worthy of the name."[8] Attacks on the corset were often linked to a campaign in favor of motherhood; and medical
arguments frequently reflected fears that if women broke away from their
traditional domestic sphere, the family and the entire social order would
be threatened.

The turn-of-the-century German dress reformers Paul Schultze-Naumberg and Christian H. Stratz combined an emphasis on health and "the
beauty of the human body" with reactionary politics, anti-feminism, and
racism. They argued that corsets impaired health and childbearing capac-
ities and that modern fashion was a "decadent" product of "artificial sen-
sibilities," engendered by urban, industrial civilization. Modern European
women were "unhealthy" and "asexual"; a "normally built woman" would

not even be able to fit into fashionable clothing. Clothes reform, for these writers, was part of a projected return to a "natural" culture, in which women would function primarily in a maternal role, in their traditional position in a rigid hierarchy of sexes, classes, and races.[9]

The connection between corsetry and reproduction was drawn not only by social conservatives, however, nor even solely by opponents of the corset. A writer for *The Queen* attacked "tight-lacing" on the grounds that "one of [women's] highest functions is that of becoming mothers." The French Ligue des Mères de Famille, which supported women's "social emancipation" and characterized the corset as an "invention of masculine despotism," also attacked the corset as "the assassin of the human race."[10]

It is difficult to know to what extent the corset posed any threat to women's health (or to the health of a fetus). Roberts mentions, without comment, a list of "over 100 illnesses caused by tight-lacing," and goes on to suggest that "Not just illness but death might be courted by the tight-lacer." Kunzle, however, is correct in pointing out the prejudices and exaggerations of many physicians and dress reformers, whose attacks on the corset and on tight-lacing were often similar in their tone and line of argument to contemporary diatribes on the terrible effects of masturbation, alcohol, and female education. Indeed, these themes were sometimes linked. The American physician, Dr. Coleman, wrote in 1899:

> Women beware. You are on the brink of destruction: You have hitherto been engaged in crushing your waists; now you are attempting to cultivate your mind: You have been merely dancing all night in the foul air of the ball-room; now you are beginning to spend all your mornings in study. You have been incessantly stimulating your emotions with concerts ... and French novels; now you are exerting your understanding to learn Greek.... Beware!! science pronounces that the woman who studies is lost.[11]

It is possible that the horror stories about the diseases caused by tight corsets derived less from any real medical danger than from fears about female sexuality and self-assertion.

Exciting the Organs of Amativeness

The American phrenologist, Orson S. Fowler, attacked tight-lacers as "suicides and infanticides." Their real crime, however, was their indulgence in "impure desires," their more or less deliberate excitement of "the organs of Amativeness"—in short, their overt sexuality. "It is high time that men who wish virtuous wives knew it [that tight-lacing stimulated female sexuality], so that they may avoid those who have inflamed and exhausted this element of their nature." (Or, one is tempted to add, those who might inflame and exhaust their husbands.) "Get natural waists or no wives." The corset, he argued, caused not only sickly and degenerate children or abortion and sterility, but also lasciviousness (of both wearer and viewer), hysteria, and insanity. Fowler was opposed to any use of the corset. Similarly, with regard to alcohol, he advised women to demand "total abstinence or no husbands."[12]

In order to understand his position, it is necessary to consider the medical-psychological theory of phrenology. According to the "science" of phrenology, virtue and "wickedness" were on a par with sanity and insanity, and were less the result of intention than of the health or sickness of the "organs" associated with the thirty-seven "faculties" of the brain. Body and mind were supposed to be kept in a proper equilibrium, if health and virtue were to be maintained. The use of the corset, tobacco, or alcohol disturbed this balance: "It is a settled principle of physiology, that nothing can stimulate or morbidly excite the body, without setting on fire the animal propensities," while simultaneously weakening the moral and intellectual faculties.[13]

Such phrenological theories were widely accepted in the nineteenth century. According to a letter in *Sylvia's Home Journal*, women who tight-laced

not only injure [the little ones] physically, but also morally, by hereditarily (and with increasing force) bestowing upon them that bump of destructiveness to their own health and happiness.

A writer for *The Rational Dress Society's Gazette* agreed that

in many cases, the cripple, the idiot, the inebriate, the profligate, would find that they owed their sufferings and their sorrows to the folly of their mothers. Tight-laced women bequeath to their children an imperfect vitality, which often leads to vicious ways.[14]

Both an ordinary fashion journal and a dress reform periodical accepted phrenological medical views on maternity. But it is rather surprising that so many modern historians should cite Fowler as a medical authority, since he "had only the crudest notions of medicine" and "resided well out toward the thickly populated lunatic fringe of science."[15]

An analysis of Fowler's work, *Intemperance and Tight-Lacing*, shows how "medicine" and "science" were marshalled against the use of the corset. According to Fowler, by squeezing the liver, the corset renders the blood "impure"; the "corrupt" and "boiling" blood then "diseases the brain," which causes "insanity." The nervous system is disordered and the brain inflamed, "which necessarily excites the organs of Amativeness, situated in the lowest point of the brain." At the same time, compression produces retention of the blood "in the bowels . . . and thereby inflames all the organs of the abdomen, which thereby excites amative desires." In short, "tight-lacing . . . necessarily kindles impure feelings . . . at the same time that it renders their possessors more weak-minded, so as the more easily to be led into temptation."[16]

All intelligent men . . . despise . . . the fashion. But fashionable young gentlemen . . . demand it . . . and their demand is acceded to by almost the whole of the opposite sex. But how happens it that this class is obeyed, while the admonitions of the other are unheeded?

It appeared that women actually preferred "a city dandy, without brains or morals, and known to be licentious, yet dressed superbly."

> Why does each strive to secure his arm, and expose all her charms to gain him as a lover? Can it be because he excites her Amativeness and Adhesiveness? . . . Are women so weak or crazy? Tight-lacing has already been shown to produce partial insanity, and also to excite impure desires.[17]

Fowler appealed to women to reject both the sexualizing corset and the sexually attractive young man, and to adopt instead the role of wife to an industrious and virtuous husband, and mother to numerous progeny. (Presumably the children could be produced without unduly arousing anyone's organs of Amativeness.)

> Will you not break away from the shackles of these fashionable libertines whose main end is to ruin you? Will you not turn your eyes and your hearts from the fashionable to the industrious—from rakes to the virtuous; from beasts to men; . . . from your destroyers to those who will save you; from the worst of husbands to be best? . . . Unloose your corset. . . . Clothe yourselves in the garb of natural beauty, and remember that you are born, not to court and please, not to be courted and pleased by, fashionable rowdies, but to become wives and mothers.[18]

Accounts of corset-induced gynecological and reproductive diseases probably reflected the doctors' anxiety about female sexuality, together with a lack of knowledge about the "mysterious" uterus. A "disease" such as hysteria that combined aspects of the reproductive and nervous systems might arouse special suspicions. Whether or not corsets increased "amativeness," they probably did not do so by exciting the "organs" thereof.

She Cut Her Liver Right in Half

In his polemic against fashionable dress, *Madre Natura versus the Moloch of Fashion*, "Luke Limner" listed ninety-seven "Diseases produced by Stays and Corsets according to the testimony of eminent medical men" (taken, however, largely from an eighteenth-century German compilation by Samuel Thomas von Soemmerring), including tuberculosis ("consumption"), cancer, scoliosis, hunchback, hysteria, melancholy, and epilepsy. Others, such as The Ladies' Sanitary Association, declared that "There ought to be the word *Torture*, or Murder, in large letters on every pair of stays." Yet many—perhaps most—doctors defended the "moderate" and "legitimate" use of the corset, while vigorously opposing tight-lacing or the "abuse" of the corset. *The Lancet*, for example, published more than an article a year from the late 1860s to the early 1890s on the medical dangers of tight-lacing, the doctors sometimes arguing that the frequency

À la Mode à la Mort. Illustration from Luke Limner, *Madre Natura versus the Moloch of Fashion* (London: Chatto & Windus, 1874).

of the practice proved that "there can be no need to adopt artificial measures for the repression of feminine brains." Nevertheless, their aversion to tight-lacing did not generally extend to ordinary corsetry, any more than their disapproval of high heels led them to advocate the abolition of shoes. Popularly also, a distinction was drawn between "the alleged injuries" caused by corsetry and "the foolish, dangerous, and unnecessary practice of *tight lacing.*"[19]

It is important to emphasize both the range of medical opinion and the commonly made distinction between "evil" tight-lacing and "necessary" or "desirable" corsetry, because many historians have concluded, on the one hand, that the medical profession was generally opposed to corsetry, and, on the other, that the medical evidence indicated (or "proved") that corsets were dangerous. This conclusion is not surprising in light of the numerous medical attacks on tight-lacing, the apparent difficulty of defining tight-lacing (or the unwillingness to do so), and the fact that a significant number of doctors were opposed to any use of the corset (except in unusual cases when orthopedic corsetry seemed required). The complexities of the corset controversy, however, were reflected (rather than elucidated) in the medical literature of the time.

Some doctors, such as Dr. Sauveur Henri-Victor Bouvier and Dr. Ludovic O'Followell, argued that the support of the bust and spine and the control of obesity, together with "woman's social destination," necessitated the corset. Other doctors responded to the controversy by inventing "improved," "hygienic" versions of the corset. Perhaps the most influential of these was the eccentric Dr. Gustav Jaeger, promoter of the Sanitary Woolen System, who argued that wool corsets had "all the advantages of girded loins without the disadvantages." Dr. Scott's "Electric Corset" was endorsed by Dr. William A. Hammond, the Surgeon General of the United States, and in 1914 the (American) Women's National Medical Association went on record in favor of corsetry. Still other doctors—moderate opponents of the corset— denied that the corset caused "most evils from cancer downwards," but thought that it did contribute to curvature of the spine, rib displacement, deformities and displacements of the internal organs, respiratory and circulatory diseases, atrophy of the abdominal muscles, diseases of the reproductive system, and "lassitude." "Even a moderate or slight amount of tight-lacing," wrote Dr. Frederick Treves, "will deform the body."[20]

The term "tight-lacing" has been used so imprecisely that it seems necessary to give examples of the variety of practices to which it was applied, which can be compared later with the very different accounts of extreme and "fetishistic" tight-lacing. The dress reformer, Mrs. Ada S. Ballin, thought that "the abuse of the corset" was "rampant"—and no wonder, since she believed that the normal female waist was 27 to 29 inches, and that women with waists of 25 inches or less were guilty of tight-lacing.[21]

The novelist Charles Reade devoted much of the plot of A Simpleton to a condemnation of tight-lacing. Dr. Staines (the hero and obvious mouthpiece for Reade's opinions) argues that the foolish heroine, Rosa, should "throw that diabolical machine into the fire." Rosa replies that stays are necessary for warmth; "it is so unfeminine not to wear them"; "a tiny waist is beautiful"; and that gentlemen (including fathers and husbands) have no business "interfering in such things." She angrily advises Staines to "go and marry a Circassian slave. They don't wear stays, and they do wear trousers; so she will be unfeminine enough, even for you."[22]

That Reade presents Rosa's behavior as self-willed and stupid is rather predictable. More interesting are her arguments, which seem to have a ring of authenticity—not, however, as an example of the beliefs of a tight-lacing "fetishist," but rather as expressions of what were probably fairly commonly held attitudes of ordinary women. Corsets, like skirts, were associated with femininity and beauty, but not generally with submissiveness.

Gordon Stables ("Medicus" of The Girl's Own Paper) described another "true story of Tight-lacing": A nineteen-year-old girl, Susie, laces more tightly after she becomes engaged—a practice that her mother views as normal, but that distresses her doctor father. "The girl is being squeezed to death ... Bother those corsets anyhow!" Worried that she is "growing more refined-like," he invites her to go to the sea-side for a vacation, and to wear her "easiest corset" for the trip. He then secretly gets rid of her other corsets, and she becomes "better, stronger, rosier, happier." Her fiancé is delighted.[23] Most instances of "tight-lacing" probably involved nothing more pernicious or *outré* than this.

Gwen Raverat recalled that, as a girl in the 1890s, she had hated her stays, taking them off whenever possible. But whenever she visited her aunt,

> soon after my arrival, I would feel her fingers fumbling in my waistbelt, to make sure that I was not tight-lacing; for she suspected every young person of a wish to be fashionable. She used to tell us a dreadful moral tale about a lady who laced herself so hard that she cut her liver *right in half*, and died in consequence. (I don't really think that there was much danger of my dying in that way.)

In the 1880s, M. Vivian Hughes was told the same story about the liver of a "young society woman."[24] Raverat's aunt and Hughes's teacher presumably shared their families' belief in the necessity of corsetry. Yet the many stories of "tight-lacing liver" reflected a widespread anxiety about the practice. (Rosa spits blood and the surgeon ascribes it to her liver.) In fact, the liver was probably chosen as the afflicted organ, because autopsies not infrequently show it to look enlarged or distorted. There exists a normal anatomic variant in which the liver has an accessory lobe.

The historian's attempts to assess medical diagnoses from the past are fraught with dangers, but we might reasonably conclude that, from the point of view of modern doctors, corsets were unlikely to have severed the liver or displaced any other organs such as the stomach or pancreas, any more than they caused epilepsy or tuberculosis (supposedly through the friction of lung and rib). Corsets probably neither supported the spine nor deformed it, although both of these beliefs indicate fears about the essential weakness of the body. The stories of crushed ribs—let alone deliberately removed ribs—have yet to be authenticated; there are some female skeletons from the 1880s at the Smithsonian Institution with what appear to be deformed ribs. Corsets probably did cause some health problems. The restriction of the chest led to upper diaphragmatic breathing, while the constriction of the waist and abdomen probably caused digestive problems, such as constipation. Although tight garters do cause varicose veins, there is no evidence that tight corsets caused heart disease either through the blockage of "impure" blood or in any other way. It is, however, possible that the use of tight corsets during pregnancy could cause complications or miscarriages; although, again, stories of the pelvic floor being pushed down or the uterus deformed should be treated with caution.

Some modern doctors have tentatively suggested that the "mechanical pressure upon the liver and upper gastro-intestinal tract from the wearing of tight-laced corsets" might have contributed to "chlorosis, an unexplained [hypochromatic iron deficiency] anemia that afflicted many young women in the late 1800s." On the other hand, it may be that better nutrition today is responsible for the disappearance of the disease, or that the condition still exists but is now known under a different name. Dr. Gerhart Schwarz, Director of Radiology at New York Eye and Ear Infirmary, believes that doctors were under social pressure to attack corsetry and that there is little or no hard medical evidence to support claims of corset-induced disease. Diseases that were more prevalent among women than men (such as tuberculosis and scoliosis) were routinely ascribed to the ill-effects of their clothing. The evidence to disprove such beliefs came in only gradually, for example, when the tubercle bacillus was discovered in 1882. Even today (when women do not wear corsets), a disease like "idiopathic scoliosis [the lateral curvature of the spine] is still eight times as prevalent among girls as boys." Interestingly, in the 1960s and 1970s, American physicians again began to publish cases of supposedly corset-related "diseases" such as "panty-girdle syndrome, i.e., swelling of legs from the constriction of the thighs" and hiatus hernia—but Dr. Schwarz, at least, argues that this development is simply part of the more general tendency today to blame the patient for his (or her) diseases.[25]

While The Ladies' Sanitary Association warned its working-class readers that "Wasps have stings" and "that sting is *Ill Health*," others thought that, health considerations aside, corsets were still an "evil" that needed to be "exorcised." Thus the American, Dr. Arabella Kenealy, argued that "It may be objected that woman is today stronger and more athletic than she has ever been. But ... not even in man, and certainly not in woman, is muscular capacity a test of health. On the contrary, its possession in very marked degree is one of the symptoms of degeneracy." The modern woman was not only excessively tight-laced, she was over-educated, over-athletic, and "over-weighted with animality."[26]

The Unnatural Can Never Be Beautiful

The corset was also attacked on aesthetic and moral grounds. Reformers insisted that "The Unnatural Can Never Be Beautiful," but they admitted that "Deformity has through long custom become to us beauty." The vehemence of the response indicated that some reformers recognized, however reluctantly, the sexual appeal of the "distorted" figure: "An artist, thoroughly in harmony with the best classic standards, said a few days ago, 'I have just seen a fashionably dressed woman, and I admit that the lines of her distorted figure, nevertheless, pleased me. Now what is the matter with *me*?'"[27]

Of course, not all opponents of the corseted waist were motivated by a desire to promote greater "chastity" of appearance and behavior. Actresses such as Ellen Terry and Sarah Bernhardt, who were avant garde in both their sartorial and sexual views, did not wear corsets. In an article on "The Artistic Aspect of Dress", Henry Holiday identified the corset with "prudery and . . . a coarse and gross conception of the human being," and deplored that so many people regarded the body "as something which is depraving to contemplate" unless "concealed and distorted . . . to make it respectable." Yet he believed that the "natural" body was characterized by "Beauty and *Purity*." A very different writer, Emile Zola, argued in *Fecondité* that women like those by Rubens and Titian were beautiful, because robust and motherly, while the attenuated, fashionable woman was defying nature and causing the "evil of depopulation."[28]

One famous artist who detested the corset was Pierre Auguste Renoir, whose feminine ideal was the illiterate, maternal housewife who enjoyed sexual intercourse. The fashionable image of femininity was as abhorrent to him as that of the athlete or "woman lawyer." He argued that the corset deformed women's ribs—"And when they become pregnant . . . I pity the poor brat inside!" —but his opposition extended to the wider artificiality of fashion, including high heels and hair styles (although he liked lacy undergarments). He objected both to women's "slavish devotion to fashion" and to the growing "vogue for the [relatively] slender figure." Women should get their physical exercise by washing clothes or scrubbing the floor: "Their bellies need movement of that sort."[29] For Renoir, corsetry (and fashion in general) was ugly, unhealthy, and associated with women's growing independence. *Both* the fashionable girl and woman *and* the advocate of woman's rights rejected woman's "natural" role.

Venus in Stays

The western ideal of physical beauty was derived, in part, from Greek art. Yet, as "Luke Limner" argued,

> In regarding the nude as depicted by Art, we have often heard ladies make observation to the effect: that, whilst admiring figures in paint and marble, they should consider the same forms frightful in frocks, a remark not untrue, as frocks and garments are constituted, being fashioned for figures of phantasy to fit those who have distorted their forms. . . . Take an antique Venus, pure as the day, and pare her down to the fashionable dimensions of a modern corset, and see how the chastity of divine truth would depart, and feelings of disgust and immodesty usurp their place.[30]

Leighton was correct in observing that the apparent "chastity" and "purity" of the Classical nude derived in part from the absence of a clearly defined waistline.

Some advocates of the Classical model actually argued that "There is positively no waist-line in the natural body." More commonly, people hedged their bets:

> The fashionable . . . waist is not the waist of nature, nor the waist of beauty. It is an absolute deformity, and in the nude figure would be actually intolerable. It is only the extraneous assistance of dress that disguises it, and enables it to pass muster in the tout-ensemble.[31]

The slim-waisted figure would be "intolerable" in the art of the nude, only insofar as the viewer might be upset by seeing a clear illustration of the current erotic ideal.

Many people tried to reconcile the two ideals, praising "natural proportions" while also expressing admiration for the "naturally small" waist. The French beauty writer Ernest Feydeau, for example, attacked as a "vulgar prejudice," propagated by "engravings in fashion journals," the idea that " a slim little waist in strange contrast with exaggerated hips and broad shoulders" constitutes a beautiful figure. He professed to be amazed that "the generality of women envy [these] elegant monstrosities." Yet, for all his emphasis on harmony, proportion, flexibility, and grace, he nonetheless concluded that "thick, large" waists are "simply hideous . . . to a man of taste."[32]

Occasionally a writer hotly defended fashion and corsetry, arguing that however beautiful the "waistless" figure might be as a nude, it would necessarily be ugly clothed. Thus, in *The Gentlewoman's Book of Dress*, Mrs. Douglas argued that

> The opponents of the corset and the waist are a little too fond of pointing to the Venus de Milo as proof of how beautiful a waistless woman can be. They forget or ignore the fact that the Venus de Milo is a charming nudity, and that it is the custom in most countries to cover oneself with clothes. Had Venus been compelled by a cold climate to drape herself, we have little doubt she would have worn stays to give her clothes the shape they lacked.[33]

Perhaps Mrs. Douglas recognized that almost any nude was already sexually "charming," but that a clothed woman wanted to display her sexual attributes.

Like dress reformers, supporters of fashion had their own ideas of what constituted a beautiful shape. The opinions of the dressmaker in "Rita's" novel *Vanity!* (1901) were probably typical of many fashionable women:

> "I hate to see a woman's figure like an hour-glass. Why can't they see that proportion is the true art of beauty? Who admires an exaggerated waist? . . .
>
> [The tightly corseted Lady Farrington enters.]
>
> "Your figure seems perfect," I said. "Perhaps the waist is a trifle too—too—"
>
> "My dear creature! not too *large*?"
>
> "Oh, no . . . Just the reverse. I was about to suggest you should not lace quite so tightly."
>
> "Tightly! I assure you my corsets are absolutely *loose* . . . Oh! don't say I look tight-laced like Mrs. Wiltshire. She boasts, you know, that she has the smallest waist of any woman in London. Of course, you know her by sight?"
>
> "Who does not? She makes me feel *sick*. I always think she's going to break in half."
>
> "I'm so glad you don't admire her. It's really too wonderful to be—nice. They say she sleeps with a steel belt round her."
>
> "What does she gain by such penance?"

"Admiration and envy."

"Not from any sensible person—of that I'm sure."

[The fitter comes in to take measurements.]

"Waist—twenty inches," she began. . . . "That will never do, you know,"
I said. "Take my advice—let out to twenty-two, or three. You won't *look*
any larger, and the fit will benefit ever so much—no strain."

"But are you *sure* I won't look clumsy?"

"On the contrary, you will have elegance and grace. The way I cut my
gowns makes your *actual* waist look quite one inch smaller than it is, but I
insist on proportion. With your bust and hips your waist could not look
large."[34]

The small waist is presented here as beautiful, especially in conjunction
with full bust and hips, but the very tightly laced waist is not beautiful or
"nice", but sickening. The image of Mrs. Wiltshire, who sleeps in a "steel
belt" and "boasts" about her waist size, comes intriguingly close to that
of the stereotyped tight-lacer of contemporary journalism.

Most of the "middle of the road" literature on corsetry implied that the
corset either veiled and protected an otherwise perfect body or corrected
minor figure flaws. The corset helped maintain "a svelte waist and a well
placed bosom." The corset supports the breasts, "augmenting their volume" and allowing them to "blossom in all their splendour and ampli-
tude." The corset was also essential for a *fashionable* appearance. There
were "Fashions in Waists." "Woman has only to change her corset. Her
waist shortens or lengthens at will. The hips are padded or flattened, the
bosom falls or rises."[35]

Supporters of the corset tended to approve of its role in the creation of
a stylish and sexually attractive image of femininity. The long, slender
waist was "one of the greatest feminine coquetries," because it seemed so
fragile and seductive: "The corsetière makes the woman—a living statue
carved by Nature—into a statuette of gracious fragility, of conventional
form, but so seductive." "A narrow waist between tasty [*savoureuses*]
hips and a proud bosom" was always admired, but even a "splendid form"
was often "transformed according to the fantasies of fashion."[36]

Trembling, Happy, Your Husband Unlaces You

But the erotic appeal of the corset extended far beyond its role in the
creation of a fashionable and seductive figure. As an item of lingerie, it
was associated with intimate moments and the act of making love. Thus,
in Balzac's *Cousin Bette*, Valérie's Brazilian lover realizes that she is
deceiving him when he discovers her "having her stays laced up by Wen-
ceslas."

It is at such moments that a woman who is neither too plump nor too slender, like the finely made, elegant Valérie, seems more than ordinarily beautiful. The rose-tinted flesh and dewy skin invite the most somnolent eye.
The lines of the body, then so lightly veiled, are so clearly suggested by the

shining folds of the petticoat and the lower part of the stays that a woman becomes quite irresistible, like every joy when we must say good-bye to it.[37]

The act of unlacing a corset (as the prelude to sexual intercourse) or lacing it up (afterwards) was the theme of many erotic prints; and the pushing of the stay lace through the holes of the corset was itself a kind of symbolic enactment of intercourse.

The periodical *La Vie Parisienne* printed a story, "La Corbeille de Mariage" (The Wedding Presents), which described the nuptial night in terms that directly link the unlacing of the corset with the act of defloration. Yet, in striking contrast to the stereotype of the frightened and sexually ignorant Victorian bride and her more or less brutal husband, the bride is portrayed here as joyful and self-assured, while her husband seems almost virginal:

> Trembling, happy, your husband unlaces you with an uncertain and clumsy hand, and you laugh, mischievously, joyously ascertaining that his confusion is caused by the sight of your beauty. You are happy to feel your omnipotence: you take care not to help him untie the knots or find his way among the lace-holes; on the contrary, you take pleasure in prolonging his tentative gropings, which tickle you deliciously.[38]

The message of the story is that the ideal married couple should be happy lovers, and that erotic lingerie contributes to their marital satisfaction. Each of the wedding presents—not only diamonds and lace, but also nightgowns, drawers, stockings, petticoats, a crêpe de chine peignoir, and several corsets—is described and then commented on by "the voice of good" and "the voice of evil," the first stressing the sexual attractiveness of the bride, and the second the probable sexual incompatibility of the couple. At the conclusion, "the voice of La Vie Parisienne" tells the bride that marriage is a compromise that should turn out very well, "especially for those, like you, with youth, health, beauty, [and] a good heart."

The "sexy" bride seems to have all the attractions of the ideal mistress. It is precisely this that disturbs "the voice of evil": "Your husband will unlace your corset? Oh! la! la! . . . You will be all the more what in the theatre one calls 'a second utility'." But it is only the evil voice that describes the marital union in terms of legal and economic bonds (together with the occasional, unwelcome sexual interlude). Such a story, of course, provides no evidence about the incidence of married lovers or their use of erotic undress and corsetry, but it does at least indicate one view of the ideal marriage.

The Embrace of the Corset

It is a view that is supported by other contemporary literature, such as the very popular work by Gustave Droz, *Monsieur, madame et bébé*. Droz argued that sexual happiness was an essential element in marriage, and he advocated that the amorous husband undress his wife after a ball or lace her into her corset—just as he had done with his mistress years before. Of the mistress he had had when he was eighteen, the narrator says:

> I adored her, and she reciprocated the sentiment. I used to dress her myself, I laced her stays, and used to feel boundless emotions as I marked [sic] her waist contract, and her figure shape itself under my hands. She would smile at me in the glass . . . all the while she was saying, "Not so tightly, dear, you will suffocate me."[39]

I do not think that it would be correct to interpret this scene as "sadistic." Certainly Droz intended it to portray shared erotic happiness, and the act of squeezing and waist contraction is not shown as painful. Nevertheless, one is entitled to ask whether women enjoyed the sensation of constriction.

Many women were so accustomed to the use of the corset that they felt uncomfortable without it. The historian Priscilla Robertson points out that "Women themselves often reported that they felt a sense of security from being all laced up . . . and any looseness of fit or relaxation of squeezing in their garments came to seem a dangerous divestment, not only of modesty, but of personal integrity."[40] There was a popular association between corsetry and morality. "The English conclude if your dress is loose, that your morals are also." And it was commonly thought that the "corsetless" period following the French Revolution was characterized both by "indecency of dress" and by a corresponding "general licentiousness of manners and morals." Of course, some people treated the issue with more levity: In 1894, the humor magazine *Le Rire* maintained that "The defense of virtue by the corset seems easily overcome if we are to judge by the number of these garments turned in at the Lost and Found."[41]

But these reasons do not entirely explain the *appeal* of the sensation of support (mild pressure or constriction). It is possible, though, that the psychological concepts of skin and muscle eroticism might be connected to the unconscious idea that the corset reproduced the sensation of being held (either by the mother or the lover). In the late nineteenth-century novel *Blix*, Frank Norris described the feelings of the heroine's young adolescent sister when she wore her stays:

> Her shoes were still innocent of heels; but on those occasions when she was allowed to wear her tiny first pair of corsets she was exalted to an almost celestial pitch of silent ecstasy. The clasp of the miniature stays around her small body was like the embrace of a little lover, and awoke in her ideas that were as vague, as immature and unformed as the straight little figure itself.[42]

The "embrace" of the corset triggered an awareness of her sexuality—a plausible hypothesis since rigid or tight clothing tends to make the individual more aware of his or her body. Equally important, though, is the association of ideas: wearing a corset equals being a grown-up woman, with a sexual role to play within marriage.

Roberts takes the modern feminist position and argues that the "erotic connotations" of the corset might well have been "closely related to ... constriction and pain," but that these connotations were probably "more appreciated by men than by women."[43] Kunzle argues that the tightly laced corset produced an extremely pleasureable sensation. Yet the obsessive and "fetishist" literature, on which they both rely, is highly atypical.

The Votaries of Tight-Lacing

I have been much interested in the correspondence in your newsy paper, in which letters have recently appeared upon the subjects of whipping girls, breast-rings, and figure-training. ... My own experiences of all three of these things when at one of the most fashionable finishing schools of the early sixties, may not be without interest to your many readers. ... [It] was one of the periodic cycles of tight-lacing, as may be gathered from the correspondence which appeared in "The Englishwoman's Domestic Magazine" about this time.[44]

Thus A WOMAN OF FIFTY wrote to *Society* magazine in 1899, referring knowledgeably to most of the cult elements that played a role in the various corset correspondences. There was the ritualistic invocation of the sexy and sadistic "mistress" of the tight-lacing "finishing school," which was populated by perverse but aristocratic young women and occasionally men dressed as women. The ubiquitous French governess, Mlle. de Beauvoir, appeared with a "thirteen-inch wasit," although otherwise "plump." "Birching ... was an openly recognised punishment." Breast-rings—the current enthusiasm among a number of correspondents to *Society*—were worn by "three French girls, daughters of a marquise."

From 1867 to 1874 a notorious corset correspondence was published in *The Englishwoman's Domestic Magazine*, previously an apparently ordinary middle- and lower-middle-class women's periodical but afterwards the focus of a furious controversy—one that has continued to this day, and that has seriously distorted our understanding of Victorian corsetry. *EDM* printed dozens of letters on the subject of tight-lacing (as well as on flagellation, high heels, particular kinds of underwear, and spurs for lady riders). Many correspondents described undergoing either voluntary or compulsory tight-lacing to extreme tenuity. Some dwelled salaciously on the painful aspects of tight-lacing, while others described the mingled sensations of pleasure and pain that they claimed to experience. The tightly corseted female body was extolled, and the use of tight corsets for men was also advocated. Not surprisingly, this correspondence (like the one on flagellation) was widely regarded as scandalous.

It was also widely perceived as genuine. In 1874, *La Vie Parisienne* described English girls with waists of "43 to 45 centimeters." In a French prose studded with English expressions, the author described "les *fashionable boarding-school*" where the girls competed for the smallest waists, so that "the majority of them retain their corsets at night"; and among the "ravishing amazons" that one saw everywhere, there were "beaucoup de *young ladies*" with pinched waists. "The waists that one can *almost* span with two hands are not the exceptions in the land of *tight-lacing*."[45]

Although many historians have also accepted the *EDM* correspondence as evidence of widespread "tight-lacing of the most outrageous kind ... amounting to torture," others, such as Doris Langley Moore, have dismissed it as "spurious" and simply the fantasies of a few "perverts," including *EDM*'s editor, Samuel Beeton. David Kunzle, however, argues that the *EDM* correspondence formed part of a genre of "fetishist" literature; and that the accounts of tight-lacing were largely authentic descriptions of "genuine experience and honestly expressed feelings."[46] Certainly, the "votaries of tight-lacing" expressed their views in a variety of periodicals, pamphlets, and books—and they often plagiarized earlier accounts in their own supposedly first-person histories. [For further information about fetishist correspondence, see the Appendix.] The *EDM* correspondence needs to be seen not only within the context of the Victorian debate about corsetry and tight-lacing, but also as a particularly notorious example of a more specialized "fetishist" interest.

To some extent, Kunzle's argument that a group of corset and tight-lacing fetishists existed may be valid. It is doubtful, however, whether the *reality* of tight-lacing (whether fetishist or not) corresponded to the picture presented by the self-proclaimed tight-lacers and others who capitalized on the scandal they provoked; let alone to Kunzle's edited and sanitized interpretation of these works, which omits or plays down the sadistic letters on "punishment corsets" and "fair flagellants," promoting instead the implausible image of the happy "fetishistic family." At the very least, a distinction should be drawn between the internal evidence of the tight-lacing letters (with their accounts of aristocratic tight-lacers such as the "Comptesse V——," 12-inch waists and 38-inch busts, and enforced tight-lacing at "fashionable" "society" finishing schools in exotic localities such as Paris and Vienna) and any external evidence that might tend to corroborate or cast doubt on the practices described.[47]

It is unclear why ordinary magazines were sometimes "taken over" by "fetishist" controversies. I suspect, however, that the regular subscribers were not the main correspondents, but rather that once a periodical opened its columns to a discussion of tight-lacing or flagellation, then a relatively small number of individuals with specialized sexual interests responded, creating controversy and temporarily increasing sales. The class origin and gender of the correspondents is thus difficult to determine. Everyone claimed to be upper-class or of the professional class while their opponents invariably denied this.

Proof, of course, is doubly difficult to obtain at this distance in time, but we may doubt the accuracy of many supposedly "factual" reports, especially when they appeared in journals engaged in the controversy. Other accounts, such as "The Sin and Scandal of Tight-Lacing," although apparently not intended to pander to the fantasies of a specialized audience, nevertheless seem deliberately sensationalistic and bizarre: Readers "will stand aghast at the widespread wickedness that is practiced by girls and women who are addicted to this pernicious habit." In some cases, journalists seem sincere but credulous. They cite previously published fetishist accounts as proof and believe the statistics given by unnamed corsetières. Photographic evidence was also offered: "The photographer ... showed my correspondent quite a number of photographs of girls and ladies (mostly of the theatrical profession or society women) with waists less than seventeen inches." It is risky to dismiss this type of testimony, yet historians of photograhy point out that photographs can be misleading and, indeed, easily altered. One Victorian photographer instructed his colleagues: "The retoucher may slice off, or curve the lady's waist after his own idea of shape and form and size."[48] Many readers were predisposed to believe lurid accounts of tight-lacing, and sexual scandal is always sure of an audience.

Both "male" and "female" correspondents extolled the erotic charms of the small waist. BENEDICT, for example, wrote to *EDM* describing himself as "a slave to a 'little waist'." PERSEVERANCE also equated a small waist with sexual attractiveness, and claimed that her husband "often laughingly tells me that I caught him with my waist." She boasted that she was "still ... able to gratify his artistic taste by displaying ... my figure." "Clumsy," "awkward" waists, on the other hand, were stigmatized as "a great detriment on the marital market."[49]

TF objected that, while men admired small waists, they were not in favor of tight-lacing "for their own wives." Instead, the wife was supposed to be "a comfort and a companion" to her husband. Other writers, however, accused anti-tight-lacing correspondents of being old gentlemen "who [are] constantly bothered to lace the stays of ... younger and more aspiring [wives]." In other words, men who were opposed to tight-lacing were simply unable to deal with female sexuality. Women opposed to the practice were dismissed as "strong minded." [50]

Yet the reaction to the pro-tight-lacing literature was not simply the hysteria of an anti-sexual society. Many people objected on the valid grounds that real marital happiness could not be based solely on a particular physical attraction. "Big, warm, masculine natures love an ordinary, natural waist." This type of man certainly sounds both virile and loving. Conversely, according to one French writer,

> Every woman who has won her husband by the fineness of her waist has married ... a fool or a depraved man, and in a little while, she will see her captive break his chain of artificial flowers.

Lady Greville agreed that such a man "belongs to the tribe of indifferent husbands who ... run after younger and handsomer women, whose waist diameters are less and their busts more largely developed."[51] And SEMPER EADUM protested:

But are women created simply to be admired by MEN? No; certainly not. They were created as helpmeets for him. ... Waists made thin by tight-lacing can only be admired by those brainless abortions who walk, or rather strut, about in patent leather boots and high collars, sucking affectionately the golden, or otherwise, heads of their canes, and who consider women as a superior sort of plaything instead of human.[52]

Tight-lacing is here associated with the *restriction* of women (and often children) to the role of sex objects or playthings. Its opponents argued that women should be valued for their personal qualities as well.

The correspondents' enthusiasm for tiny waists went far beyond that of the average person, and accounts of impossibly small waists seem to represent fantasy extensions of the widespread admiration for small waists. NORA claimed to have attended "a fashionable school in London" where "it was the custom for the waists of the pupils to be reduced one inch per month ... When I left school ... my waist measured only thirteen inches." The correspondents competed, asking "What is the smallest size waist that one can have?"[53]

Despite their obsession with tiny waist measurements, the majority of tight-lacing advocates paid relatively little attention to the bosom as an erogenous zone. The corsetières quoted in *The Gentlewoman* were unusual, in giving bust and hip as well as waist measurements: 40–14–38 and 37–13–38. Yet a number of other nineteenth-century sources indicate that the *primary* purpose of the corset was to support and accentuate the bust. The corset could have been an adjunct to breast fetishism, as well as being fetishistic "in its own right," but this is not usually evident from the pro-tight-lacing literature.[54]

The sexual appeal of the small-waisted female torso was sometimes transferred to the corset. Correspondents argued that "half the charm in a small waist comes, not in spite of, but on account of, its being tight-laced"; "—the tighter the better"; "well-applied restraint is in itself attractive." Here we see the erotic appeal of bondage and waist confinement for its own sake, rather than for the effect it produces.[55]

One letter that lends credence to the idea that, for the fetishist at least, the corset functioned as a substitute for the (nonexistent) female phallus was written by A MALE WASP WAIST, whose extreme revulsion at the idea of a non-corseted waist seems like a transferrence of his uneasiness and fear of the female genitalia: "To my mind a non-stayed waist is horrid. ... What man enjoys a dance holding a flabby waist, where his fingers sink into fat? ... We men love a stiff, hard, well-boned waist to hold"— preferably one that measured "twelve-and-a-half inches." The shape of the corset—essentially that of the female torso—is not an obvious phallic symbol, yet it transforms the soft and pliant torso into something hard and rigid. The possible symbolism of the corseted body as an erect penis is reinforced by nineteeth-century references to corsets as "armor," which is associated with the idea of weapons. A MALE WASP WAIST not only admired corseted women but also wore corsets himself and dressed "like a lady." He enjoyed being mistaken for a woman (or fantasizing about this): "I have been struck by the number of men who admired me, and would, no doubt, have liked to put their arms round my small waist. If they had only known I was also one of their sex!" His fantasy seems to focus on the joys of being a phallic woman embraced by men, and at the same time remaining a man. The place that he imagined men touching was his waist.[56]

The tight-lacing letters should also really be seen in conjunction with those on whipping. The scenarios are similar: girls are undisciplined or uncorseted for years, perhaps because their "relatives" are "abroad." They rebel but are forced to submit—often at finishing schools or at the hands of a governess. Just as the best methods of tight-lacing are debated at length—are handcuffs or locked corsets useful?—so also do correspondents argue whether it is best to, say, strap a girl across the "horse" or chain her to the ceiling; to leave her underwear on or strip her naked. Specifics of discipline are combined with a dream-like vagueness of narrative. FANNY, for example, wrote

> Up to the age of fifteen, I was . . . suffered to run . . . wild. . . . Family circumstances and change of fortune . . . led my relatives to the conclusion that my education required a continental finish. . . . I was packed off to a highly-genteel and fashionable establishment for ladies, situated in the suburbs of Paris . . . [where] I was subjected to the strict and rigid system of lacing "[57]

Many of the corset and tight-lacing letters recount scenarios that could easily have been part of a pornographic novel, and any temptation to feel indignant about historical tight-lacing gives way to the belief that these letters need to be analyzed as sexual fantasies. The accounts of "Tight-Lacing as a Punishment" and of "punishment corsets"—very tight, heavily boned, and often locked with a padlock—became increasingly outrageous. One letter described what happened to WASP-WAIST when she rebelled against being laced smaller than eighteen inches:

> The French mistress, on hearing this, became very angry, for it was her special business to see that all the girls should have wasp waists. I then received a punishment which thoroughly subdued me, and it most certainly did me a lot of good. The weight of my body was suspended from my wrists, which were fastened above my head, while my feet, which were encased in tight, high-heeled boots, were fastened to a ring in the floor. In this position, only protected by my stays, I received a severe whipping across the back, which gave me intense pain, but left no mark, owing to my being tightly laced. After this castigation I was very humble, but before the French mistress would untie my hands, she reduced the size of my waist to fifteen inches.[58]

For votaries, such as ALFRED, the appeal of the tightly corseted waist derived from the sadistic fantasies associated with tight-lacing:

> There is something to me extraordinarily fascinating in the thought that a young girl has for many years been subjected to the strictest discipline of

the corset. If she has suffered, as I have no doubt she has, great pain . . . from their extreme pressure, it must be quite made up to her by the admiration her figure excites.

Another correspondent, MORALIST, tried to explain what was so "fascinating" about this thought: The "discipline of the corset" implied that "a valuable lesson of self-abnegation has been taught; that patience and endurance of pain and inconvenience for the sake of others has been inculcated; that the crude spirit has been . . . tamed." In other words, the girl had been trained to be submissive—or, in his terms, to be "a womanly woman," rather than "a 'strong-minded woman' or a tomboy":

> The corset is an ever-present monitor, indirectly bidding its wearer to exercise self-restraint. The restraint of the corset may be said to be insensibly imitated by the mental faculties over the moral character. . . . If you want a girl to grow up gentle and womanly in her ways and her feelings, lace her tight.

He argued that "men do not admire this continual struggle on the part of women to shake off conventionalities," and the corset helped keep women in their place.[59]

MORALIST's letter has been frequently quoted, and superficially it seems to lend support to the traditional historical position—that the tight corset was an instrument of women's oppression. But most people thought that, far from being womanly and morally upright, tight-laced women were, in MORALIST's own words, "devoid of brains and hearts." The most extreme claims for the morality of the corset often came from such suspect sources.

Indeed, the popular image of the tight-lacer was so negative that it seems to have provoked something of a backlash, since attacks on tight-lacing often seemed to include ordinary fashionable women. For example, in *The Gentlewoman's Book of Dress*, Mrs. Fanny Douglas indicated that, while many people perceived tight-lacers as "vicious" and "criminal," she herself saw them as self-respecting, pleasant, and attractive— especially in comparison with the "hygienic faddist." Mrs. Douglas did not, however, advise her readers to tight-lace: "The probability is that, being a sensible woman, you have stays loose enough for health and tight enough for neatness."[60] And she would probably *not* have approved of the fetishists' emphasis on enduring *pain* to tame the spirit—or to arouse pleasurable sensations.

The most notorious aspect of the fetishist literature was its emphasis on *pain and pleasure*. Many of the tight-lacing letters have a pronounced sado-masochistic tone. References to "discipline," "confinement," "compulsion," "suffering," "torture," "agony," "submission," and the "victim" abound—as do references to the mingled sensations of pleasure and pain. For, although pain is frequently mentioned, it is also true that in letter after letter the self-proclaimed tight-lacers of both sexes declared that the practice produced "delightful," "delicious," "exquisite," and "pleasurable" feelings.

Do these expressions tell us anything about ordinary corset wearing, or are they largely distinct from it? Throughout the nineteenth century and into the twentieth, the opponents of tight-lacing referred to the "torture" and "suffering" that it created. In part, this reflected a sincere effort to minimize the discomfort sometimes created by dress. References to suffering probably also functioned as warnings or threats of the painful consequences of not obeying the reformers' advice, a phenomenon also apparent in the purity literature of the time. Corset advertisements, however, constantly stressed that their products gave a "sense of ease, comfort, and support."

The idea that the average woman *wanted* to be hurt by her corset finds no substantiation in the orthodox literature of the time. On the other hand, the idea that one must be willing to suffer (at least a little) to be beautiful was much more common: "Whatever the apparent paradox, the best way to love women is to ask them to suffer a little in order that our eyes continue to be charmed."[61] Women wanted elegance *and* comfort, but they were willing to compromise to some extent on comfort for the sake of greater beauty. Some men liked to imagine (and perhaps exaggerate) the extent of their suffering.

Other correspondents stressed that tight-lacing was "very exciting and pleasant," and they asserted that they would do it for the "delicious feeling . . . if no other reason."

> To me the sensation of being tightly laced in a pair of elegant, well-made, tightly fitting corsets is superb. . . . I rejoice in quite a collection of these much-abused objects, in silk, satin, and coutil of every style and colour, and never feel prouder or happier, so far as matters of the toilette are concerned, than when I survey in myself the fascinating undulations of outline that art in this respect affords to nature.[62]

The auto-eroticism of this account might well have been apparent even to pre-Freudian readers.

Thus, even though *The Family Doctor* printed numerous testimonials to this aspect of tight-lacing, its editors also published a column, signed by HYGEIA, that sternly denounced any practice that had such effects:

> It is our custom to avoid any correspondence, but in an issue of some weeks back a young lady referred to the "pleasurable sensation" caused by tight-lacing. We cannot enter, for obvious reasons, into any detailed explanation in these pages, but must content ourselves by most earnestly warning her or any others in like case to discontinue a practice with, this admission shows, to those who are acquainted with physiology and the ailments of the sex, will lead to moral as well as physical degeneracy and debasement.[63]

Eventually, in an article on "Fatal Corsets," Miss Mayard quoted "a great French physiologist" who stated quite openly that

> For the corset habit one must look . . . deeper than that of mere feminine Vanity. By experiments I have been able to prove that the sensation upon

certain organs of the feminine body produced by tight-lacing, even of a
severe character, are not merely free from unpleasantness, but even, under
certain and frequent conditions, pleasant. . . . For example, Mdlle. B——, a
pretty *fille de boutique*, experienced only heightened orgasmic pleasure
when encased in a corset seven centimeters smaller in the waist than the
one (of forty-two centimeters) usually worn. A corset of nine centimeters
less produced considerable pain and discomfort. . . . It is to this fact—*i.e.*,
the pleasure, at most the excitations, experienced by tight-lacers—that
observers must look for the reason that the corset still reigns supreme as an
article of feminine clothing and fancy.[64]

Was this "heightened orgasmic pleasure" at all generally experienced
by ordinary corset wearers? What *"organs of the feminine body"* specifically were affected? Or was it that the *mind* was affected? The ordinary
woman's feelings of "support" and mild "compression" differed significantly from the sensations reported by the tight-lacers. The connection
between pain/pleasure and discipline/confinement indicates that the plea-
sures experienced by the "fetishist" tight-lacers may have been related to
other sexual aberrations, such as sado-masochism and transvestism.

Punch frequently adopted a sarcastic tone when discussing women's
fashions, but these accounts of tight-lacing struck a nerve in the author
of "The Elasticity of Young Ladies," who compared the practice with
hanging and tight-lacers with the notorious murderess, Mrs. Maria Manning (who killed her husband):

To lace quite as tight as perhaps some women would like, to be sure , is not
in their power. If you were to take a woman, put a strap or a girdle round
her neck, and pull it in several inches, you would seriously inconvenience
her, as we know, indeed, from the case of MARIA MANNING and a few others.[65]

Punch, indeed, still focused on female folly, just as others have emphasized female masochism and powerlessness. Yet much of the tight-lacing
correspondence was apparently written by men, and many letters describe
men who claim to tight-lace. Corsetry for men was unusual, except in the
form of "belts" for "hygienic" purposes, such as the prevention or cure of
obesity and the support of "the loins and abdomen" during athletic activities. The idea of tight-laced men has little to do with either fashion or
feminism, but it may have a great deal to do with fetishism.[66]

As another correspondent to *Society* wrote, regarding an account of
Girton girls flogged by Eton boys, "I don't believe a word of these stories."[67] Perhaps an unknown number of individual "fetishists" did many
of the things they described—tight-laced, had themselves whipped,
pierced their nipples—but not under the circumstances that they
described—at the foreign boarding school, in the bosom of the fetishist
family, at the hands of Mlle. de Beauvoir, and not to the degree of tenuity
that they claimed to have achieved. Nor do I think that their sexual fantasies and acting out of these fantasies had very much to do with sensa-

tions and experiences of the average corseted woman— any more than the average glove-wearer endured tiny, padlocked gloves.

Most cases of "tight-lacing" probably involved nothing more than girls and women lacing a little more closely to achieve smaller waists. I have devoted so much attention to bizarre accounts of tight-lacing not because I think there existed many actual fetishists (quite the reverse), but in order to demonstrate how these letters cannot be accepted at face value (as they have been). It is nevertheless true that the corset had potential as a symbol, in part because the small corseted waist was widely regarded as erotic. As lingerie became more seductive in the later nineteenth century, it too became incorporated into more and more erotic fantasies.

Hail, O Corset! Symbol of Femininity

In the wider society, the corset seemed to represent female sexuality. If we turn from the bizarre fantasies of *EDM* to the *Playboy* of its day—*La Vie Parisienne*—it appears that some of the hostility to the perceived threat of dress reform undoubtedly derived from fears that women would reject a sexual role:

> The corset will live as long as the innate desire to please lives in woman's heart . . . They have tried to combat it. . . . Vain efforts! Useless furies! The corset, more powerful than its enemies, has not ceased for a single instant from making proselytes. . . . One can destroy a religion, overthrow a government; against the corset one can do nothing! Hail, then, intimate and mysterious garment that increases the charm of women. . . . Hail, O corset! You are blessed by all women, and even those whom nature has overwhelmed with gifts can not pass your competitive exam. Your reign has come without having been predicted by the prophets, and the clamors of hell do not prevail against you! May your power grow still greater, if this is possible, and may your name be glorified all over the earth. . . . Amen![68]

The blasphemy strikes a strange note, but the perception that the corset was being attacked, but would (must?) emerge victorious, may not have been that uncommon. It is possible that the reference to competitive exams was a passing blow at the idea of education for women, but the overall emphasis seems to be not so much anti-feminist as pro-female sensuality.

A cartoon of 1885, "Le Dernier Chateau Fort," shows a stone fortress in the shape of a corset. Besieged, it yet resists Royal ordinances, Imperial decrees, Papal excommunications, the exhortations of priests, the *conseils* of doctors, the enlightened advice of scholars and philosophers, and the voice of painters and poets—swearing to "Live Captive or Die!" The artist seemed to fear that an end to corsets would mean an end to sexual beauty and the bondage of sexual desire.[69]

Early twentieth-century cartoons on "costume reforme" show a fat woman in baggy trousers; a woman in Greek dress with a thick waist and short sleeves being approached by several men including a policeman; and "the man of the future" reduced to wearing a corset. The implication is that if women give up the true corset (in favor of no corset or a girdle), they will become ugly, obscene, and masculine, and men will then necessarily become quasi-feminized. Better that women should continue to wear "the feminine corset" that "renders the eternal feminine more troubling "—but not, presumably, troublesome.[70]

Was this overreaction a response to male fears about women's rights? An article on "Corset et Féminisme" in *Les Dessous Elégants* suggests that male apprehension centered more on changes in women's attitudes and style of behavior, on propriety and allure, than on actual political or socioeconomic demands. The corset imposed "elegance of deportment" and had a "salutary " effect on women's "physical and moral allure."

> A slackening in the bearing of the individual produces a looseness in manners and speech . . . Certain young women, extremely twentieth-century . . . by deliberately abandoning the corset, have abandoned the majority of good manners.

These "emancipated" women use vulgar slang, cross their legs like men, even smoke in public. The author concluded:

> For the woman who wants to remain womanly moderate corsetry is indispensable. . . . This is good feminism, infinitely more profitable to women than the *"bon garçonnisme"* with which certain women try to dress themselves.[71]

A Woman in a Corset Is a Lie

"A woman in a corset is a lie, a falsehood, a fiction, but for us this fiction is better than the reality."[72] The belief that the female body was seriously flawed may explain some of the hyperbolic praise lavished on the corset, as well as some of the expressions of discontent when it was used to create a false figure. In some cases the deception was accepted, indeed demanded, but in others it aroused disappointment, since the fiction was too transparent.

It may be that the corset was the focus of a peculiar ambiguity toward female sexuality in the nineteenth century. Evidence that some men were profoundly ambivalent about the female body can be found in a series of illustrated and annotated centerfolds (most of them by Henri de Montaut) in the periodical *La Vie Parisienne*.

The centerfold "Before and After the Corset" (9 September 1882) presents neither as satisfactory. The woman at the upper left is "large" and *"svelte,"* but with a waist that is "rather short and not very slim . . . not at all the fashionable waist." "She puts on a corset that pinches and spoils the young, fresh body," making her "stiff as a post." Now she will look well-dressed. Here Montaut seems to admire the natural woman and to be critical of corsetry, but the other figures are more seriously defective, and his comments become increasingly derogatory. One woman is "Thin,

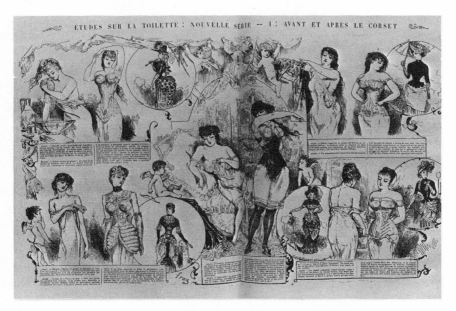

Études sur la Toilette: Nouvelle Serie. Avant et Après le Corset. Illustration from *La Vie Parisienne* (9 September 1882).

bony; no bosom, no hips, no nothing." So she equips herself with "rubber breasts that palpitate" automatically when touched, rubber hips and derriere, even long padded gloves. The final product is so obviously artificial as to be repulsive: "With this corset, one often has adventures, but never a *rendez-vous.*"

Another woman is fat. Her "waist seems like a succession of double chins." Squeezed into a reinforced corset, "the double chins disappear, dispersing themselves one knows not where." Still another has a "large" waist, a "falling" bosom, and hips that are "scarcely indicated." The corset "flattens the stomach which spreads out on the sides and forms fantasy hips, that can be taken for real ones"; a "steel bar raises the bosom."

The central and largest figure is that of a "grand, still majestic" woman, but her "plumpness [*embonpoint*] . . . is a little too overflowing." Specifically, her "low and remarkably voluminous bosom tend[s] to approach the stomach which, itself, is beginning to be lost in the bulging hips." In her corset, though, she is "Splendid!"—but this estimation is immediately qualified: her flesh only "gives the illusion of marble." The fat on her stomach and hips has not disappeared, but only been pushed down, and her breasts require a harness to hold them up. If she appeared in a dress cut low in back, her fat would swell out. In short, whatever her clothed appearance, the real woman was usually ugly.[73]

Occasionally, Montaut portrayed a naturally attractive woman. The central figure in "Considérations sur le Corset" (19 April 1879) is a young

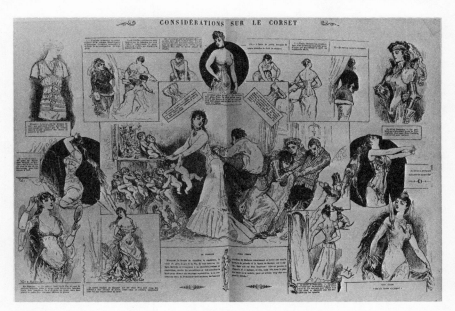

Considérations sur le Corset. Illustration from *La Vie Parisienne* (19 April 1879).

and pretty woman who laces tightly, not to improve a defective figure, but to achieve "the smallest waist in society." This is presented not as deceit, but as a dedication to fashion and vanity, and Montaut's tone is mocking but not bitter.

In "Les Corsets" (15 January 1881), the central figure is uncorseted and wears only a "silk *maillot.*" She has a "very well-made" body and a naturally small waist—or rather an unnaturally small waist. "The best is, without any doubt, not to wear a corset, but is necessary to be able to do without it, and this is extremely rare. One has more or less need of it (generally more than less)." Thus even when Montaut extols the uncorseted woman, her figure is automatically stylized to correspond to the corseted ideal.[74]

The Desire To Please the Gentlemen

In the centerfolds "Les Corsets" and "Les Dessous" (2 May 1885), the focus shifts to the characterization of different categories of women and corsets. On the most basic level, some corsets "are poems," while others are "stupid and ugly"; some women are sexually attractive, others most definitely are not. There is also a quite subtle analysis of the kinds of corsets thought to be appropriate for various women.

The "*femme comme il faut et honnête*"—the proper and virtuous woman, respectable, truly elegant, a married woman of the upper class—

Études sur la Toilette: Les Corsets. Illustration from *La Vie Parisienne* (15 January 1881).

wore "a white satin corset; never a colored corset." The white satin is praised as "The king of corsets! Flexible, shimmering, soft against the body that it delineates without sqeezing." Like its wearer, it was elegant and seductive, soft and white, but not too overtly sexual.

There was a subtle, but important, difference between the ideal corset and "the decent corset," although this, too, was generally "white satin or silk, sometimes pearl grey." But the decent corset encased a figure of which "there is always too much or not enough"; consequently it had "numerous bones that hide the absences or disperse the assemblages" of flesh. Although cleverly made, this corset "does not succeed in deceiving anyone"—or not for long. It is at least possible that the association of deception with the *decent* corset was, in part, a veiled attack on the sexual deceptions practiced by allegedly decent women.

The plain black satin corset was "forbidding" and "decent" like its wearer. But the black satin corset was also "the ideal of the little laundress who is considering going bad."

The *cocotte*, a woman whose social role was primarily sexual, wore underclothing that reflected this. She was addicted to "*jeu de corsets*," loosely translatable as "freaky corsets." One has a design of peacock feathers. Another of "tea-rose" colored satin was also apparently designed for the woman of easy virtue: "Very elegant and extremely becoming. Evidently designed to be seen and ... looked at!" The "true corset of combat," it was scented with a perfume that "smells stronger as it grows warmer." Its wearer, though, was warned that if she laced too tightly, her corset would "vein the skin . . . [and] create . . . red lines and creases that are very slow to fade." Tight-lacing, then, was not erotic, although an attractive corset was.

The *parvenue* also wore ornate "brocade corsets" with embroidery, lace, and bows. It is unclear whether this indicated personal immorality, but it did demonstrate a lack of breeding: "a display of unprecedented luxury, but no real elegance." She was quite mistaken in believing that she dressed in the "manner" of the aristocratic Faubourg Saint-Germain.

The simplest corset was sometimes best, particularly for "the young girl," who was advised to wear a "corset of white coutil—the one that almost always contains the prettiest things." It was judged to be "more provocative, despite all, than many others that attempt to be more"—a conclusion that might apply to its wearer as well. "The little girl" naturally wanted to abandon her boneless waistband order to wear a "true" corset, "which crowns her a young woman."

Other categories of corsets and their wearers tended to be more satirical. It is no surprise to see "The Provincial" and "The Foreigner" ridiculed in a Parisian paper. But the most negative figure was that of the *gratineuse*, who sought "to reform the feminine toilette" and so abandoned the corset for a "very solid and tight" silk jersey. Such a woman had a "total absence of the desire to please or agitate the gentlemen." And that, after all, was perhaps the primary function of the corset, at least as far as *La Vie Parisienne* was concerned.[75]

Clearly, both the traditional interpretation of the relationship between the women's rights movement and opposition to the corset, and Kunzle's inversion of that interpretation are oversimplified. Many "enemies of the corset" were men (like Renoir) with "an attachment to the concept of the 'natural woman'"; but it is a distortion to argue that the anti-corset party was primarily anti-feminist, anti-sexual, and misogynist.[76] Socially conservative males formed one component of the anti-corset party, but they also formed a part of the middle ground in favor of the corset—and, according to their testimony in the fetishist correspondence, some of them advocated forcing girls to be tight-laced.

The popular perception in the nineteenth and early twentieth centuries was that the movement for women's rights was fairly closely associated with the movement for rational dress.[77] To a considerable extent this was correct, although most major feminists did not make dress and corset reform one of their highest priorities. The traditional interpretation of feminism and dress reform errs, however, in its conclusion that female emancipation went hand in hand with the progressive reform of women's dress and in particular the abandonment of the corset. In fact, as Robert Riegel points out, by the close of the nineteenth century, "no major dress

reform had occurred." Changes in the position of women "had come without the assistance of 'rational' costume."[78] The corset was not abandoned,
but it gradually changed shape, and evolved into different forms of body-
structuring undergarments. Meanwhile other intimate undergarments
gained in erotic significance.

10

The Attractions
of Underclothes

High Victorian and Edwardian Underwear

No study of the relationship between fashion and eroticism can omit the
subject of women's lingerie, a type of clothing whose associations with
intimacy, the naked body, and the act of making love have given them an
enduring attraction. The fashion historian Anne Buck described the
"period, 1890–1914, and particularly between 1900 and 1908" as "the
great epoch of underwear."[1] Contemporaries were also of this opinion. In
1898, Octave Uzanne maintained that "The most special characteristic of
contemporary dress is the elaboration of undergarments." He was only
one of many to rhapsodize about "the exquisite, subtle, adorable art . . .
of filmy, beautiful underclothing." And month after month, in *The Lady's
Realm*, Mrs. Pritchard elaborated on the theme, "Lingerie is an enthrall-
ing subject." Indeed, at one point she enthusiastically—if, perhaps, blas-
phemously—argued that "The Cult of Chiffon has this in common with
the Christian religion—it insists that the invisible is more important than
the visible."[2]

Meanwhile, the underclothing of the past was maligned as ugly and
unflattering: "Think of the old days, when the bulky flannel petticoat
[and] thick long-clothes . . . were *de rigueur*." The fashion designer,
Lucille, likewise dismissed nineteenth-century underwear as consisting
solely of "flannel underclothes, woolen stockings, and voluminous petticoats."[3] The manifest inaccuracies and prejudices in this characterization
of Victorian underwear have been blithely ignored by most fashion historians, together with the obvious tendency in fashion journalism to promote the current style at the expense of earlier fashions. Designers and
publicists also derided past styles in order to exaggerate their own importance in the history of fashion. But this picture of Victorian underwear fit
so well into the stereotype of sexual repression, while descriptions of the

extravagance of early twentieth-century lingerie fit equally into the popular view of the Edwardian period, that they have been widely accepted as valid.

Yet the Victorians were by no means unaware of the appeal of seductive and luxurious undergarments. For a long time, however, elaborate underclothing tended to be associated with women of easy virtue. Since the courtesan's business was sexual, her use of deliberately seductive underclothing was not surprising.[4] In general, though, public opinion held that, however elaborate and even coquettish outerwear might be, the underwear of the respectable woman should be relatively plain and modest. In 1861, Doctor Daumas, for example, argued that "The woman's chemise is an object of respect not of censure; it is the white symbol of her modesty, that one must neither touch nor look at too closely."[5]

Edouard Manet, *Nana* (1877). Courtesy of the Hamburger Kunsthalle, Hamburg.

Ordinary fashion journals and other women's magazines devoted relatively little attention to the subject of underclothing, and illustrations tended to show these items of clothing discreetly folded, rather than on the human figure. The majority of examples of underlinen from the mid-Victorian period that have survived—chemises, petticoats, drawers, camisoles, and nightgowns—are white cotton or linen, of varying degrees of fineness and with a gradual but subtle increase of decoration over time. Decoration might include insertions of embroidery or lace, tucks, or *broderie anglaise*. Although they were sometimes quite attractive, these garments seem essentially modest and unassuming.

The great exception was petticoats, which were often more decorative and colorful, because they were often glimpsed. As early as 1858, the American magazine *Home Journal* suggested in the article "The Red Petticoat Connubially Whip-Up-Alive" that the red petticoat had first been used by Queen Victoria "to reawaken the dormant conjugal susceptibility of Prince Albert."[6]

During the 1870s and 1880s, however, women's underclothing developed simultaneously in two contrasting directions—on the one hand, toward a "healthy," "rational" style, epitomized by Doctor Jaeger's woolen garments, and, on the other, toward greater luxury of material and decoration. According to Anne Buck, the introduction of wool and silk "reflected the two different purposes which underwear is acquiring at this time"—permitting greater physical activity and the display of luxury.[7]

The vogue (one is tempted to call it a "cult") for woolen underwear led some fashion historians to characterize the 1880s as a period of "healthy" underwear, in sharp contrast to the "sexy" Edwardian period, when luxurious silk lingerie received tremendous emphasis in the fashion press. This picture, implying a sudden, drastic change, misinterprets the developments of the High Victorian period.[8] For it was during the High Victorian period that the increase in luxury began to be accompanied by the belief that more decorative and seductive underwear was perfectly appropriate for the respectable married woman. When hidden garments became more luxurious, it seems to indicate that more women were dressing attractively for intimate moments and for their own pleasure.

In *L'Art de la toilette chez la femme. Bréviaire de la vie élégante*, the French fashion writer Violette argued that

> Underwear [*les 'dessous'*] occupies a very large place in modern elegance. A true Revolution has taken place in this very intimate side of the feminine toilette. In the past, the law that ruled *lingerie* was absolutely unchangeable. Chemises and stockings traversed centuries without undergoing the least Revolution.

But she claimed that this situation had recently changed dramatically: Underwear was now as elegant and luxurious as outer clothing—or even more so. To be pretty "is only half of seduction. Luxury has become the indispensable complement of beauty."[9]

Not surprisingly, fashion magazines tended to emphasize the *elegance* of underwear, more than its potentially seductive qualities. As late as 1902, Mrs. Pritchard stressed repeatedly that "lovely lingerie" did not belong "only to the 'fast'," and that "dainty undergarments . . . are not necessarily a sign of depravity." "The most virtuous of us are now allowed to possess pretty undergarments, without being looked upon as suspicious characters." "Ugliness no longer represents virtue," she insisted, adding somewhat disingenuously that "A wish for dainty underwear is generally actuated by a desire for cleanliness."[10]

Yet by this point Mrs. Pritchard also explicitly linked "exquisite lingerie" and sexual satisfaction within marriage. Mrs. Pritchard was not a "typical" Edwardian fashion writer, since she was unusually outspoken about being sexually attractive to one's husband. (Similar advice seems to appear in America about a decade later.) Nevertheless, she was perfectly respectable. For more than a decade, she wrote a monthly column on "The London and Paris Fashions" for the upper-class periodical *The Lady's Realm*, and was later Fashion Editress for *The Daily Telegraph*.

She was most outspoken in her appropriately named book, *The Cult of Chiffon*, in which she blamed failed marriages on the wife's unwillingness to adopt more seductive lingerie and, by implication, a more seductive attitude toward her husband: "Can one wonder that marriage is so often a failure, and that the English husband of such a class of women goes where he can admire the petticoat of aspirations?" Mrs. Pritchard advised "the irreconcilables among my married friends not to shriek loudly with the company of disappointed spinsters . . . but to try . . . the expedient of a much-befrilled petticoat or some illusions in *robes de nuit*." She was aware that such advice might appear "coarse and unpleasant," but she asked her readers to consider "the pathetic side of the matrimonial life of many of your intimate friends." If a couple were unhappily married, would it not be worthwhile for the wife to attempt to charm her husband with "pretty arts and subtleties," rather than leaving such attractions "to a class of women less favoured than ourselves"? A woman might be "the most virtuous and careful of wives," but if she were "without mystery and without coquetry," she would be "far from attractive to the ordinary man."[11]

La Vie Parisienne

The desirable eroticism of lingerie was recognized some two decades earlier by writers and illustrators for *La Vie Parisienne*. In the 1860s and early 1870s, the focus tended to be on outerwear (theatre dress, ball gowns, coiffures), but in the course of the 1870s and increasingly in the 1880s, the emphasis shifted to lingerie and *déshabillé*. Thus in the story, "The Wedding Presents," the bride's nightgowns introduced themselves as "fine nightgowns of batiste with lace insertions, [and with] a large monogram embroidered on the heart." According to "the voice of good,"

"They will scarcely veil with their pearly transparency your rosy and plump body. Your husband will prefer them to the most sumptuous toilettes and your mirror will tell you that [this style] is . . . what suits you best." Both the wife's economic dependence on her husband and her sexual power over him were indicated next: "It is when you are dressed in them that you will confess the little debts and the large bills . . . . The transparent nightgown is for the woman what the robe is for the lawyer." Her role is presented as a sexual one—as a kind of married mistress, not a housekeeper or mother.

"The voice of evil," on the other hand, warned that sexual relations in marriage were a legal obligation for a wife, and therefore not a pleasure: "You will dread the instant of putting on these too diaphanous nightgowns, because they call to mind the favorable moment for the lover . . . an hour perhaps charming for a lover free to escape . . . but hateful to the one for whom the law imposes it." He implied that a woman obliged to submit to her husband has little chance of manipulating him financially: "And you can acknowledge some bills . . . . This scanty costume will not at all prevent your husband from telling you 'Zut' [No way!]." But existing examples of nightgowns from this period scarcely bear out these descriptions. They remained fairly voluminous and concealing, but presumably the relatively lighter fabrics were perceived as revealing. Both the lace insertions and the monogram were typical of better-quality underclothing of the period. When attempting to elucidate the erotic qualities of garments from the past, the historian must try to see the clothing as it was seen then. Viewed only from the modern perspective, it is difficult to see anything remotely erotic about High Victorian (or even Edwardian) nightgowns. Much of their appeal stemmed from their role as clothing for bed—and thus, by implication, for making love.

Every item of lingerie could arouse the husband's desire for his bride. When the woman wears her crepe de chine peignoir, her husband will give her "a quantity of kisses on the less well defended places." More intimate garments inspired even greater enthusiasm. *Les pantalons*, "decorated with lace and bows of white watered silk" were

> dainty and pretty tight . . . showing the shape of your round thighs and half veiling with their lace your fine, straight knees . . . Your husband will watch you going and coming in the bedroom, smart and coquettish. . . . This will be the moment of hoydenish caresses and of crazy pursuits full of charm.

"How pretty are these cloudy petticoats," murmured "the voice of good":

> You will never be more seductive than when enveloped in their vapor. Your husband, always amorous, would like to put them on you himself, to see you in the form of a 'little dancer,' [in] a corset of white satin and multiple transparent skirts, from which your legs will emerge, rosy under their stockings. . . . He will tell you again that there is nothing comparable to you at the Opera . . . or in Eden!

The image of the husband dressing his wife seems less surprising than his open comparison of her with the dancers at the Opera. "The voice of evil" ignores any possible impropriety, arguing only that "Your luxury of petticoats will shock your husband!"[12] But luxury was part of their appeal.

La Vie Parisienne insisted that "The absolutely elegant *pantalon* in good taste" was "simplicity itself"— but it "can easily cost 20 louis." Certain fabrics, such as linen, batiste, nansouk, or "fine percale" were good, but silk, surah, and chiffon were still less than respectable. Lace, embroidery, pleats, and ribbons were good when applied with discretion (and when the lace was expensive and real)—a petticoat should give "a cloudy effect when the dress is raised "—but overly "frothy" trim or "a large ruff of lace" was tasteless.

The elegant undergarment was "always white," but someone's mistress might wear, say, "the Irresistible" *pantalon* in "flesh-colored batiste" with "rose-colored bows," or "Provocation" in "peach-flower surah." For "high fantasy," drawers might be colored "in nymph's thigh, or blue Danube, or blue Nile, or sickly heliotrope"—but these were really only suitable for the *cocotte* or the *bourgeoise parvenue*. Again, degrees of eroticism and class distinctions are inextricably mixed. Indeed, one puff described "beautiful lingerie" as "aristocratic lingerie."[13]

Other writers of La Vie Parisienne were not always so careful to distinguish between simple and elegant underclothes and those of "fantasy." A puff for "intimate lingerie" from the Maison Berte, for example, used sexual imagery to describe

> the conjugal chemise in Oriental silk or batiste, all shivering with lace, with great tracks of insertions ... transparent crossroads to good places ... Its indiscretions would shock the young girl radiant with seraphic beauty, flower turning into fruit.

Similarly "the *pantalon cherubin*" was described as being "clasped at the knee by a ribbon under which quivers a long flounce of lace," and the flannel night gown with its *jabot* of lace (which sounds modest enough) is called "the *combat* nightgown."[14]

It is somewhat risky, of course, to rely on La Vie Parisienne for accurate descriptions of what married women really wore, since the magazine was directed to the man-about-town, and catered to his erotic fantasies. Some figures are fantastic, and perhaps represent neither wife nor mistress: "The great priestess" seemed to represent the sexual ideal. She wore a "*décolletée* nightgown in black satin ... decorated with mechlin lace (a type that resists more ...)." Perhaps the implication is that other sorts of lace might rip under the strain of sexual intercourse. Most strikingly, this imaginary nightgown is open all down the front: "A true sacerdotal garment. But how to close this jewel-case? No one has ever spoken of that." The nightgown as jewel-case could be interpreted as symbolizing the vagina, as well as implying that the body was a jewel.

Accounts of foreign women often reflected contemporary fantasies about exotic feminine types. The Oriental woman (here, as usual, Middle Eastern or Turkish) was described as spending her days "naked or nearly so"—but at night she is covered with rich fabrics and furs. The woman of the Sudan was virtually naked, but for her jewelry and slippers. Even other Europeans could be shown as being so uninhibited as to dispense with all night-time apparel: "In Italy.—A fig for nightgowns or any other covering! Has she not the mosquito-net crowning the . . . bed like the sail of a schooner? Ah! The mosquitos aren't bored!"[15]

Although nightgowns and lingerie could be erotic, the appeal of the naked body also exerted a strong influence. During the 1890s, when censorship in France was further relaxed, more nudes appeared in *La Vie Parisienne*. To some extent, the magazine's emphasis on lingerie in the 1880s may have represented the closest thing to nudity that the law permitted. Nevertheless, there are also indications that the partially clad female figure was often perceived as *more* erotic than the nude.

The Case of Underpants

Women's underpants (known in England as "drawers" and by the 1880s also as "knickers," and in France as *le caleçon, le culotte, les pantalons,* and *le pantalon féminin*) were only slowly accepted in the course of the nineteenth century, in the face of long and powerful resistance. They were widely perceived as a "demi-masculine" article of dress, and in the early part of the century were worn primarily by some courtesans, actresses, and dancers. Long underpants were then adopted by little girls, and as an infantile mode spread from England to France, to be gradually adopted by respectable women for sporting pursuits, such as horseback riding, and for more active dances, such as the polka and the waltz. But as late as 1873, *Le Sport* argued that while it might be "necessary" for certain pursuits, "it is never gracious . . . . *Le pantalon*, in a word, is a man's article of clothing . . . and because of that, women who have the true intuition of elegance of their sex will always abstain from it."[16]

The development of the swaying crinoline-cage in mid-century may have led to a more general acceptance of feminine underpants, as the immodesty of female trousers began to be outweighed by the danger of being exposed without them. *L'inexpressible* became termed *l'indispensable*. (Although drawers were open up the inside of the legs, a yard or so of chemise was tucked into the drawers, thus shielding the thighs from view.) Doctors also argued that reasons of hygiene (such as the dangers of cold and germs) necessitated the use of drawers, in addition to the chemise and petticoat(s).[17]

As the issue of its indecency faded, it became fashionable and "absolutely modern" to wear drawers. Increasingly, however, drawers were adopted by women of the middle and working classes, from whom the fashionable sought to distinguish themselves. A degree of eroticism was reintroduced to the garment in conjunction with greater elegance of material. Thus Violette maintained that "our *pantalons* of silk, clasped at the knee by a ribbon above a wreath of frothy lace, have lost all resemblence with those *pantalons* made of percale and covering the leg as far as the ankles—very decent, but hideously ugly and bourgeois."[18]

Part of the perceived "ugliness" of the old style of drawers apparently derived from their very decency and modesty, their concealment of the leg. Were the new, fashionable drawers intended to be at least slightly indecent? This perspective appears in the 1887 novel *L'Adorée* by René Maizeroy: "So light, so brief, with cascades of Valenciennes lace and frills of ribbons, these *pantalons* which do not descend beyond the lace garters ... drive a lover crazy better than the immodest state of nudity."[19]

There were dissenters, however, or at least those who pretended to prefer the state of affairs prior to the widespread acceptance of drawers. An article of 1890, "De l'Adultère; conseils pratiques" in the magazine *Gil Blas* presented a negative picture of drawers—from the point of view of an old voyeur:

> ... in my youth, under the Empire, women did not wear drawers ... [and] our imagination climbed the length of their stockings and seduced us into ecstasies toward those regions as intimate as they are delicious. We did not see, but we knew that we could see, should the occasion arise. ... But today ... we know that there our view would be irremediably arrested by an obstacle, that our suggestive voyage would end at a hollow of batiste and we come to a stop at the base of the wall.[20]

If the opportunity for the sight of women's sexual organs had decreased, nevertheless a voyeurism directed toward the sight of the underpants themselves to some extent replaced it. Much of the appeal of dances like the *can can* and the *chahut* derived from the intentional exhibition of the dancers' underpants. Numerous erotic postcards from the 1890s and the early twentieth century showed women exposing their elaborate underpants that made the derriere appear to be enormously expanded. In *My Apprenticeships*, Colette described Willy's apartment as "strewn" with postcards "celebrating the attractions of underclothes ... ribboned drawers, and buttocks."[21]

Modern Society: The Fantasy and "Fetishism" of Underwear

Even the earliest "fetishist" correspondence paid some attention to the subject of underwear. A few *EDM* correspondents, for example, advocated women wearing visible underpants, like those of little girls. By the early 1890s, the correspondence in journals such as *Modern Society* emphasized not only tight-lacing, but also such subjects as the "delicious swish and entrancing rustle" of the silk petticoat. Accounts of "dainty underwear" described "the very thinnest and filmiest" garments, nightgowns in "a kind of silk gauze—so filmy that they can only be worn once," chemises in "coloured gauze," each with a matching "frou-frou jupe." Even *La Vie Parisienne* would have disputed that such garments were worn by "French *grandes dames*." One French woman, for example, was described as wearing "black stockings, black satin drawers trimmed with ecru lace, a black silk chemise . . . yellow satin stays, trimmed with black lace, and yellow garters": "Tout cela c'est pour mon mari, qui adore les peaux blanches!" Another suggestion was to wear crimson drawers and a matching chemise with black stays.[22]

Like the corset correspondents, underwear enthusiasts argued that the modern man resisted marriage, "putting his attentions in quarters where the question of intentions is never raised"; so it was necessary to use erotic lingerie to "pique" his imagination. Alternatively, he might be most attracted by the "diaphanous and cobwebby lace petticoat" *itself*—going to the extent of stealing it from the "high kicking dancer." In reality, such erotic lingerie was still probably mostly worn by courtesans: for example, an "amber silk" chemise was called "the Liane de Pougy chemise."[23]

In other respects, however, this correspondence apparently reflected more specialized erotic interests. Thus, although the "rustle" of the "frou frouing" petticoat was cited by later fashion journalists, here it seemed to form part of a kind of fabric fetishism. Satin, for example, exerted a "fascination" that was related to its texture ("fine," "stiff," "soft"), the "nice noise" it made ("a vague creaking sound"), and its sado-masochistic associations ("satin skin" cried out to be caned), and sometimes transvestism and theft. In a turn-of-the-century medical account, one kleptomaniac reported, "When I can grab some silk, then I am just as if I were drunk. I tremble, although not from fear. . . . I can only think of one thing, to go into a corner where I can rustle it at my ease, which gives me voluptuous sensations even stronger than those I feel with the father of my children."[24] Can such a woman be considered a fetishist, or is this phenomenon a product of the development of the department store, with its peculiarly seductive atmosphere?

The most important point, though, is that these descriptions of lingerie look ahead to those printed in more orthodox fashion journals of the early twentieth century, when color and silk had become more widely accepted. The budding popular interest in erotic lingerie spread throughout society, and may even have influenced sexual fantasies. The corset began to be less important in its own right than as an element of seductive lingerie.

The Iconography of the Corset Advertisement

What was it that *women* wanted for themselves from lingerie and corsets? Although much of the literature on fashion was prescriptive and moralistic (and the literature on corsetry was particularly combative and polarized), advertisements were designed to appeal to the consumer's perceived *desires*, whether or not these conflicted with prescribed behavior. An examination of corset advertisements indicates that the vast majority were directed toward women who were neither dress reformers nor tight-lacers.

Of course, not even children believe all the promises made by advertisers. But even if we assume a degree of exaggeration and outright duplicity, as well as attempts to *create* consumer desires, nevertheless, corset names, images, and product descriptions tell us what manufacturers thought would appeal to women; and they may also provide a clue to the self-images and fantasies of the corsets' wearers.[25] Advertisements also provide an indication of the changing shape of the corset and the ideal torso, as well as the degree of body exposure and erotic imagery permissible in periodicals at any given date.

Trade names of corsets tend to fall readily into thematic groups. Many corset names, such as The Rival Corset ("perfect shape") and Thomson's La Fiancée, promised physical beauty and success in marital competition. The Kyoto Costume Institute has an example of La Fiancée (circa 1884) that is made of cherry pink silk satin with black decorative stitching.

The name "Swanbill" and the logo of a swan gliding past waterplants were probably intended to conjure up the image of a gently curving figure. One Swanbill advertisement shows a bride and a baby, perhaps suggesting that the corset would help a woman win a husband, without injuring their child. Another popular model was Thomson's Glove-Fitting Corset, the name indicating a trim and perfect fit. The sexual symbolism of the swan and the glove are obvious.

One much heralded feature of corset design (evident in the Swanbill advertisement) was the development of slightly different styles of corsets for different figure types—the "stout," the "slim," the "full," the "graceful"—a development that did not necessarily indicate a greater acceptance of alternatives to the "ideal" figure. If anything, the reverse seems more likely, as the various corsets were apparently intended to make their wearers seem to approximate one particular figure type. The Ideal and The Configurateur Corsets, for example, were both designed to "transform" a "thin bust," by lacing padded "regulators" inside the breast gores. Others, such as The Bon Ton Corset and Dr. Warner's Patent Flexible Hip Corset, had "self-adjusting or laced hips" that could also be "regulated at the desire of the wearer." The Empress Corset was "extra long" and "clasps the hips tightly."

Corsets that were possibly intended for would-be tight-lacers are Giraud's Small Waist Corset (sizes 15 to 23) for "exceptional figures," The Willowaist Corset, The Ringwaist Corset, and The Princess Wasp Waist (the last by Madame Dowding, who also produced a corset called The Little Black Cat, as well as a number of corsets for men). These were in the minority, however. The only popular corset with such associations was Thomson's Glove-Fitting Corset, which was recommended in *EDM* and *The Corset and the Crinoline*.

More commonly, beauty, rather than a small waist per se, was emphasized: The Enchantress, The May Queen, The Mignon, The Perfection,

The Statuesque, L'Irrésistible, La Délice, Le Svelte, The Serpentine, The Radiant. Corset names evoked images of mythical or even divine beauty, among them CP à la Sirène (after the dangerous water-spirits), Le Corset Diane (named after the virginal moon goddess Diana and billed as fulfilling "The dream of pretty Parisiennes"), and The IC Persephone Corset (after the fertility goddess).

The range of names seems to have expanded in the early twentieth century. Many evoked figures from mythology, history, and historical legend: Le Corset Déesse, The Venus Corset, The Diana, The Leda ("Queen of Corsets" and, of course, Jupiter's lover, whom he took after assuming the form of a swan), The Cleopatra, The Sappho, La Samothrace, La Sylphide, The Portia, The Ninon, and Le Corset Marie Antoinette.

Two corsets that probably referred to famous women of the day were The Corset Liane (after the courtesan Liane de Pougy) and The Rejane (after the actress). By the early twentieth century, acting was perceived less as a scandalous profession, and more as an exciting one. Thus the boringly named H. S. Corsets were advertised in *Myra's Journal* (January , 1901) with the recommendation that "Among Actresses these beautiful Corsets are held in high favour. . . . Testimonials from all the Leading London Actresses, the Elite, and the Medical Profession." Some corsets carried ordinary female names such as Jessica, Lilian, and Stella, but others had a distinctly exotic sound: Idilia, Batyra, and Minuska.

Many corset names were romantic, such as L'Aimée, Le Rêve, and L'Apparition. Some in this category were named for jewels, such as The Sapphire, or compared to jewels, as when The Specialité Corset was "likened to that Gem of Gems, the Diamond." L'Écrin was a suggestive name, since in dream symbolism a jewelbox is thought to refer to the vagina. Flower names such as The Columbine and The Asphodel were feminine, while The Grand Calyx Corset of Madame Guillot, "creator of mystery," implied more specifically that the woman was a flower within the corset.

The Papillon Corset was also romantic, but some names present a surprising contrast to this theme: there was also La Militaire and Le Corset à la victoire. The Oracle Corset hinted at a mysterious (but presumably happy) future—and was specifically associated with "the pretty Mantle sisters" at the Opera and with "Madame la Comtesse d'H——, née de B——, known for having the prettiest waist in Paris."

Corset names also evoked status—The Princess, La Châtelaine, The Lady Vivian, The Prima Donna, The Duchess Corset and Thomson's Empress Corset. The box top for the ABC Empress Queen Corset showed a picture of Queen Victoria, perhaps indicating fantasies of power and patriotism rather than sex appeal. On the other hand, it was thought by some that "The possession of a slender waist is a question of race,"[26] so that corsets with "aristocratic" names might also implicitly have promised a "refined" figure.

Some corset names emphasized chic—such as The Bon Ton Corset, or indeed, in English-speaking countries, any corset with a French name.

The International Corset presumably had cosmopolitan connotations, while The Corset of the Future was undoubtedly supposed to be ultra-fashionable. Other names referred to a specific type of corset, such as Le Corset Louis XV, and the supposedly "classical" (i.e., quasi-Empire) Ceinture Athenienne. Could The Sunflower Corset have been intended for Aesthetes?

Illustrations also formed an important component of corset advertisements. Prior to the mid–1880s, most advertisements did not portray the corseted female figure, but rather only an illustration of the corset itself, sometimes accompanied by a picture of a clothed female figure. It seems likely that publishers were reluctant to print "indecent" illustrations of women in their underwear. (There were, however, some fashion plates that showed corsets being worn.) By the 1880s and early 1890s, it became more acceptable to show women wearing corsets. The half-length female figure in a corset, while remaining popular into the twentieth century, seems to have formed the link between the earlier illustrations of an isolated corset and those that showed the full-length corseted figure. At first rather sketchy and small in scale, these illustrations became more detailed and elaborate. By the turn of the century, they were often fairly erotic genre scenes of one or more women in a state of undress in boudoirs or bedrooms, engaged in a variety of activities—such as looking in a mirror, sleeping on a sofa, being laced up by a maid, and so on. This development probably did not go unprotested. In the 1890s, the National Vigilance Association (a prominent English social purity organization) attempted to censor theatre posters and "corset and lingerie displays" of which it disapproved. Certain corset advertisements in America were also censored.[27]

There is sometimes a note of voyeurism in the portrayal of semi-clad women in an intimate setting. This appears quite clearly in an American corset card of the mid–1880s: "THE SECRET OUT AT LAST—WHY *MRS. BROWN* HAS SUCH A *PERFECT* FIGURE," which shows a woman peeking through a key-hole into Mrs. Brown's bedroom. Mrs. Brown stands in her corset, looking at herself in a mirror. This voyeurism focused on self-admiration or on the image of one or more clothed or corseted women (never men) looking at a woman friend in her new corset.

Illustrations sometimes portrayed the woman in conjunction with some suitably appealing familiars, such as kittens or cupids. The woman herself could be transformed into a fantasy image, such as a mermaid in a striped corset, rising from the sea. Some illustrations imply a romantic story, such as the reception of a love letter. One especially erotic corset advertisement appeared in 1901 in *The Gentlewoman*, showing a beautiful sleeping woman on a sofa. Her lacy peignoir is open, revealing her corseted torso above a smooth petticoat ending in a mass of frills. The caption reads: "THE SPECIALITÉ CORSET IS A DREAM OF COMFORT."

While illustrations and corset names often appealed subliminally to women's fantasies and desires, the accompanying text focused on issues of conscious concern to women. Descriptions generally included claims of quality and novelty, and information on available materials, colors, shapes, prices, and (sometimes) sizes. Almost always touted were the improved and elegant appearance produced by the corset, and its support and comfortable fit. Durability, stylishness, and patented improvements referring either to corset construction or the correction of particular figure problems were also often cited. Toward the end of the century, the attractive appearance of the corset as an item of lingerie was increasingly stressed.

It seems that what women wanted most from a corset was "A perfect figure guaranteed with ease" (circa 1881). They wanted "Corsets that make my figure so much admired" (1885)—not so much a *very* small-waisted figure, as an "elegant" figure on which a fashionable dress would fit well, since "The object of dress is . . . to display to the best advantage the female form divine" (1884).

Different corsets were desirable for different occasions. For mornings at home, for summer, for sport and for wearing beneath a tea-gown, a woman wanted a short and lightly boned corset or corselet permitting "perfect ease and comfort," flexibility, and support for the bust; for daytime, an elegant design; and for evening, a low-cut, well-boned, and especially stylish corset—one that was chic in design and made of beautiful material, perhaps matching her petticoat.

In general, although "uncomfortable and troublesome" corsets were condemned, the vast majority of advertisements focused primarily on appearance. There were relatively few advertisements for corded (rather than boned) corsets or for other "healthy" corsets, such as those made of wool or "cellular" material, or those with shoulder straps. Some women

The Specialité Corset is a Dream of Comfort. Advertisement from *The Gentlewoman* (1901). Courtesy of The Gallery of English Costume, Platt Hall, Manchester.

(and men) with health problems—such as "nervous exhaustion," 'Brain Fag," gout, "female irregularities," lumbago, hysteria, and consumption— did have recourse to "the marvellous health-giving properties" of the "Electric Corset (1880s through 1905). These extensive claims may be a response to the equally sweeping indictments of the corset. Many of the same illnesses are cited. Nevertheless, although most women apparently ignored the attacks on the corset, a number of advertisers believed that many women wanted a "hygienic" corset—as long as it was also seductive and elegant.

Indeed, *the* fashionable corset of the early twentieth century was intended to be a "hygienic corset." A French corsetière with a degree in medicine, Madame Inez Gâches-Sarraute, designed the new corset with a straight busk, because she believed the busk that curved inward at the waist was unhealthy. The inward pressure at the waist "forced the organs downward," whereas her straight-fronted corset would support the abdomen and "add to the effects of nature." Furthermore, her corset, being lower on top, would not suppress the bust.[28] In theory, it might have been a better design, but when laced even moderately tightly, it produced if anything a *more* "distorted" figure, known as the S-bend, with the stomach pushed back, the breasts thrown forward, and the back arched. Yet the straight-fronted corset seems to have been adopted quite rapidly:

> There is in Paris a new corset, which is the rage. . . . The new straight-fronted corset . . . is likely to create a new style of waist and figure entirely, and it is in every way, a more hygienic and healthy garment than any of the old-fashioned stays. . . . The waist is not nearly so small as formerly, a much more important point in the figure now being the long, straight-sloping line in the front. The new cut of corset, of course, drops the bust, and to attain that curved look so essential to a good figure it is necessary for thin women to have a ruching or even two ruchings of ribbon put inside the new, low-busted corset.[29]

The focus of the figure begins to shift from the waist to the bosom.

The Eroticism of Lingerie

The intimate quality of lingerie is a valued erotic consideration. It lies next to the skin, and is only seen by the wearer and the lover. Octave Uzanne compared the woman in lingerie to "a tinted flower, whose innumerable petals become more and more beautiful and delicate as you reach the sweet depths of the innermost petals. She is like a rare orchid, who surrenders the fragrance of her mysteries only in the intimacies of love." And Emile Zola described at length the lingerie on display at a department store, that looked "as if a group of pretty girls had undressed, piece by piece, down to the satin nudity of their skin."[30]

Mrs. Pritchard, of course, believed that attractive negligée garments "are a pretty compliment to your husband." And at least some Victorian brides agreed. When the Englishwoman Ellen Peel married in 1890, her uncle gave her £100 for a wedding present, and she recorded in her diary that she spent £90 on *under* linen, but it is lovely, nightgowns especially, I hope *he* will like them." Lady Naomi Mitchison also recalled buying her trousseau during the First World War, and leaving the store in tears when her mother and the saleswoman began to comment on her nightgowns.[31]

Marguerite d'Aincourt, author of *Études sur le costume féminin* (1883), assumed that the bride would initially be too modest and shy to wear seductive lingerie and *déshabillé*; but that they should still be part of her trousseau, because she would come to appreciate them, just as, implicitly, she would come to enjoy sex:

> Do not describe [the conjugal chemise] to young girls; one should respect the exquisite and a little inordinate modesty of these seraphims, but have it placed in their bridal trousseau. They will not wear it at first, but after some time, they will understand the value of this Orient silk or batiste . . . [with] insertions of lace, all quivering with the Valenciennes which decorates it in flounces at the hem. They will get used to this transparent web, which, in front—from the start of the throat to the waist—reveals the charming graces of a young and supple bust.[32]

In Elinor Glyn's racy novel, *The Vicissitudes of Evangeline* (1905), the character Mary Mackintosh is shocked by Evangeline's Doucet nightgown, which is described as being virtually see-through and cut low in the neck: "I consider this garment not in any way fit for a girl—or for any good woman, for that matter." When Evangeline points out that it is very becoming, she replies, indignantly, "But no nice-minded woman wants to look becoming in bed!"[33] Glyn, though, presents Mackintosh as a ridiculous prude, a view that she presumably expected her readers to share. More unrealistic is her portrayal of the unmarried but independent Evangeline in such a nightgown. For most women, lovely lingerie came, if it came at all, as part of the erotic initiation of marriage.

In early twentieth-century France, the authors of books and articles on beauty and dress were sometimes surprisingly insistent about the erotic qualities of lingerie and its role in lovemaking. In *Tous les secrets de la femme* (1907), the Baronne d'Orchamps maintained that "Nothing equals the voluptuous power of feminine underwear [*les dessous*]." It plays a crucial role in the continued seduction of the husband: "At the apparition of these veils," an "ineluctible rapture . . . comes over the masculine brain." Their "vaporous ingenuity and involved style add to the mysterious and tempting power of the desired treasures in proportion that the woman feigns to protect and distance them."[34]

Similarly, in *Le Bréviaire de la femme* (1903), the Comtesse de Tramar argued that the very difficulty of "the dismantling of the fortress," by "exasperating anticipations," functioned "to convince the mortal of the supreme favor that he is going to receive." The act of slowly undressing marked "the amorous stations of desire." Yet, she believed, many women were still afraid that they would be "compromised if they began to appear in those *déshabillés* that seemed to be reserved only for those whose profession is to seduce." Tramar insisted, though, that "The husband has the right to see pretty things"—"elegant and gay" lingerie was at least as important as "good silver" or "a well decorated house" with a "pretty nuptial chamber." In other words, the wife should be not only a homemaker, but also a lover. As a good lover, she should know that fine underwear was of "essential importance":

> It is the veiled, secret part, the desired indiscretion conjured up; the man in love expects silky thrills, caresses of satin, charming rustles, and is disappointed by an unshapely mass of rigid lingerie. . . . It is a disaster![35]

This type of advice, taken together with the fact that by the Edwardian period lingerie had become both increasingly luxurious and a focus of journalistic interest, lends support to the idea that people were becoming more open about their sexuality. Materials that had been *risqué* in the 1880s became increasingly acceptable over the next decades, and fine Edwardian lingerie was made of "all the downy and delicate fabrics of *froufroutage*." The poem "Frou-Frou" in *The Lady's Realm* exemplified the related emphasis on auditory eroticism: "The very rustle of her gown as she goes by I love to hear . . . I wait your coming 'Frou-Frou—Frou-Frou.'" [36]

Even color became more acceptable, although there were still those who argued that "Color, in the secret clothing of women, is an entirely modern taste, deriving no doubt from the nervousness that torments our imagination, from the dulling of our sensations, from that unceasingly unsatisfied desire that causes us to suffer . . . and that we apply to all manifestations of our feverish life."[37] It all sounds rather ominous, and if colored underwear were at all widely perceived as an expression of a decadent and neurasthenic craving, it is not surprising that some fashion journalists advised their readers to choose white. Even *La Vie Parisienne* had warned that men who liked black underwear "need to see white skin emerging from a black sheath, because white skin in itself hardly arouses [them] any more"—and women were advised that white underwear sufficed for the virile man.[38]

In addition to being an element of seduction, "elegant underclothes" were also a source of "personal satisfaction" for the woman herself. "This paradise of fine and soft lingerie . . . this warm and luxurious temple that shakes at our least shiver; this little fortune that the elegant woman hides under her dress" serve "to tranquilize" her. "This consciousness of our femininity" only develops "when, in all disinterestedness, for ourselves alone . . . we have obtained from the lightly touching and delicate underclothes" certain sensations "for our skin"—"the discreet lightness of breath and the penetrating savor of the caress."

Here D'Orchamps anthropomorphizes the lingerie; it produces tactile sensations akin to those of a lover, and responds to the body it envelops:

In its silky thrill, this luminous and glittering froth overflows from beneath the prudish, enveloping exterior clothing—does it not appear as if animated by the warmth and clandestine caresses that it ceaselessly exchanges with the palpitating silhouette within?[39]

Sensations of softness and warmth and of silky materials gently rubbing against the skin, an intimate connection with the body, a combination of secrecy and visual effect, and a justifiable sense of luxury—a "little fortune"—were all components of lingerie that contributed to reinforcing a sense of femininity.

Fashion historians have referred to the "body-clothes unit," but d'Orchamps distinguished sharply between underwear, which has a close connection with the body and "shakes at our least shiver," and exterior clothing that is "prudish" and "enveloping." Some contemporaries, indeed, suggested that "The beauty and elegance of the 'underneath' developed in logical proportion" to the "severity and simplicity" of the increasingly popular "English tailor-made style." If the tailor-made was somewhat austerely elegant, luxurious lingerie was overtly feminine. Then, too, although the tailor-made could be an expensively understated garment, characterized by "elegance of cut," it had also been widely copied, "producing a leveling effect on the exterior clothing." Lovely lingerie reasserted both femininity and status.[40]

If the intimate quality of underwear was itself a valued erotic consideration, such garments were also partially revealed in less intimate situations. "Without knowing it perhaps, assuredly without wanting it—never confess it!—we have all, one day or another, benefited" from the effect of the sight of a petticoat, produced when "the sudden overflowing of the indiscreet flood . . . of our silky muslins" was glimpsed "under the lifting of the skirt": it had a "stupefying effect on the imagination of the adored master." Part of the appeal of this flood of petticoats derived from their being hidden under a "quite simple, quite modest dress."[41]

That petticoats were in fact designed to be exhibited and heard is clear from the lively interest and detailed descriptions offered by fashion journalists and novelists. Like tea-gowns (which also became a "mania" in the early twentieth century), petticoats hovered on the borderline between secret clothing and fashionable dress. Corsets, although hidden, became increasingly elegant—made of silk in "a prism of delicious colors," embroidered with flowers, and often matching the elaborately decorated petticoat. Indeed, it was this elegance of lingerie and corsetry that seems to have appealed most to women. Who could have resisted a petticoat of "pale blue satin . . . painted with bunches of violets and cut with a curved edge . . . below which falls a shaped flounce of coffee-coloured lace, mounted on a blue silk flounce," or a corset of "beautiful brocade in a Louis Seize design of violets and ribbons on a ground of palest pink and blue shot cream"? And these were by no means the most extravagant creations of the time.[42]

Giovanni Boldini, *Crossing the Street* (1875). Courtesy of The Sterling and Francine Clark Art Institute, Williamstown, Massachusetts.

If the austerity of mid-Victorian lingerie indicated not a dislike of sexuality, but an attitude of relative reserve toward its expression, the growing acceptance of erotic and luxurious lingerie and *déshabillé* seemed to indicate a greater willingness to celebrate erotic beauty and marital sexuality. The expansion of colors, materials, and decorations in underwear was paralleled by a growing acceptance of artificial beauty aids after 1880, and again especially after 1900. Although outer clothing continued to balance sexual display and sexual modesty in the manner characteristic of the nineteenth century as a whole, intimate garments and those worn in semi-private settings became more disphanous, soft, and overtly seductive. One garment in particular—the *robe d'interieur* or tea-gown—assumed a special importance, since it alone was not primarily confined "to the bedroom and the boudoir."[43] It is my belief that the tea-gown played a significant role in the development of modern fashion, due to its unique position halfway between dress and undress. Initially akin to the humble dressing gown, the tea-gown became an increasingly elaborate but still private dress. Not only did it evade the otherwise almost universal requirement of corsetry, but its image as an "artistic" garment of "poetry" and "fantasy" permitted designers and wearers a greater degree of experimentation that helped pave the way for the radical "new look" in female fashion and beauty. To a large extent, it was via the tea-gown that many of the design ideas associated with the "aesthetic" or "healthy and artistic" dress movement entered the mainstream of fashion, in the process shedding any connatations of minority anti-fashion and austere sartorial morality. The "Cult of Chiffon" extended beyond lingerie to embrace evening gowns, blouses, tea-gowns—and, most important, attitudes toward feminine beauty in general.

Into the Twentieth Century

11

The Changing Ideal of Feminine Beauty

In the late nineteenth and early twentieth centuries, the High Victorian ideal of feminine beauty developed into something that we might call the Edwardian or Belle Epoque ideal. This almost immediately began to evolve further; and between about 1908 and 1910, a new look had appeared that was popularly associated with the designer Paul Poiret, and that in retrospect can be seen as the precursor of the Twenties look. There was a reciprocal influence between the changing attitudes toward sexual beauty and the evolving ideal of feminine physical beauty, on the one hand, and the development of women's fashions, on the other.

The New Religion of Beauty

The literature on feminine beauty changed significantly during the last decade of the nineteenth century and the first decade of the twentieth. Fashion and beauty writers increasingly stressed the erotic elements of feminine beauty—not yet, as in the Twenties, by reference to "sex appeal," but more obliquely, by emphasizing the importance of "personal magnetism," "fascination," and "charm"—terms that strongly implied the property of attracting others, and in particular members of the opposite sex:

> A woman's greatest attraction lies in her femininity. Far above symmetry of form or the most perfect features must certainly be placed that wonderful and mysterious psycho-physical quality of personal magnetism, which, for lack of a better definition, we will designate as soul-beauty.[1]

"Soul-beauty" appears to have been very different from the inner spiritual beauty that so many Victorian writers had praised. By the turn of the century, writers were much less likely to posit a rigid distinction between "true" inner beauty and its "false" and artificial counterpart. On the contrary, they usually argued that "the aids of adventitious arts and the advantages of a fine setting" were both necessary and desirable.[2]

Some writers went so far as to argue that devotion to personal appearance constituted a "new religion" for women. One of the most outspoken proponents of this view in Great Britain was Mrs. Eric Pritchard, who argued that physical beauty attracted men more than "the cultivation of intellect alone." Although most women were not "gloriously fashioned by Nature . . . fortunately . . . there has arisen a cult which has become nearly as effectual . . . as personal beauty. . . . And this new religion is 'smartness'." With the aid of dress, women could achieve an approximation of beauty that would give them (sexual) "power" over men.[3]

Many of her contemporaries gave similar advice. Even Mrs. Pritchard's quasi-mystical stress on the "cult of chiffon" and the "new religion" of chic had their counterparts elsewhere. The Comtesse de Tramar wrote books on feminine beauty with deliberately "religious" titles, such as *Le Bréviaire de la femme. Pratiques secrètes de la beauté* (1903) and *L' Évangile profane. Rite féminin* (1905). Just as Mrs. Pritchard had compared the cult of chiffon with the Christian religion, so also did Tramar compare the feminine rite of beautification and adornment with the sacred rites of the Catholic Church. She maintained that in the past the "fathers of the Church" had not scorned to occupy themselves with the "frivolous questions" of dress and adornment,

> finding in them a thrilling, immediate interest. This interest, it is true, revealed itself on the whole in a severe censure; alongside sacred rites, was born a special rite, which effaces them, *le rite féminin*; it is, in effect, an essentially feminine religion, which woman will practice across the centuries, a devotee of this cult, of this ceremony, which creates her happiness, placing in her soul infinite ecstasys.[4]

The severe censure of churchmen was apparently irrelevant to modern women. But religious terminology—"gospel," "rite," "cult," "ceremony," "breviary," etc.—must have retained some kind of significance. Perhaps it implied the force of revealed truth, the dedication of "devotees," and the promise of some kind of salvation.

In the overheated prose typical of this type of literature, Mrs. Pritchard focused on pleasing men, while Tramar emphasized the pleasure that women obtained from adorning themselves. At least in part, the feminine rite of self-beautification was auto-erotic. The old strictures against "vanity" seem to have disappeared altogether. Of course, Tramar also meant that beauty inspired love, and that this produced happiness, but happiness was associated with ruling men through their sexual passion, and not with either feminine submission or the moral improvement of men. Indeed, one of her later books was titled *Que veut la femme? Être jolie, être aimée et dominer* (1911). The Baronne d'Orchamps also maintained in *Tous les secrets de la femme* (1907) that the purpose of her book was "to augment woman's chances of happiness through a knowledge of her

amorous resources . . . [and] means of seduction." Her elegance would be
"alluring" and her beauty would be constantly adapted "to the fantasies
and gestures of love."[5] Although there is little hard evidence, it is possible
that this new tone was related to the wider use of contraceptives, which
began to free women from fear of unwanted pregnancies.

As the conscious pursuit of sexual satisfaction within marriage was
increasingly emphasized, men also offered advice on what Max O'Rell
called "the gentle art of ruling a husband." In his very popular book, *Her
Royal Highness Woman* (1901), he playfully maintained that "Men are
ruled, as children are, by the prospect of a reward. The reward of your
husband is your amiability, your sweetness, your devotion, and your
beauty, of which you should take a constant care."[6] The message for
women was that happiness lay in loving and being loved—and to win love,
a woman should be beautiful, seductive, and elegant. Yet this was also the
period in which increasing numbers of women were following careers and
avocations in the wider world. Even fashion magazines joined the chorus,
proclaiming the appearance of the "New Woman" and the "girl of
Today"—figures regarded with considerable ambivalence by the general
society.

Occasionally, a writer would insist, a little defensively, that her beauty
advice was directed only toward virtuous married women. There was,
apparently, still something slightly suspect about this new type of beauty
book. Thus, the Baroness Staffe maintained in her book *The Lady's
Dressing Room* (1892):

> I recognise only the woman anxious to preserve the love of the man of her
> heart, . . . the woman whose wish it is to remain attractive only to the father
> of her children. . . . I flatter myself that . . . the book . . . may be useful to
> virtuous women who wish to be happy.

She specifically rejected those "women . . . who, led astray by a perverted
desire to please, obtain their power by injurious means. . . . The sanctum
where a goddess dwells" [the lady's dressing room] should not be
"defile[d] . . . by the mention of tricks and falsehood." It is difficult to
determine what deceits she disapproved of, however, since, although she
professed to deplore the "unbecoming mania for painting," she gave
advice on rouge, powder, and certain "harmless" hair dyes, such as henna,
walnut juice, and tea. She also defended the use of the corset, when laced
moderately. If she was lenient about petty deceptions, it was because they
were employed in a good cause: "It is not enough to be a good wife and a
good mother in order to retain the affections of your husband . . . ; you
must also be an attractive and pleasant woman."[7]

Artifice was far more acceptable than hiterto. According to S——
G——, author of *The Art of Being Beautiful* (1903), "Complaints against
artificiality will not hold in these modern times where we are bound to
accept civilization altogether or leave it." The "entirely unaided face" was
superceded by the *discreet* use of rouge, powder, and colored lip salve;

while hair dyes and the use of false hair built up over pads gave the impression that women were "crowned with a coronet of . . . hair." Max Beerbohm suggested that these changes signaled that "The season of the unsophisticated is gone by" and "a new epoch of artifice" had begun.[8]

As for "the ethical side of clothes," for many writers this seemed to have evolved into the problem of whether "dress is, or is not, part of our duty to society." The answer seemed to be positive. As Lillian Joy put it, "Afterall, most of us *is* dress, so we may as well do what we can to make it beautiful. There is only just our head of our real selves sticking out at the top, and that we can't remake in a superior fashion." (Except, others might have added, through cosmetics and the employment of a good hairdresser.) In her book *Usages du monde; Règles du savoir-vivre dans la société moderne* (1899), Staffe added that elegance was more than a question of clothes. There also existed "moral elegance," which was the opposite of vulgarity, mercantilism, and egoism.[9] The element of class distinction was clearly important in the sartorial code, and may have reflected growing social tensions below the surface of the "Belle Epoque."

The significance of the "new religion of beauty," the greater openness about sartorial "amorous resources," and the increased acceptability of "artifice," are difficult to interpret in terms of attitudes toward sexuality. Similarly, the corresponding lessening (but by no means disappearance) of emphasis on strictures about spiritual beauty, true versus false beauty, and the connection between the beautiful and the good cannot be viewed as meaning that dress was now perceived as morally neutral. There were still many strict rules governing the manners and morals of dress and adornment. On the other hand, more people were apparently willing to accept that the "sophisticated" married woman could be erotically attractive without being in any way immoral.

Yet just as the "prudishness" of the Victorians has been grossly overstated, so also (in popular histories at least) has the sexual liberation of the Edwardian period. Much has been made of the lives and loves of society beauties like Lily Langtry and courtesans like Cleo de Merode, but their experiences prove as little about the lives of the majority of women as did the experiences of earlier "pretty horsebreakers" like Cora Pearl. Staffe, for example, emphasized that, whether married or single, a woman had to maintain considerable reserve with "le gentleman." She could never be alone with a man, without compromising her honor and (if married) the honor of her husband. Even if a woman were unhappy with her husband, she should never aspire to be another man's friend, "even in all innocence." "It is playing with fire. . . . Resign yourself, lose yourself completely in your children."[10]

Changing attitudes toward the erotic aspects of beauty had only a subtle influence on fashion. The tea-gown (which had existed since the 1870s) was very popular in some circles and lingerie became more seductive. But outer dress covered as much of the body as previously. Materials, colors,

Advertisement for The London Corset Company's Tricot Corset (1905). Courtesy of the Musée des Arts Décoratifs, Paris, Maciet Collection.

and decoration became simultaneously more dainty and more magnificent—as, in a way, did the ideal woman herself.

The Cult of Chiffon

Le style 1900 was characterized by a curvilinear line that was somewhat more subtly "flowing" than that of the Victorian period(s). It was a sinuous Art Nouveau line, and, indeed, the ornamentation on dress and fashion plates often was derived from the Art Nouveau style in the other decorative arts. The hourglass figure of the Victorian beauty evolved into an S-shape, as the Junoesque curves of the Edwardian beauty were forced into a corset that threw her bosom forward and her hips back, and elongated her waist. Tight, boned bodices were often replaced by soft blouses and shirt-waists. Fashion magazines described the "blouse as "all-important," "the be-all and end-all of the average wardrobe." "No material was too gorgeous for it, no elaboration was held superfluous." The petite Early Victorian beauty grew steadily taller and somewhat sturdier over the course of the nineteenth century; by the turn of the century, the ideal beauty was tall and statuesque, "superb," "magnificent," "splendid." Similarly, the bonnet of the Mid-Victorian period and the pretty and even frivolous hats of the High Victorian period gave way to very large and elaborate hats, often decorated with feathers, and worn pinned onto masses of upswept hair. Large amounts of magnificent jewelry (sometimes imitation), and over-sized accessories (purses, stoles, muffs, fans) also contributed to the Edwardian woman's larger-than-life image.

The ideal feminine image was not only one of "magnificence and splendour," however, but also one of "exquisite daintiness" and *froufrou* seductiveness. "*Le style 1900* . . . assure[d] the triumph of *déshabillé*." Evening dresses, tea-gowns, and lingerie were often made of soft, light, "clinging," and even semi-"transparent" materials (such as chiffon, lawn, muslin, faille, and thin silks such as crepe de chine, together with much lace). The most popular colors were tender, delicate pastels. Fashion journalists described dresses as "simple evening seductions . . . irresistible confections of tulle and net . . . painted mousselines de soie, delicately tinted chiffon" that were intended to produce an effect of "adorable frothiness" and "delicacy." Presumably, the wearers were also supposed to look seductive, adorable, and irrisistible. Perhaps uncharitably, the fashion historian Alison Gernsheim has characterized the ideal Edwardian beauty as a woman of "massive daintiness."[11]

Superb Physical Proportions

The physical ideal at the turn of the century was the woman with "fascinating and beautiful curves." The "fine figure" was "perfectly free from all scrawny and hollow places," with "a bust as full, plump, and firm as you could desire." Lucille recalled that her fashion models were "six foot one of perfect symmetry" and "statuesque": "No one of them weighed under eleven stone, and several of them weighed considerably more. They were 'big girls' with 'fine figures.' . . . It was the day of tall women with gracious curves." The thin woman was given short shrift and was rudely told to "cover some of her angles." If anything, the Edwardian beauty was taller, weighed more, and had a larger bosom than her predecessor.[12]

The Victorians had favored a curvacious hourglass figure, with a full bosom, small waist, and wide hips. By the turn of the century, the ideal

Tea-Gown. Photograph courtesy of The Gallery of English Costume, Platt Hall, Manchester.

Unidentified English Corset Advertisement (ca. 1903). Courtesy of the Musée des Arts Décoratifs, Paris, Maciet Collection.

figure apparently had an even more well-developed bosom but perhaps somewhat slimmer hips. Although a small waist remained highly desirable, there were far fewer of the long discussions on its merits and demerits that had previously been so common. The changing shape of the corset, and in particular the development of the straight-front corset around 1900, resulted in a somewhat different stylization of the female torso. The long, straight busk pushed the stomach in and threw the bust forward. Perhaps because of this new corset shape and the forward leaning stance that it promoted, the waist, per se, became less of a focal point, while the bosom was emphasized to a greater extent.

Alexander Walker's early Victorian trinity of beauties—Diana, Venus, and Minerva—was replaced by Juno, Venus, and Psyche. The third, the slender "girlish figure," was least admired, and while some preferred Venus with her "well-developed and prominent" bust and slim waist, others favored the Junoesque woman, whose bust was full "even to embarassing opulence." Or, as Sonia Keppel recalled, "In those days, the contours of Ceres were more fashionable than those of Venus, and my mother's ripe curves were much admired. To conform to such standards, handkerchiefs padded out some of the bodices of her flatter-chested friends."[13]

A plethora of advertisements for creams, potions, and pills promised to produce "a perfectly formed BUST." "Royal Creme" was supposed to increase the size of the bosom by "four to five inches." Another advertisement claimed that its (rather mysterious) product "increases the bust . . . six inches and makes the arms and neck plump and round." The user would "gain fifteen to thirty pounds more in weight and round out the entire form . . . until [she was] entirely developed." Widely advertised in France were "les Pilules Orientales," which promised to provide "that . . . opulence of . . . the bust" that is "regarded as the most perfect expression of Beauty, and a certain sign of flourishing health."[14]

Bust improvers became more common. Many were, in essence, boned or padded camisoles, but more elaborate devices were also available, such as "pneumatic bust forms," alleged to be "light as air" and undetectable "by sight or touch," that promised to give the wearer "the admirable and superb proportions of the ideal figure." To some extent, the design of the new corset made some form of bust bodice a necessity, since the straight busk would have made a corset that was high in the front too uncomfortable. Bust bodices were not designed to lift the bosom up, but only to support and pad it. In fact, the Edwardian bosom was worn conspicuously low.

The design of the dress bodice was somewhat loose and pouched, tending to conceal the division between the breasts, and producing the effect of a mono-bosom, in contrast to the more recognizable curves of the Victorian bosom. It has been suggested that this "mono-bosom" reflected an unwillingness to admit that women had two breasts, and that it was intended to present "an impressive but innocuous outline." Such a conclusion is probably unwarranted. Although some bust bodices were in the form of a single rounded bolster, others padded each breast; furthermore, even during the Victorian period, the boning and lining of the dress bodice had not emphasized the shape of the individual breasts as much as the curve of the bosom as a whole. The fashions of the early twentieth century "had the advantage, from a mature woman's point of view, of allowing the bust to be very big without distracting from the impression of elegance."[15] The long, sloping sine-curve of the Edwardian bosom complemented the line of the corset, whereas breasts that protruded straight out would have tipped the figure too far forward. But there should be no historical confusion between the definition of the ideal bosom, per se, and the *stylization* of the dress bodice, with its pouched and even drooping front.

Not only the bosom, but the ideal woman herself, was "pink and white and rounded in form." According to the Baroness Staffe, "An angular form and a want of flesh that displays the skeleton under the skin are considered a disgrace in a woman."[16] Although the dress and petticoat(s) hid the shape of the legs, these, too, were supposed to be round and plump. D'Orchamps described the ideal leg in some detail, since "its ample and pale pink roundness . . . is certainly one of the most incontestible ornaments of the feminine body." She maintained that a "plump" thigh attracted the admiration of "the contemplator." This would, of course, be a very private view, the thigh being "at the supreme center of modesties." Modesty did not, however, prohibit her from tracing the line of the leg: "Delicately shaded, at the summit, by the secret fleece of Venus, [the thigh] is delineated as far as the graceful nodosity of the knee . . . end[ing] in the elegant and round calf." Tramar's description was more prosaic: "The thighs are round, the knees smooth, allowing the calf to stand out, in order to give an elegant line to the leg."[17]

These descriptions indicate once again that the ideal of physical beauty can not simply be translated into the terms of fashionable dress. If to some extent the shifting erogenous zone *of fashion* moved gradually from the waist to the bosom, nevertheless the slender waist and well-padded legs and derriere remained important in erotic terms. With regard to dress, the emphasis on the full bosom was reflected in the extreme popularity of the soft blouse.

The ideal bosom may also have reflected the social and erotic importance of the matron. There is considerable evidence that fashions were designed with the mature woman in mind, not only because she tended to have more money, but because she represented the feminine ideal. We read that "The typical woman of today, admired and quoted [is] the woman of thirty or thereabouts." An essay on "Love at 35" suggested that girls experience only "puppy love," while older women learn the art of loving through experience: "We feel the appeal of differing manifestations of sexual attraction." The many descriptions of society women overwhelmingly focused on older women, who were described as "handsome," "regal," "magnificent," and "beautiful" in fashions that are "singularly suggestive," "tempting," and "captivating." Lucille recalled that "As a general rule the fashions were created for older women, and were only adapted for the *jeune fille*, often very unsuitably at that."[18]

It was quite common for fashion writers to compare the debutante's figure unfavorably with that of the matron. An article in *The Queen* maintained that "La jeune fille is a lady the chief defect of whose figure is the lack of it! . . . The general run of girls suffer from a paucity of curves and contours." Girls tended to have "scraggy" figures and "callow shoulders—I am being truthful but unkind!" The author described one dress that, in her opinion, would have been "a charming gown for a woman of thirty! . . . It was exceedingly pretty, but it would have wanted the shoulders of a woman of the world, if you know what I mean . . . not the probably too visible collar-bone and shoulder-blades of a child of seventeen!" The debutante needed dresses that were "specially designed to help in the

matter of flat bust and hips [and] to conceal sharply-pointed elbows."
Happily, given a little time, "a girl generally fills out wonderfully."[19]

Her filling out was not merely a matter of gaining weight, however; nor can it be said that the older woman entirely eclipsed the younger one. By the 1890s and increasingly in the early twentieth century, beauty books emphasized the relationship between "physical culture" and physical beauty. D'Aubigny argued that "There are more good-looking girls today than ever before" and "healthy exercise is undoubtedly the real cause and secret of this increase of good looks." She advised young women to "Give the body a chance to do the beautifying. . . . Use every function and power of the body . . . indulge in every kind of sport, and develop into beautiful women."[20]

Similarly, Ella Fletcher, author of *The Woman Beautiful* (1899), saw the development of a "modern type" of beauty, the product of "twenty years of endeavor looking to the improvement of women mentally and physically." She maintained that

> When we come to consider the present type of women's beauty, we find that . . . the last quarter of the nineteenth century has witnessed a wondrous change; one which, though it seems gradual to us, will, when viewed in the historic light, appear phenomenally rapid.

The "cult of Hygeia," she argued, has produced a new type of ideal beauty, who is not only healthy, but actively athletic. "The reigning English beauty of this closing season of the nineteenth century" was "tall, with a graceful figure developed by all manner of outdoor sports, in which she excells." Remarkably, Fletcher then described a variety of sports and exercises that the reader could do to "develop" her figure (arms, chest, shoulders, legs), "to become muscular and strong," to improve her posture, and to become more graceful.[21]

Although fashion magazines at the turn of the century can hardly be said to have *urged* their readers to exercise, they did occasionally advise them of the benefits to health and beauty of sports such as rowing, riding, bicycling (although this was controversial), swimming, walking, and gymnastics. The figure as a whole was to be developed. (On the other hand, "over-exercise" was deplored as unhealthy, unattractive, and masculine.) The vogue for physical culture, however (which was much less noticeable in France), had little direct or immediate effect on the design of fashion, bicycle costumes notwithstanding. The new ideal beauty might have had better muscle tone than her predecessor, but, dressed, she hardly projected an athletic image—quite the reverse. Neither the "smart" skirt and shirt (that Americans associate with the Gibson Girl) nor the simultaneously "magnificent" and "dainty" dress of the Edwardian lady were particularly *sportif*.

Yet the growing popularity of exercise and the ideal of the healthy, athletic beauty may have had a delayed influence on fashion. It seems at least plausible that the "long and flowing" line of Edwardian fashion would not have developed to the extent that it did if the ideal woman had not become at least *somewhat* more "willowy," even if her corset played a role here. I would not want to overstate the influence of exercise on the ideal of physical beauty at this time. The point is that it *began* to have an influence; people thought it should have an influence, and that later this influence became considerable. *Style* was apparently more effective than ideology in ultimately changing appearance and behavior.

At this time, though, the *image* was probably more in evidence than the reality. Fletcher, for example, referred to the ideal modern beauty as a "Diana"—the name itself implying health, strength, and physical activity—and she specifically contrasted the modern beauty with the ideal beauty of the early nineteenth century, criticizing the latter as "timid" and "weak." She also believed that there was a "modern type of face" that was no longer characterized by "weakness and insipidity." The new ideal woman was not one of "sylph-like fragility," not "an ultra-etherealized type"; "taste" had evolved and, perhaps, "the race" itself had improved. Elsewhere, a similar comparison was made between the "steel-engraving lady" and the "Gibson Girl"—but was unusual in criticizing the latter as unfeminine and ugly.[22]

It was not so much that women's actual faces and bodies had changed significantly (although with better nutrition, they probably were taller), but rather that, as the ideal evolved, women tried to approximate it. Some historians seem to have assumed, naively, that in the 1840s women's shoulders sloped; in the 1880s they were shaped like an hourglass; in 1900 their bosoms grew; and in 1920 they shrank. In fact, of course, women had the same range of body types that they have now; but as particular figures and "looks" became popular, most women used foundation garments, diets, the optical illusions of dress, and particular stances and gestures in an attempt to approximate the current ideal. In short, there seems to have been (and continues to be) a reciprocal relationship between fashion and the current ideal of feminine beauty.

The design of Edwardian dresses and the physical stance that accompanied them—shoulders back, bosom leading, and stomach and derriere pushed back—were intended to give an impression of buxom stateliness. Edwardian dress could be worn to proper effect only on a body that was itself carried magnificently. Without correct posture and the general effect of physical well-being, the wearing of these opulent clothes loses much of its effect. In many cases, the very same women who wore Edwardian fashion would change their entire look when they adopted the so-called Poiret figure (and fashion), and still later the classic Twenties look.

The Poiret Figure and the Beginnings of Modern Fashion

The First World War was in many respects the dividing line between the nineteenth century and the modern era. The differences between fashion and beauty in 1905 and in 1925 are so striking as to lead one to assume, at least initially, that the war must somehow have *caused* a revolutionary change in fashion, and in attitudes toward the female body. Yet although the war did significantly affect the clothing of both men and women, it is also true that "changes had already begun before 1914 and ... the war merely hastened and developed them." In fact, the new look began to appear by about 1908, and has been primarily associated with the French fashion designer, Paul Poiret. It entailed not only a new fashion, but also a new physical ideal. As a journalist for *The Queen* wrote in 1911, "*The New Figure* ... may, I think, be called the Poiret figure, for it is certainly in his salons that the boneless corset is most in vogue."[23]

Paul Iribe, *Two Gowns*. Illustration for *Les Robes de Paul Poiret* (Paris, 1908).

Of course no single designer—however indefatigable a propagandist—
is entirely responsible for a significantly new look. Dress reformers had
attacked the corset for decades, and aesthetes had tried without notable
success to promote flowing draperies that hung from the shoulders and
followed the lines of the body. The first few years of the twentieth century
saw the revival of fashions based on high-waisted Directoire and Empire
models— but initially primarily for private or semi-private dress: nightgowns, chemises, and tea-gowns. Others were moving in the same direction, particularly individuals in the theatre and art worlds. Mario Fortuny
was designing Greek-inspired dresses and Isadora Duncan was dancing,
corsetless and with bare limbs, in her version of Greek dress. Thus, people
were somewhat prepared when in 1907 there came from Paris "the glad
tidings of the rising star Poiret, an eccentricity, a new word, and a new
mania."[24]

Recent research indicates that Poiret's personal influence has been
greatly exaggerated. Dorothy Behling's close study of fashion illustrations
indicates that "Between 1892 and 1908, a definite trend toward the
empire silhouette began to emerge from many couture houses." The
change was evolutionary, not revolutionary; the House of Doucet was perhaps most consistent in this regard, while Drecoll and Beer were at least
as avant-garde as Poiret. Lanvin was also adventurous in promoting a new
silhouette. Once the change began to take hold. it accelerated rapidly in
popularity:

> In 1908, the gown with an "S" silhouette, a high neck, a train, and three
> quarter or elbow sleeves was featured by most of the couture houses. . . . By
> 1909, the Neo-Directoire silhouette and the "S" shape were almost equally
> popular. . . . The Neo-Directoire style by the year 1910 was almost twice as
> popular as the S-shape. . . . However, the Edwardian "S" . . . was shown by
> Paquin as late as 1911.[25]

Poiret was not the only designer to reject what had been the starting point
for fashion design—the full figure with the constricted waist. Nevertheless, he was influential, and if we take his statements with more than a
grain of salt, they are revealing of changing attitudes toward women's
fashion.

In his autobiography, Poiret boasted, "It was still the age of the corset.
I waged war upon it. . . . It was . . . in the name of Liberty that I proclaimed the fall of the corset and the adoption of the brassiere which,
since then, has won the day. Yes, I freed the bust."[26] Others also claimed
credit, in statements as self-serving as Poiret's own. Lucille, for example,
recalled that she had "brought in the brassiere in opposition to the hideous corset." And Caresse Crosby even claimed to have "invented" the
brassiere.[27] (Of course, the brassiere developed gradually out of the bust
bodice, and was first worn *with* the corset, although Poiret prefered his
customers to wear a short, light, and boneless corset that was little more
than a girdle.)

The fashionable Edwardian figure was gradually replaced by a slender and sinuous body type with smaller breasts, slimmer hips, and long legs. In an unpublished manuscript Poiret explained, "I favour small breasts that rise forth from the bodice like an enchanting testimonial to youth. Can anything be more captivating than this beauteous roundness? It is unthinkable for the breasts to be sealed up in solitary confinement in a castle-like fortress like the corset, as if to punish them."[28]

Poiret believed that the corset of the day gave women a deformed appearance: "It divided its wearer into distinct masses; on the one side there was the bust . . . on the other, the whole behindward aspect, so that the lady looked as if she were hauling a trailor. It was almost a return to the bustle." He also disliked the way the corset and décolleté evening gown seemed to serve up the breasts. Madame Poiret recalled his injunction, "From now on the breasts will no longer be worn."[29]

Once the tightly cinched waist was no longer the focal point of fitted dress, the designer could work with a new vocabulary of shapes and styles. Thus, for example, although the breasts were not to be "worn," Poiret's high-waisted dresses (often with *bateau* necklines) subtly emphasized the bosom, without requiring either that it be padded or exposed, or that the waist below should be constricted. Clothing could be designed from the shoulders down instead of, in effect, upwards and downwards from the waist. But unlike the rather loose and heavy dresses associated with Aesthetes and Dress Reformers, the new designs were softly draped and sheath-like—"just touching the outline of the figure . . . to underscore the endowments of [the woman's] body." "To dress a woman is not to cover her with ornaments." Rather, he wanted to use the light-weight rubber girdle, brassiere, and dress "to reveal nature in a significant contour."[30]

The twentieth-century "fashion revolution" consisted of two phases. In the first, Directoire, period, the old, corseted look developed into a straight but sinuous silhouette, with an easy and often raised waistline and a narrow skirt that in 1911 became the notorious "hobble skirt." In the second (but related) phase, Orientalism was in fashion. The 1909 Paris debut of the Ballets Russes with its costumes by Leon Bakst contributed to both the infamous *jupes-culottes* (known also as trouser-skirts and harem-skirts) and the so-called "lamp-shade tunic" (a short tunic-crinoline worn over a long, narrow skirt), as well as the use of brilliant colors and richly textured fabrics, turbans, aigrettes, beads, and tassels.[31]

In the long run, the most important development was the promotion of the slender figure. As early as May, 1908, *Vogue*'s Paris correspondent wrote:

> The fashionable figure is growing straighter and straighter, less bust, less hips, more waist, and a wonderfully long, slender suppleness about the limbs. . . . The long skirt . . . reveals plainly every line and curve of the leg from hip to ankle. The petticoat is obsolete, pre-historic. How slim, how graceful, how elegant women look! The leg has suddenly become fashionable.[32]

Yet the corset, per se, did not immediately disappear, nor did the skirt rise. Instead, "the desire for the natural uncorseted effect" resulted in the development of new forms of corsets, some more or less lightly boned, others elastic. Corset advertisements stressed that their product "gives the corsetless figure so much admired." Their function, indeed, was not so much to constrict the waist—since the "waistless effect" was fashionable—as to produce "long," "straight" hips. According to the 1914 Peter Robinson catalogue, the woman with an "average figure" (one with a "20 to 30 inch" waist) or a plumper figure might want a "Hip-Confiner" corset or a "Thigh-Diminishing" model with both bones and "elastic insets." Those with "slender figures" (19 to 26 inch waists) could wear the "new 'Boneless' Tricot models [which give] . . . extreme flexibility." Every corset was intended to be worn with "a Brassiere to save the figure from going unshapely"; these well-fitting camisoles came in bust sizes of 32, 34, 36, and soon up to 44 inches.[33]

It is unclear how many women wore more or less unboned corsets or narrow *ceintures* (and brassieres) and how many wore long, straight, boned corsets (also with bust bodices). The Victoria and Albert Museum has a French corset from about 1914 that is a good example of the shorter and very lightly boned variety of corset. Made of pink cotton with a "doe-skin" finish, it extends from waist to hip, laces in back and has an expandable panel in the front. The Musée de la Mode et du Costume in Paris has an example of the type of corset that extends from just below the bosom to mid-thigh; cream colored satin with a pattern of yellow irises, it is moderately boned. It dates from about 1910 and was sold at the Galeries Lafayette.

Until 1914, the standard corset "became more and more enveloping below, to the point of hampering walking and movements." It was only during the war years that the girdle, as opposed to the long corset, became *generally* worn. As the corset manufacturer Fernand Libron put it, "The general upheaval of life and manners occasioned by the Great War led to an unconstraint [*laisser-aller*] that one could only compare to that of the revolutionary period." Nevertheless, in the years prior to the war many women began to wear lighter and less constricting foundation garments, particularly if they had *relatively* slender figures, or liked to tango. Lady Naomi Mitchison, for example, recalled that when she was sixteen (in 1913) her mother made a "half-hearted" attempt to put her into a whale-boned corset, but when she refused to wear it, her mother backed down. The small waist was simply far less important than it had been; in 1914, one corset manufacturer asserted that "Today Polaire's wonderful waist leaves us unmoved or amused; yesterday it thrilled men and roused women to prodigies of emulation."[34]

Certainly, verbal acceptance of the new line came quickly. The woman of "serpentine" or feline slenderness had supposedly ousted her "opulent" and "wasp-waisted" predecessor. Her greater flexibility and grace were praised—and, sometimes, her "comfortable" new figure was equated with her social emancipation. Advertisements showed "surprising pictures of serpent-like beings in stays"; and stressed that "Our modern silhouettes, those silhouettes à la Helleu or à la Drian . . . have . . . the suppleness of a cat." Corset manufacturers stressed that "Woman has thrown off her shackles"—although they hastened to add that *their* corsets offered perfect "freedom to woman."[35]

The author of a 1914 catalogue for Marshall & Snellgrove, *Towards New Liberty*, actually argued that the new corset showed that woman "is a new creature, a new sex almost," no longer "wasp-waisted, wasp-minded," but "daily becoming more and more of a companion and equal to man." He stressed, though, that it was crucial to retain her charm:

> The sporting girl and the new woman can go too far. . . . Woman's appeal to man must always, I think, contain an element of the physical in it. In the old days that appeal was obligatory, yet almost passive, the appeal of the slave girl in the Babylonian market—toneless, a degradation. Today woman can make of herself what she will. She is making her mind as free as her body. Let her see to it that both are attractive. . . . Freedom does not necessitate laxity. The question today is: "How can women's figures have free play in every movement, and yet be kept trim and neat?"[36]

The answer: By wearing a "boneless or lightly boned corset" in that strong yet pliant fabric—Balloon Silk. The same pamphlet also shows a rather smug-looking young lady of 1914 comparing herself with an irate and crinolined ancestor.

Perhaps more than any other single factor, the popularity of the tango and similar dances led many women to abandon orthodox corsetry in 1913 and 1914. Some corset advertisements complained that, "at balls . . . one sees a number of women who affect an excessive unconstraint . . . [and] have abandoned all support; the bust undulates to the rhythm of the dance in a loose fashion." Other advertisements—such as one on "Chiffons and Tango"— bowed to the trend and promoted short elastic corsets, maintaining that they "prevent muscle fatigue," so "dancers prefer them." Indeed, one "all elastic" model that slipped on over the head was called the "tango."[37] Also in 1913, the professional dancer Irene Castle started a minor fashion for bobbed hair—another precursor of the Twenties.

Ideals of beauty changed slowly, though. All arguments that "The slender [*mince*] woman is the queen of the century!" should be taken with more than a grain of salt. If the "abundant [*plantureuse*] woman" was less fashionable than previously, most people were apparently still critical of "excessive *sveltesse*." The French fashion historian Marylène Delbourg-Delphis argues convincingly that the early twentieth-century woman was only *beginning* to want to be thin, and that this was still "more a desire than a reality." The "idealizing" graphic art of 1908 to 1914, characteristic of Poiret's deluxe pamphlets and certain avant-garde French fashion magazines, did not accurately portray the figures that most women had at the time. And some people complained that the new "sheath-like" fashions were "very trying to the average figure."[38]

Yet "the slimming craze" gradually gained adherants. In 1912, *Journal des Dames et des Modes* (one of the new periodicals) wavered between the belief that "fashion . . . only modifies very little the voluptuous silhouette of women of fashion"—and the more radical insistence that "thinness [*la maigreur*] triumphs," the "new beauty" has a "tanagraesque silhouette":

> Your glances no longer go to anyone but the willowy, slender woman. . . . It is no longer a question of breasts or hips, or so little! . . . I challenge you to notice a fat woman today, so much has the tyranny of fashion imperiously formed and strangled our preferences.

For centuries the ideal had been the "fat" woman, who "symbolised the family." Now the new ideal of beauty had resulted in "a different conception of love." "At present the thin woman seduces us with her disquieting and alert glamour. She comes and goes. . . . Nothing rejuvinates like thinness, and . . . youth is *a priori* thin."[39] Statements like these clearly presage the ideal of the Twenties—the thin, young woman, who was so far from symbolizing the family that her dress minimized the maternal bosom, while exposing the legs, in the manner of a little girl.

The new physical ideal is clearly shown in an illustration from *Gazette du Bon Ton* (1912), which is devoted to underwear à la mode. It shows two very young women with tiny breasts, one in a thigh-high pink silk chemise, the other in combinations. Stockings are shown, hinting at an open interest in legs. A corset advertisement from the 1914 *Gazette du Bon Ton* also indicates the dramatic changes of fashion and physique.

As early as 1908, *Vogue* declared that the leg was fashionable. Although not exposed, it was indicated by the tight skirt. In his memoirs Poiret boasted that, having freed the bust, he then "shackled the legs":

> Women complained of being no longer able to walk. . . . Have their complaints or grumblings ever arrested the movement of fashion, or have they not rather, on the contrary, helped it by advertising it? Everyone wore the tight skirt.[40]

The hobble skirt *was* very popular, especially in 1911 and 1912. It was tighter than the tied-back skirts of the late 1870s, and it did prevent the wearer from taking full strides. But it was hardly as restrictive as legend has it. A great deal of nonsense has been written about the "meaning" of the hobble skirt—that it expressed the intention of male designers to keep women in bondage, and women's unconscious desire to resist emancipation. Since fashion tends to go to extremes, once the raised waist and narrow skirt were adopted, it was unsurprising, but not especially significant, that for several years the skirt became very narrow. In any case, it was often modified with devices such as that of Madame Paquin—"cunning

Within the illustration:

LES DESSOUS
A
LA MODE

L A mode actuelle
impose des dessous
légers.

Sur la chemise courte,
en fin tissu de soie, une
combinaison de soie éga-
lement, à mailles serrées.
Chemise et combinai-

H. Martin, *Les Dessous à la Mode*. Fashion plate from *Gazette du Bon Ton* (1912). Copyright Condé Nast Publications, Ltd. Courtesy of Condé Nast Publications and the Victoria and Albert Museum Library.

pleats at the side," so that although the skirt "looked slim," "walking was a pleasure." Alternatively, the skirt was slit either at the side or the front with "inner skirts of chiffon or lace that fill the openings made for ease of movement." Some dresses, however (especially for evenings), had slits that revealed "an ample display of feet and hosiery," necessitating "a variety of slippers and shoes."[41]

Even the raising of hemlines in 1915–1916 was anticipated by this style of narrow, slit skirts, which was known in Germany as the "naked mode."

Paul Brissard, Advertisement for Le Corset Bon Ton. From *Gazette du Bon Ton* (1914). Copyright Condé Nast Publications, Ltd. Courtesy of Condé Nast Publications and the Victoria and Albert Museum Library.

According to the fashion historian Max von Boehn, there were clerical protests against it in 1913, with the Prince Bishop of Lainbach (Austria) arguing that "The newest fashions in clothes are designed to serve the cause of lust." More surprisingly, in early 1914 a group of aristocratic French women also protested against "the indecency of exposing the leg completely to view." There were also cries of anguish over the 1913 introduction of modest V-necklines for daytime dress. Although *de rigueur* for evening wear, the lower décolletage for daytime was thought to be unhealthy and immoral.[42]

Of course, the notorious *jupe-culotte* (or harem trouser-skirt) of 1911 also indicated the legs, but this was more of a *succès de scandale* than a significant influence on fashion. The style, however, like the "lamp-shade tunic" (1912–1913)—a short full overskirt like a miniature crinoline above a narrow longer skirt—reflected the importance of Orientalism in dress in the prewar years. A recurring minor theme for decades, "the aesthetic of the Far East" became a rage in France and England from about 1909 until the First World War. Both Poiret and Diaghilev's Ballets Russes were influential in replacing the Belle Epoque look with an alternative look of "Turkish, Persian, [and] Hindu modes."[43]

Cecil Beaton recalled that

A fashion world that had been dominated by corsets, lace, feathers, and pastel shades soon found itself in a city that overnight had become a seraglio of vivid colours, harem skirts, beads, fringe, and voluptuousness.[44]

There was a strong element of theatricality in all this, and, indeed, the more *outré* costumes were worn at popular fancy dress parties. But romantic fantasies of the "exotic" East did affect people's perceptions of themselves. Sonia Keppel described how "many of those who saw [Nijinsky and Karsavina in *Scheherazade*] were powerfully affected by it, and some of the most unlikely people suddenly saw themselves as pagan gods and enchantresses. An exotically Eastern element began to percolate into typically English homes." The "influence of Bakst-in-the-home" soon extended from cushions and incense to "Persian jackets," turbans, "an improvised 'yashmak' and scarves." "They all dressed up in Eastern dress, and, to this day, my childhood's recollection of Lady Juliet is of a very tall, willowy siren, in Turkish trousers."[45]

These fashion fantasies were not entirely new, of course; many Edwardian ladies had imagined that in their tea-gowns they looked like "graceful houris clad in gauze and gorgeous draperies," that gave "a man a sort of luxurious feel of being an Oriental Pasha." Or, as Loelia, Duchess of Westminster, put it more cynically, women acted "as if they were odalisques trying to fascinate a Pasha, instead of respectable matrons tied up to British gentlemen whose minds were entirely fixed on guns, dogs, and birds." By the teens, though, innumerable women seemed to picture themselves as "the favorites of the harem."[46]

Harem imagery seems today to be rather silly and having little or nothing to do with the modern world, but Orientalism continued to be popular throughout the Twenties—when women wore "Oriental" perfumes and cosmetics, "slave" bracelets and "barbaric jewelry," turbans, and other "exotic" accoutrements. In 1926, for example, Liane de Pougy described seeing women at luncheon at the Lido who "looked as though they were acting in a fairy tale: Scheherazade, Salome, Salammbo—Oriental ladies from rich harems . . . in sumptuous pyjamas, . . . brilliantly coloured, glittering . . . fantasy reigned at its wildest."[47]

The mental associatins between the exotic and the erotic led to an increased emphasis on the desirability of a kind of mysterious sensuality that replaced both the pretty flirtatiousness of the Victorians and the froufrou seductiveness of the Edwardians. Consider, for example, the question of color. Although colors may have an actual physiological effect, all that can definitely be said is that their significance is interpreted differently at different times. While the Edwardians found pastels "refined" and "elegant," and bright colors almost "vulgar," by the teens pale shades seemed "enervated"; "clear, true colors" appeared in "reaction." Even "violent" "extraordinary" colors or "an excess of color" was fashionable. Poiret dismissed the Edwardian palette as

> Nuances of nymph's thigh, lilacs, swooning mauves, tender blue hortensias, niles, maizes, straws, all that was soft, washed out, and insipid. . . . I threw into this sheepcote a few rough wolves; reds, greens, violets, royal blues, that made all the rest sing aloud. I had to . . . put a little gaity, a little new fresh-

ness, into their colour schemes. . . . On the other hand the morbid mauves were hunted out of existence.[48]

It is difficult to know whether there was any direct connection between fashion and the art of the Fauves (which gained attention at the 1905–6 Salon d'Autumn), but the fashionable colors were definitely perceived as wild. Furthermore, some pre-war artists like Robert and Sonia Delauney and the Futurist Marinetti specifically advocated the use of bright and even clashing colors for both men's and women's clothes.

Twenties fashion writers continued to praise "Oriental," "exotic," "vivid," "strong," "clean," "wonderful and dangerous," "rainbow" colors. Presumably by using these adjectives, they were appealing to women's desire to look dangerously attractive, since men, by and large, did not respond to the challenge to abandon the dull-colored suit. Many of the same bright colors had been popular in the High Victorian era, but fashion writers then had stressed that while "gladdening" colors were pretty, anything too garish was unladylike. By the Twenties, though, writers felt free to describe a beige as "flesh coloured" or to dub a blue-green "turquoise *morte*." The *colors* were not new, but their associations and their juxtapositions had changed, and people presumably felt that they were presenting a particular new image through their choice of color and style.

Yet despite the many similarities between the pre-war look and the look of the Twenties, the First World War did intervene and it did have an influence on fashion and the feminine ideal—but its effects were more complex than has been supposed.

The First World War

It has frequently been asserted that the war forced women to adopt "functional" dress (so that they could work), and that it created social conditions that "liberated" them sexually. The war gave women economic independence, and an "increased sense of their own capacity," while destroying "all the old arguments about women's proper place." The appearance of the short skirt and the "abandonment" of the corset have been heralded as signs of these dramatic changes. Shortages of material supposedly led to shorter dresses, while shortages of metal helped bring and end to stays and "tight-lacing"—but that, in any case, "the exigencies of a wartime situation led to a reduction of interest in high fashion, together with a new "acceptance of the human body."[49] This was not quite how it appeared to people at the time, nor is this interpretation convincing now.

The most striking change in fashion occured in 1915–1916, when the narrow styles (the hobble skirt, the peg-top skirt, the narrow skirt worn with the lamp-shade tunic, and the draped panier styles) gave way to a flared and shortened skirt, with a hem that ranged from mid-calf to just above the ankle. The new style was referred to at the time as the Louis

Seize style or the "war crinoline." In 1917, the rather loose, straight "barrel [*tonneau*] line" took over, with the waist-line gradually moving down toward the natural position. By 1918, the House of Worth showed dresses with a dropped waistline, but the styles of 1919 were an eclectic mixture, favoring "sack" dresses with V-necks. But high-waisted, just above ankle-length dresses were still common. Increasingly, the tendency was toward one-piece dresses, which were simple to make and easy to wear. Post-war fashion looked similar to the easy-fitting and even sometimes rather voluminous late-war styles, with the hemline rising slightly up the calf in 1921, but falling to near the ankles again in 1923, before beginning its notorious rise toward the knees. Dresses were often very full in the skirt and hips, had raised waistlines almost as often as lowered ones, and were frequently ruffled. The classic Twenties look actually existed only from about 1924 to 1928.

Functional explanations of these sartorial changes are unsatisfactory on a number of grounds. To begin with, the full "crinoline" skirt took up more, not less material. Clothing was not rationed or government-directed during World War I. There were numerous substitutes for metal "bones," but the trend *before* the war was toward less constricting and even boneless corsets, and this trend continued. Although we cannot know how fashion would have evolved had there been no war, the pattern of fashion change makes it likely that having been so narrow, the skirt would have become full in any case. Simply in terms of the internal dynamics of fashion, it seems plausible that if we remove the narrow underskirt, the lampshade tunic-overskirt remains, perhaps slightly lengthened to somewhere between mid-calf and just above the ankle.

It is true that the shorter, fuller skirt worn with a less constricting corset was more practical (although women had been perfectly capable of working in previous styles). A writer for *The Illustrated London News* believed that "Women's dress will very likely be permanently affected by the War." So many women were working, and "their dress must be suitable for the work that they must do." But it was also admitted (unhappily) that "the tendency to shortness . . . is affecting many of the evening gowns as well." As late as 1916, *La Femme Chic* printed an article "on reconciling one's husband to short skirts when he came home on leave." The same year, the English periodical, *The Lady,* presented the brassiere in terms of the wartime alliance: "The French and American women all wear them and so must we."[50]

In fact, the war fashions were not so much rational as they were stylish. Lady Cynthia Asquith noted with some surprise in her diary (April, 1915) that "the clothes have undergone enormous change since the war and have become practically early Victorian with real full skirts. I thought war would produce reactions to womanliness." Later entries also show how the short style was perceived as "ultra-fashionable," not functional. Thus, at a dinner party, her friend Ettie appeared "very disfigured by short fashionable skirt. It looked like an accident." But a few weeks later she herself gave in and bought one to wear at a luncheon party, "though I felt rather absurd in new-fashioned, full, short, black taffeta dress."[51]

It is likely that the short skirt was accepted both because the pre-war styles had paved the way for it, and because wartime seemed to necessitate "practical" innovations. Although the war changed the operation of the world of couture, the evolution of fashion continued on its way. Recognizing that the idea of fashion might seem unduly frivolous, even offensive, at a time of social crisis, the French fashion industry emphasized both the aesthetic and patriotic aspects of the new and "altogether practical and plucky" style. There is a certain air of rationalization in the argument that

> Paris has innovated a warlike elegance, jovial, sportive, and easy, leaving every gesture free, either to raise the unhappy wounded, or, if need be, to handle a weapon. . . . [Women's] figures [are] uncompressed, allowing them easily to bend over suffering men . . . [and] they have made themselves look . . . pretty . . . so as to bring with them a ray of light and cheerfulness.[52]

In fact, of course, nurses wore uniforms, and Lady Diana Cooper recalled, "I did look horrible. The dress was just off the floor," while for out of doors, the nurse wore "a bonnet not unlike the Salvation Army but less becoming, and a long, tubular, narrow cape to the ankles—no arm-movement possible. We looked like caterpillars." Other working women also often wore uniforms, which tended to be ankle-length skirts and medium-length jackets, although munitions workers wore boiler-suits.[53]

Yet more women did work during the war years, and working-class women especially gained a greater degree of economic independence. (A working-class woman who made £35 a year in 1900 could make £5 a week during World War I.) Furthermore, restrictions on women's social activities lessened, so women had more personal independence and opportunities to meet men outside family-sponsored and chaperoned affairs. But despite both official claims that women were now participating in all facets of public life, and hysterical denunciations of a rising tide of immorality, the degree of economic and sexual liberation achieved either during the war years or in their aftermath seems to have been greatly exaggerated. In America, for example, only 5% of women workers joined the labor force for the first time in the war years; most simply changed jobs. There was certainly more discussion of sex and probably also more pre-marital sex, but it was hardly promiscuity. If historians have tended to over-estimate the pervasiveness of the ideology of domesticity and the double standard of morality during the pre-war period, so also have they tended to exaggerate the extent to which these were overthrown in the course of the war.[54]

The Twenties

Why have so many people then and now believed that the war created a completely new woman? The historian James McMillan suggests that

"Probably the main reason for the new image of women in the post-war period was the fact that, thanks to changes in fashion, they looked different . . . and contemporaries can hardly be blamed if they took fashion to be only the external manifestation of more profound changes." There is much to be said for this hypothesis, although McMillan undercuts his own argument when he maintains that wartime fashions had been "functional," and that this "had led to shorter skirts, unaccentuated waists . . . flat breasts and a vogue for slim, boyish figures [with] . . . close-cropped hair."[55]

Certainly many contemporaries felt that short skirts equalled virtual nudity and loose girdles, loose morals; and the "straight" figure was widely perceived as an aberration in the history of feminine beauty. These ideas were further exaggerated by fashion historians, such as James Laver, who argued that

> The disappearance of corsets is always accompanied by . . . promiscuity . . . [and] is connected with another phenomenon characteristic of all periods following a great upheaval. . . . [T]he emancipated woman . . . tri[es] to look . . . like a man . . . [and] cut[s] her hair short.[56]

This view completely misinterprets the significance of Twenties fashion and the effect of the First World War. Historians who have focused on the "promiscuity" of the postwar woman and the "boyishness" (sexual ambiguity) of the Twenties look have erred as much as those who have insisted that, because of the war, "functional " dress and "healthy" sexuality supplanted irrational and body-denying fashion. The war did *not* mark the transition from the wasp waist to the boyish look. Such a view ignores the crucial importance of the pre-war transition period.

What the war really *caused* was the disruption of the pre-war social and economic hierarchy, and this had an indirect but significant effect on fashion. Mrs. I., an Englishwoman born in the late 1890s, recalled that what was really striking after the war was how much harder it was to tell what class someone belonged to by looking at their clothes. At the very highest levels of fashion, distinctions remained clear, however. If Coco Chanel was and remains famous for her simple "poor look," the wealthy Mrs. D. recalls that it was nonetheless a *very* expensive style. What it did, though, was to make the wearer look young and casual.[57]

What actually happened in the Twenties, and what did it mean? The slimmer, younger physical ideal that was beginning to appear before 1914 gained ground rapidly. Yet accounts of extreme thinness and boyish figures are suspect. The Duchess of Westminster, for example, recalled:

> Bosoms and hips were definitely *out*. A lovely figure meant a perfectly straight figure and the slightest suggestion of a curve was scorned as *fat*. The ideal woman's vital statistics would probably have been something like 30–30–30.[58]

But this was an exaggeration.

Most contemporary accounts show a definite ambivalence about both the ideal weight and the ideal bust-size. In 1922, Florence Courtenay, the American author of *Physical Beauty: How to Develop and Preserve It*, defined the ideal figure as "a lithe, well-rounded form, graceful yet not so plump as to be called voluptuous. . . . Round, firm, well-modeled breasts of medium size cannot be improved upon. . . . The ideal waist is one not contracted by too tight a corset. . . . The hips should be broader than the shoulders." More specifically, a woman of five foot three inches should weigh approximately one hundred nineteen pounds and have measurements of 28.8–24.7–35.2. We would certainly not consider a bust measuring less than thirty inches to be "of medium size." On the other hand, while she thought that most women needed to reduce their weight, she argued that the *ideal* weight for a woman of five foot seven inches was one hundred and forty-eight pounds, which seems very heavy by today's standards, and that weight had to go somewhere. But for all her ambiguity about actual statistics, she did make it clear that

> Physical beauty is a definite part of the feminine sex appeal. And a happy marriage depends largely on a normal and happy sex appeal on the part of the woman and corresponding sex interest on the part of the man.

The ideal figure was not supposed to be asexual, androgynous, or masculine, and clothes (including corsets) were also supposed to be "an important [element] in . . . physical beauty."[59]

The anonymous author of *Le Nouveau Bréviaire de la beauté* also described the ideal figure as "deliciously undulating," and praised "the opulent and firm bosom with marvelous contours." He (for the author seems to have been male) went on to assert that "There is nothing more charming than two beautiful breasts, well-rounded, firm, and of a striking whiteness." Yet the rather erotic illustrations show girls with small breasts. *Figures, Faces, and Folds*, a book for art students, described "the ideal type of the present" as "slim and muscularly perfect," with a "slim waist" and "rounded hips," but added, "It is no fault if the breasts are only small."[60]

Throughout the Twenties many people remained unhappy about the new look. Ironically, even Poiret looked back on some of the love affairs of his youth, and was more appreciative of the full corseted figure: Raymonde was

> as lissome as she was shapely, like they made them at that time. . . . [She] had pretty forms in front and behind (this was still appreciated and in demand at that time). I found in these attractions an infinite charm, and if I had been able to imagine that they were on the point of disappearing, perhaps I would have taken better advantage of them.[61]

With his career failing rapidly, Poiret regretted the new look that he had helped to create.

Writers cautioned women against wearing "flat" brassieres that were too small, say "size thirty-four when their correct bust measurement is thirty-six." They worried that "the revenge of thin women" meant that others had been "reduced" to a "severe regime" of diet and exercise. In fact, the problem was not so much that the ideal of *physical* beauty was too thin or too flat-chested, but rather, on the one hand, that the contrast with the earlier ideal seemed too extreme, and, on the other, that many of the fashions of the Twenties were widely—and understandably— regarded as not "suited to anyone who was not really slender, or quite young." [62] The tubular line of the dress was determined by the widest or most prominent part of the body; and if a woman had even an average figure and bosom by pre-war standards, her Twenties dress hung in such a way that she looked fat.

The feminine ideal of the Twenties was not so much "boyish" as *youthful*. As the social hierarchy that had placed the rich middle-aged woman at its pinnacle crumbled after the war, the Diana of the Edwardians and the Tanagra of the pre-war period became still more important. In the Twenties, as young women began to lead more active, independent lives, *they* became fashionable society's trend-setters. The post-war disillusionment with the "old" people who had sent the young off to die may also have contributed to the apotheosis of youth. "Youth rules the world today and in no phase of life is it more apparent than in fashion." Thus, Twenties fashions minimized the breasts, which were associated with the mature woman and the mother, and emphasized the "long," "straight," "shapely" legs, which were associated with youth. Although only the daring showed their knees, and then only for a few years in the mid–1920s, even daytime fashions (traditionally much less revealing than evening dress) exposed bare arms and "well-moulded calves and slender ankles" in "nude silk hose." Previously, only dresses for very young girls had exposed so much of these limbs.[63]

The clothing of the Twenties not only revealed more of the body (particularly the limbs), but also emphasized the "easy" movement of the unconstrained body beneath the clothing itself. A woman wearing Twenties dress was much more *touchable* than a woman in Victorian or Edwardian dress. Clothing weighed a fraction of what it had previously, and little lingerie was worn, especially if a woman was able to dispense with a corset. Even if she did wear foundation garments, they were usually made of elastic or rubber: "See how short . . . are our skirts, how loose our girdles, how flowing and untrammeled the lines of our frocks."[64]

For both the High Victorian and the Edwardian periods, the ideal of feminine beauty (though different in details of physique and fashion) was a draped ideal—the existence of a beautiful body had largely to be inferred from the appearance of a woman in fashionable dress. The Twenties illustrates a shift to the opposite extreme: Much more of the body was revealed, so that, in effect, clothing only succeeded in its object of enhancing feminine beauty when worn on a nearly ideally suitable body.

Another characteristic of the style of the Twenties was "the natural, extremely casual manner of wearing clothes," and of presenting oneself;

but it was an image composed of several very different elements. On the one hand, it was asserted that "Girlish immaturity is the correct pose," and that "the charm of schoolgirl days is now carried past the 30's." Yet the "modern ideal of womanhood" was not the innocent young girl, but rather the girl who "adopted boyish mannerisms and slang," while simultaneously projecting a "*soignée*" sophistication that implied a certain sexual availability.[65]

Literary depictions of the Twenties anti-heroine are unreliable as a guide to women's behavior, but perhaps legitimate as the portrayal of a popular "pose." Certainly, one may doubt whether Monique Lerbier, the promiscuous, bisexual, drug addict protagonist of Victor Margueritte's best-selling novel *La Garconne*, was typical of her period. Yet the virginal heroines of Michael Arlen's *The Green Hat* and Aldous Huxley's *Antic Hay* also tried hard to project an *image* of disillusioned post-war depravity.[66]

Their appearance was quintessentially Twenties, and shows the interaction between the physical ideal, fashion, and the image of the self. Huxley's heroine, for example, was slender, but "it was a rounded slenderness" —"flexible and tubular, like a section of a boa constrictor. She dressed in clothes that emphasized this serpentine slimness." Unornamented, completely covered from her metallic hat to her snakeskin shoes, her "person" seemed both "severe" and attractive in a dangerous, strong way. Like a figure in a contemporary fashion plate, she projected a streamlined, highly artificial *chic*.[67]

Iris Storm, wearer of the "green hat," was specifically compared to "the women in George Barbier's almanacks, *Falbalas et Fanfreluches*, who know how to stand carelessly," and who wear clothes that appear to be "pour le sport." She was an odd combination of childishness, with her dress printed with red elephants, and sophistication, with her diamond-studded powder box and jade cigarette case. Her "thick, tawny," wavy hair was "shingled"; it had "died a very manly death . . . above her neck." Yet she wore earrings. Thus, her body also combined chic and sexuality. "She was without hips, according to the fashion," but had naturally "boyish breasts." Some might like the "Reubens" figure, but it was Iris's that represented the narrator's ideal of the "demoiselle." To his praise, she replied simply, "I am proud of my breasts, because they are so beautiful."[68]

Twenties fashions may have caused such controversy at the time, because they projected an image whose connotations were objectionable and confusing to many people. It was not only that women looked immodest, immoral, and ugly, a lack of "mystery" seeming to equal a lack of "sex appeal." There also seemed to be a contradiction between the popular and traditional ideal of feminine physical beauty and the fashionable ideal of dress, which was chic and casual, very young and "semi-masculine," and certainly not traditionally "feminine" and "beautiful."

There must have been many women like Lady Troubridge, who complained in 1925 that, although she "admire[d] the present-day type of beauty, with its reedlike slimness ... a perfect machine moved by the elixer of youth," she found it hard that "no one is allowed to be middle-aged." To corset oneself into an approximation of the tubular line was only a partial solution, since even boneless corselettes caused a certain rigidity, antagonistic to "the kinetic silhouette" and "the principle of movement" and "suppleness" promoted by the fashion press. Furthermore, while the thin young Edwardian girl could pad and cover herself, the ample matron of the Twenties was less able to cope successfully with an era when (as Lady Troubridge put it), "the worship of the body is in the ascendent."[69]

It would be a mistake to interpret this "worship of the body" simply as Kern's post-Victorian "acceptance of the body." To a considerable extent, it signified greater demands on the body. The change from the admiration for the ample, mature female body to that of the slim, young, active body meant partly that the corset was internalized in the form of dieting, while the need to look young fed the growing beauty industry.

Victorian beauticians (like the notorious Rachel of the 1860s) had been satirized as dangerous witches, who "enameled" their customers' complexions. But as early as the 1890s, the "scientific culture of beauty" had become a significant force. *Harper's Bazar* (1893) maintained that "Public opinion, aided by masseuses, hairdressers, complexion specialists, and manicure and pedicure professors, has undergone a great change in the last few years." By 1910 there were "make-up parlours" all over London, and other large cities. The (relative) democratization of fashion was paralleled by the wider use of cosmetics and professional hair stylists. The nineteenth-century "ladies' paradise"—the department store—opened beauty sections, and visiting them became a popular pastime. The wealthy had always had access to lady's maids and professional hairdressers and manicurists. Now these and related professions became part of a vast commercial network. Even before the Twenties, the flapper openly wore rouge, powder, lipstick, eyeshadow, mascara, and perfume. Her hair was bobbed, marcelled, and given permanent waves. Advertisements proliferated in magazines and newspapers of the 1920s—and became increasingly direct in claiming that their products added to the wearer's sex appeal. By the Twenties, women were even criticized for leaving their faces in a "raw state." Without cosmetics, they did not look dressed.[70]

"Summer Evening," a fashion plate from *Style Parisien* (circa 1925–1926), shows perhaps the quintessential Twenties beauty—slim, sophisticated, streamlined, and modern. Nothing could be further from the demure prettiness of an 1850s fashion plate than this casual chic. And yet her appearance was the product of a long evolution, rather than a sudden, cataclysmic change. Throughout the second half of the nineteenth cen-

Soir d'Été, Dresses by Jenny. Fashion plate from *Style Parisien* (ca. 1926).

tury, there was an increasingly open acceptance of artificial and erotic beauty. The concept of style goes beyond the formal elements of body and dress to create a far more complex image of the ideal self. The form of self-presentation expressed through fashion and adornment changed, but it was always intended to be sexually attractive.

12

Conclusion

In the preceding chapters, I have tried to analyze nineteenth and early twentieth-century fashion on its own terms, asking "What did the women of the time think and feel about their clothes?" I have been at pains to prevent as much as possible the intrusion of late twentieth-century assumptions about Victorian dress, on the grounds that such assumptions entail serious historical distortions. But contemporary perceptions of fashion are also worthy of attention, since styles of appearance and ideals of feminine erotic beauty did not freeze in 1910, with the beginning of modern fashion and the greater acceptance of more overt sexual display.

The look of the Twenties gave way to a more traditionally "feminine" mode in the Thirties. The Forties saw the ambivalent appearance of the war worker, "manning" the factories in trousers, but also wearing heavy cosmetics—to say nothing of the "sweater girl" of pin-up fame. The decade of the Fifties was characterized by an ideological emphasis on conformity, and by fashion images that were sharply age- and gender-specific, such as the wife, the teen-ager, and the man in the grey flannel suit. The Sixties were "liberated" in rather the same way as the Twenties, with short skirts and birth control at the forefront of the popular imagination. Then with the development of to a new women's movement came a growing sense that fashion was somehow intrinsically anti-feminist epitomized by stories of bra-burning. It therefore seems valid, and perhaps even necessary, in closing, at least to touch on the issue of the relationship between fashion, femininity, and feminism in the world today.

Recent works, such as Lois Banner's *American Beauty* and Susan Brownmiller's *Femininity*, have attacked fashion and ideals of feminine beauty as deeply oppressive to women—not only in the past, but today as well. According to the neo-feminist critique, fashion is bad because it is sexually exploitive and artificial. It is also conducive to self-absorption, and it is a waste of time. In fact, fashion and beauty culture form the *basis* for all other inequalities that women face. Fashion and feminism have always been at war, and to the extent that fashion has become less oppressive, it is due to the influence of the women's movement. But although women no longer wear "tight" corsets and long skirts, nevertheless trousers are still superior to modern skirts, on both practical and ideological grounds. As Brownmiller writes, "A skirt, any skirt, has a feminizing mission."

> To care about feminine fashion, and to do it well, is to be obsessively involved in inconsequential details on a serious basis. ... The desperate unending absorption in the drive for a perfect appearance—call it feminine vanity—is the ultimate restriction on freedom of mind.[1]

Far better, Banner argues, to adhere to the "feminist" ideal of the "natural" woman, and the beauty of "spiritual qualities, healthy bodies, and useful lives." That these books have been, on the whole, well received, indicates that many presumably more-or-less fashionable people are nevertheless inclined to think badly of feminine fashion. Even *Vogue* (America's best known fashion magazine) treated *Femininity* with respect—although probably *none* of *Vogue's* readers would enjoy a world stripped of dresses, earrings, and eye make-up (to mention only three items that Brownmiller disapproves of).[2]

But is fashion intrinsically anti-feminist? Certainly fashion is erotic and artificial, but are those necessarily negative features? It is apparently a difficult concept for most people to accept that there is no "natural" way for men and women to look. But if you compare, say, a medieval Adam and Eve by Hugo van der Goes with a Renaissance example, by Dürer, you see very different bodies—bodies that have been stylized in part by the clothes that they would have worn, which in turn reflected cultural conceptions of the ideal body type. The "natural" human body does not exist; but most people accept as natural the clothed figures that they are accustomed to seeing, or, to some extent, what they would like to see. All that can definitely be said is that men and women differ in their primary and secondary sexual characteristics, but the degree of difference can be relatively large or small, depending on the individual and racial type. Beyond this, there exists a range of possible body types, which are products of both heredity and environment.

The contemporary belief that athleticism equals feminism and is "based on sound medical knowledge" is as culture-bound as an Edwardian doctor's approval of "healthy" fatness for both men and women, and is as ideologically derived as the feminist hostility toward large breasts. To minimize gender distinctions and to emphasize a mesomorphic body type is no more "natural" than fashion's various exaggerations or stylizations of the sexual body. Most people today exercise less for any pleasure that they might get out of doing sit-ups than because they want to look good. It is absurd to blame fashion, as such, for turning women into sexual objects.

In practical terms, the alternative to fashion involves hiding the female body—either completely, as with the Iranian *chador*, or in any sexual sense, as with the revolutionary Mao uniform. Islamic dress—or indeed, the clothing of other fundamentalist religions—indicates a belief that women's sexuality should not be displayed publicly, because women are the dangerously erotic possessions of their fathers and husbands. This is obviously unacceptable to the modern feminist, who tends, instead, to prefer unisex clothing. But the most celebrated experiment in the promotion of an anti-fashion uniform began to crumble after Mao Zedong died, as increasing numbers of men and women abandoned their identical blue cotton jackets and trousers—arguing that they wanted to look beautiful and individual.[3]

Historically, attacks on the artificiality of fashion have been almost as common as attacks on its immorality. Yet why should the idea of artificiality arouse such deep hostility? In fact, as the Balinese myth of the origin of clothing indicates, the artificial creation of the self is human, even super-human, whereas the natural and unmodified is equivalent to remaining in an uncivilized, animal state. Or, as Nietzsche wrote in *The Birth of Tragedy*, "We derive such dignity as we possess from our status as art works." In the western world, there is evidence that this attitude was and remains stronger in France than in the Anglo-Saxon countries. In his recent study of the French, Theodore Zeldon suggests that many French people believe that "to be French [is] to be, above all, artificial," that it is a national characteristic, like the snobbishness of the English and the practicality of Americans.[4]

Yet it was also in Enlightenment France that the idealization of the natural reached its most extensive philosophic elaboration: nature, simplicity, and virtue were united, while the artificial, exaggerated, and luxurious were denigrated as the product of "corrupt" civilizations. There is some sense that there exists a "psychological affinity between amorous desires and the craving for luxuries." Werner Sombart expanded this ancient moral critique to develop a theory of capitalism that argued that the liberation of sexual libido promoted the demand for luxury items, and spurred industrialization. Although as an economic theory this is simplistic, it does seem that the hostility to artificiality may itself be derivative from the hostility to sexual display.[5]

The so-called Calvinist work ethic combines with the theory of utilitarianism to introduce yet another reason for the denigration of the artificial: Work is a moral imperative, and it is a sinful waste of time to shop or to adorn and admire oneself. Beyond a certain minimum attention to the appearance necessary for social and self respect, dressing up is dismissed as "play-acting," with the implication that women have nothing more important to do. It is interesting that the traditional attacks on "feminine vanity" or "narcissism" (as well as falsehood and laziness) have been so uncritically adopted by modern feminists. Few argue today that both male and female attitudes toward adornment should change, but rather that women should adopt the "utilitarian" male standard. Thus homosexual men are also criticized for their attention to their appearance; only lesbians and heterosexual men are supposedly free from the need to be sexually attractive to men. Clearly, practicality is not really the issue.

Obviously, comfort and health are important to most people, but both terms are interpreted differently at different times and by different people. Both men's and women's fashions have at times restricted free movement, but significant physical constriction has been more characteristic of female fashions. At present , however, western women have much *greater* leeway than men to choose the clothing they feel happiest in. Comfort does not only entail the negative freedom from physical pain or constraint, but also positive feelings of physical and psychological pleasure. Today, despite some unhappiness with fashion, there are no actual dress reform proposals. Brownmiller herself admitted that many "backsliding" feminists ultimately concluded that straight-legged pants were "boring"; they "returned to dresses because they felt that life was getting grey without some whimsical indulgence in the feminine esthetic" and "the frivolous gaity of personal adornment."

The naiveté of the neo-feminist critique of fashion seriously cripples any attempt to understand the significance of changing ideals of beauty and styles of dress. But the critique is not irrelevant, nor do I mean to make fun of it. Many intelligent people believe that fashion and social definitions of femininity have limited the potential of the individual woman, and this is a legitimate concern. (Far fewer men appear to feel oppressed by cultural definitions of masculinity, although the minority that do are subject to perhaps the harshest social restrictions.) Every society has some kind of sex/gender system, by which biological males and females become social men and women. We do not know if biological distinctions determine the functions of the sexes within society—beyond the sexual function of procreation—because in every case, artificial distinctions are also made. Men and women look differently and do different things. Clothing may reinforce or merely reflect sex role ascription. But "the idea of the oppression of women, while certainly a historical fact, is of limited usefulness to historical inquiry. More important are questions like: What were women doing? How were they doing it? What was their own understanding of their place in the world?"[6]

It is absurd to blame *clothing* for limiting women, and pointless to blame "men" or "society" for *forcing* women to wear restrictive or "feminine" dress. What Marx said of men applies to women as well:

> Men make their own history, but they do not make it just as they please; they do not make it under circumstances chosen by themselves, but under circumstances directly encountered, given, and transmitted from the past.

The historian Nancy Cott has demonstrated that women, too, were and are neither "passive receivers of changing definitions of themselves," nor "totally mistresses of their destinies." Social and economic change affected women in many—not always "progressive" or direct—ways; and when they could, women seized the opportunities that they perceived for ends that they desired.[7] More women have perceived fashion in a positive than in a negative light, or (if ambivalent) as being more positive than negative. This continues to be true, for although many women today verbally dismiss fashion as an irrelevant vestige from the past, in practice, they adhere to it.

Nor is it that women have been brainwashed into literally regarding themselves as they are regarded by men; although there may be an element of truth in John Berger's suggestion that

> Men act and women appear. Men look at women. Women watch themselves being looked at. . . .The surveyor of woman in herself is male; the surveyed female. Thus she turns herself into an object—and most particularly an object of vision: a sight.[8]

But the libido for looking is more complex than this. For both men and women, whenever sex is an issue, so also is looking and being seen. Every woman who has ever been accosted on the street knows the temporary desire to be invisible, just as every person of either sex has posed in public, hoping to be regarded as attractive by his or her peers.

Fashion change occurs, in large part, because novelty arouses sexual curiosity and causes the individual to be *seen* more clearly again. This has very little to do with the so-called shifting erogenous zone, but instead is a characteristic of visual and psychological perception. Fashion also changes in response to previous and competing styles, and less directly with cultural attitudes toward the body, sexuality, and concepts of masculinity and femininity. Fashion change does not directly reflect changes in society or the position of women. In investigating how social (and fashion) change occurs, it appears that "attitudes, especially those involving emotional matters such as race or sex, almost never change except under compulsion, and that behavior is a more promising fulcrum for change than attitudes." Put differently, people are "converted by the *fait accompli*."[9] As women moved into the public world in a variety of ways—from shopping at department stores and lunching in town to participating in women's organizations and working at jobs, new styles evolved that seemed appropriate to these situations, yet also reflected traditional ideals of femininity. Ideals of beauty changed imperceptibly as women changed—the socialite Gibson Girl who was taller than her mother, went to college, and played golf with male friends gave a new look to the young woman, so people began to think that this is how beautiful young women *should* look.

The ideal image constantly interacted with the reality of women's lives. The goal was always to be attractive—both slender and rounded, modest and erotic. Thus, for example, the image of the Romantic ballerina affected the look of the 1830s and 1840s, but the frailty, thinness, and innocence of the early-Victorian woman have been greatly exaggerated.

The other important influence of that era, the evangelical movement of the early nineteenth century, was often harshly anti-sexual in tone, but was more often *prescriptive* than descriptive. The "new" buxom voluptuousness and overt sensuality of the Mid-Victorian woman was not really new, but indicated a shift in emphasis, both away from its immediate predecessor and toward a greater female presence. The purity movement of the later nineteenth century represented a minority backlash against the growing popular acceptance of erotic and personal expression. The social and sexual modernity of the Gibson Girl and the Poiret flapper were, to some extent, more a question of image than reality—but they became more real by virtue of people's growing acceptance of the pose. "Emancipation" and "exercise" were significant but rarely direct influences on fashion, unless the wildly popular tango could be considered a feminist dance.

Style, as much or even more than ideology, causes changes in women's appearance and in their lives. The erotic root of fashion manifests itself by means of the choices of countless individuals. Or as the author of *La Mode et la coquetterie* expressed it in 1912: "It is without doubt the desire to please which creates the mode, but it is the desire to please oneself that follows it."[10]

Appendix

In the third part of this book, in discussions of the eroticism of the corset and of the tight-lacing controversy, I referred frequently to the centerfold illustrations of *La Vie Parisienne*, and to the "tight-lacing correspondence." Additional bibliographical and historiographical information on these sources is presented in this appendix. Important centerfolds in *La Vie Parisienne* include: "Comment Elles S'Habillent de Nuit" (9 November 1878, pp. 650–651); "Considérations sur le Corset" (19 April 1879, pp. 224–225); a very popular seven-part series, "Études sur la Toilette," starting with "Les Chemises" (18 December 1880, pp. 746–747), and continuing with "Les Corsets" (15 January 1881, pp. 38–39), "Pantalons, Bas et Chaussures" (19 February 1881, pp. 108–109), "Les Corsages Décolletés" (2 April 1881, pp. 198–199), "Les Bas et la Manière de S'en Servir" (14 May 1881, pp. 286–287), "Dessus et Dessous—Conjectures sur les Sorties de Bal" (28 May 1881, pp. 316–317), "Les Postiches" [deceptive additions such as bust improvers, wigs, pads for the derrière, etc.] (11 June 1881, pp. 344–345); "Avant et Après le Corset" (9 September 1882, pp. 522–523); "Intimités—Toilettes d'Intérieur Offensives et Defensives (2 June 1883, pp. 308–309); and "Les Dessous" (2 May 1885, pp. 252–253).

Any attempt to analyze these centerfolds must take into account that *La Vie Parisienne* was a rather unusual magazine. A useful synopsis of its history appears in David Kunzle's article, "The Corset as Erotic Alchemy," in Thomas Hess and Linda Nochlin, eds., *Woman as Sex Object: Studies in Erotic Art, 1730–1970* (Art News Annual 38, New York: Newsweek, 1972.) Both the founder-editor, Marcelin, and the primary illustrator, Henri de Montaut, seem to have been almost obsessed with the theme of Woman and Fashion, but their views were typical neither of ordinary fashion journalism nor of the usual caricature magazines. In its treatment of feminine fashion, *La Vie Parisienne* was often overtly erotic, even quasi-fetishistic and bizarre—and cannot be considered representative of contemporary opinion. Nevertheless, its extreme emphasis on the eroticism of dress and underwear can potentially tell us something about more widespread cultural attitudes (and male fantasies). In a period when reticence about the subject of erotic dress was the general rule, we cannot afford to ignore a source that focuses so single-mindedly on this very subject. Furthermore, it is still closer in sensibility to, say, *Playboy* Magazine than to *Bizarre*.

The tight-lacing correspondence in *The Englishwoman's Domestic Magazine* has received a great deal of attention from historians. But to be read with real understanding, that correspondence must be seen in a larger bibliographical context. In the 1840s, *The Family Herald* printed a few tight-lacing letters. *EDM*-style letters on tight-lacing and corporal punishment appeared in the fashion magazine *The Queen* between 1862 and 1865. The role of Samuel Beeton, the editor of *EDM*, has been widely misinterpreted. Although he founded *The Queen* in 1861, he sold it in April 1862 to E.W. Cox, publisher of *The Field*. Beeton was, therefore, not in charge of *The Queen* during the period in which the tight-lacing letters appeared there and so he cannot be said to have launched the trend, although in *EDM*, in July 1862 and November 1863, he mentioned accounts of tight-lacing. It seems at least plausible that in 1867 Beeton recalled the correspondence in *The Queen*, and, in an attempt to boost circulation, printed several similar letters and waited for a response. There was apparently a deliberate policy to restrict such letters to *EDM*, as a note appeared in *The Young Englishwoman* in May, 1867 (p. 277), inviting those who wanted to discuss corsetry to write to *EDM*. Among the few exceptions were two tight-lacing poems that appeared in *The Young Englishwoman*.

There were, though, some identifiable connections between the various tight-lacing sources. One correspondent to *The Queen*, a Madame de la Santé, went on to publish a pamphlet, *The Corset Defended* (London: T.E. Carler, 1865). Furthermore, Ward, Lock, & Tyler, the publishers of *EDM*, also put out *The Corset and the Crinoline* (London, n.d. [1868]) by W. B. L. [William Barry Lord], which was reprinted in 1871, this time anonymously, under the more pejorative title, *The Freaks of Fashion*. This book reproduced a number of the letters from *The Queen* and from *EDM*. Beeton solicited more correspondence on "figure training" in *EDM* (October, 1870, p. 254), and several months later Ward, Lock, & Tyler brought out another text, *Figure Training; or Art the Handmaid of Nature* (London, n.d. [1871]), by "E. D. M.." Again correspondence from *The Queen* and *EDM* was quoted, and *The Corset and the Crinoline* was cited as an authoritative history of corsetry. None of these works quoted letters opposed to tight-lacing.

It is also worth pointing out that *EDM* printed so many letters on corporal punishment that a supplement devoted to that topic ran from April to December 1870. Both the corset and whipping literature clearly appealed to special-interest groups and aroused anger and incredulity elsewhere. *The Daily Telegraph*, *Saturday Review* ("The Birch in the Boudoir"), and *Punch*, for example, published articles on the correspondence on the "whipping of girls." According to Samuel Beeton (*EDM*, March 1, 1869, p. 165), "The three papers ... all express their belief that the letters that have been printed in *EDM* are feigned, false, due, the *Saturday* [*Review*] fancied, to the fertile brain of the Editor." He maintained, however, that he had received "letters from a hundred pens," and that "All the correspondence is genuine, absolutely and without reserve of any kind." Presumably, controversy helped to sell books and magazines.

Kunzle presents Beeton in a highly favorable light, on the grounds that he provided a public forum for a persecuted sexual minority: although "not averse to a certain sensationalism," Beeton was motivated primarily by "the spirit of fair play" when he published the pro-tight-lacing letters. He was "bowing to pressures from his young female readership." If he did print a few "suspect" letters—such as those "recounting enforced tight-lacing"—it was merely to "provoke correspondence." Kunzle concludes that, by publishing these letters, "Beeton opened the door a chink to the sexual liberation of both sexes." Take this as you will.

Another similar correspondence on tight-lacing, corporal punishment, high heels, ear and nipple-piercing, underwear, and dress reform (which was regarded as titillating) appeared in *The Family Doctor and People's Medical Advisor* in the 1880s. Although *FD* frequently printed articles on the dangers of tight-lacing, they are not orthodox medical articles, and seem to have been designed to provoke more correspondence. *The Family Doctor* (published 1885–1918) was put out by the publishers of *The Illustrated Police News*, and, like it, seems to have been an example of sensationalist popular journalism. Some correspondents mention *EDM* or use the same pseudonyms.

"Fetishist" correspondence on tight-lacing (for men and women), dress reform, gloves, lingerie, spurs, etc., also appears in *Modern Society* (1880–1917) off and on between 1884 and 1911, with a series on "Slaves of the Stay-Lace" lasting from November 1909 to January 1910. This women's magazine with a large circulation also carried advertisements for Madame Dowding's corsets for men—as did *Society* (1879–1900). *Society* printed numerous letters on tight-lacing, "Birching Young Ladies," transvestism, gloves, lingerie, high heels, and breast rings, especially in 1894, 1896, and 1899 to 1900. In 1898–1899 there appeared a serial exposé of "Massage in the West-End." Clearly this magazine was for several years more than a vehicle for social and theatrical gossip.

Other periodicals that included occasional letters, stories, and even photographs devoted to tight-lacing include (but are not limited to) *Photo-Bits* (especially from 1909 to 1912), *Tit-Bits* (1894), *Answers* (1893), and *Bits of Fun* (from 1910 to 1920). *London Life* was a late example of a fetishist forum, lasting until 1941, and dealing with a range of fetishist topics. The author of "The Vogue of the Wasp-Waist" (26 April 1930, p. 29) looked back nostalgically to Victorian waists of nine and ten inches.

Some works that purported to be exposés and critiques of tight-lacing were actually either fetishistic or deliberately sensationalist. *How to Train the Figure and Achieve Perfection of Form* by F. B. (London: The Central Publishing Co., 1896), for example, included a selection of tight-lacing letters (that have been cut out of the copy at the British Museum Library).

I have been unable to find any comparable French confessions or defenses of tight-lacing. A twenty-page pamphlet, *Monographie du corset* (published in 1887 in Louvain, Belgium) *did* defend tight-lacing, but the author, a "Miss Seeker," was apparently English. She argued (pp. 8, 19–20) that the history of the corset was far from being a "martyrology of women." On the contrary, the tight corset was necessary for health and beauty, and she gave as an example a "Madame de la R***," who had a waist of fifty centimeters at the age of sixty, and after having had six children. Her own sixteen-year-old sister, Jenny, wore a heavily boned and rigid corset and had the "waist of a nymph"—forty-six centimeters.

Toward the end of the century, the bust became more of a focus of interest in the fetishist correspondence. The "governess" at "Madame La B——'s school just outside Paris" wrote "Tight-Lacing and the Latest Craze"— that of having one's *"tetons"* pierced by "jewelers in the Rue St. Honoré"—a practice, she pointed out, that had been described in *La Vie Parisienne* and in "a recent *roman*." Breast-rings and "the friction of my *lingerie*" caused her bust to grow (*Society*, 16 December 1899, p. 2109).

AN ENGLISH SCHOOLGIRL wrote to *The Family Doctor* to describe her experiences of "Corset Discipline" at a "fashionable girls' college at Eastbourne." She mentioned several times that her "bust was (for a girl) beautifully rounded, quite filling out the bodice of my dress." She wanted to lace to thirteen inches: "My new black satin corsets were taken out of their box. . . . Mademoiselle herself [the French governess] draped them on me, then the servant took hold of the long and strong silken lace. I felt the latter slipping through the holes, my stomach being squeezed in and forced downwards and saw my waist get gradually smaller, and my bosom and hips more prominent." It was still impossible to close the corset completely, supposedly because her underclothing took up too much space. "Mademoiselle said, 'Gertie you must take off your drawers'." She removed her silk knickerbockers and wore only her chemise and corset. "I could now easily clasp my hands round my waist, and I saw my hips looked very large and full, whilst my bust filled my chemise, and my breasts looked as if they would burst through the lace and silk" (27 September 1890, p. 73.)

Notes

Notes to Introduction

1. By 1868, the front of the crinoline had flattened, forming a half-cage that evolved into the first bustle; in 1878 the bustle shrunk to a small pad, but dresses had trains behind; in about 1880, the bustle reappeared, rather higher than before, and grew larger and larger, until it suddenly disappeared.

2. *Zum Fünfundzwanzigjährigen Bestehen der "Modenwelt," 1865–1890.* (Berlin, 1890.)

3. Lois Banner, *American Beauty: A Social History . . . Through Two Centuries . . . Of the American Idea, Ideal, and Image of the Beautiful Woman* (New York: Alfred A. Knopf, 1983).

4. Jules David Prown, "Mind in Matter: An Introduction to Material Culture Theory and Method," *Winterthur Portfolio* 17 (Spring, 1982): 1–19.

5. Philippe Perrot, *Les Dessus et les Dessous de la bourgeoisie. Un histoire du vêtement au XIXᵉ siècle* (Paris: Librairie Arthème Fayard, 1981). See also Philip Thody, "The Semiotician in the Wardrobe," *The Times Literary Supplement* (October 16, 1981): 1199; Roland Barthes, *Système de la Mode* (Paris: Editions de Seuil, 1967); Terence Hawkes, *Structuralism and Semiotics* (Berkeley and Los Angeles: University of California Press, 1979), pp. 135, 125; Ingrid Brenninkmeyer, *The Sociology of Fashion* (Winterthur: P. G. Keller, 1962), pp. 95–96; Prown, "Mind in Matter," p. 12.

6. See Quentin Bell, *On Human Finery* (New York: Schocken Books, 1976), pp. 58–60; Yvonne Deslandres, *Le Costume, image de l'homme* (Paris: Albin Michel, 1976), pp. 86, 105; René König, *A La Mode: On the Social Psychology of Fashion* (New York: Seabury Press, 1973), pp. 128–146; Edward Sapir, "Fashion," in *Encyclopedia of the Social Sciences*, Vol. 6, p. 141; William Bridgewater and Elizabeth J. Sherwood, eds., *The Columbia Encyclopedia* (New York: Columbia University Press, second edition, 1950).

7. Walter Fairservis, *Costumes of the East* (Riverside, Connecticut: Chatham Press, in association with The American Museum of Natural History, 1971); Shen Congwen, *Zhongguo gudai fushi yanjiu* [Researches on Ancient Chinese Costume] (Beijing and Hong Kong: The Commercial Press, 1981).

Notes to Chapter 1

1. Genesis 3: 7, 21. Saint Augustine's "lust-shame theory," developed in *The City of God,* is characterized as such in Robert H. Lauer and Jeanette C. Lauer, *Fashion Power. The Meaning of Fashion in American Society* (Englewood Cliffs, New Jersey: Prentice-Hall, 1981), p. 41, and is described at length in Stanford M. Lyman, *The Seven Deadly Sins: Society and Evil* (New York: St. Martin's Press, 1978), pp. 55–58.

2. An interesting study could be done on clothing myths. The image of the woman as weaver is quite common, and a number of cultural groups regard all textiles as essentially female and metal instruments as essentially male.

3. Isaiah 3: 16–24; I Timothy 2: 9–10; Tertullian, "On the apparel of women," cited by Lauer and Lauer, *Fashion Power,* p. 42.

4. Havelock Ellis, *Studies in the Psychology of Sex,* first published in 1898, 1899, 1936 (New York: Modern Library Edition, 1949), Vol. 1, Part 1, "The Evolution of Modesty," pp. 63, 59; Ernest Crawley, *Dress, Drinks, and Drums. Further Studies of Savages and Sex* (London: Methuen & Co., 1931), pp. 9–11.

5. Casanova, cited by Ellis, "The Evolution of Modesty," p. 1; Mrs. Merrifield, *Dress as a Fine Art* (London: A. Hall Virtue, 1854, and Boston: Jewett & Co, 1854), p. 16; G. Woolliscroft Rhead, *Chats on Costume* (London: T. Fisher Unwin, 1906), p. 20.

6. Anthropological theories cited in Havelock Ellis, "The Evolution of Modesty," pp. 61, 47, 59; William Graham Sumner, *Folkways. A Study of the Sociological Importance of Usages, Manners, Customs, Mores, and Morals,* first published in 1906 (New York: Mentor Books, 1960), pp. 3636–3634; E. A. Westermarck, *The History of Human Marriage,* first published in London in 1891, cited by Ruth Benedict, "Dress," in Edwin R. A. Seligman, ed., *Encyclopedia of the Social Sciences* (New York: Macmillan, 1931), Vol. 5, p. 236.

7. Lois M. Gurel and Marianne S. Beeson, eds., *Dimensions of Dress and Adornment: A Book of Readings* (Dubuque, Iowa: Kendell/Hunt, 1975), p. 4.

8. Sigmund Freud, *Totem and Taboo* (1912–1913), *The Standard Edition of the Complete Psychological Works,* translated and edited by James Strachey, et al. (London: The Hogarth Press and the Institute of Psycho-Analysis, 1953–1975), 24 volumes, vol. 13; René König, *A La Mode: On the Social Psychology of Fashion* (New York: Seabury Press, 1973), pp. 26, 32–33.

9. Herbert G. Blumer, "Fashion," in David L. Sills, ed., *International Encyclopedia of the Social Sciences* (New York: The Macmillan Company & The Free Press, 1968), Vol. 5, p. 342. See also Ruth Benedict, "Dress," in *Encyclopedia of the Social Sciences* (New York: Macmillan & Co., 1931), Vol. 5, p. 236.

10. Lauer and Lauer, *Fashion Power,* pp. 73–93; Doris Langley Moore, *The Woman in Fashion* (London: B. T. Batsford, 1949), p. 11.

11. Langley Moore, *The Woman in Fashion,* p. 5; Paul H. Nystrom, *Economics of Fashion* (New York: Ronald Press, 1928), pp. 10–13.

12. Ingrid Brenninkmeyer, *The Sociology of Fashion* (Winterthur: P. G. Keller, 1962), p. 8; Nystrom, *Economics of Fashion,* p. 25.

13. Fernand Braudel, *Capitalism and Material Life, 1400–1800*, first published Paris, 1967, translated by Miriam Rochan (New York and London: Harper & Row, 1973), pp. 231, 226; Mary Ellen Roach and Joanne Eicher, *Dress, Adornment and the Social Order* (Englewood Cliffs, New Jersey: Prentice-Hall, 1973), p. 28.

14. Blumer, "Fashion," p. 342.

15. Herbert Spencer, "Fashion," in *The Principles of Sociology*, first published in 8 parts in 3 volumes, 1876–1896 (New York: D. Appleton & Co., 1899); Thorstein Veblen, "Dress as an Expression of the Pecuniary Culture," Chapter 7 of *The Theory of the Leisure Class*, first published in 1899 (New York: Random House, The Modern Library, 1934), p. 179.

16. Veblen, *The Theory of the Leisure Class*, pp. 179, 149, 171–172.

17. Quentin Bell developed an intelligent and sophisticated revision of Veblen's theory; see *On Human Finery* (London: Hogarth Press, 1947, 1976), especially pp. 182–185, and Langley Moore, *The Woman in Fashion*, pp. 1–15.

18. Roach and Eicher, *Dress, Adornment, and the Social Order*, pp. 219–222; Georg Simmel, "Fashion," *International Quarterly* 10 (October, 1904): 130–155.

19. Blumer, "Fashion," pp. 342–343; Lauer and Lauer, *Fashion Power*, pp. 6, 22.

20. Georg Simmel, "Exkurs über den Schmuck," trans. as "Adornment," in Kurt H. Wolff, trans. and ed., *The Sociology of Georg Simmel* (Glencoe: The Free Press, 1950), pp. 338–344.

21. Louis Octave Uzanne, *Fashion in Paris. The Various Phases of Feminine Taste and Aesthetics from 1797 to 1897* (London: William Heinemann, 1898), p. v; Max von Boehn, *Modespiegel* (Berlin: Braunschweig, & Hamburg: G. Westermann, 1919), p. 4.

22. Max von Boehn, *Modes and Manners of the Nineteenth Century*, English translation of *Die Mode: Menschen und Moden im neunzehnten Jahrhundert* (London: Dent, 1927), 4 volumes, vol. 3, p. 48.

23. James Laver, *Taste and Fashion: From the French Revolution to Today* (London: George G. Harrap & Co., 1937, revised ed., 1945), pp. 198–199.

24. Bell, *On Human Finery*, p. 102.

25. Ernst Gombrich, *The Sense of Order. A Study in the Psychology of Decorative Art* (Ithaca, New York: Cornell University Press, 1979), p. 200; Ernst Gombrich, *Ideals and Idols. Essays on Values in History and in Art* (Oxford: Phaidon Press, 1979), pp. 51, 46, 61, 50, 43; Karl Popper, *The Poverty of Historicism*, cited by Gombrich, *Ideals and Idols*, p. 61.

26. Ernst Gombrich, "Style," in David Sills, ed., *International Encyclopedia of the Social Sciences* (New York: Macmillan, 1968), Vol. 15, p. 357.

27. Peter Gay, *Art and Act. On Causes in History—Manet, Gropius, Mondrian* (New York: Harper & Row, 1976), pp. 14–16.

28. Agnes Brooks Young, *Recurring Cycles of Fashion 1760–1937* (New York: Harper & Bros., 1937), p. 3.
    See also A. L. Kroeber and Jane Richardson, "Three Centuries of Women's Dress Fashions: A Quantitative Analysis," in *The Nature of Culture* (Chicago: University of Chicago Press, 1955), pp. 358–378.

29. Lauer and Lauer, *Fashion Power*, pp. 14–15, 20; Edward Sapir, "Fashion," in *Encyclopedia of the Social Sciences* (New York: Macmillan & Co., 1931), Vol. 6, p. 141.

Notes to Chapter 2

1. Edmund Bergler, *Fashion and the Unconscious* (New York: Brunner, 1953), pp. vii, viii; Lawrence Langner, *The Importance of Wearing Clothes* (New York: Hastings House, 1959).

2. J. C. Flügel, *The Psychology of Clothes* (London: The Hogarth Press, 1930); René König, *A La Mode: On the Social Psychology of Fashion* (New York: Seabury Press, 1973).

3. Sigmund Freud, *The Interpretation of Dreams* (1900), *The Standard Edition of the Complete Psychological Works*, translated and edited by James Strachey, et al. (London: The Hogarth Press and the Institute of Psycho-Analysis, 1953–1975), 24 volumes, vol. 4–5; Freud, "Fetishism" (1927), *S.E.*, vol. 21, pp. 149–158; J. C. Flügel, "Clothes Symbolism and Clothes Ambivalence," *International Journal of Psychoanalysis*, vol. 10 (Spring, 1929): 205–214; Flügel, *The Psychology of Clothes*, p. 27.

4. Flügel, *The Psychology of Clothes*, pp. 20–22, 26.

5. König, *A La Mode*, pp. 26, 32–33.

6. Ernest Crawley, *Dress, Drink, and Drums. Further Studies of Savages and Sex* (London: Methuen & Co., 1931), p. 54; Havelock Ellis, quoted in Elizabeth Hurlock, *The Psychology of Dress. An Analysis of Fashion and Its Motive* (New York: Ronald Press, 1929), p. 144.

7. Deuteronomy 22: 5; Philip Stubbs, *The Anatomy of Abuses*, quoted in Mary Lou Rosencranz, *Clothing Concepts: A Social-Psychological Approach* (New York: Macmillan, 1972), p. 166.

8. Sigmund Freud, "Instincts and Their Vicissitudes" (1918), *S.E.*, vol. 14, pp. 126–130.

9. Sigmund Freud, *Jokes and Their Relation to the Unconscious* (1905), *S.E.* vol. 8, p. 98.

10. Flügel, *The Psychology of Clothes*, p. 107; Flügel, "Clothes Symbolism," p. 205.

11. Flügel, *The Psychology of Clothes*, pp. 106, 160, 107–108; Flügel, "Clothes Symbolism," p. 211.

12. Flügel, *The Psychology of Clothes*, pp. 213, 86, 115. But see also Freud, "On Narcissism: An Introduction" (1914), *S.E.*, vol. 14, pp. 73–105; Helene Deutsche, *The Psychology of Women* (New York, 1944), p. 194.

13. Flügel, *The Psychology of Clothes*, pp. 108–121, 208, 211–215.

14. Laver, *Modesty in Dress*, p. 119.

15. See, for example, Philippe Perrot, *Les Dessus et les Dessous de la bourgeoisie. Une histoire du vêtement au XIXe siècle* (Paris: Librairie Arthème Fayard, 1981), p. 21. Perrot goes on to suggest that when the legs were uncovered "in the 1920s," there developed a "very candid fetishism for those parts." The use of the word "fetishism" is so broad as to be almost meaningless.

16. David Kunzle, *Fashion and Fetishism: A Social History of the Corset, Tight-Lacing and Other Forms of Body Sculpture in the West* (Totowa, New Jersey: Rowman and Littlefield, 1980), Introduction and Chapter One. See "The Corset Controversy" for an analysis of Kunzle's theories.

17. Jeffrey Weeks, *Sex, Politics and Society. The Regulation of Sexuality since 1800* (London & New York: Longman Group Limited, 1981), pp. 141–156.

18. Dr. Richard von Krafft-Ebing, *Psychopathia Sexualis with Especial Reference to the Antipathic Sexual Instinct. A Medico-Forensic Study*, originally published in 1886, English translation of the 12th German edition by F. J. Rebman (Brooklyn, New York: Physicians and Surgeons Book Co., 1926), pp. 17–24, 218, 224, 222, 234, 238, 247–269.

19. Weeks, *Sex, Politics, and Society*, pp. 148–149; Havelock Ellis, "Erotic Symbolism," in *Studies in the Psychology of Sex*. 7 parts in 2 volumes, 1898–1936 (New York: Modern Library Edition, 1942), vol. 2, pp. 8–9, 15, 32.

20. Dr. Wilhelm Stekel, *Sexual Aberrations. The Phenomena of Fetishism in Relation to Sex*, translated by Dr. S. Parker from the first German edition of 1922 (New York: Horace Liveright, 1930), pp. 3–37, 72–76, 130–132, 202–224, 225–275, 300, 305.

21. Freud, *Three Essays on the Theory of Sexuality*, pp. 153–154.

22. Freud, "Fetishism" (1927), *S.E.*, vol. 21, pp. 152–154.

23. Freud, "Fetishism," pp. 155, 157.

24. Alfred Kinsey, cited by Sherry Magnus, "Feet, Shoes & Power . . . The Last Erogenous Zone," *Vogue* (April, 1982), p. 384.

25. William A. Rossi, *The Sex Life of the Foot and Shoe* (London: Routledge & Kegan Paul, 1977), pp. 20, 3, 19, 37, 121, 146.

26. James Laver, *Dress. How and Why Fashions in Men's and Women's Clothes have Changed during the Past Two Hundred Years* (London: John Murray, 1950), p. 47; James Laver, *Modesty in Dress* (Boston: Houghton Mifflin, 1969), p. 14.

27. Laver, *Modesty in Dress*, pp. 37, 97, 96.

28. C. Willett Cunnington, *Feminine Attitudes in the Nineteenth Century* (London: William Heineman, 1935). Doris Langley Moore has made some very intelligent and witty objections to this approach in *The Woman in Fashion* (London: B. T. Batsford, 1949), p. 10.

29. C. Willett Cunnington, *The Perfect Lady* (London: Max Parrish & Co., 1948), pp. 39, 49–51.

30. Langley Moore, *The Woman in Fashion*, p. 13.

31. Freud, *Three Essays on the Theory of Sexuality*, pp. 183–184, 169, 171, 207. Freud used the term in association with the concept of "component instincts." An erotogenic zone is an organ or part of the body (such as the oral and anal orifices) from which arise sensations of sexual excitation. Different types of sexual constitution derive in part from "the innate preponderance" of a particular erotogenic zone or component instinct. Hence, the development, for example, of the oral and anal personality types. In cases of voyeurism and exhibitionism, "the eye corresponds to an erotogenic zone; while in the case of those components of the sexual instinct which involve pain and cruelty, the same role is assumed by the skin." Normally, at puberty, the separate "erotogenic zones become subordinated to the primacy of the genital zone," and the sexual aim of pleasure leads to actual sexual intercourse.

32. Alison Lurie, *The Language of Clothes* (New York: Random House, 1981); Prudence Glynn, *Skin to Skin: Eroticism in Dress* (New York: Oxford University Press, 1982), p. 17.

33. Glynn, *Skin to Skin*, pp. 31–57, 62.

34. Lurie, *Language of Clothes*, pp. 230–261.

35. Glynn, *Skin to Skin*, pp. 15–16.

36. Langley Moore, *The Woman in Fashion*, p. 1.

Notes to Chapter 3

1. Philip Malcolm Waller Thody, *Roland Barthes: A Conservative Estimate* (Atlantic Highlands, New Jersey: Humanities Press, 1977), p. 112.

2. Gordon Rattray Taylor, *Sex in History* (London: Thames & Hudson, 1953), cited by Jeffrey Weeks, *Sex, Politics and Society. The Regulation of Sexuality since 1800* (London and New York: Longman, 1981), p. 2.

3. Sigmund Freud, *Three Essays on the Theory of Sexuality* (1905), *S.E.*, vol. 7, p. 156. See also Freud, *Civilization and Its Discontents* (1930), *S.E.*, vol. 21, p. 83; C. Fouquet and Y. Knibiehler, *La Beauté pour quoi faire? Essai sur l'histoire de la beauté féminine* (Paris: Temps Actuel, 1982), pp. 18–19; Havelock Ellis, "Sexual Selection in Man," *Studies in the Psychology of Sex* (New York: Modern Library Edition, 1942), vol. 1, p. 156.

4. Freud, "Leonardo da Vinci and a Memory of His Childhood" (1910), *S.E.*, vol. 11, pp. 97, 96; Freud, *Civilization and Its Discontents*, p. 83.

   Freud's analysis is based primarily on psychological evidence, and secondarily on hypotheses about the pre-historic period, ancient history, and "primitive" cultures.

5. René König, *A La Mode: On the Social Psychology of Fashion* (New York: Seabury Press, 1973), p. 82.

6. Robert Herrick (1591–1674), "Upon Julia's Clothes" and "Delight in Disorder."

7. Freud, *Three Essays on the Theory of Sexuality*, p. 156.

8. König, *A La Mode*, p. 91. "The New Temptation of St. Anthony" (1895) is reproduced in Friedrich Wendel, *Weib und Mode* (Dresden: Paul Aretz Verlag, 1928), p. 258.

9. James Laver, *Modesty in Dress* (Boston: Houghton Mifflin, 1969), p. 97.

10. König, *A La Mode*, pp. 93, 134–135.

11. Robert Musil, *The Man Without Qualities*, 4 vols., translated by Eithne Wilkins and Ernst Kaiser from the German edition, *Der Mann ohne Eigenschaften* (London: Secker & Warburg, 1953, 1954, 1960), vol. 1, pp. 331–332, 337.

12. Anne Hollander, *Seeing Through Clothes* (New York: Viking Press, 1978), pp. 447–448.

13. Marcel Proust, *Le Côté de Guermantes*, cited by Marylène Delbourg-Delphis, *Le Chic et le Look* (Paris: Hachett, 1981), p. 42. See also Remy Q. Saisselin, "From Baudelaire to Christian Dior: The Poetics of Fashion," *Journal of Aesthetics and Art Criticism*, 18 (1959–1960).

14. Urs Ramseyer, *The Art and Culture of Bali* (Oxford: Oxford University Press, 1977), pp. 60, 70.

15. Lois M. Gurel and Marianne S. Beeson, eds., *Dimensions of Dress and Adornment: A Book of Readings* (Dubuque, Iowa: Kendell/Hunt, 1975), p. 4; Justine Cordwell, "The Very Human Arts of Transformation," and Ronald Schwarz, "Uncovering the Secret Vice: Toward an Anthropology of Clothing and Adornment," both in Cordwell and Schwarz, eds., *The Fabrics of Culture: The Anthropology of Clothing and Adornment* (New York: Mouton, 1979), pp. 45, 26–30.

16. Thody, *Roland Barthes*, p. 103.
17. Domna Stanton, *The Aristocrat as Art: A Study of the Honnête Homme and the Dandy in Seventeenth and Nineteenth-Century French Literature* (New York: Columbia University Press, 1980), p. 5.
18. Stanton, *The Aristocrat as Art*, pp. 110, 150.
19. Hollander, *Seeing Through Clothes*, pp. xi–xvi, 311–314, 454.

Notes to Chapter 4

1. Betty-Bright P. Low, "Of Muslins and Merveilleuses. Excerpts from the Letters of Josephine du Pont and Margaret Manigault," *Winterthur Portfolio* 9 (Charlottesville: Published for the Henry Francis Dupont Winterthur Museum by the University Press of Virginia, 1974), p. 29; N. G. Dufief, *Nature Displayed in Her Mode of Teaching Language to Man (etc.)* (Philadelphia, 1806), p. 15.
2. Valerie Steele, "The Social and Political Significance of Macaroni Fashion," unpublished paper presented at the Annual Meeting and Symposium of the Costume Society of America, Oakland, California, May, 1982. Forthcoming in *Costume. The Journal of the Costume Society*.
3. Anne Buck, *Victorian Costume and Costume Accessories* (London: Herbert Jenkins, 1961), p. 19.
4. Theophile Gautier, *De la mode* (1958), quoted in Marylène Delbourg-Delphis, *Le Chic et le Look* (Paris: Hachette, 1981), p. 23.
5. Phyllis Cunnington, *Costume in Pictures* (London: The Herbert Press, 1964), pp. 99–103; Jane Welsh Carlyle (1839), quoted by Anne Buck, "Clothes in Fact and Fiction 1825–1865," *Costume. The Journal of the Costume Society* 17 (London, 1983), p. 91.
6. Marina Warner, ed., *Queen Victoria's Sketchbook* (New York: Crown Publishers, 1979), p. 88. It is unclear from this quotation exactly what Albert was wearing. He might, in fact, have been in uniform.
7. *Aglaia. The Journal of the Healthy and Artistic Dress Union* (Spring, 1894), p. 16.
8. Georgiana Hill, *A History of English Dress* (New York: G.P. Putnams Sons, 1893, and London: Richard Bentley & Son, 1893), p. 276.
9. *The Ladies Treasury for 1877*, pp. 474, 29.
10. Sarah Levitt, unpublished paper presented at a meeting of The Costume Society, London, January, 1982.
11. *La Mode Illustrée* (1876) and *Myra's Journal* (1876), cited by Norah Waugh, *Corsets and Crinolines* (London: B. T. Batsford, 1954), pp. 106, 124; Doris Langley Moore, *The Woman in Fashion* (London: B. T. Batsford, 1949), p. 113.
12. English fashion journalist (1876), cited without attribution by Janet Arnold, "The Cut and Construction of Women's Dresses c. 1860–1890," in Ann Saunders, ed., *High Victorian Costume 1860–1890* (London: Published for The Costume Society, Victoria and Albert Museum, 1969), p. 28.
13. Charles Blanc, *Art in Ornament and Dress* (London: Chapman and Hall, 1877), pp. 110–112.
14. Louis Octave Uzanne, *The Fan* (London: J. C. Nimmo and Bain, 1884), p. 10; J. Augustin Challamel, *The History of Fashion in France* (London: S. Low, Marston, Searle, and Rivington, 1882), p. 230.

15. *The Englishwoman's Domestic Magazine* (1 August 1870), p. 99.
16. Challamel, *The History of Fashion in France*, p. 230; Louis Octave Uzanne, *The Sunshade, Muff, and Glove* (London: J. C. Nimmo and Bain, 1883), p. 61.
17. Langley Moore, *The Woman in Fashion*, pp. 79–115.
18. *The Queen* (1878), quoted by Madeline Ginsbrug, *Victorian Dress in Photographs* (New York: Holmes & Meier, 1982), p. 85.
19. See Musée de la Mode et du Costume, *Secrets d'élégance 1850–1970* (Paris, 1978), p. 42; *The Lady's Magazine* (September, 1901), p. 272; *The Queen* (10 January 1903), p. 74.
20. *Les Modes* (May, 1901), p. 13.
21. Friedrich Engels, *Condition of the Working Class in England in 1844* (1892), p. 66, quoted by Anne Buck, "Clothes in Fact and Fiction 1825–1865," p. 93.
22. Thomas Wright, *Some Habits of the Working Classes*, by a Journeyman Engineer (1867), pp. 189, 119, quoted by Anne Buck, "Clothes in Fact and Fiction 1825–1865," p. 93.
23. P. Emerson, *A Son of the Fens*, quoted by Jane Grove, "Victorian Respectability and the Etiquette of Dress," *Strata of Society*. Proceedings of the Seventh Annual Conference of the Costume Society, April 6–8, 1973 (London, 1974), p. 18.
24. C. H. Ward Jackson, *A History of Courtaulds* (1941), p. 56, and Elizabeth Gaskell, "The Cage at Cranford" (1863), both quoted by Anne Buck, "Clothes in Fact and Fiction 1825–1865," pp. 99–100. The information on slaves is from a talk given by Carol Kregloh at Smith College, February, 1984.
25. Jane Welsh Carlyle, *Letters and Memorials*, III (1864), p. 231, quoted by Anne Buck, "Clothes in Fact and Fiction 1825–1865," p. 99.
26. See the photographs reproduced in Madeleine Ginsburg, *Victorian Dress in Photographs*, pp. 140–143, 149–151. "Dinner Hour, Wigan" by Eyre Crowe, 1874, is in the Manchester City Art Galleries. See also Michael Hiley, *Victorian Working Women: Portraits from Life* (Boston: David R. Godine, 1979), pp. 14–15, 18.
27. Challamel, *The History of Fashion in France*, p. 224; Louis Octave Uzanne, *Fashion in Paris* (London: William Heinemann, 1898), pp. 128–140; Uzanne, *The Modern Parisienne* (London: William Heinemann, 1912), pp. 29–32, 37–38, 170–175.
28. *The Queen* (1878), quoted by Madeleine Ginsburg, *Victorian Dress in Photographs*, p. 172.
29. *Cornhill Magazine* (1901) and *Family Budgets* (1896), quoted by E. Royston Pike, *Human Documents in the Age of the Forsytes* (London: George Allen & Unwin, 1969), pp. 145–175, especially pp. 149, 159.
30. Madeleine Ginsberg, "Rags to Riches: The Second Hand Clothes Trade 1700–1978," *Costume* 14 (1980), p. 128; Wendy Forrester, *Great-Grandmama's Weekly: A Celebration of The Girl's Own Paper* (Guildford and London: Lutterworth Press, 1980), pp. 92, 94, 108.
31. *Cornhill Magazine*, quoted by Pike, *Human Documents*, p. 162. See also *How to Dress on £15 a Year as a Lady*, by A Lady (London: Frederick Warburg & Co., 1878).

32. *The Life and Labour of the People of London*, 17 vols. (1902–1903), quoted by Pike, *Human Documents*, p. 78.

33. Bruno de Roselle, *La Mode* (Paris: Imprimerie nationale, 1981), pp. 1–6. See also Philippe Perrot, *Les Dessus et les Dessous de la bourgeoisie. Une histoire du vêtement au XIXᵉ siècle* (Paris: Librairie Arthème Fayard, 1981).

34. Diane de Marly, *The History of Haute Couture* (New York: Holmes & Meier, 1980), especially pp. 126–127; Ewing, *The History of Twentieth-Century Fashion*, pp. 12–15. See also Diane de Marly, *Worth. Father of Haute Couture* (New York: Holmes & Meier, 1980).

35. Roselle, *La Mode*, p. 85.

36. For America, see Claudia B. Kidwell and Margaret C. Christman, *Suiting Everyone: The Democratization of Clothing in America* (Washington, D.C.: Smithsonian Institution Press, 1974); and a forthcoming study of the department store by William Leach; for England, Ewing, *The History of Twentieth-Century Fashion*; and Alison Adburgham, *Shops and Shopping, 1800–1914* (London: George Allen & Unwin, 1964); and for France, Boucher, *A History of Fashion in the West*; Michael Miller, *The Bon Marché. Bourgeois Culture and the Department Store, 1869–1920* (Princeton: Princeton University Press, 1981); Henrietta Vanier, *La Mode et ses métiers: Frivolités et luttes des classes, 1830–1890* (Paris: Armand Colin, 1960).

37. de Marly, *The History of Haute Couture*, pp. 110–111; Perrot, *Les Dessus et les Dessous de la bourgeoisie*, pp. 111–154.

38. *The Draper* (1871), quoted by Madeleine Ginsburg, *Victorian Dress in Photographs*, p. 172.

39. Doris Langley Moore, *Fashion Through Fashion Plates 1771–1970* (London: Ward, Lock, 1970), pp. 10, 28, 27. See also the classic study by Vyvyan Holland, *Hand Coloured Fashion Plates 1770 to 1899* (London: B. T. Batsford, 1955); Charles Gibbs Smith, *The Fashionable Lady in the Nineteenth Century* (London: Her Majesty's Stationery Office, 1960); and Madeleine Ginsburg, *An Introduction to Fashion Illustration* (Owings Mills, Maryland: Stemmer House Publishers, 1982); Alison Gernsheim, *Fashion and Reality 1840–1914* (London: Faber & Faber, 1963); Richard Ormond, "The Sources for the Study of Belle Epoque Costume," in Ann Saunders, ed., *La Belle Epoque. Costume 1890–1914* (London: Published for The Costume Society, Victoria and Albert Museum, 1968), pp. 5–13; Richard Ormond, "Pictorial Sources for a Study of Costume, 1860–1890," in Ann Saunders, ed., *Victorian Costume 1860–1890*, pp. 10–15.

40. Ewing, *The History of Twentieth-Century Fashion*, p. 12.

Notes to Chapter 5

1. Stephen Kern, *Anatomy and Destiny: A Cultural History of the Human Body* (New York: Bobbs-Merrill Co., 1975), p. 10.

2. Peter Quennell, *Victorian Panorama. A Survey of Life and Fashion from Contemporary Photographs* (London: B.T. Batsford, 1937; New York: Charles Scribner's Sons, 1937), pp. 92, 97.

3. Irene Clephane and Alan Bott, *Our Mothers. A Cavalcade in Pictures, Quotation and Description of Late Victorian Women, 1870–1900* (London: Victor Gollancz Ltd., 1932), pp. 199, 4.

4. Duncan Crow, *The Victorian Woman* (New York: Stein & Day, 1972), pp. 25, 123.

5. Cyril Pearl, *The Girl with the Swansdown Seat* (New York: Bobbs-Merrill Co., 1955), pp. 12, 79, 204–211.

6. Ronald Pearsall, *The Worm in the Bud. The World of Victorian Sexuality* (London: Weidenfield and Nicolson, 1969), pp. ix–xv, 110–122.

7. Peter Cominos, "Late Victorian Sexual Respectability and the Social System," *International Review of Sociology*, vol. 8 (1963): 18–48, 216–250; R. S. Neale, "'Middle-Class' Morality and the Systematic Colonizers," in *Class and Ideology in the Nineteenth Century* (London: Routledge & Kegan Paul, 1972), pp. 121–142. See also Stephen Marcus, *The Other Victorians. A Study of Sexuality and Pornography in Mid-Victorian England* (New York: Basic Books, Inc., 1964).

8. Kern, *Anatomy and Destiny*, p. 1.

9. Kern, *Anatomy and Destiny*, pp. 10, 12, 2, 3.

10. Kern, *Anatomy and Destiny*, pp. 12, 2, 17.

11. Philippe Perrot, *Les Dessus et les Dessous de la bourgeoisie. Une histoire du vêtement au XIXᵉ siècle* (Paris: Librairie Arthème Fayard, 1981), p. 21.

12. Kern, *Anatomy and Destiny*, pp. 6, 10.

13. Kern, *Anatomy and Destiny*, p. 10.

14. Helene E. Roberts, "The Exquisite Slave: The Role of Clothes in the Making of the Victorian Woman," *Signs: Journal of Women in Culture and Society*, vol. 2, no. 3 (Spring, 1977): 554–569; see especially pp. 554–557. See also Helene E. Roberts, "Submission, Masochism, Narcissism: Three Aspects of Women's Role as Reflected in Dress," in Virginia Lussier and Joyce Walstedt, eds., *Women's Lives: Perspectives on Progress and Change* (Newark, Delaware: University of Delaware Press, 1977).

15. Roberts, "The Exquisite Slave," p. 555.

16. For men's clothing, see Ellen Moers, *The Dandy* (London: Seeker & Warburg, 1960), pp. 181, 203, 272; Perrot, *Les Dessus et les Dessous*, pp. 56–63; Penelope Byrde, *The Male Image. Men's Fashion in Britain 1300–1970* (London: B. T. Batsford, 1979); The "Major" (of *Today*), *Clothes and the Man. Hints on the Wearing and Caring of Clothes* (London: Grant Richards, 1900).

   For women's clothing, see Doris Langley Moore, *The Woman in Fashion* (London: B. T. Batsford, 1949), pp. 79, 115; Anne Buck, *Victorian Costume and Costume Accessories* (London: Herbert Jenkins, 1961), p. 32; Anne Hollander, *Seeing Through Clothes* (New York: Viking, 1978), pp. 365–390.

17. Roberts, "The Exquisite Slave," pp. 554, 557; James Laver, *Clothes* (New York: Horizon, 1953), p. x; Mrs. Margaret Oliphant, *Dress* (London: Macmillan & Co., 1878), pp. 4, 7.

18. Kern, *Anatomy and Destiny*, pp. 19, 12.

19. Bonnie G. Smith, *Ladies of the Leisure Class. The Bourgeoises of Northern France in the Nineteenth Century* (Princeton: Princeton University Press, 1981), p. 78.

   Some of Smith's explanations recall Cunnington's implausible suggestion that the 1870s bustle was "maternal" (because low-slung), while the 1880s bustle was "aggressive" (because it jutted out).

20. Roberts, "The Exquisite Slave," pp. 567, 569.

21. Kern, *Anatomy and Destiny*, p. 11; Perrot, *Les Dessus et les Dessous*, pp. 17–19.

22. Bradley, *The Eternal Masquerade*, p. 227; Peter T. Cominos, "Innocent Femina Sensualis in Unconscious Conflict," in Martha Vicinus, ed., *Suffer and Be Still. Women in the Victorian Age* (Bloomington and London: Indiana University Press, 1972), pp. 171–172.

23. John S. and Robin M. Haller, *The Physician and Sexuality in Victorian America* (Urbana, Chicago, and London: University of Illinois Press, 1974), pp. xii, 102; William Leach, *True Love and Perfect Union. The Feminist Reform of Sex and Society* (London and Henley: Routledge & Kegan Paul, 1981), pp. 76, 90; Jeffrey Weeks, *Sex, Politics and Society. The Regulation of Sexuality Since 1800* (London and New York: Longman, 1981), pp. 160–165.

24. Kern, *Anatomy and Destiny*, p. 17 [emphasis added].

25. Weeks, *Sex, Politics and Society*, p. 19.

26. H. Dennis Bradley, *The Eternal Masquerade* (London: T. Werner Laurie, 1922), pp. 227, 4, 15, 17, 229, 9, 245.

27. Carl Degler, "What Ought to Be and What Was: Women's Sexuality in the Nineteenth Century," *American Historical Review*, vol. 79, no. 5 (December, 1974): 1467–1490, p. 1467; F. Barry Smith, "Sexuality in Britain, 1800–1900: Some Suggested Revisions," in Martha Vicinus, ed., *A Widening Sphere: Changing Roles of Victorian Women* (Bloomington and London: Indiana University Press, 1977), p. 182.

28. James F. McMillan, *Housewife or Harlot: The Place of Women in French Society, 1870–1940* (Brighton, Sussex: The Harvester Press, 1981); Theodore Zeldin, *France 1848–1945*, 2 vols. (London: Oxford University Press, 1973, 1977), vol. 1, Chapters on "Marriage and Morals" and "Women."

29. Degler, "What Ought to Be and What Was," pp. 1467–1490; Peter Gay, "Victorian Sexuality," *The American Scholar* (Summer, 1980): 372–378; Neale, "'Middle-Class' Morality and the Systematic Colonizers"; F. Barry Smith, "Sexuality in Britain," pp. 182–198; Martha Vicinus, "Introduction: New Trends in the Study of the Victorian Woman," in Vicinus, ed., *A Widening Sphere*.

30. Degler, "What Ought to Be and What Was," pp. 1471–1472; Ian Bradley, *The Call to Seriousness. The Evangelical Impact on the Victorians* (New York: Macmillan & Co., 1976), pp. 13, 27.

    See also Charles Rosenberg, "Sexuality, Class, and Role in 19th-Century America," *American Quarterly*, vol. 25, no. 2 (May, 1973): 131–153.

31. A. Debay, *Hygiène et physiologie du mariage* (Paris, n.d.; went through 173 printings between 1848 and 1888); William Acton, *The Functions and Disorders of the Reproductive Organs in Youth, in Adult Age, and in Advanced Life* (London: John Churchill, 1857); William Acton, *Prostitution* (London, 1857); Mrs. Eliza Lynn Linton, "The Girl of the Period," *Saturday Review* (14 March 1868); Mrs. Hugh Reginald (Mary Eliza) Haweis, *The Art of Beauty* (London: Chatto & Windus, 1878).

Notes to Chapter 6

1. Mrs. E. M. King, *Rational Dress; or, The Dress of Women and Savages* (London: Kegan, Paul, Trench & Co., 1882), p. 13; Mme. Marie-Elizabeth

Cavé, *Beauté physique de la femme* (Paris: Paul Leloup, [1868]), p. 11; John Stuart Mill, cited by Priscilla Robertson, *An Experience of Women. Pattern and Change in Nineteenth-Century Europe* (Philadelphia: Temple University Press, 1982), p. 19.

2. Mrs. C. E. Humphrey, *How to be Pretty Though Plain* (London: James Bowden, 1899), p. 9; "The Art of Dress," *The Quarterly Review* 79 (March, 1847), p. 379.

3. Gabriel Prevost, *Le Nu, le vêtement, la parure chez l'homme et chez la femme* (Paris: C. Marpon et E. Flammarion, 1883), pp. 35–36. See also "The Art of Dress," *The Quarterly Review* (1847), p. 373.

4. Yvonne Knibiehler, "Le Discours médical sur la femme: Constants et ruptures," in *Mythes et representations de la femme au dix-neuvième siècle*, special number of *Romanticisme* (Paris: Librairie Honoré Champion, 1976), pp. 45–46.

5. Edmund and Jules de Goncourt, *Journal* (1851–1896), entry of 13 October 1855; edited and translated by Robert Baldick, *Pages from the Goncourt Journal* (Oxford: Oxford University Press, 1978), p. 18.

6. Herbert Spencer, cited by Priscilla Robertson, *An Experience of Women*, p. 25; Knibiehler, "Le Discourse médical sur la femme," pp. 45–46.

7. Alexander Walker, *Beauty; Illustrated Chiefly by an Analysis and Classification of Beauty in Women* (London: E. Wilson, 1836), pp. 357, 161, 225, 209, 287, 249, 226.

8. C. Fouquet and Yvonne Knibiehler, *La Beauté pour quoi faire? Essai sur l'histoire de la beauté féminine.* (Paris: Temps Actuels, 1982), pp. 18, 73–82, 95–97.

9. Arnold James Cooley, *The Toilet and Cosmetic Arts in Ancient and Modern Times* (London: R. Hardwick, 1866, and Philadelphia: Lindsay & Blackiston, 1866; reprinted, New York: Burt Franklin, Research and Source Works Series 511, 1970), pp. 100, 129.

10. Prevost, *Le Nu, le vêtement*, pp. 37, 81.

11. *How to be Beautiful.* Oliphant's Juvenile Series (Edinburgh: W. Oliphant & Co., and London: Hamilton, Adams, & Co., 1866), pp. 5, 26.

12. Humphry, *How to be Pretty Though Plain*, p. 12; Mrs. C. E. Humphry, *Beauty Adorned* (London: T. Fisher Unwin, 1901), p. 2; C. T., *How to Dress Well. A Manual of the Toilet for the Use of Both Sexes* (London: George Routledge & Sons, 1868), p. 10.

13. Frances Mary Steele and Elizabeth Livingston Steele Adams, *Beauty of Form and Grace of Vesture* (London: B. F. Stevens, and Cambridge, Massachusetts: University Press, 1892), pp. 10, 49, 53.

14. *Sylvia's Home Journal* (February, 1878), p. 58; Mrs. Hugh Reginald (Mary Eliza) Haweis, *The Art of Beauty* (London: Chatto & Windus, 1878; reprinted, New York and London: Garland Publishing Inc., 1978), pp. 3, 9.

15. A Lady, *Beauty: What it is, and How to Retain It* (London: Frederick Warne & Co., 1873), pp. 1–2; Mrs. Sewell (1869), cited by Priscilla Robertson, *An Experience of Women*, p. 63; R., *Dress in a Nutshell* (London: Greening & Co., 1901), p. 1; Carolyn C. Lougee, *Le Paradis des femmes. Women, Salons, and Social Stratification in Seventeenth-Century France* (Princeton: Princeton University Press, 1976), p. 38.

16. Mrs. Aria, "Dressing as a Duty and an Art," *The Woman's World* (July, 1890), pp. 476–477.

17. John S. Haller and Robin M. Haller, *The Physician and Sexuality in Victorian America* (Urbana, Chicago, and London: University of Illinois Press, 1974), p. 141.
18. *The Delineator* (1897), p. xii.
19. Cited without attribution by Elizabeth Ewing, *Dress and Undress: A History of Women's Underwear* (New York: Drama Book Specialists, 1978), p. 86.
20. A Professional Beauty, *Beauty and How to Keep It* (London: Brentano's, 1889), pp. 47, 49.
21. Mlle. Pauline Mariette, *L'Art de la toilette* (Paris: Librairie Centrale, 1866), pp. 40–41.
22. George Frederick Watts, "On Taste in Dress," originally published in *The Nineteenth Century* (January, 1883), reprinted in Mary Watts, ed., *George Frederick Watts*, vol. 3 (London: Macmillan & Co., 1912), pp. 218, 203–204, 224.
23. *The Queen* (11 September 1869), p. 157.
24. H. Rider Haggard, *She. A History of Adventure.* [first published in 1886] (London: Longmans, Green, and Co., 1916), p. 187.
25. George Moore, *A Drama in Muslin* [first published in 1886] (Gerrards Cross, Buckinghamshire: Colin Smythe Ltd., 1981), p. 4; *My Secret Life* (New York: Grove Press, 1966; abridged edition, New York: Ballantine Books, 1973), pp. 166–167.
26. Honoré de Balzac, *Cousin Bette*, trans. by Marion Ayton Crawford. (Harmondsworth, Middlesex: Penguin Books, 1965), p. 183; *La Mode Illustrée* (1876), cited by Norah Waugh, *Corsets and Crinolines* (London: B. T. Batsford, 1954), p. 124.
27. *How to Dress or Etiquette of the Toilette* (London: Ward, Lock & Tyler, n.d. [1877]), p. 14.
28. Baronesse [Blanche A. A.] Staffe, *Usages du monde; règles du savoir-vivre dans la société moderne* (Paris: Ernest Flammarion, 1899), p. 261; Munby's diary, quoted by Michael Hiley, *Victorian Working Women: Portraits from Life* (Boston: David Godine, 1979), p. 29; Moore, *A Drama in Muslin*, p. 30.
29. Moore, *A Drama in Muslin*, pp. 172–173.
30. Jean-Philippe Worth, *A Century of Fashion*, trans. by Ruth Miller. (Boston: Little Brown & Co., 1928), p. 71.
31. Emile Zola, *Au bonheur des dames* (Paris, 1883), trans. by April Fitzlyon, *Ladies' Delight* (London and New York: Abelard-Schuman, 1958), p. 386; Mrs. C. S. Peel, *Life's Enchanted Cup. An Autobiography (1872–1933)* (London: John Lane, 1933), p. 47.
32. *The Habits of Good Society* (1855), cited by Louis Stanley, *The Beauty of Woman* (London: W. H. Allen, 1955), p. 180.
33. "Crinoline," cited by Alison Gernsheim, *Fashion and Reality: 1840–1914* (London: Faber & Faber, 1963), p. 46.
34. "How to Choose a Wife by Her Legs," The Sir Basil Liddell Hart "Scrapbooks," in The Liverpool Polytechnic Art Library.
35. *How to Dress or Etiquette of the Toilette*, p. 57; Humphry, *Beauty Adorned*, p. 100.
36. "The Lady with the Little Feet," *London Society* (June, 1869), pp. 504, 495.
37. *The Ladies' Treasury for 1877*, pp. 108–109; Haweis, *The Art of Beauty*, pp. 118–120; A. Cazenave, *Beauty, or the Art of Human Decoration*, trans. by

Marie Courcelles. (Cincinnati and New York: Chase & Hall, 1877), pp. 100, 114.

38. Moore, *A Drama in Muslin*, pp. 88, 85.
39. *La Vie Parisienne* (13 March 1875), p. 152.
40. Cazenave, *Beauty, or the Art of Human Decoration*, pp. 91, 22; Cooley, *The Toilet and Cosmetic Arts*, p. 287.
41. Humphry, *Beauty Adorned*, p. 76; *The Englishwoman's Domestic Magazine* (April, 1866), p. 113. (Hereafter *EDM*.)
42. Cooley, *The Toilet and Cosmetic Arts*, pp. 311, 294–295, 308; *EDM* (January, 1866), p. 16.
43. Humphry, *Beauty Adorned*, pp. 27, 67, 69.
44. C. T., *How to Dress Well*, p. 84; *EDM* (February, 1866), p. 48; Cooley, pp. 230–231, 257–258; Cazenave, p. 35; Haweis, *The Art of Beauty*, p. 172; Charles Baudelaire, "Un Fantôme" (1860), "Un Hémisphère dans une Chevelure" (1862), and "La Chevelure" (1859); Prevost, *Le Nu, le vêtement*, p. 99.
45. Charlotte Yonge, *Womankind* (London, 1877), p. 112.
46. Georgine de Courtois, *Woman's Headdress and Hairstyle in England from AD 600 to the Present Day* (London: B. T. Batsford, 1973), p. 128; [Mrs. Elizabeth Lynn Linton], "The Girl of the Period," *Saturday Review* (14 March 1868), p. 340.
47. Robert Hillestad, "The Underlying Structure of Appearance," *Dress* 5 (1980): 117–125; A Professional Beauty, *Beauty and How to Keep It*, p. 44; *My Secret Life*, pp. 166–167.
48. A Professional Beauty, *Beauty and How to Keep It*, pp. 56–57.

Notes to Chapter 7

1. Theodore Zeldin, *France: 1848–1945*, 2 vols. (Oxford: Oxford University Press, 1973, 1977), vol. 2, p. 441; A Lady, *Beauty: What It Is and How to Retain It* (London: Frederick Warne & Co., 1873), p. 92.
2. Gabriel Prevost, *Le Nu, le vêtement, la parure chez l'homme et chez la femme* (Paris: C. Marpon et E. Flammarion, 1883), pp. 38, 3–4.
3. Madame Roxy Caplin, *Health and Beauty, or corsets and clothing constructed in accordance with the physiological laws of the human body* (London: Darnton & Co., 1854), pp. 35–36; Mrs. Hugh Reginald (Mary Eliza) Haweis, *The Art of Beauty* (London: Chatto & Windus, 1878; reprinted, New York and London: Garland Publishing, Inc., 1978), p. 36.
4. Charles Blanc, *Art in Ornament and Dress* (London: Chapman and Hall, 1877), p. 53; Mrs. Margaret Oliphant, *Dress* (London: Macmillan and Co., 1878), p. 4.
5. Arnold James Cooley, *The Toilet and Cosmetic Arts in Ancient and Modern Times* (London: R. Hardwick, 1866, and Philadelphia: Lindsay and Blackiston, 1866; reprinted, New York: Burt Franklin, Research and Source Works Series 511, 1970), p. 160; Haweis, *The Art of Beauty*, pp. 273, 11, 16, 13.
6. Haweis, *The Art of Beauty*, pp. 128–129.
7. *Godey's Lady's Book* 9 (August, 1834), p. 90.
8. Charlotte Mary Yonge, *Womankind* (London: Mozley, 1877), pp. 116–117; *Godey's Lady's Book* 7 (December, 1833), p. 310; John Todd, *The Young Man: Hints Addressed to the Young Men of the United States* (Northamp-

ton, Massachusetts, 1850), quoted by Karen Halttunen, *Confidence Men and Painted Women: A Study of Middle-Class Culture in America, 1830–1870* (New Haven: Yale University Press, 1982), p. 40.

9. The Sir Basil Liddell Hart "Scrapbooks," in the Liverpool Polytechnic Art Library.

10. *Godey's Lady's Book*, quoted in Halttunen, *Confidence Men and Painted Women*, p. 89; Mrs. Hugh Reginald (Mary Eliza) Haweis, *The Art of Dress* (London: Chatto & Windus, 1879; reprinted, New York and London: Garland Publishing Inc., 1978), p. 126; Haweis, *The Art of Beauty*, pp. 263, 195–196, 257.

11. *Sylvia's Home Journal* (January, 1878), pp. 6–7.

12. Yonge, *Womankind*, p. 117; *How to Dress or Etiquette of the Toilette* (London: Ward, Lock & Tyler, n.d. [1877]), p. 87.

13. *The Art of Beauty* (London, 1825), quoted by Richard Corson, *Fashions in Make-Up from Ancient to Modern Times* (New York: University Books, 1972), p. 295; Gordon Stables, M.D., *The Girl's Own Book of Health and Beauty* (London: Jarrold & Sons, 1892), preface, no page numbers; "Medicus" [Stables], cited by Wendy Forrester, *Great Grandmama's Weekly. A Celebration of the Girl's Own Paper* (Guilford and London: Lutterworth Press, 1980), pp. 50–54; *How to Dress or Etiquette of the Toilette*, p. 50; Frances Mary Steele and Elizabeth Livingston Steele Adams, *Beauty of Form and Grace of Vesture* (London: B. F. Stevens, and Cambridge, Massachusetts: University Press, 1892), pp. 50, 53.

14. Mrs. C. E. Humphry, *How to be Pretty Though Plain* (London: James Bowden, 1899), pp. 10–11; Mrs. C. E. Humphry, *Beauty Adorned* (London: T. Fisher Unwin, 1901), pp. 4–5.

15. For information on Madame Rachel, see Richard Corson, *Fashions in Make-Up*; Advertisement in *The Queen* (18 February 1871), no page number.

16. *The Ugly-Girl Papers; or Hints for the Toilet* by S.D.P. Reprinted from *Harper's Bazar* (New York: Harper & Brothers, 1874), p. 60; Gwen Raverat, *Period Piece. A Cambridge Childhood* (London: Faber & Faber, 1952), pp. 266–267.

17. Charles Baudelaire, "In Praise of Cosmetics" (1863), in *The Painter of Modern Life and Other Essays*, trans. and ed. by Jonathan Mayne. (London: Phaidon Press, 1964), pp. 31–34.

18. [Mrs. Elizabeth Lynn Linton], "Costume and its Morals," *Saturday Review* (13 July 1867), p. 44.

19. [Mrs. Elizabeth Lynn Linton], "The Girl of the Period," *Saturday Review* (14 March 1868), pp. 339–340; Leonore Davidoff, *The Best Circles. Society Etiquette and the Season* (London: Croom Helm, 1973), p. 114; *The Girl of the Period and the Fashionable Woman of the Period*. Reprinted from *Saturday Review*. (New York: J. R. Redfield, 1869), especially pp. 17–19.

20. *The Tomahawk. A Saturday Journal of Satire* (12 March 1870), no page number, in The Sir Basil Liddell Hart "Scrapbooks." Other cartoons and articles are also in The Sir Basil Liddell Hart "Scrapbooks."

21. W.L. Burn, *The Age of Equipoise. A Study of the Mid-Victorian Generation* (London: George Allen & Unwin, 1964), p. 26.

22. "On Vanity and Love of Dress," *Family Herald* (3 June 1843), p. 60. [Emphasis added.]

23. *Dress, Health and Beauty* (London: Ward, Lock & Co., 1878), pp. 134, 17.

24. Mrs. Beecher Stowe, "What are the Sources of Beauty in Dress," *The Queen* (12 December 1868), p. 345.

25. F. T. Vischer, cited in Friedrich Wendel, *Weib und Mode: eine Sittengeschichte im Spiegel der Karikatur* (Dresden: Paul Aretz Verlag, 1928), pp. 173–175.

26. "Who Is To Blame? A Few Words on Ladies' Dress, in its Moral and Aesthetic Aspects. Addressed to the 'Fast' of Both Sexes," reprinted from *The Journal of Social Science* (London: L. Booth, n.d. [ca. 1866), pp. 4–5, 7; Haweis, *The Art of Beauty*, p. 263.

27. C. T., *How to Dress Well*, pp. 13, 94; Haweis, *The Art of Beauty*, pp. 11, 17.

28. "The Art of Dress," *The Quarterly Review* 79 (March, 1847), pp. 375–376.

29. "Nice Girls," *Harper's Bazar* (11 April 1868), p. 382. [Emphasis added.]

30. *Sylvia's Home Journal* (January, 1878), p. 11.

31. "A Lady's Question—What Shall We Wear?," *London Society* (May, 1869), p. 413.

32. Miss Oakey (Mrs. Maria Richards Dewing), *Beauty in Dress* (New York: Harper, 1881), p. 145; *The Art of Dressing Well. A Book of Hints*, p. 62.

33. *The Rational Dress Society's Gazette* (October, 1888), p. 2.

34. Theodore Zeldin, ed., *Conflicts in French Society. Anticlericalism, Education and Morals in the Nineteenth Century* (London: George Allen & Unwin, 1970), p. 32.

35. Martha Vicinus, "Introduction," in Vicinus, ed., *A Widening Sphere: Changing Roles of the Victorian Woman* (Bloomington and London: Indiana University Press, 1977), pp. xi, xix; Jeffrey Weeks, *Sex, Politics, and Society. The Regulation of Sexuality since 1800* (London and New York: Longman, 1981), pp. 27, 41; Mrs. Merrifield, *Dress as a Fine Art* (London: A. Hall Virtue, 1854, and Boston: Jewitt & Co., 1854), p. 24

36. C. T., *How to Dress Well*, p. 44; *Etiquette of Good Society*, p. 79.

37. Henry James, *The Awkward Age*, Book Two: Little Aggie. [first published in 1899] (Harmondsworth, Middlesex: Penguin Books, 1966), p. 87; Mlle. Pauline Mariette, *L'Art de la toilette* (Paris: Librairie Centrale, 1866), p. 2.

38. *La Reforme par les dames* (Paris: J.-L. Paulmier, 1865), p. 23, cited by Philippe Perrot, "Le Jardin des modes," in Jean-Paul Aron, *Misérable et glorieuse. La Femme du XIXe siècle* (Paris: Librairie Arthème Fayard, 1980), p. 104.

    See also Erving Goffman, "Attitudes and Rationalizations Regarding Body Exposure," in Roach and Eicher, *Dress, Adornment, and the Social Order*, p. 50.

39. One of the Aristocracy, *Etiquette for Women. A Book of Modern Modes and Manners* (London: C. Arthur Pearson, 1902), p. 14.

40. Louis Octave Uzanne, *The Modern Parisienne* (London: William Heineman, 1912); Sylvaine Marandon, *L'Image de la France dans l'Angleterre victorienne 1848–1900* (Paris: Armand Colin, 1967); Marylène Delbourg-Delphis, *Le Chic et le Look* (Paris: Hachette, 1981).

41. Trevor Fairbrother, "The Shock of John Singer Sargent's 'Madame Gautreau,'" *Arts Magazine*, vol. 55, no. 5 (January, 1981), p. 90; Albert Woolf, quoted in Evan Charteris, *John Sargent* (New York: Scribners, 1927), p. 62.

42. *The Art Amateur* (1889), quoted in Fairbrother, "The Shock," p. 94; Ralph Curtis, quoted in Charteris, *John Sargent*, pp. 61–62; Fairbrother, p. 91, in the context of an analysis of *Gazette des Beaux-Arts* (1884).

43. C. T., *How To Dress Well. A Manual of the Toilet for the Use of Both Sexes* (London: George Routledge & Sons, 1868), p. 11. [Emphasis added.]

44. Henry James, *The Portrait of a Lady*, Chapter 19 [first published in 1881] (Cambridge, Massachusetts: The Riverside Press, 1956), pp. 172–173.

45. C. T., *How To Dress Well*, p. 21; W. L. Burn, *The Age of Equipoise*, pp. 253–254.

46. A Lady, *How to Dress on £15 a Year as a Lady* (London: Frederick Warne & Co., 1873), p. 4.

47. "A Lady's Question—What Shall We Wear?," *London Society* (May, 1869), p. 410; *The Woman's World* (May, 1890), p. 349; *The Art of Dressing Well. A Book of Hints* (London: Lockwood & Co. and Simpkin, Marshall & Co., n.d. [ca. 1870]), p. 66; C. T., *How to Dress Well*, p. 43; Mrs. Aria, "Dressing as a Duty and an Art," *The Woman's World* (July, 1890), p. 476.

48. C. T., *How to Dress Well*, p. 19; Clarke, p. 10; C. T., *How to Dress Well*, p. 14; *The Art of Dressing Well. A Book of Hints*, p. 2; *Sylvia's Home Journal* (February, 1878), p. 59.

49. Mrs. Aria, "Dressing as a Duty and an Art," p. 476.

50. *Etiquette of Good Society* (London, Paris, & New York: Cassell, Peter Galpin & Co., n.d. [ca. 1880]), pp. 77–79.

51. Derek Hudson, *Munby. Man of Two Worlds. The Life and Diaries of Arthur J. Munby 1828–1910* (London: John Murray, 1972), pp. 40–41; C. T., *How to Dress Well*, pp. 22–24.

52. J. Erskine Clarke, *Over-Dress*. Tracts for the Family, No. IX (London: John Morgan, n.d.), pp. 4–9.

53. Rosa Nouchette Carey, "Aunt Diana," *The Girl's Own Paper* (20 June 1885), p. 595.

54. Louisa Twining, "Dress," *The Sunday Magazine*, ed. by Thomas Guthrie D.D. (London: Strahan & Co., 1872), p. 467.

55. *Dress, Drink, and Debt. A Temperance Tale* (London: Society for Promoting Christian Knowledge, n.d. [ca. 1878]), p. 11.

56. John Forbes Moncrieff, *Our Domestics and Their Mistresses. A Contribution to "The Servant Question"* (Edinburgh: Andres Stevenson; and London: Dyer Brothers, n.d. [ca. 1895]), p. 55.

57. C. T., *How to Dress Well*, p. 27; Moncrieff, *Our Domestics*, pp. 82, 54.

58. Wilkie Collins, *The Moonstone*, Third Narrative and The Loss of the Diamond. [first published in 1868] Ed. by J.I.M. Stewart. (Harmondsworth, Middlesex: Penguin Books, 1966), pp. 363, 86.

59. Mrs. Eric Pritchard, *The Cult of Chiffon* (London: Grant Richards, 1902), cited in Doris Langley Moore, *The Woman in Fashion*, p. 177. Mrs. M. E. W. Sherwood, *A Transplanted Rose* (New York, 1882), cited in The Museum of the City of New York, *The House of Worth. The Gilded Age, 1860–1918*. Text by Jo Anne Olian. (New York, 1982), p. 8.

60. *Sylvia's Home Journal* (February, 1878), p. 58; *The Queen* (15 November 1879), p. 457; F. Adolphus, *Some Memories of Paris* (Edinburgh and London: William Blackwood and Sons, 1895), p. 189.

61. Anthony Trollope, *The Eustace Diamonds*, Chapter 35 [first published in 1873] (Harmondsworth, Middlesex: Penguin Books, 1969), pp. 358, 348.

62. Blanc, *Art in Ornament and Dress*, p. 151.

63. Haweis, *The Art of Beauty*, pp. 21, 18, 20, 22, 23.

64. Haweis, *The Art of Beauty*, pp. 23–24; Haweis, *The Art of Dress*, pp. 13–14.

65. Haweis, *The Art of Dress*, p. 29.
66. Bea Howe, *Arbiter of Fashion* (London: Harvill Press, 1967). [A biography of Mrs. Haweis]
67. Helen Gilbert Ecob, *The Well-Dressed Woman: A Study in the Practical Application to Dress of the Laws of Health, Art, and Morals* (New York: Fowler and Wells, 1893), p. 261

Notes to Chapter 8

1. *The Englishwoman's Domestic Magazine* (February, 1871), p. 99; *Sylvia's Home Journal* (Christmas, 1878), p. 45, (June, 1878), p. 246.
2. Ada S. Ballin, *The Science of Dress in Theory and Practice* (London: Sampson Low, Marston, Searle, & Rivington, 1885), pp. 6, 9.
3. Stella Mary Newton, *Health, Art and Reason. Dress Reformers of the Nineteenth Century* (London: John Murray, 1974), p. 3; Shelly Foote, "Bloomers," *Dress. The Journal of the Costume Society of America* 5 (1980), pp. 1–12; Mary E. Tillotson, *Progress vs. Fashion. An Essay on the Sanitary and Social Influences of Women's Dress* (Vineland, New Jersey, 1873), p. 20; *The New York Times*, cited by Jeanette C. and Robert H. Lauer, "The Battle of the Sexes. Fashion in 19th Century America," *Journal of Popular Culture*, Vol. XIII, No. 4 (Spring, 1980), p. 583.
4. Robert E. Riegel, "Women's Clothes and Women's Rights," *American Quarterly*, Vol. XV, No. 3 (Fall, 1963): 390–401.
5. William Leach, *True Love and Perfect Union. The Feminist Reform of Sex and Society* (London and Henley: Routledge & Kegan Paul, 1981), pp. 246–247, 20; Tillotson, *Progress vs. Fashion*, pp. 23, 5.
6. Leach, *True Love and Perfect Union*, pp. 243, 249.
7. Tillotson, *Progress vs. Fashion*, pp. 1–2, 5.
8. Leach, *True Love and Perfect Union*, p. 91; Riegel, "Women's Clothes and Women's Rights," p. 397; James F. McMillan, *Housewife or Harlot: The Place of Women in French Society 1870–1940* (Brighton, Sussex: The Harvester Press, 1981), p. 91; Tillotson, *Progress vs. Fashion*, pp. 5, 8, 2.
9. *The Lancet*, quoted in *Sylvia's Home Journal* (April, 1878), p. 150; Frederick Treves, *The Dress of the Period in its Relations to Health* (London: Published for the National Health Society by Allman & Son, n.d. [1882]), pp. 6–8; *Dress, Health and Beauty* (London: Ward, Lock & Co., 1878), pp. 18–22; Abba Gould Woolson, ed., *Dress-Reform: On Dress as it Affects the Health of Women* (Boston, 1874), pp. 10, 13.
10. *The Rational Dress Society's Gazette* (April, 1889), p. 2.
11. *Dress, Health and Beauty*, p. 123.
12. Mrs. E. M. King, *Rational Dress; or, The Dress of Women and Savages* (London: Kegan, Paul, Trench & Co., 1882), pp. 3, 4, 25.
13. King, *Rational Dress*, pp. 6, 4.
14. King, *Rational Dress*, pp. 26, 27.
15. *Dress, Health, and Beauty*, pp. 86–87.
16. *Dress, Health, and Beauty*, p. 89.
17. Leach, *True Love and Perfect Union*, p. 250.
18. King, *Rational Dress*, pp. 27, 12.
19. King, *Rational Dress*, p. 13.
20. *Sylvia's Home Journal* (June, 1878), p. 247; (July, 1878), p. 293.

21. *The Englishwoman's Domestic Magazine* (March, 1871), p. 163; *Sylvia's Home Journal* (January, 1878), p. 11.
22. Mrs. Hugh Reginald (Mary Eliza) Haweis, *The Art of Beauty* (London: Chatto & Windus, 1878; reprinted, New York: Garland Publishing, Inc., 1978), pp. 25–26; Benjamin Disraeli, *Lothair,* cited by Richard Jenkins, *The Victorians and Ancient Greece* (Oxford: Basil Blackwell, 1980), p. 324.
23. *The Queen* (18 October 1879), p. 366; (6 December 1879), p. 544.
24. Oscar Wilde, cited by Jenkins, *The Victorians and Ancient Greece,* p. 363.
25. *Sylvia's Home Journal* (June, 1878), p. 247.
26. *The Queen* (18 October 1879), p. 366; *Woman's World* (1888), p. 142.
27. Mrs. Hugh Reginald (Mary Eliza) Haweis, *The Art of Dress* (London: Chatto & Windus, 1879; reprinted, New York: Garland Publishing, Inc., 1978), pp. 26–27.
28. Jenkins, *The Victorians and Ancient Greece,* pp. 67–69, 302.
29. Mrs. Margaret Oliphant, *Dress* (London: Macmillan & Co., 1878), pp. 68–69.
30. C. Willett and Phillis Cunnington, *Handbook of English Costume in the 19th Century* [originally published in 1959] (Boston: Plays Inc., 1970), p. 28. See also Diane de Marly, *The History of Haute Couture 1850–1950* (New York: Holmes & Meier, 1980), pp. 63–80; Elizabeth Ewing, *Dress and Undress. A History of Women's Underwear* (New York: Drama Book Specialists, 1978), pp. 88–95; Stella Mary Newton, *Health, Art and Reason.*
31. E. P. Thompson, *William Morris. Romantic to Revolutionary* (London: Lawrence & Wishart Ltd., 1955), pp. 84, 122.
32. William Morris, cited by Alison Adburgham, *A Punch History of Manners and Modes* (London: Hutchinson, 1961), p. 134.
33. *Sylvia's Home Journal* (December, 1879), p. 420; Walter Crane, "Of the Progress of Taste in Dress in Relation to Art Education," *Aglaia. The Journal of the Healthy and Artistic Dress Union,* Number 3 (Autumn, 1894), reprinted in Walter Crane, *Ideals in Art* (London: George Bell and Sons, 1905), pp. 175–176.
34. *The Queen* (6 December 1879), p. 544; *Sylvia's Home Journal* (December, 1879), p. 420.
35. Newton, *Health, Art and Reason,* p. 56.
36. Barbara Baines, *Fashion Revivals from the Elizabethan Age to the Present Day* (London: B.T. Batsford, 1981), pp. 129–130; *The Queen* (12 July 1879), p. 41; Diane de Marly, *The History of Haute Couture,* p. 77.
37. Mrs. J. Comyns Carr, *Reminiscences* (London: Hutchinson & Co., 1925), p. 151.
38. Peter Gunn, *Vernon Lee. Violet Paget, 1856–1935* (London: Oxford University Press, 1964), p. 78; F. E. Francillon, *Mid-Victorian Memories* (London: Hodder & Stoughton, 1913), p. 212. See also *The Queen* (16 August 1879), p. 151; *The Queen* (2 August 1879), p. 114; *Sylvia's Home Journal* (9 December, 1879), p. 420.
39. Haweis, *The Art of Beauty,* pp. 273–275. See also A. C., "Individuality in Dress," *The Queen* (6 December 1879), p. 544; A. C., "The Influence of Aesthetics on English Society," *Sylvia's Home Journal* (December, 1879), p. 420.

Mrs. Haweis approved of some aspects of Aesthetic dress for attractive as well as plain women. She also approved of Dr. Jaeger's all-wool clothing (as underwear only, however) and Kate Greenaway-style children's clothes, which her daughter failed to appreciate. Mrs. Haweis was very briefly Treasurer of the Rational Dress Society. Her own style of dress was apparently original and "artistic," but neither Aesthetic nor Rational in any meaningful sense. She wrote to her mother in 1875, "My eccentric dresses make me quite celebrated." Her clothing included features from past styles; for example, in 1881 she designed a dress for her "Musical Evenings" that was made from Japanese brocade bought at Liberty's and modeled after the dress of a Court lady of Charles II's reign. Her hairstyle matched and was derived from the coiffure in a portrait by Lely. She was also fond of fancy dress parties, and held at least one with a fourteenth-century theme. Bea Howe, *Arbiter of Elegance* (London: The Harvill Press, 1967), pp. 133, 154, 161.

40. *Sylvia's Home Journal* (April, 1878), p. 173.

41. *Sylvia's Home Journal* (September, 1879), p. 296; *Sylvia's Home Journal* (December, 1879), pp. 420–421; *The Queen* (16 August 1879), p. 151; *The Queen* (2 August 1879), p. 114.

42. W. Graham Robertson, *Time Was* (London: Hamish Hamilton, 1931), pp. 67–68.

He went on to describe male Aesthetes: "The men, after abortive efforts to look like Greek gods, tried medieval saints instead and cultivated pale, ascetic faces with dreary eyes and unkempt locks; the more daring soaring to Liberty silk ties and brown velvet coats."

43. A. C., "Individuality in Dress," *The Queen* (6 December 1879), p. 544.

44. David Sonstroem, *Rossetti and the Fair Lady* (Middletown, Connecticut: Wesleyan University Press, 1970), pp. 3, 41, 198; Mario Praz, *The Romantic Agony* [first published in English in 1933] (London: Oxford University Press, 1970), pp. 228–229.

45. Mrs. Humphrey Ward, *Robert Elsmere* (London and New York: Macmillan & Co., 1888), p. 161.

46. G. J. Barker-Benfield, *The Horrors of the Half-Known Life. Male Attitudes Toward Women and Sexuality in Nineteenth-Century America* (New York: Harper & Row, 1976), pp. 258–259.

47. Robert H. Lauer and Jeanette C. Lauer, *Fashion Power. The Meaning of Fashion in American Society* (Englewood Cliffs, New Jersey: Prentice-Hall, 1981), pp. 263–264; see also Herbert Blumer, "Fashion: From Class Differentiation to Collective Selection," *The Sociological Quarterly*, 10 (Summer, 1969), 290–296.

48. Newton, *Health, Art and Reason*, pp. 166–167. [Emphasis added.]

49. Johan Huizinga, *Homo Ludens: A Study of the Play Element in Culture* (London: Routledge & Kegan Paul, 1949), pp. 193–194.

Notes to Chapter 9

1. David Kunzle, "Dress Reform as Antifeminism: A Response to Helene E. Roberts's 'The Exquisite Slave: The Role of Clothes in the Making of the Victorian Woman'," *Signs: Journal of Women in Culture and Society*, vol. 2, no. 3 (Spring, 1977), pp. 570, 575; David Kunzle, *Fashion and Fetishism. A Social History of the Corset, Tight-Lacing, and Other Forms of Body-Sculpture in the West* (Totowa, New Jersey: Rowman & Littlefield, 1982), pp. 2, 40–43, 45, xvii.

2. Kunzle, *Fashion and Fetishism*, pp. viii, 1–4; Kunzle, "Dress Reform as Antifeminism," p. 577; Helene E. Roberts, "Reply to David Kunzle's 'Dress Reform as Antifeminism'," *Signs* (Winter, 1977), p. 519.

3. Roberts, "Reply to David Kunzle's 'Dress Reform as Antifeminism'," p. 519; Kunzle, "Dress Reform as Antifeminism," p. 574; Kunzle, *Fashion and Fetishism*, Appendix B.

4. C. Willett and Phillis Cunnington, *The History of Underclothes* (London: M. Joseph, 1951), p. 179; revised edition, edited by A.D. Mansfield and Valerie Mansfield (London: Faber & Faber, 1981), pp. 113, 110; Irene Clephane and Alan Botts, *Our Mothers. A Cavalcade in Pictures, Quotation and Description of Late Victorian Women 1870–1900* (London: Victor Gollancz, 1932), p. 192; Alison Lurie, *The Language of Clothes* (New York: Random House, 1981), p. 220; Elizabeth Ewing, *Dress and Undress. A History of Women's Underwear* (New York: Drama Book Specialists, 1978), p. 69; Bernadine Morris, "A History of Discomfort Told by Corsets," *The New York Times* (October 1, 1980).

5. I am indebted to Ms. Annette Carruthers, Assistant Keeper of Decorative Arts at the Leicestershire Museum and Art Gallery in New Walk, Leicester, for the lists and summary of waist sizes of corsets from the Symington Collection. I would also like to thank Miss Penelope Byrde, Keeper of Costume at the Museum of Costume at Bath, who assured me that most museum people agree that stories of 15 or 16 inch waists are fantasies; and Ms. Jane Tozer, Keeper at The Gallery of English Costume, Platt Hall, Manchester, who showed me many corsets and provided a goldmine of information.

6. E. Ward & Co., *The Dress Reform Problem A Chapter for Women* (London: Hamilton, Adams & Co., and Bradford: John Dale & Co., 1886), pp. 52–53.

7. Doris Langley Moore reported that the smallest dress in her collection was twenty-one inches; the average for young women's dresses was twenty-four. Doris Langley Moore, *The Woman in Fashion*, p. 17; Doris Langley Moore, *Fashion Through Fashion Plates* (London: Ward Lock, 1970), p. 92.

   Other museums such as The Gallery of English Costume in Manchester and The Merseyside County Museum in Liverpool, contain some dresses with smaller waist measurements. Unlike Mrs. Langley Moore, Anthea Jarvis, Assistant Keeper of Decorative Art at the Merseyside County Museum, Liverpool, reported that she had some difficulty finding models who could wear the Victorian dresses in her collection: One of the smallest dresses was an evening dress from the 1890s with a waist of just under twenty inches, indicating a corset measurement of about eighteen inches.

8. Charles Roux, *Contre le corset* (Paris: Imprimerie de E. Brière et Cie., 1855), pp. 4, 1–3, 8.

9. Paul Schultze-Naumberg, *Die Kultur des weiblichen Körpers als Grundlage der Frauenkleidung* (Jena, 1901), and Christian Stratz, *Die Frauenkleidung und ihre natürliche Entwicklung* (Stuttgart, 1900), cited by Stephen Kern, *Anatomy and Destiny. A Cultural History of the Human Body* (New York: Bobbs-Merrill Co., 1975), pp. 14–16, 263.

   Although they professed to admire the "natural" female body, both Schultze-Naumberg and Stratz included in their works grotesque photographs and descriptions of the supposed physical effects of corset wearing. This preoccupation might indicate at least an ambivalence about the female body. The work of Schultze-Naumberg was favorably reviewed in the journal

274

Notes to Chapter 9

of The Healthy and Artistic Dress Union, *The Dress Review* (April, 1903), pp. 39–42.

10. *The Queen* (11 September 1869), p. 157; *Pour la beauté naturelle de la femme contre la mutilation de la taille par le corset* (Paris: Ligue des Mères de Famille, 1909), pp. 3, 12.

11. Helene E. Roberts, "The Exquisite Slave," *Signs: Journal of Women in Culture and Society*, vol. 2, no. 3 (Spring, 1977), pp. 561–562; Dr. Coleman, cited by John S. Haller and Robin M. Haller, *The Physician and Sexuality in Victorian America* (Urbana: University of Illinois Press, 1974), p. 39.

12. Orson S. Fowler, *Intemperance and Tight-Lacing; Founded on the Laws of Life, as Developed by Phrenology and Physiology* (Originally published, New York, ca. 1846; Manchester: John Heywood, n.d. [ca. 1899]), pp. 40, 35–39.

13. John D. Davies, *Phrenology Fad and Science. A 19th-Century American Crusade* (New Haven: Yale University Press, 1955), pp. 111, 106, 4; Madeleine Stern, *Heads and Head Lines. The Phrenological Fowlers* (Norman: University of Oklahoma Press, 1971), pp. 41, 47–48; Fowler, *Intemperance and Tight-Lacing*, p. 36.

14. *Sylvia's Home Journal* (September, 1878), p. 419; *The Rational Dress Society's Gazette* (April, 1889), p. 2.
    A REFORMER saw women as breeding machines, and argued that since men "would reject a deformed and feeble animal of any kind to produce the young ones for their farms, one can hardly understand their anxiety to see their own children born of such mothers." *The Family Doctor* (March 10, 1888), p. 23.

15. Davies, *Phrenology: Fad and Science*, pp. 47, 154. Fowler's own attitudes toward women were rather complex: He certainly expressed considerable anxiety about "excessive" female sexuality, but in *Creative and Sexual Science* (1870), he advocated "summa bonum enjoyment" in coition. He also argued that "Women's Sphere of Industry should ... be enlarged till it equals that of men." Fowler, cited by Stern, *Heads and Head Lines*, pp. 193, 167.

16. Fowler, *Intemperance and Tight-Lacing*, pp. 33, 36.

17. Fowler, *Intemperance and Tight-Lacing*, pp. 36–39, especially p. 38.

18. Fowler, *Intemperance and Tight-Lacing*, p. 39.

19. Luke Limner (pseud. of John Leighton), *Madre Natura versus the Moloch of Fashion* (London: Chatto & Windus, 1874), pp. 70–73; The Ladies' Sanitary Association, *Wasps Have Stings; or, Beware of Tight-Lacing* (London: Published by the Ladies' Sanitary Association, and by John Morgan, n.d.), pp. 11, 6, 8; *The Lancet* (10 January 1880), cited by Kunzle, *Fashion and Fetishism*, p. 160; John Plummer, "Stays," *Once A Week* (12 April 1862), p. 446. See also Kunzle, *Fashion and Fetishism*, p. 189.

20. Dr. Sauveur Henri-Victor Bouvier, *Études historiques et médicales sur l'usage des corsets* (Paris: J.-B. Baillière, Librairie de l'Academie Imperiale de médecine, 1853), pp. 32–34; Dr. Ludovic O'Followell, *Le Corset. Histoire—médecine—hygiène* (Paris: A. Maloine, Editeur, 1905); Gustav Jaeger, M.D., *Selections from Essays on Health Culture and the Sanitary Woolen System* (London: Dr. Jaeger's Sanitary Woolen System Co., 1884), p. 165; C.E. Wheeler, M.D., untitled article in *The Dress Review*, issued quarterly by The Healthy and Artistic Dress Union (July, 1906), p. 54; W.

Wilberforce Smith, M.D., "Corset Wearing: The Medical Side of the Attack," *Aglaia* (July, 1893), p. 7, (Spring, 1894), pp. 31–35; Frederick Treves, F.R.C.S., *The Dress of the Period in its Relations to Health* (London: Published for the National Health Society, by Allman & Son, n.d. [1882]), pp. 15–20.

21. Ada S. Ballin, *The Science of Dress in Theory and Practice* (London: Sampson Low, Marston, Searle, & Rivington, 1885), pp. 142, 327; Ada S. Ballin, "Tight-Lacing," *Womanhood* (April, 1903), p. 327.

22. Charles Reade, *A Simpleton*, originally serialized in *London Society* (August 1872 to September 1873). "At the Author's particular request this story is not illustrated." It was then published as a book in 1873 (Boston: Dana Estes & Co., n.d.), pp. 43, 37, 36, 44–45, 181.

23. Gordon Stables, *The Girl's Own Book of Health and Beauty* (London: Jarrold's & Sons, 1892), p. 113.

24. Gwen Raverat, *Period Piece. A Cambridge Childhood* (London: Faber & Faber, 1952), p. 259; M. Vivian Hughes, *A London Girl of the Eighties* (London: Oxford University Press, 1936), p. 52.

25. Edward D. Kilbourne, "Are New Diseases Really New?," *Natural History* (December, 1983), p. 32; Gerhart S. Schwarz, M.D., "Society, Physicians, and the Corset," *Bulletin of the New York Academy of Medicine*, vol. 55, no. 6 (June, 1979): 551–590, especially pp. 555–557, 584.

My thanks to Dr. Kilbourne, Chairman of the Department of Microbiology at the Mount Sinai School of Medicine, for referring me to additional information in *The American Journal of Medicine* 88 (1980). In a private communication, Dr. Kilbourne observed that it was difficult "to relate [chlorosis] to effects of mechanical constriction."

26. The Ladies' Sanitary Association, *Wasps Have Stings; or, Beware of Tight-Lacing*, p. 12; Dr. Arabella Kenealy, "The Curse of Corsets," *The Nineteenth Century and After*, vol. 55 (January, 1904), pp. 131, 135, 132.

27. *Dress, Health, & Beauty* (London: Ward, Lock, & Co., 1878), p. 79; Ada S. Ballin, *The Science of Dress in Theory and Practice*, p. 151; Frances Mary Steele and Elizabeth Livingston Steele Adams, *Beauty of Form and Grace of Vesture* (London: B. F. Stevens, 1892), pp. 19, 20–21.

28. Henry Holiday, "The Artistic Aspect of Dress," *Aglaia. The Journal of the Healthy and Artistic Dress Union* (July, 1893), pp. 15, 23 [emphasis added]; Emile Zola, *Fecondité*, translated as *Fruitfulness* (New York, 1900), p. 42. See also *The Dress Review* (April, 1903), p. 41.

29. Jean Renoir, *Renoir, My Father*, trans. by Randolph and Dorothy Weaver (London: Wm. Collins, Fontana Books, 1965), pp. 85–87.

30. Luke Limner, *Madre Natura versus the Moloch of Fashion*, pp. 40–41. See also A.F. Crell and W.M. Wallace, *Family Oracle of Health* (London, 1824–1825), 2 vols., vol. 2, p. 414, in which stays are blamed for marring "the chaste beauty of the Grecian model."

31. Steele and Adams, *Beauty of Form*, p. 26; Arnold James Cooley, *The Toilet and Cosmetic Arts in Ancient and Modern Times* (London: R. Hardwick, 1866, and Philadelphia: Lindsay & Blackiston, 1866), p. 353.

32. Ernest Aimé Feydeau, *The Art of Pleasing*, translated from the French by Marie Courcelles. (New York: G.W. Carlton & Co., 1874), pp. 18–19, 46.

33. Mrs. Fanny Douglas, *The Gentlewoman's Book of Dress* (London: Henry & Co., n.d. [ca. 1894]), pp. 123–124.

34. "Rita," *VANITY! The Confessions of a Court Modiste* (London: T. Fisher Unwin, 1901), pp. 31, 38–39, 40.

35. Marguerite d'Aincourt, *Études sur le costume féminin* (Paris: Roveyre & G. Blond, 1885), pp. 24–25; Robert Machray, "Fashions in Waists," *The Lady's Realm* (December, 1902), p. 274; *La Vie Parisienne* (13 March 1875), p. 152.

36. Ernest Leoty, *Le Corset à travers les ages* (Paris: Paul Ollendorff, 1892), pp. 84, 102; Octave Uzanne, *L'Art et les artifices de la beauté* (Paris: Belix Juven & Bibliothèque Femina, 1902), pp. 92–94, 127.

37. Honoré de Balzac, *Cousin Bette*, trans. Marion Ayton Crawford (Harmondsworth, Middlesex, England, and New York: Penguin Books, 1965), p. 410.

38. "La Corbeille de mariage," *La Vie Parisienne* (17 May 1884), p. 271.

39. Gustave Droz, *Papa, Mamma and Baby*, trans. without abridgement from the 130th French printing of *Monsieur, madame, et bébé*, first published in 1866 (London: Vizetelly & Co., 1887), p. 9.

40. Priscilla Robertson, *An Experience of Women. Pattern and Change in Nineteenth-Century Europe* (Philadelphia: Temple University Press, 1982), p. 115. See also La Baronne d'Orchamps, *Tous les secrets de la femme* (Paris: Bibliothèque des Auteurs Modernes, 1907), p. 84; *Les Dessous Elégants* (February, 1903), p. 26.

41. A letter from Mrs. Sarah Anstin to Miss Senior (June, 1862), quoted without further attribution in Duncan Crow, *The Victorian Woman* (New York: Stein & Day, 1972), p. 334; "The History of the Corset," *The Queen* (5 December 1879), p. 375; *Le Rire* (1894), quoted in Cornelia Otis Skinner, *Elegant Wits and Grand Horizontals. Paris—La Belle Epoque* (London: Michael Joseph, 1963), p. 39.

42. Frank Norris, *Blix* (Garden City, New York: Page & Co., 1899), p. 5.
    The heroine herself is both pure and womanly, "healthy-minded" and "healthy-bodied"—and her clothing is presented as an expression of her personality and erotic appeal. There is, though, something almost fetishistic about the details of dress on which Norris dwells so lovingly: "She wore a heavy black overskirt that *rustled in a delicious fashion* over the coloured silk skirt beneath, and a white shirt-waist . . . *starched to a rattling stiffness.* Her neck was *swathed tight and high* with a broad ribbon of white *satin.* . . . He loved her because she was so pretty . . . and because she wore the great dog-collar [of a Saint Bernard] around her *trim, firm, corseted waist.*" [emphasis added]. Norris, pp. 7, 133.

43. Roberts, "Reply to David Kunzle's 'Dress Reform as Antifeminism'," p. 519.

44. A WOMAN OF FIFTY, "The Cult of Beauty in a Girl's School Forty Years Ago," *Society* (7 October 1899), p. 1911.

45. *La Vie Parisienne* (5 September 1874), p. 507.

46. Doris Langley Moore, *The Woman in Fashion* (London: B. T. Batsford, 1949), pp. 17–18; David Kunzle, "Dress Reform as Antifeminism," pp. 572–573, 577.

47. Contrary to Kunzle's belief, the serial article on "The Sin and Scandal of Tight-Lacing. A Crusade Against This Modern Madness," in *The Gentlewoman* (10 December 1892 to 18 March 1893), does not constitute "hard statistics" about the incidence and practice of tight-lacing. Indeed, Kunzle admits that he never actually read this exposé (which can be found in the Library of The Gallery of English Costume, Platt Hall in Manchester, England), but only excerpts from it, compiled by Sir Basil Liddell-Hart, who

himself strongly believed in the existence of tight-lacing (as well as believing that it was morally advantageous). See David Kunzle, *Fashion and Fetishism*, pp. 311–320; ETHEL, *The Family Doctor* (10 March 1888), p. 23; HYGEIA, "Does Tight-Lacing Really Exist," *FD* (3 September 1887), p. 7; HYGEIA, "Tight-Lacing in Brighton and Parisian Schools," *FD* (24 December 1887), p. 266.

48. "The Sin and Scandal of Tight-Lacing," *The Gentlewoman* (10 December 1892), p. 807; Ada S. Ballin, "Tight-Lacing," *Womanhood* (April, 1903), p. 324; Elise Maynard, "Fatal Corsets, or The Perils of Tight-Lacing," *Womanhood* (April, 1903), pp. 319–323, photographs on pp. 321–323; Helmut and Alison Gernsheim, *The History of Photography, 1865–1914* (New York: McGraw-Hill, 1969), p. 235.

49. BENEDICT, *EDM* (November, 1867), p. 614; PERSERVERANCE, *EDM* (August, 1868), p. 111; "Clumsy," *EDM* (November, 1867), p. 614.

50. T.F., *EDM* (February, 1868), p. 109; A CORRESPONDENT, *EDM*, (April, 1868), p. 224; A YOUNG BARONET, *EDM* (October, 1867), p. 558, reprinted in William Barry Lord, *The Corset and the Crinoline*, p. 184; *EDM* (November, 1867), p. 613.

51. *Schild's Monthly Journal* (January, 1894), p. 6; Charles Dubois, *Considérations sur cinq fleaux: l'Abus du corset, l'usage du tabac, la passion du jeu, l'abus des liqueurs fortes et l'agiotage* (Paris: E. Dentu, 1857), p. 14, cited in Philippe Perrot, *Les Dessus et les Dessous de la bourgeoisie. Une histoire du vêtement au XIXᵉ siecle* (Paris: Librairie Arthème Fayard, 1981), pp. 278–279; Lady Violet Greville, from an article in *The National Review*, quoted in *The Gentlewoman* (18 March 1893), p. 331.

It is worth noting that the *later* sections of *The Gentlewoman*'s serial article on tight-lacing appear to have been written by a different person.

52. SEMPER EADUM, *FD* (12 June 1886), p. 231.

53. NORA, *EDM* (May, 1867), p. 279; CONSTANCE, *The Queen* (18 July 1863), p. 44. See also ANOTHER CORRESPONDENT, *EDM* (September, 1867), p. 502; W. H. JOHNSON, *FD* (27 October 1888), p. 131. "The Waist of the Period," on the front cover of *FD* (3 March 1888) was a sketch allegedly taken "from photos" of one sister in a "tight-lacing family."

54. *The Gentlewoman* (24 December 1892), p. 852 and (31 December 1892), p. 884; James Laver, *Modesty in Dress* (Boston: Houghton Mifflin, 1969), p. 119. See also ALFRED, *EDM* (January, 1871), p. 62.

55. *EDM* (September, 1868), p. 166; *EDM* (March, 1871), p. 191; "E. D. M.," *Figure-Training; or Art the Handmaid of Nature* (London: Ward, Lock & Tyler, 1871), p. 18. See also A FAIR TIGHT-LACER, *FD* (12 June 1886), p. 231.

56. A MALE WASP WAIST *FD* (June 26, 1886), p. 263. See also AN OLD STAY-WEARER AND TIGHT-LACER, *FD* (12 June 1886), p. 231.

57. FANNY, *The Queen* (25 July 1863), quoted in William Barry Lord, *The Corset and the Crinoline* (London: Ward, Lock, & Tyler, n.d. [1868]), pp. 157–158. See also PRO-ROD, *EDM* (September, 1868), p. 168; *EDM* (May, 1867), p. 277; *EDM* (February, 1870), pp. 126–127; *EDM* (March, 1870), pp. 188–191; *EDM* (November, 1868), p. 280; *EDM* (August, 1870), p. 126; *EDM* (October, 1867), p. 558.

58. WASP WAIST, *Society* (23 September 1899), p. 1871. See also "Tight-Lacing as a Punishment," *FD* (3 September 1887), p. 7; "punishment corsets," *Modern*

Society (26 October 1895), p. 1585; "foot corsets" and "locked gloves," *Modern Society* (12 October 1895), p. 1523.

59. ALFRED, *EDM* (January, 1871), p. 62; MORALIST, *EDM* (February, 1871), p. 127.
60. Mrs. Fanny Douglas, *The Gentlewoman's Book of Dress* (London: Henry & Co., n.d. [ca. 1894]), pp. 14–15, 16, 17.
61. Preface to Dr. Ludovic O'Followell, *Le Corset. Histoire—médecine—hygiène* (Paris: A. Maloine, Editeur, 1905), p. vii.
62. STAYLACE, *EDM* (June, 1867), p. 224. See also *The Gentlewoman* (10 December 1892), p. 807; *FD* (12 June 1886), p. 231; *FD* (10 March 1888), p. 23; BENEDICT, *EDM* (November, 1867), p. 614.
63. *FD* (7 April 1888), p. 82. See also CONFESSIONS OF A MAN CORSET WEARER, *Answers* (21 October 1893), p. 384.
64. Miss Maynard, "Fatal Corsets," *Womanhood* (April, 1903), p. 322.
65. *Punch* (18 September 1869), p. 111.
66. SATIN WAIST, *Society* (23 December 1899), p. 1871; "Les Corsets pour Hommes," *Les Dessous Elégants* (August, 1904), pp. 137–139.
67. *Society* (28 January 1899), p. 1176.
68. An unofficial advertisement for Leoty corsets, *La Vie Parisienne* (27 February 1886), p. 127.
69. "Le Dernier Chateau Fort" (1885) is reproduced in Fernand Libron and Henri Clouzot, *Le Corset dans l'art et les moeurs du XIIIe au XXe siècle* (Paris: published by Libron, 1933), p. 107.
    Libron was President de la Chambre Syndicale des Fabricants de Corsets en gros de Paris; Clouzot was Conservateur du Musée Galliera.
70. *Les Dessous Elégants* (November, 1904), p. 205.
71. G. Viterbo, "Corset et Féminism," *Les Dessous Elégants* (September, 1904), pp. 155–156.
72. Eugene Chapus, *Manuel de l'homme et de la femme comme-il-faut* (Paris, 1862), cited by Philippe Perrot, *Les Dessus et les Dessous de la bourgeoisie. Une histoire du vêtement au XIXe siècle* (Paris: Librairie Arthème Fayard, 1981), p. 259.
73. "Études sur la Toilette: Nouvelle Série. Avant et Après le Corset," *La Vie Parisienne* (9 September 1882), pp. 522–523.
74. "Considérations sur le Corset," *La Vie Parisienne* (19 April 1879), pp. 224–225; "Études sur la Toilette: Les Corsets" *La Vie Parisienne* (15 January 1881), pp. 38–39.
75. "Les Corsets," *La Vie Parisienne* (15 January 1881), pp. 38–39; "Les Dessous," *La Vie Parisienne* (2 May 1885), pp. 252–253.
    In fact, the silk jersey of the dress reformer [not shown here] is actually rather similar to the silk *maillot* of the central figure in "Les Corsets." Their bodies, though, and even more important, their *attitudes,* are very different.
76. Robert E. Riegel, "Women's Clothes and Women's Rights," *American Quarterly,* vol. XV, no. 3 (Fall, 1963), pp. 390–401; David Kunzle, "Dress Reform as Antifeminism," p. 570.
77. There were, for example, endless cartoons in *Punch* portraying the "strong-minded woman" who favored both women's rights and rational dress (including some form of supposedly healthy substitute for the ordinary corset). In reality, many members of The Rational Dress Society were in favor

of greater opportunities for women, as were many members of The Healthy
and Artistic Dress Union.
78. Riegel, "Women's Clothes and Women's Rights," pp. 397, 401.

Notes to Chapter 10

1. Anne Buck, "Foundations of the Active Woman," in Ann Saunders (ed.), *La Belle Epoch, Costume 1890–1914* (London: Published for the Costume Society, 1968), p. 43.
2. Louis Octave Uzanne, *Fashion in Paris 1797–1897* (London: Heinemann, 1898), p. 172; Louis Octave Uzanne, *The Modern Parisienne* (London: Heinemann, 1912), p. 23; *The Lady's Realm* (April, 1903), p. 767; Mrs. Eric Pritchard, *The Cult of Chiffon* (London: Grant Richards, 1902), p. 16.
3. *The Lady's Realm* (December, 1902), p. 291; Lady Lucy Christiana Duff-Gordon (Lucille), *Discretions and Indiscretions* (London: Jarrolds, 1932), p. 66.
4. In 1857, for example, the Goncourts described a courtesan's expensive and erotic lingerie. *Pages from the Goncourt Journal*, trans. and ed. by Robert Baldick (New York: Oxford University Press, 1978), p. 26.
5. Dr. Daumas, "Hygiène et médecine," in *Fashion-Théorie* (March, 1861), cited in Philippe Perrot, *Les Dessus et les Dessous de la bourgeoisie. Une histoire du vêtement au XIXᵉ siècle* (Paris: Librairie Arthème Fayard, 1981), p. 267.
6. *Home Journal* (13 February 1858), quoted in William Leach, *True Love and Perfect Union* (London and Henley: Routledge and Kegan Paul, 1981), p. 219.
7. Anne Buck, "Foundations of the Active Woman," p. 43.
8. See, for example, Elizabeth Ewing, *Dress and Undress. A History of Women's Underwear* (New York: Drama Books, 1978).
9. Violette [Alice de Laincel], *L'Art de la toilette chez la femme. Bréviaire de la vie élégante* (Paris, 1885), pp. 4, 37.
10. Mrs. Eric Pritchard, *The Cult of Chiffon*, p. 15; *The Lady's Realm* (April, 1901), p. 776; (November, 1901), p. 115; and (September, 1901), p. 648.
11. Mrs. Eric Pritchard, *The Cult of Chiffon*, p. 20.
12. "The Wedding Presents," *La Vie Parisienne* (17 May 1884), p. 270.
13. "Pantalons, Bas, et Chausseurs," *La Vie Parisienne* (19 February 1881), pp. 108–109; "Les Dessous," *La Vie Parisienne* (2 May 1885), pp. 252–253; "Petite Chronique," *La Vie Parisienne* (14 February 1874), p. 102.
14. "Petite Chronique," *La Vie Parisienne* (2 December 1882), p. 700.
15. "Comment Elles S'Habillent de Nuit" [How They Dress at Night], *La Vie Parisienne* (9 November 1878), pp. 650–651.
16. Pierre Dufay, *Le Pantalon féminin. Un Chapitre inedit de l'histoire du costume* (Paris: Charles Carringdon, 1906), pp. 110–111, 117–118; *Le Sport*, quoted in Romi, *Histoire pittoresque du pantalon féminin* (Paris: Jacques Grancher, 1979), p. 68.
17. Romi, *Histoire pittoresque du pantalon féminin*, pp. 58, 154; Dufay, *Le Pantalon féminin*, pp. 134, 163.
18. Violette, *L'Art de la toilette*, p. 41.
19. Rene Maizeroy, *L'Adorée*, quoted in Romi, *Histoire pittoresque du pantalon féminin*, p. 74.

20. "De l'Adultére: Conseils pratiques," *Gil Blas* (10 February 1890), quoted in Dufay, *Le Pantalon féminin*, p. 114.

21. Colette, *My Apprenticeships*, trans. by Helen Beauclerk (London: Martin Secker & Warburg, 1957; New York: Farrar, Straus, & Giroux, 1978), p. 21.

22. *Modern Society* (26 December 1891), p. 171; *Modern Society* (20 August 1892), p. 1263; *Modern Society* (17 December 1892), p. 148; *Modern Society* (1 July 1893), p. 1034.

23. Clara Bell; *Modern Society* (11 June 1892), p. 937; "The Strange History of a Lace Petticoat," *Modern Society* (23 April 1892), p. 713; *Modern Society* (24 November 1894), p. 52.

24. *De la Kleptomanie*, quoted by Michael Miller, *The Bon Marché. Bourgeois Culture and the Department Store, 1689–1920* (Princeton: Princeton University Press, 1981), p. 204. See also *Modern Society* (25 February 1893), p. 461; SATIN SKIN, *Society* (14 October 1899), p. 1931, and the cases described in Richard Krafft-Ebing, *Psychopathia Sexualis*; William Stekel, *Sexual Aberrations. The Phenomena of Fetishism in Relation to Sex*; and Havelock Ellis, *Studies in the Psychology of Sex*.

25. A few advertisements for women's corsets may have been directed toward men—who would then, presumably, buy the corsets for their wives or mistresses. These are very different from women's advertisements. One such "puff" or veiled advertisement for Madame Billaud's Corset (in *La Vie Parisienne*, 14 February 1874, p. 102) uses the technique, familiar to pornography, of comparing the woman's body with a landscape: "No engineer would know how to transform an ungrateful terrain with as much art. . . . Mme Billaud . . . relieves the monotony of a desert plain by the movements of the soil . . . to align the highs, fill in the valleys, separate the hillocks by creating a ravine, to prevent landslides—that is only play for the clever corsetière."

     Few men wore corsets at this time. Those who did wore corsets with names that had military, aristocratic, and god-like associations. An 1899 advertisement in *Society* promoted men's corsets with the names The Marlboro, The Kitchener, and The Carlton—famous aristocratic generals. At the Kyoto Costume Institute, I saw a man's grey linen corset from the 1890s or early twentieth century with the label, "Celebrated Apollo [brand] [with] fitted Spartan unbreakable steels." Apollo was the personification of male love and beauty, while the Spartans, of course, had been famous as warriors. At this time in Britain, references to the Greeks could have had homosexual connotations. Another English corset from the same period was labeled the "Double Axe Brand"—another warlike name. There is some evidence that military officers (and sportsmen) were prominant among the handful of men who continued to wear corsets in the later nineteenth century. These corset names, per se, indicate only that their wearers wanted to associate themselves with the military and the aristocracy.

26. Lady Violette Greville, *The Gentlewoman in Society* (London: Henry & Co., 1892), p. 131.

27. Edward J. Bristow, *Vice and Vigilance. Purity Movements in Britain since 1700* (Dublin: Gill & Macmillan, 1977), p. 206. See also Arthur W. Pearce, *The Future Out of the Past. An Illustrated History of the Warner Brothers Company on its 90th Anniversary* (Bridgeport, Connecticut: The Warner Brothers Company, 1964).

28. Madame Inez Gâches-Sarraute, *Le Corset. Étude physiologique et pratique* (Paris: Librairie de l'Academie de Médecine, 1900), pp. 12, 17, 1.

29. *The Lady's Magazine* (February, 1901), p. 217; *The Lady's Magazine* (March, 1901), p. 304.

30. Uzanne, quoted in Gertrude Aretz, *The Elegant Woman from the Rococo Period to Modern Times*, trans. James Laver. (London: G. G. Harrap, 1932), p. 273; Emile Zola, *Au bonheur des dames* [originally published 1883] (Paris: Fasquelle. Le Livre de Poche, n.d.), p. 478.

31. Mrs. Eric Pritchard, "Bridal Trousseaux," *The Lady's Realm* (April, 1903), p. 711; Ellen Peel, quoted in Betty Asquith, *A Victorian Young Lady* (Salisbury: Michael Russell, 1978), p. 142 [A selection from the letters and diaries of Ellen Peel, covering the period 1886–1908.]; interview with Lady Naomi Mitchison, London, 1981.

32. Marguerite d'Aincourt, *Études sur le costume féminin* (Paris: Rouveyre et G. Blond, 1883), pp. 14–15.

33. Elinor Glyn, *The Vicissitudes of Evangeline* (London: Duckworth & Co., 1905), pp. 99–100.

34. Baronne d'Orchamps, *Tous les secrets de la femme* (Paris: Bibliothèque des Auteurs Modernes, 1907), pp. 78, 79.

35. Comtesse de Tramar, *Le Bréviaire de la femme. Pratiques secrètes de la beauté*, eighth edition. (Paris: V. Havard, 1903), pp. 115, 169–171.

36. Uzanne, *Fashion in Paris 1797–1897*, p. 172; Cecil Lorraine, "Frou-Frou," *The Lady's Realm* (December, 1904), p. 170.

37. Pierre de Lano, *L'Amour à Paris sous le Second Empire* (Paris: Simonis Empis, 1896), p. 182, quoted in Perrot, *Les Dessous et les Dessous*, p. 282.

38. *La Vie Parisienne* (1888), pp. 88–89, quoted in Kunzle, *Fashion and Fetishism*, p. 60.

39. d'Orchamps, *Tous les secrets de la femme*, pp. 78–79.

40. Uzanne, *The Modern Parisienne*, pp. 25–26.

41. d'Orchamps, *Tous les secrets de la femme*, pp. 78–79.

42. *The Lady's Magazine* (February, 1901), p. 217; *Womanhood* (May, 1903), p. 433.

43. *The Lady's Realm* (December, 1902), p. 286.

Notes to Chapter 11

1. H. Ellen Browning, *Beauty Culture* (London: Hutchinson & Co., 1898), p. 15.

2. Mrs. Eric Pritchard, *The Cult of Chiffon* (London: Grant Richards, 1902), p. 4.

3. Mrs. Eric Pritchard, *The Cult of Chiffon*, pp. 5–6.

4. Comtesse de Tramar [Marie-Fanny de Lagarrigue, Baronne d'Ysarn de Capdeville, Marquise de Villefort, who also wrote under the names Comtesse de Marca and Baronne d'Ormal], *Le Bréviaire de la femme. Pratiques secrètes de la beauté*, eighth edition. (Paris: Victor Havard, 1903); and *L'Évangile profane. Rite féminin* (Paris: Victor Havard, 1905), p. 5.

5. Comtesse de Tramar, *Que veut la femme? Être jolie, être aimée et dominer* (Paris: Malet, 1911); Baronne d'Orchamps, *Tous les secrets de la femme* (Paris: Bibliothèque des Auteurs Modernes, 1907), p. xi.

6. Max O'Rell, *Her Royal Highness Woman* (London: Chatto & Windus, 1901), pp. 36–37.

7. Baroness Blanche A. A. Staffe, *The Lady's Dressing Room*, trans. Lady Colin Campbell. (London: Cassell & Co., 1892), pp. 13, 18.
   Staffe also wrote the column "Notes Mondaine" for *Annales*.

8. S— G—, *The Art of Being Beautiful. A Series of Interviews with a Society Beauty* (London: Henry J. Drane, n.d. [1903]), p. 47; *The London Journal of Fashions* (1895), quoted in Neville Williams, *Powder and Paint: A History of the Englishwoman's Toilet* (London: Longman's, Green, & Co., 1957), p. 115; Max Beerbohm, *The Yellow Book* (April, 1894), quoted in Neville Williams, *Powder and Paint*, pp. 116–117.

9. Lillian Joy, *The Well-Dressed Woman* (London: Cassell & Co., 1907), pp. 1–2; Baroness Blanche A. A. Staffe, *Usages du monde; règles du savoir-vivre dans la société moderne* (Paris: Flammarion, 1899), p. 7.

10. Staffe, *Usages du Monde*, pp. 315–316.

11. Musée de la Mode et du Costume, *Secrets d'élégance 1750–1950* (Paris, 1978), p. 42; *The Lady's Magazine* (September, 1901), p. 272; *The Queen* (10 January 1903), p. 74; Alison Gernsheim, *Fashion and Reality: 1840–1914* (London: Faber & Faber, 1963), p. 85.

12. *Pictorial Review* (October, 1905), p. 49; Madame Estelle d'Aubigny, *The Woman Beautiful in the Twentieth Century* (London and New York: Street & Smith, 1902), p. 10; Lady Lucy Christiana Duff Gordon [Lucille], *Discretions and Indiscretions* (London: Jarrolds, 1932), pp. 76, 78, 71; *The Lady's Realm* (April, 1903), p. 768.

13. A Toilet Specialist, *The Art of Beauty. A Book for Women and Girls*, edited by "Isobel" of *Home Notes*. (London: C. Arthur Pearson, 1899), pp. 3–4; Sonia Keppel, *Edwardian Daughter* (London: Hamish Hamilton, 1958), pp. 14–15.

14. Advertisements in *The Delineator* (December, 1894), p. xxxiii; *Pictorial Review* (October, 1905), p. 49; *Les Dessous Elégants* (October, 1901), n.p.

15. James Laver, *Edwardian Promenade* (London: Edward Holton, 1958), pp. 147–148.

16. Staffe, *The Lady's Dressing Room*, pp. 282, 281.

17. d'Orchamps, *Tous les secrets de la femme*, p. 282; Tramar, *La Bréviaire de la femme*, p. 135.

18. *The Queen* (3 January 1903), p. 26; "Love at 35," *The Queen* (14 February 1903), p. 244; Duff Gordon, *Discretions and Indiscretions*, p. 90.

19. Mrs. Nepean,"La Jeune Fille," *The Queen* (23 May 1903), p. 807.

20. d'Aubigny, *The Woman Beautiful in the Twentieth Century*, pp. 9–10, 35.

21. Ella Fletcher, *The Woman Beautiful* [first published in 1899] (New York, 1901), pp. 34, 24, 32–33.

22. Fletcher, *The Woman Beautiful*, pp. 35, 24–27, 11; Caroline Ticknor, "The Steel-Engraving Lady and the Gibson Girl," *Atlantic Monthly* 88 (July, 1901), pp. 105–108.

23. C. Willett Cunnington and Phillis Cunnington, *The History of Underclothes* (London: M. Joseph, 1951), p. 219; *The Queen* (March, 1911), cited by Norah Waugh, *Corsets and Crinolines* (London: B. T. Batsford, 1954), p. 112.

24. Lady Diana Cooper, *The Rainbow Comes and Goes* (London: Rupert Hart-Davis, 1958), p. 61; see also Barbara Baines, *Fashion Revivals from the Elizabethan Age to the Present Day* (London: B.T. Batsford, 1981), pp. 55–58;

Guillermo de Osma, *Mariano Fortuny. His Life and Work* (New York: Rizzoli International Publications, 1980).

25. Dorothy Behling, "French Couturiers and Artist/Illustrators: Fashion from 1900 to 1925," Ph.D. dissertation, Ohio State University, 1977, pp. 40–47.

26. Paul Poiret, *King of Fashion. The Autobiography of Paul Poiret*, trans. by Stephen Haden Grasset (Philadelphia and London: J. B. Lippincott Co., 1931), pp. 76–77. Originally published as *En habillant l'époque*, 1930.

27. Duff Gordon, *Discretions and Indiscretions*, p. 66; Caresse Crosby, quoted in Elizabeth Ewing, *Dress and Undress*, p. 115.

28. Unpublished manuscript, quoted in Palmer White, *Poiret* (New York: Clarkson N. Potter Inc., 1973), p. 28; unpublished manuscript, quoted in White, *Poiret*, p. 31.

29. Poiret, *King of Fashion*, p. 76; Madame Poiret, quoted in White, *Poiret*, p. 31.

30. *Vogue* (15 October 1913), quoted in White, *Poiret*, p. 39.

31. Erté, *Things I Remember. An Autobiography* (New York: Quadrangle/The New York Times Book Co., 1975), p. 26.

32. *Vogue* (May, 1908), quoted in White, *Poiret*, p. 41.

33. "The desire," advertisement for Le Papillon Corset, *Vogue* (1 June 1913), p. 85; "Gives the corsetless figure," advertisement for La Resista Corset, *Dress and Vanity Fair* (September, 1913), p. 65; "The 'waistless' effect," Catalogue for Peter Robinson, Ltd., *The Curtain is Drawn—The Fashion Line for 1914 is Revealed* (London, 1914), no page numbers.

34. Fernand Libron and Henri Clouzot, *Le Corset dans l'art et les moeurs du XIIIᵉ au XXᵉ siècle* (Paris: published by Libron, 1933), pp. 110, 112; Lady Naomi Mitchison, *All Change Here. Girlhood and Marriage* (London: The Bodley Head, 1975), p. 31; "Polaire," Sidney Mannor (for) Marshall & Snellgrove, *Towards New Liberty. A Comment on Modern Tendencies* (London, 1914), pp. 15–16.

35. Mrs C. S. Peel, *Mrs Barnet, Robes* (London: John Lane, The Bodley Head, 1915), p. 171; advertisement for Mme. Rabeau's *corset-maillot*, "The Apotheosis of the Line," *Les Modes* (December, 1911), p. 1911; Mannor, *Towards New Liberty*, pp. 12, 5.

36. Mannor, *Towards New Liberty*, pp. 7, 9–10, 13.

37. "At balls," puff for Vertus Soeurs Corsets, *Les Modes* (March, 1914), p. 40; "Chiffons and Tango," also promoting Vertus Soeurs Corsets, *Les Modes* (January, 1914), p. 36; the "Tango" corset was promoted in *Dress and Vanity Fair* (September, 1913), p. 5.

38. d'Orchamps, *Tous les secrets de la femme*, pp. 45–46; Marylène Delbourg-Delphis, *Le Chic et le Look* (Paris: Hachette, 1981), pp. 32–33; *Harrison's Complete Dressmaker* (February, 1909), p. 33.

39. *Journal des Dames et des Modes* (10 September 1912), p. 88, and (10 August 1912), p. 57.

40. *Vogue* (May, 1908); Poiret, *King of Fashion*, p. 76.

41. *The Gentlewoman* (16 May 1914), p. 670; *Dress and Vanity Fair* (October, 1913), pp. 29, 80.

42. Max von Boehn, *Modes and Manners of the Nineteenth Century*, 4 volumes [originally published in 1919] (London: Dent, 1927), vol. 4, pp. 119, 123.

43. *Les Modes* (January, 1914), p. 10.

44. Cecil Beaton, *The Glass of Fashion* (London: Weidenfeld and Nicolson, 1954), p. 109.

45. Keppel, *Edwardian Daughter*, p. 89.

46. "Lamia," *Country Life* (28 September 1907), quoted in Pauline Stevenson, *Edwardian Fashion* (London: Ian Allan, 1980), p. 41; Loelia, Duchess of Westminster, *Grace and Favour* (London: Weidenfeld and Nicolson, 1961), p. 41; *Vogue* (1 June 1913), p. 22.

47. Liane de Pougy, *My Blue Notebooks*, trans. by Diana Athill. (London: Andre Deutsch, 1979), p. 206.

48. Poiret, *King of Fashion*, p. 93. See also *Journal des Dames et des Modes* (1 June 1912), p. 5; *L'Art et la Mode* (30 September 1911), p. 750.

49. Arthur Marwick, *War and Social Change in the Twentieth Century* (New York: Macmillan, 1974); Stephen Kern, *Anatomy and Destiny. A Cultural History of the Human Body* (New York: Bobbs-Merrill Co., 1975), pp. 16–17, 20. See also Arthur Marwick, *The Deluge. British Society and the First World War* (Harmondsworth, Middlesex: Penguin Books, 1967).

50. *Illustrated London News* (21 August 1915), p. 252, and (16 October 1915), p. 506; *La Femme Chic* (1916), cited by Doris Langley Moore, *The Woman in Fashion*, p. 170; *The Lady* (1916), cited by Elizabeth Ewing, *Dress and Undress*, p. 123.

51. Lady Cynthia Asquith, *Diaries 1915–1918*, ed. by E.M. Horsley (New York: Alfred A. Knopf, 1969), pp. 11, 51, 14, 31.

52. *The 1915 Mode as Shown by Paris* (New York and Paris: Conde Nast, 1915), pp. 8, 17.

53. Lady Diana Cooper, *The Rainbow Comes and Goes*, pp. 120, 124.

54. James F. McMillan, "The First World War and the Social Condition of Women in France," Part Two of *Housewife or Harlot: The Place of Women in French Society, 1870–1940* (Brighton, Sussex: The Harvester Press, 1981), pp. 101–192; William Chafe, *The American Woman. Her Changing Social, Economic, and Political Roles, 1920–1970* (New York: Oxford University Press, 1972); Jeffrey Weeks, "Belief and Behavior 1914–39," Chapter 11 of *Sex, Politics and Society. The Regulation of Sexuality Since 1900* (London and New York: Longman, 1981), pp. 199–231.

55. McMillan, *Housewife or Harlot*, p. 163.

56. James Laver, *Taste and Fashion from the French Revolution to the Present Day* (London: George G. Harrap, 1937, revised ed., 1945), p. 101.

57. Interview with Mrs. I. (born in the late 1890s) in Cambridge, England, 1981; interview with Mrs. D. (born in 1896) in London, England, 1981.

58. The Duchess of Westminster, quoted in Elizabeth Ewing, *History of Twentieth Century Fashion* (London: B.T. Batsford, 1979), p. 93.

59. Florence Courtenay, *Physical Beauty: How to Develop and Preserve It* (New York: Social Mentor Publications, 1922), pp. 8–9, 6, 13, 10, 54.

60. *Le Nouveau Bréviaire de la beauté* (Paris, n.d. [ca. 1926]), pp. 8, 58; Adolphe Armand Braun, *Figures, Faces and Folds* (London: B.T. Batsford, 1928), pp. 1–2.

61. Paul Poiret, *Revenez-y* (Paris: Librairie Gallimard, 1932), p. 122.

62. Josephine Huddleston, *Secrets of Charm* (New York and London: G.P. Putnam's Sons, 1929), p. 277; Marcel Braunschvig, *La Femme et la beauté* (Paris: Librairie Armand Colin, 1929), p. 129; *Art-Goût-Beauté* (September, 1926), no page numbers.

63. "Youth," Elizabeth Hurlock, *The Psychology of Dress* (New York: Ronald Press, 1929), p. 165; "long," "straight," Courtenay, *Physical Beauty*, p. 9; "shapely," *The Queen* (20 March 1920), p. 11; "well-moulded calves," Margaret Story, *How to Dress Well* (London and New York, 1924), p. 397; "nude silk hose," *Eve* (12 January 1927), no page numbers.

64. *Vogue* (May, 1922), p. 69.

65. "The natural," Emily Burbank, *The Smartly Dressed Woman; How She Does It* (New York: Dodd, Mead & Co., 1925), p. 1; "girlish immaturity," *A History of Feminine Fashions* (London, n.d. [ca. 1926]), p. 52; "the charm," *Pictorial Review* (October, 1926), p. 41; "modern ideal," Duff-Gordon, *Discretions and Indiscretions*, pp. 272, 259, 80.

66. Victor Margueritte, *La Garçonne* (Paris: E. Flammarion, 1922); Michael Arlen, *The Green Hat* (New York: George H. Doran, 1924); Aldous Huxley, *Antic Hay* [first published, 1923] (New York: Modern Library Edition, 1933).

67. Huxley, *Antic Hay*, pp. 133–134.

68. Arlen, *The Green Hat*, pp. 18, 26, 53, 186, 305.

69. Lady Troubridge, *Memories and Reflections* (London: William Heineman, 1925), pp. 63, 118; "The kinetic silhouette," *Art-Goût-Beaute* (April, 1926) and (September, 1926), no page numbers.

70. Neville Williams, *Powder and Paint; Harper's Bazar* (1893), cited by Lois Banner, *American Beauty*, p. 215; Richard Corson, *Fashions in Make-Up*, p. 479.

Notes to Chapter 12

1. Susan Brownmiller, *Femininity* (New York: Simon and Schuster, 1984), pp. 51, 80–81. See especially the chapters on the body and clothes.

2. Lois Banner, *American Beauty. A Social History . . . Through Two Centuries . . . of the American Idea, Ideal, and Image of the Beautiful Woman* (New York: Alfred A. Knopf, 1983). See the Introduction (pp. 3–16) and Chapter 13; *Vogue* (February, 1984).

3. Valerie Steele, "Fashion in China," *Dress. The Journal of the American Costume Society* (1983), pp. 8–15.

4. Friedrich Nietzsche, *The Birth of Tragedy*, quoted in Domna C. Stanton, *The Aristocrat as Art. A Study of the Honnête Homme and the Dandy in Seventeeth and Nineteenth-Century France* (New York: Columbia University Press, 1980), no page number. Theodore Zeldin, *The French* (New York: Pantheon Books, 1982), p. 33.

5. Werner Sombart, *Luxury and Capitalism*, translated by W. R. Dittmar. (Ann Arbor: University of Michigan Press, 1967), described in Carolyn C. Lougee, *Le Paradis des femmes. Women, Salons, and Social Stratification in Seventeenth-Century France* (Princeton: Princeton University Press, 1976), p. 39.

6. Gerda Lerner, *The Majority Finds Its Past. Placing Women in History* (New York: Oxford University Press, 1979), p. xxv.

7. Karl Marx quoted and analyzed in Nancy Cott, *The Bonds of Womanhood. "Women's Sphere" in New England* (New Haven: Yale University Press, 1977), p. 4.

8. John Berger, *Ways of Seeing* (1972), cited by Griselda Pollock, *Mary Cassatt* (New York: Harper & Row, 1980), p. 18.

9. William H. Chafe, *The American Woman. Her Changing Social, Economic, and Political Roles, 1920–1970* (London: Oxford University Press, 1972), p. 245.

10. E. M. Green, *La Mode et la coquetterie* (Paris: Devambez, 1912), p. 15.

Bibliography

PRIMARY SOURCES

I. Interviews

Interview with Mrs. D., an Englishwoman born in 1896, who married into the Anglo-French aristocracy. She wore a Callot Soeurs wedding dress, and her favorite designer was Vionnet. London, England, 1981.

Interview with Mrs. I., an Englishwoman born in the late 1890s into a well-to-do religious family in York. Cambridge, England, 1981.

Interview with Lady Naomi Mitchison, born in 1897. Her memoirs and those of her mother, Louisa Kathleen Haldane, have been published. London, England, 1981.

II. Unpublished Sources

Département des Estampes, Series 0a20. Bibliothèque Nationale, Paris.

Duff Gordon, Lady Lucy Christiana [Lucille], "Private Collection Scrapbooks." The Library of The Fashion Institute of Technology, New York.

The Vyvyan Holland Collection of Fashion Plates. The Cooper-Hewitt Museum, New York.

Liddell-Hart, Sir Basil. "Scrapbooks." The Liverpool Polytechnic Art Library.

Maciet Collection. The Library of the Musée des Arts Décoratifs, Paris.

Paquin, Mme. "Designs" and "Publicité." The Costume and Fashion Research Centre, Bath.

"Pictorial History of the Corset." Vol. 1 The Early Period; Vol. 2 From 1880 to 1914; Vol. 3 From 1915 to 1929. The Brooklyn Museum Art Library.

Warshaw Collection of Business Americana. National Museum of American History, The Smithsonian Institution.

House of Worth. "Albums of Photographs." The Costume and Fashion Research Centre, Bath. "Costume Sketches." The Costume Institute, Metropolitan Museum of Art.

III. Books and Articles

A. C. "Individuality and Dress," *The Queen* (6 December 1879).

—————. "The Influence of Aesthetics on English Society," *Sylvia's Home Journal* (December, 1879).

A Lady. *Beauty: What It Is, and How to Retain It.* London: Frederick Warne & Co., 1873.

A Lady. *How to Dress on £15 a Year as a Lady.* London: Frederick Warne & Co., 1873.

A Lady of Rank. *The Book of Costume: or, Annals of Fashion, from the Earliest Period to the Present Time.* London: Henry Colburn, 1847.

A Professional Beauty. *Beauty and How to Keep It.* London: Brentano's, 1889.

A Toilet Specialist. *The Art of Beauty. A Book for Women and Girls.* Edited by "Isobel" of *Home Notes.* London: C. Arthur Pearson Limited, 1899.

Abraham, Karl. "Remarks on The Psycho-Analysis of a Case of Foot and Corset Fetishism" [1910]. In *Selected Papers of Karl Abraham.* Translated and edited by Douglas Bryan and Alix Strachey. New York: Basic Books, 1960.

Adami, J. G. and C. S. Roy. "The Physiological Bearing of Waist-Belts and Stays," *The National Review* 12 (November, 1888):341–349.

Adolphus, F. *Some Memories of Paris.* Edinburgh and London: William Blackwood and Sons, 1895.

Janine Aghion. *The Essence of the Mode of the Day Paris 1920.* Paris: The Books of La Belle Edition, n.d. [1920].

Marguerite d'Aincourt. *Études sur le costume féminin.* Paris: Ed. Rouveyre et G. Blond, n.d. [ca. 1885].

Alexandre, Arsène. *Les Reines de l'aiguille: Modistes et couturières.* Paris: Théophile Belin, 1902.

Alq, Louise d'. *Les Secrets du cabinet de toilette, conseils et recettes par une femme du monde.* Paris: Bureau des Causeries Familières, 1881.

Anstruther, Elizabeth. *The Complete Beauty Book.* New York: D. Appleton and Co., 1906.

Aria, Mrs. "Dressing as a Duty and an Art," *The Woman's World* (July, 1890).

—————. *Costume: Fanciful, Historical, Theatrical.* London: Macmillan and Co., 1906.

Arlen, Michael. *The Green Hat.* New York: George H. Doran, 1924.

Art of Beauty, or The Best Methods of Improving and Preserving The Shape, Carriage and Complexion, Together with the Theory of Beauty. London: Knight and Long, 1825.

The Art of Dress, or Guide to The Toilette, with Directions for Adapting the Various Parts of the Female Costume to the Complexion and Figure. London: Charles Tilt, 1834.

"The Art of Dress," *The Quarterly Review* 79 (March, 1847):372–399.

The Art of Dressing Well: A Book of Hints. London: Lockwood and Co., and Simpkin, Marshall and Co., n.d. [ca. 1870].

Asquith, Lady Cynthia. *Remember and Be Glad.* London: James Barrie, 1952.

—————. *Diaries 1915–1918.* New York: Alfred A. Knopf, 1969.

Aubigny, Madame Estelle d'. *The Woman Beautiful in the Twentieth Century.* London and New York: Street & Smith, 1902.

Avenel, Vicomte George d'. *Le Méchanisme de la vie moderne.* 4 vols. Paris: Librairie Armand Colin, 1900–1905.

Baldwin, Monica. *I Leap Over The Wall. Contrasts and Impressions after Twenty-eight Years in a Convent.* New York: Rinehart and Company, 1950.

Ballin, Ada S. *The Science of Dress in Theory and Practice.* London: Sampson Low, Marston, Searle, and Rivington, 1885.

————. "Tight-Lacing," *Womanhood* (April, 1903).

Balsan, Consuelo Vanderbilt. *The Glitter and The Gold.* Maidstone: George Mann, 1953.

Balzac, Honoré de. *Cousin Bette.* Translated by Marion Aytors Crawford. Harmondsworth, Middlesex: Penguin Books, 1965.

Baudelaire, Charles. *The Painter of Modern Life and Other Essays.* Translated and edited by Jonathan Mayne. London: Phaidon Press, Ltd. 1964.

Beaton, Cecil. *The Glass of Fashion.* London: Weidenfeld and Nicolson, 1954.

Bennett, Arnold. *The Journal of Arnold Bennett 1896–1910.* New York: The Viking Press, 1932.

Bertall [Charles Albert d'Arnoux]. *La Comédie de notre temps.* 2 vols. Paris: E. Plon, 1874.

Bibesco, Princess. *Noblesse de robe.* Paris: Bernard Grasset, 1928.

Bigg, Ada Heather. "The Evils of 'Fashion,'" *The Nineteeth Century*, vol. 3, no. 3 (1893). Reprinted in Gordon Wills and David Midgley, eds., *Fashion Marketing.* London: George Allen & Unwin Ltd., 1973, pp. 35–46.

Black, Alexander. *Miss America: Pen and Camera Sketches of the American Girl.* New York: Charles Scribner's Sons, 1898.

Blanc, Charles. *L'Art dans la parure et dans le vêtement.* Paris: Librairie Renouard, 1875. Translated under the title *Art in Ornament and Dress.* London: Chapman and Hall, 1877.

M. R. Bobbitt, ed. *With Dearest Love to All. The Life and Letters of Lady Jebb.* London: Faber and Faber, 1960.

Boehn, Max von. *Modespiegel.* Berlin, Braunschweig, and Hamburg: G. Westermann, 1919.

————. *Die Mode: Menschen und Moden im neunzehnten Jahrhundert.* Munich: F. Bruckmann, 1919. Translated by M. Edwardes, under the title *Modes and Manners of the Nineteenth Century.* With additional chapters by Grace Thompson. 4 vols. London: Dent, 1927.

————. *Modes and Manners: Ornaments.* London: Dent, 1929.

Book of Beauty, Vigor, and Elegance, The Science and Art of Dressing with Taste. New York: Hurst & Co., 1875.

Bourdeau, Louis. *Histoire de l'habillement et de la parure.* Paris: Félix Alcan, 1904.

Boutet, Henri. *Les Modes féminines du XIXᵉ siècle.* Paris, Société Française d'editions d'art, 1902.

Dr. Sauveur Henri-Victor Bouvier. *Études historiques et médicales sur l'usage des corsets.* Paris: Chez J.-B. Baillière, Libraire de l'Academie Imperiale de Médecine, 1853.

Bradley, H. Dennis. *The Eternal Masquerade.* London: T. Werner Laurie, 1922.

Braunschvig, Marcel. *La Femme et la beauté.* Paris: Librairie Armand Colin, 1929.

Brockett, Dr. Linus Pierpont. *Woman: Her Rights, Wrongs, Privileges, and Responsibilities, etc.* First published 1869. Plainview, New York: Books for Libraries Press, 1976.

Browning, H. Ellen. *Beauty Culture.* London: Hutchinson & Co., 1898.

C. T. *How To Dress Well. A Manual of the Toilet for the Use of Both Sexes.* London: George Routledge & Sons, 1868.

Campbell, Lady Colin. *Etiquette of Good Society.* London & New York: Cassell & Co., 1911.

Campbell Dauncey, Mrs. Enid. "The Functions of Fashion," *The Contemporary Review* (May, 1911):603–607.

Caplin, Madame Roxey. *Health and Beauty, or Corsets and Clothing Constructed in Accordance with the Physiological Laws of the Human Body.* London: Darnton and Co., 1854. Revised edition, *Health and Beauty, or Woman and Her Clothing.* London: Kent & Co., 1864.

Carlyle, Thomas. *Sartor Resartus.* London: Reprinted for friends from *Fraser's Magazine,* 1833.

Carr, Mrs. J. Comyns. *Reminiscences.* London: Hutchinson and Co., n.d. [1925].

Mme. Marie-Elizabeth Cavé. *Beauté physique de la femme.* Paris: Paul Leloup, n.d. [1868].

Cazenave, Dr. Pierre Louis Alphée. *De la décoration humaine: Hygiène de la beauté.* Paris, 1867. Translated by Marie Courcelles under the title *Beauty, or The Art of Human Decoration.* Cincinnati and New York: Chase & Hall, 1877. Also translated by Miss T. Nash as *Female Beauty, or The Art of Human Decoration.* New York: G. W. Carlton & Co., 1874.

Challamel, J. Augustin. *Histoire de la mode en France.* Paris: A. Hennuyer, 1881. Translated under the title *The History of Fashion in France.* London: S. Low, Marston, Searle, and Rivington, 1882.

Chevasse, P. H., Fellow of the Royal College of Surgeons, England. *Man's Strength and Woman's Beauty, or the Royal Road to Life, Love, and Longevity.* Cincinnati, Philadelphia, Chicago: Jones Brothers & Co., 1880.

Clarke, J. Erskine, M. A. *Over-Dress.* Tracts for the Family. London: John Morgan, n.d. [ca. 1865].

"The Confessions of a Tight Lacer," *Tit-Bits* (October 27, 1894).

Cooley, Arnold James. *The Toilet and Cosmetic Arts in Ancient and Modern Times.* London: R. Hardwick, 1866; Philadelphia: Lindsay & Blackiston, 1866. Reprint. New York: Burt Franklin, Research and Source Works Series 511, 1970.

Cooper, Diana. *The Rainbow Comes and Goes.* London: Rupert Hart-Davis, 1958.

"La Corbeille de mariage," *La Vie Parisienne* (17 May 1884).

"Corsets and Corpulence," *London Society* (October, 1869).

Courtenay, Florence. *Physical Beauty: How to Develop and Preserve It.* New York: Social Mentor Publications, 1922.

Crane, Walter. "On the Progress of Taste in Dress in Relations to Art Education," *Aglaia. The Journal of the Health and Artistic Dress Union* (1894). Reprinted in Walter Crane, *Ideals in Art.* London: George Bell and Sons, 1905.

Crawley, Ernest. *Dress, Drinks, and Drums: Further Studies of Savages and Sex.* London: Methuen, 1931.

Darfeu, Docteur. *Hygiène de la Parisienne.* Paris: Ed. Rouveyre et G. Blond, n.d. [ca. 1885].

"Distortion by Tight-Lacing." In *Chambers Miscellany of Useful and Entertaining Tracts.* Vol. 10. Edinburgh: William and Robert Chambers, 1846.

Douglas, Mrs. Fanny. *The Gentlewoman's Book of Dress*. London: Henry and Co., n.d. [ca. 1894].

Dress, Drink, and Debt. A Temperance Tale. London: Society for Promoting Christian Knowledge, n.d. [ca. 1878].

Dress, Health & Beauty. London: Ward, Lock, & Co., 1878.

Droz, Gustave. *Monsieur, madame et bébé*. Paris: Hetzel, 1866. Translated as *Papa, Mamma and Baby*. London: Vizetelly, 1887.

Dufay, Pierre. *Le Pantalon féminin. Un Chapitre inedit de l'histoire du costume*. Paris: Charles Carrington, 1906.

Duff Gordon, Lady Lucy Christiana [Lucille]. *Discretions and Indiscretions*. London: Jarrolds, 1932.

E. D. M. *Figure Training; or, Art the Handmaid of Nature*. London: Ward, Lock, and Tyler, 1871.

Earle, Alice Morse. *Two Centuries of Costume in America*. 2 vols. New York: Macmillan, 1903.

Ecob, Helen Gilbert. *The Well-Dressed Woman: A Study in the Practical Application to Dress of the Law of Health, Art, and Morals*. New York: Fowler and Wells, 1893.

Ellington, George [pseud.] *The Women of New York or Social Life in the Great City*. New York: The New York Book Company, 1870.

Ellis, Havelock. *Studies in the Psychology of Sex*. 7 parts in 2 volumes. 1898–1936. New York: Modern Library Edition, 1942.

Erté. *Things I Remember. An Autobiography*. New York: Quadrangle/The New York Times Book Co., 1975.

Etiquette of Good Society. London, Paris, and New York: Cassell Petter Galpin & Co., n.d. [ca. 1880].

Evans, Maria Millington. *Chapters on Greek Dress*. London and New York: Macmillan & Co., 1893.

F. B. *How to Train the Figure and Attain Perfection of Form*. London: The Central Publishing Co., 1896.

Farnsworth, Eva Olney. *The Art and Ethics of Dress. As Related to Efficiency and Economy*. San Francisco: Paul Elder & Co., 1915.

Feydeau, Ernest Aimé. *L'Art du plaire: Étude d'hygiène, de goût, et de toilette*. Paris, 1873. Translated by Marie Courcelles under the title *The Art of Pleasing*. New York: G. W. Carleton and Co., 1874.

Fletcher, Ella. *The Woman Beautiful*. New York: Brentano, 1900.

Flower, William Henry. *Fashion in Deformity, as Illustrated in the Customs of Barbarous & Civilised Races*. London: Macmillan & Co., 1881.

Fowler, Mrs. Lydia F. *Dress, Its Uses and Influence. A Lecture*. London: W. Tweedie, n.d. [1864].

Fowler, Orson S. *Tight-Lacing, Founded on Physiology and Phrenology: Or, The Evils Inflicted on Mind and Body, by Compressing the Organs of Animal Life, Thereby Retarding and Enfeebling the Vital Functions*. New York: O. S. & L. N. Fowler & S. R. Wells, 1846.

————. *Intemperance and Tight-Lacing; Founded on the Laws of Life, as Developed by Phrenology & Physiology*. New York, 1846. Manchester: John Heywood, n.d. [ca. 1899].

————. *Amativeness; or, Evils and Remedies of Excessive and Perverted Sexuality; Including Warning and Advice to the Married and Single*. New York, 1846. Manchester: John Heywood, n.d. [ca. 1897].

Fox, George P. *Fashion: The Power that Influences the World.* New York: American News Co., 1871.

Francillon, R. E. *Mid-Victorian Memories.* London: Hodder and Stoughton, 1913.

Fred, W. *Psychologie der Mode.* Berlin: Richard Munter, 1905.

French, Lillie Milton. "Shopping in New York," *The Century Magazine* (March, 1901): 644–658.

Freud, Sigmund. *The Standard Edition of the Complete Psychological Works.* Translated and edited by James Strachey, et al. 24 vols. London: The Hogarth Press and the Institute of Psycho-Analysis, 1953–1975.

Gâches-Sarraute, Mme Inez. *Le Corset. Étude physiologique et pratique.* Paris: Masson et cie. editeurs, Libraire de l'academie de médecine, 1900.

The Gibson Girl and Her America. The Best Drawings of Charles Dana Gibson. Selected by Edmund Vincent Gillson, Jr. New York: Dover Publications, 1969.

Glenard, Dr. Frantz. *Le Vêtement féminin et l'hygiène.* Paris: Editions de la Revue Scientifique, 1902.

Glyn, Elinor. *Visits of Elizabeth.* London: Duckworth & Co., 1900.

————. *The Vicissitudes of Evangeline.* London: Duckworth & Co., 1905.

————. *Three Weeks.* London: Duckworth & Co., 1907.

Grand-Carteret, John. *Le Decolleté et le retroussé. Quatre siècles de Gauloiserie (1500–1870).* Paris: E. Bernard et cie., n.d.

————. *Les Moeurs et la caricature en France.* Paris: Librairie Illustrée, 1888.

————. *XIXᵉ Siècle en France. Classes—moeurs—usages—costumes— inventions.* Paris: Librairie de Firmin, Didot et cie., 1893.

————. *La Femme en culotte.* Paris: Ernest Flammarion, n.d. [1899].

————. *L'Histoire, la vie, les moeurs et la curiosité par l'image, le pamphlet et le document (1450–1900).* Vol. 5. Paris: Librairie de la Curiosité et des Beaux-Arts, 1928.

Green, E. M. *La Mode et la coquetterie.* Paris: Devambez, 1912.

Greville, Lady Violet. *The Gentlewoman in Society.* London: Henry and Co., 1892.

Grey, Mrs. William. *Idols and Society; or Gentility and Femininity.* London: William Ridgway, 1874.

Haldane, Louisa Kathleen. *Friends and Kindred.* London: Faber and Faber, 1961.

Hardy, Lady Violet. *As It Was.* London: Christopher Johnson, 1958.

Haweis, Mrs. Hugh Reginald [Mary Eliza]. *The Art of Beauty.* London: Chatto & Windus, 1878. Reprint. New York and London: Garland Publishing, 1978.

————. *The Art of Dress.* London: Chatto & Windus, 1879. Reprint. New York and London: Garland Publishing, 1978.

Heard, Gerald. *Narcissus: An Anatomy of Clothes.* London: Kegan Paul, 1924.

Hegermann-Lindencrone, Lillie de. *In the Courts of Memory: Musical and Social Life During the Second Empire in Paris.* 1912. Reprint. New York: Da Capo Press, 1980.

Hiler, Hilaire. *From Nudity to Raiment.* London: W. & G. Foyle, 1929.

Hill, Georgiana. *A History of English Dress.* 2 vols. New York: G.P. Putnam's Sons, 1893; London: Richard Bentley & Son, 1893.

A History of Feminine Fashion. London, n.d. [ca. 1926].

"The History of the Corset," *The Queen* (5 December 1863).

Holiday, Henry. "The Artistic Aspect of Dress," *Aglaia. The Journal of the Healthy and Artistic Dress Union* (July, 1893).

Holt, Ardern. *Fancy Dresses Described, or What to Wear at Fancy Balls.* London: Debenham and Freebody, 1879.

How to be Beautiful. Oliphant's Juvenile Series. Edinburgh: W. Oliphant & Co., 1866; London: Hamilton, Adams, & Co., 1866.

How to Dress or Etiquette of the Toilette. London: Ward, Lock, & Tyler, n.d. [1877].

Hughes, M. Vivian. *A London Girl of the Eighties.* London: Oxford University Press, 1936.

Mrs. C. E. Humphry. *Manners for Women.* London: James Bowden, 1897.

————. *How to be Pretty Though Plain.* London: James Bowden, 1899.

————. *Beauty Adorned.* London: T. Fisher Unwin, 1901.

Hurlock, Elizabeth. *The Psychology of Dress: An Analysis of Fashion and Its Motives.* New York: Ronald Press, 1929.

Hygeia, "Does Tight-Lacing Really Exist?," *The Family Doctor* (3 September 1887).

————. "Tight-Lacing in Brighton and Parisian Schools," *The Family Doctor* (24 December 1887).

Iribe, Paul. *Les Robes de Paul Poiret.* Paris: Société Générale d'Impression, for Paul Poiret, 1908.

Jaeger, Gustav. *Selections from Essays on Health-Culture and the Sanitary Woolen System.* London: Dr. Jaeger's Sanitary Woollen System Co., 1884.

Joy, Lilian. *The Well-Dressed Woman.* London: Cassell and Co., 1907.

Kenealy, Dr. Arabella. "The Curse of Corsets," *The Nineteenth Century and After* 15 (January, 1904):131–137.

Keppel, Sonia. *Edwardian Daughter.* London: Hamish Hamilton, 1958.

King, Mrs. E. M. *Rational Dress; Or, The Dress of Women and Savages.* London: Kegan Paul, Trench, & Co., 1882.

Kingsford, Anna, M.D. *Health, Beauty, and The Toilet. Letters to Ladies from a Lady Doctor.* London and New York: Frederick Warne & Co., 1886.

Krafft-Ebing, Dr. Richard von. *Psychopathia Sexualis with especial reference to the Antipathic Sexual Instinct. A Medico-Forensic Study.* 1886. Translated from the 12th German edition by F. J. Rebman. Brooklyn: Physicians and Surgeons Book Co., 1926.

Ladies' Sanitary Association. *Wasps Have Stings; or, Beware of Tight-Lacing.* London: Published by the Ladies' Sanitary Association, and by John Morgan, n.d.

————. *Dress and Its Cost.* London: Published by the Ladies' Sanitary Association, and by John Morgan, n.d.

"The Lady with the Little Feet," *London Society* (June, 1869).

"A Lady's Question—What Shall We Wear?" *London Society* (May, 1869).

Leoty, Ernest. *Le Corset à travers les ages.* Paris: Paul Ollendorff, 1893.

Lepape, Georges. *Les Choses de Paul Poiret vues par Georges Lepape.* Paris: Maquet, for Paul Poiret, 1911.

Libron, Fernand, and Henry Clouzot. *Le Corset dans l'art et les moeurs du XIIIᵉ au XXᵉ siècle.* Paris: Published by the authors, 1933.

Limner, Luke. [John Leighton]. *Madre Natura versus the Moloch of Fashion.* London: Chatto and Windus, 1874.

Linton, Mrs. Elizabeth Lynn. "The Girl of the Period," *Saturday Review* (14 March 1868).

————. "The Follies of Fashion." In *Ourselves. Essays on Women*. London, 1884.

[Lord, William Barry]. *The Corset and the Crinoline*. London: Ward, Lock & Tyler, n.d. [1868]. Reprinted under the title *The Freaks of Fashion*. London: Ward, Lock, & Tyler, 1871.

Lorentz, Mme E., and Mlle. A. Lacroix. *Cours complet d'enseignement professionel de la coupe*. Vol. 1. *Corset*, Vol. 2 *Lingerie*. Paris: École Moderne de Coupe de Paris, 1911–1912.

M. M. *How to Dress and What to Wear*. London: Methuen & Co., 1903.

Machray, Robert. "Fashions in Waists," *The Lady's Realm* (December, 1902).

The "Major" of *Today. Clothes & The Man. Hints on the Wearing and Caring of Clothes*. London: Grant Richards, 1900.

Mallarmé, Stephane. *La Dernière Mode. Gazette du Monde et de la Famille*. September-December, 1874. Reprint. Paris: Éditions Ramsay, 1978.

Mariette, Mlle. Pauline. *L'Art de la toilette*. Paris: Librairie Centrale, 1866.

Maynard, Elise. "Fatal Corsets, or The Perils of Tight-Lacing," *Womanhood* (April, 1903).

McClellan, Elizabeth. *Historic Dress in America 1800–1870*. Philadelphia: George W. Jacobs, 1910.

Melanzie. *How to be Beautiful. Dietetics, Exercise, and Hygiène*. London: V. Victorsen, 1909.

Merrifield, Mrs. *Dress as a Fine Art*. London: A. Hall Virtue, 1854; Boston: Jewett & Co., 1854.

Mitchison, Naomi. *Small Talk. Memories of an Edwardian Childhood*. London: The Bodley Head, 1973.

————. *All Change Here. Girlhood and Marriage*. London: The Bodley Head, 1975.

A Modern Hygeian. Boston: G. Frost & Co., Specialists in Hygienic Underwear, 1891.

Mohrbutter, Alfred. *Das Kleid der Frau*. Darmstadt and Leipzig: Verlags-Astalt Alexander Koch, 1904.

Moncrieff, John Forbes. *Our Domestics and Their Mistresses. A Contribution to the "Servant Question."* Edinburgh: Andrew Stevenson; London: Dyer Brothers n.d. [ca. 1895].

Moore, George. *A Drama in Muslin*. 1886. Reprint. Gerrards Cross, Buckinghamshire: Colin Smythe Ltd., 1981.

Musil, Robert. *The Man Without Qualities*. Vol. 1. 1930. Translated by Eithne Wilkins and Ernst Kaiser. London: Secker and Warburg, 1953.

Mustoxidi. *Qu'est-ce que la mode?* Paris: Picart, 1921.

"Nice Girls," *Harper's Bazar* (April 11, 1868).

The 1915 Mode as Shown by Paris. New York: Condé Nast, 1915.

Nothing to Wear; A Satire on the Present Extravagance in Ladies' Dress. London: Rock & Co., 1858.

Le Nouveau Bréviaire de la beauté. Paris, n.d. [ca. 1926].

Oakley, Miss. [Mrs. Maria Richards Dewing]. *Beauty in Dress*. New York: Harper, 1881.

O'Followell, Dr. Ludovic. *Le Corset. Histoire-médecine-hygiène*. Preface by Paul Ginisty. Paris: A. Malosne, 1905.

Oliphant, Mrs. Margaret. *Dress*. London: Macmillan and Co., 1878.

One of the Aristocracy. *Etiquette for Women. A Book of Modern Modes and Manners*. London: C. Arthur Pearson, 1902.

Orchamps, La Baronne d'. *Tous les secrets de la femme*. Paris: Bibliothèque des Auteurs Modernes, 1907.

O'Rell, Max. *Her Royal Highness Woman*. London: Chatto & Windus, 1901.

Paris: Exposition universelle internationale de 1900. *Les Toilettes de la collectivité de la couture*. Paris: Société de Publications d'Art, 1900.

Peel, Mrs C. S. *Mrs Barnet, Robes*. London: John Lane, The Bodley Head, 1915.

——. *Life's Enchanted Cup. An Autobiography (1872–1933)*. London: John Lane, 1933.

[Peel, Ellen]. *A Victorian Young Lady*. [Diaries and Letters, 1886–1908]. Edited by Betty Askwith. Salisbury: Michael Russell, 1978.

"The Philosophy of Tight-Lacing," *The Saturday Review* (17 December 1887).

Philpott, Edward. *Crinoline from 1730 to 1864*. London, 1864.

Poiret, Paul. *En habillant l'époque*. Paris: Bernard Grasset, 1930. Translated by Stephen Haden Guest, under the title *King of Fashion. The Autobiography of Paul Poiret*. Philadelphia and London: J. B. Lippincott Co., 1931. Also published under the title *My First Fifty Years*. London: Victor Gollancz Ltd., 1931.

——. *Revenez-y*. Paris: Librairie Gallimard, 1932.

Potter, Beatrix. *The Journal of Beatrix Potter from 1881 to 1897*. Transcribed from her code writing by Leslie Linder. London & New York: Frederick Warne & Co., 1966.

Potter, Cora Brown. *The Secrets of Beauty and the Mysteries of Health*. San Francisco and New York: Paul Elder and Co., 1908.

Liane de Pougy. *My Blue Notebooks*. Translated by Diana Athill. London: Andrew Deutsch, 1979.

Pour la beauté naturelle de la femme contre la mutilation de la taille par le corset. Preface by Edmond Harancourt. Paris: Ligue des Mères de Famille, 1909.

Praga, Mrs. Alfred. *Appearances. How to Keep Them Up on a Limited Income*. London: John Long, 1899.

——. *What to Wear and When to Wear It*. London: George Newnes, 1903.

Prevost, Gabriel. *Le Nu, le vêtement, la parure chez l'homme et chez la femme*. Paris: C. Marpon et E. Flammarion, 1883.

Price, Julius M. *Dame Fashion, Paris-London (1789–1912)*. London: Low Marston, 1913.

Pritchard, Mrs. Eric. *The Cult of Chiffon*. London: Grant Richards, 1902.

Proust, Marcel. *A la recherche du temps perdu*. Paris, 1913–1922. Translated by C. K. Scott Moncrieff and Frederick A. Blossom, under the title *Remembrance of Things Past*. 7 books in 2 vols. New York: Random House, 1927–1932.

Quicherat, Jules. *Histoire du costume en France*. Paris: Libraire Hachette et cie, 1875.

Quigley, Dorothy. *What Dress Makes of Us*. London: Hutchinson & Co., 1898.

'R.' *Dress in a Nutshell*. London: Greening & Co., 1901.

Rational Dress Association. *The Exhibition of the Rational Dress Association. Catalogue of Exhibits and Lists of Contributors*. London, 1883.

Raverat, Gwen. *Period Piece. A Cambridge Childhood*. London: Faber and Faber, 1952.

Reade, Charles. *A Simpleton*. 1873. Boston: Dana Estes & Co., n.d.

Rhead, G. Woolliscroft. *Chats on Costume*. London: T. Fisher Unwin, 1906.

"Rita." *Vanity! The Confessions of a Court Modiste*. London: T. Fisher Unwin, 1901.

Robertson, W. Graham. *Time Was*. London: Hamish Hamilton, 1931.

Robida, A. *"Yester-year." Ten Centuries of Toilette*. Translated by Mrs. Cashel Hoey. London: Sampson Low, Marston & Co., 1892.

Rosary, Eugene. *Nos vêtements*. Rouen: Megard et cie., 1881.

Roux, Charles. *Contre le corset*. Paris: Imprimerie de E. Brière et cie., 1855.

S. D. P. *The Ugly-Girl Papers; or Hints for the Toilet*. Reprinted from *Harper's Bazar*. New York: Harper & Brothers, 1874.

S-G-. *The Art of Being Beautiful. A Series of Interviews with a Society Beauty*. London: Henry J. Drane, n.d. [1903].

Sacchetti, Enrico. *Robes et femmes*. Paris: Dorbon-Aine, 1913.

Santé, Madame de la. *The Corset Defended*. London: T. E. Carler, 1865.

Schidrowitz, Leo. *Sittengeschichte des Intimen*. Vienna and Leipzig: Verlag fur Kulturforschung, n.d.

See, Raymonde. *Le Costume de la Revolution à nos jours*. Paris: Éditions de la Gazette des Beaux Arts, 1929.

Seeker, Miss. *Monographie du corset*. Louvain: Imprimerie Lefever, frères et soeur, 1887.

Sem [Georges Marie Goursat]. *Le Vrai et le Faux Chic*. Paris, Succès, n.d. [ca. 1914].

Sherwood, Mrs. Mary Elizabeth Wilson. *A Transplanted Rose: A Story of New York Society*. New York: Harper & Brothers, 1892.

Un Siècle de modes féminines, 1794–1894. Paris, 1896.

Simmel, Georg. "Fashion," *International Quarterly* 10 (October, 1904): 130–155.

"The Sin and Scandal of Tight-Lacing. A Crusade Against This Modern Madness," *The Gentlewoman* (10 December 1892 to 18 March 1893).

Spencer, Herbert. "Fashion." In *The Principles of Sociology*. 8 parts in 3 vols. 1876–1896. New York: D. Appleton & Co., 1899.

Stables, Gordon, M.D. *The Girl's Own Book of Health and Beauty*. London; Jarrold & Sons, 1892.

Staffe, Baroness Blanche A. A.. *The Lady's Dressing-Room*. Translated by Lady Colin Campbell. London: Cassell and Company, 1892.

————. *Usages du monde; règles du savoir-vivre dans la société moderne*. Paris: Ernest Flammarion, 1899.

Steele, Frances Mary, and Elizabeth Livingston Steele Adams. *Beauty of Form and Grace of Vesture*. London: B. F. Stevens, and Cambridge, Massachusetts: University Press, 1892.

Stekel, Dr. Wilhelm. *Sexual Aberrations. The Phenomena of Fetishism in Relation to Sex*. Translated by Dr. S. Parker from the first German edition of 1922. New York: Horace Liveright, 1930.

Stratz, Dr. C. H. *Die Schönheit des Weiblichen Korpers*. Stuttgart: Verlag von Ferdinand Enke, 1898.

————. *Die Frauenkleidung und ihre natürliche Entwicklung*. Stuttgart: Verlag von Ferdinand Enke, 1900.

————. *Die Rassenschönheit des Weibes*. Stuttgart: Verlag von Ferdinand Enke, 1901.

Sumner, William Graham. *Folkways. A Study of the Sociological Importance of Visages, Manners, Customs, Mores, and Morals*. 1906. Reprint. New York: Mentor Books, 1960.

Sylvia. *How to Dress Well on a Shilling a Day. Ladies' Guide to Home Dress-Making and Millinery*. London: Ward, Lock, and Co., n.d. [ca. 1873].

Ticknor, Caroline. "The Steel-Engraving Lady and the Gibson Girl," *The Atlantic Monthly* (July, 1901), pp. 105–108.

Tillotson, Mary E. *Progress vs. Fashion. An essay on the Sanitary & Social Influences of Woman's Dress*. Vineland, New Jersey, 1873.

The Toilet Editress of "The Lady." *The Figure and Complexion. The Lady Handbooks. Toilet Series, No. 2*. London: "The Lady" offices, n.d. [1893].

Tramar, La Comtesse de. [Marie-Fanny de Lagarrigue, Baronne d'Ysarn de Capdeville, Marquise de Villefort.] *Le Bréviaire de la femme. Pratiques secrètes de la beauté*. Paris: Victor Havard, 1903.

————. *L'Évangile profane. Rite féminin*. Paris: Victor Havard, 1905.

Traphagen, Ethel. *Costume Design and Illustration*. New York: John Wiley and Sons, 1918.

Treves, Frederick. *The Dress of the Period in its Relations to Health*. London: Published for the National Health Society, by Allman & Son, n.d. [1882].

Troubridge, Lady Laura. *Memories and Reflections*. London: William Heinemann, 1925.

————. *Life Amongst the Troubridges*. London: John Murray, 1966.

Twining, Louisa. "Dress," *The Sunday Magazine*, ed. by Thomas Guthrie D. D. London: Stehan & Co., 1872.

Uzanne, Louis Octave. *L'Éventail*. Paris: A. Quantin, 1882. Translated under the title *The Fan*. London: J. C. Nimmo, 1884.

————. *L'Ombrelle, le gant, le manchon*. Paris: A. Quantin, 1883. Translated under the title *The Sunshade, Muff, and Glove*. London: J. C. Nimmo, 1883.

————. *La Française du siècle. Modes—moeurs—usages*. Paris: A. Quantin, 1886. Translated under the title *The Frenchwoman of the Century, Fashions—Manners—Usages*. London: J. C. Nimmo, 1886.

————. *The Mirror of the World*. London: J. C. Nimmo, 1890.

————. *La Femme à Paris. Nos contemporaines. Notes successives sur les Parisiennes de ce temps dans leurs divers milieux, états, et conditions*. Paris: Librairies-Imprimeries Réunies, 1894. Translated under the title *The Modern Parisienne*. London: William Heinemann, 1912.

————. *Les Modes de Paris, variations du goût et de l'esthétique de la femme, 1797–1897*. Paris: Société Française d'Éditions d'Art. Translated under the title *Fashion in Paris. The Various Phases of Feminine Taste and Aesthetics, 1797–1897*. London: Heinemann, 1898. Also published under the title *Fashion in Paris in the Nineteenth Century. The various phases of feminine taste and aesthetics from the Revolution to the end of the XIXth century*. London: William Heinemann, 1901.

————. *L'Art et les artifices de la beauté*. Paris: Félix Juven et Bibliothèque Femina, 1902.

Veblen, Thorstein. *The Theory of the Leisure Class*. 1899. New York: Random House, The Modern Library, 1934.

Viterbo, F. "Corset et Feminism," *Les Dessous Elégants* (September, 1904).

Violette [Alice de Laincel]. *L'Art de la toilette chez la femme. Bréviaire de la vie élégante*. Paris: E. Dentu, Libraire de la Société des gens de lettres, 1885.

Walker, Alexander. *Beauty; Illustrated Chiefly by an Analysis and Classification of Beauty in Women*. London: E. Wilson, 1836.

Walker, Mrs. A. *Female Beauty, as preserved and improved by Regimen, Cleanliness and Dress*. London: Thomas Hust, 1837.

E. Ward & Co. *The Dress Reform Problem. A Chapter for Women*. London: Hamilton, Adams & Co., and Bradford: John Dale & Co., 1886.

Watts, George Frederick. "On Taste in Dress," *The Nineteenth Century* (January, 1883). Reprinted in Mary Watts, ed., *George Frederick Watts*, Vol. 3. London: Macmillan and Co., 1912.

Webb, Wilfred Mark. *The Heritage of Dress*. London: E. G. Richards, 1907.

Welch, Margaret. "Corsets Past and Present," *Harper's Bazar* (September, 1901): 450–454.

Wendel, Friedrich. *Weib und Mode: eine Sittensgeschichte im Spiegel der Karikatur*. Dresdin: Paul Aretz Verlag, 1928. Also published under the title *Die Mode in der Karikatur*.

Westminster, Loelia, Duchesse of. *Grace and Favour*. London: Weidenfeld and Nicolson, 1961.

Who is to Blame? A Few Words on Ladies' Dress, in its Moral and Aesthetic Aspects. Addressed to the 'Fast' of Both Sexes". London: L. Booth, n.d. [ca. 1866].

Wilberforce Smith, W., M.D. "Corset Wearing: The Medical Side of the Attack," *Aglaia* (July, 1893).

Williams, Mrs. Hwfa. *It Was Such Fun*. London: Hutchinson, 1935.

Winterburn, Florence Hull. *Principles of Correct Dress. Including Chapters by Jean Worth and Paul Poiret*. New York and London: Harper & Brothers Publishers, 1914.

Woolson, Mrs. Abba Gould, ed. *Dress-Reform: On Dress as it Affects the Health of Women*. Boston: Roberts Brothers, 1874.

Worth, Jean Philippe. *A Century of Fashion*. Translated by Ruth Miller. Boston: Little, Brown and Co., 1928.

Yonge, Charlotte Mary. *Womankind*. London: Mozley, 1877; New York: Macmillan, 1877.

Young, John H. *Our Deportment, or the Manners, Conduct, and Dress of the Most Refined Society*. Detroit, Michigan and St. Louis, Mo.: F. B. Dickerson & Co., 1882.

Zola, Emile. *Au bonheur des dames*. Paris, 1883. Translated by April Fitzlyon under the title *Ladies' Delight*. London and New York: Abelard-Schuman, 1958.

IV. Periodicals

French

L'Art et la Mode. Journal de la Vie Mondaine. [1880–1967]
Art, Goût, Beauté. [1920–1932]
Le Bon Ton. [1834–1884]
Chiffons. [1907–1932]
Comoedia Illustré. [1908–1914, 1919–1921]

La Dernière Mode. Gazette du Monde et de la Famille. [1874–1875]
Les Dessous Elégants. [1901–the present] Now called *Le Corset de France*
Les Elégances Parisiennes. [1916–1924]
Fémina. [1901–1956]
Le Figaro-Modes. [1903–1906]
Le Follet. [1829–1882]
La Gazette du Bon Ton. [1912–1925] The American Version—also in French—
     was *La Gazette du Bon Genre* [1920–1922]
Le Grande Dame. Revue de l'Elégance et des Arts. [1893–1900]
Les Grandes Modes de Paris. [1901–1933]
Les Idées Nouvelles de la Mode. [1922–1932]
Le Jardin des Modes Nouvelle. [1912–1914]
Le Journal des Dames et des Modes. "Costumes Parisiens". [1797–1839]
Le Journal des Dames et des Modes. [1912–1914]
Le Journal des Demoiselles. [1833–1922]
La Mode. [1829–1854]
La Mode Artistique. Revue de Toutes les Elégances. [1869–1892, 1895–1907]
La Mode [dessinée] par Fried. [1918–1919]
La Mode Illustrée. [1860–1937]
La Mode Pratique. [1891–1938]
*Les Modes. Revue Mensuelle Illustrée des Arts Décoratifs Appliques à la
     Femme.* [1901–1937]
Modes et Manières d'Aujourd'hui. [1912–1922]
Le Moniteur de la Mode. [1843–1913]
Le Petit Courrier des Dames. [1821–1868]
Le Petit Echo de la Mode. [1879–1955]
Revue de la Mode. [1872–1913]
Le Sourire de France. [Early twentieth century]
Le Style Parisien. [July 1915–February 1916]
La Toilette de Paris. [1859–1873]
Très Parisien. [1920–1936]
La Vie Parisienne. [1863–1939. See especially 1879–1883]

English

Aglaia. The Journal of the Healthy and Artistic Dress Union. [1893–1894]
Ackermann's Repository of Arts. [1809–1828]
*Answers. A Weekly Journal of Interesting Facts, Smart Sayings, Amusing
     Anecdotes and Jokes.* [Early twentieth century]
La Belle Assemblée, or Bell's Court and Fashionable Magazine. [1806–1868]
Daily Telegraph. [See especially 1910]
The Dress Review. [1903–1906]
The Englishwoman's Domestic Magazine. [1852–1877. See especially 1867–
     1874]
Eve. [Early twentieth century]
The Family Doctor and People's Medical Advisor. [1885–1917]
Fashion. [Late nineteenth century]
Fashion For All. [Late nineteenth century]
Fashion Illustrated. [Late nineteenth century]
Fashion London. An Illustrated Journal for Ladies. [Late nineteenth century]

Fashions of Today. The English edition of *La Mode Pratique.* [1892–1894]

Le Follet. Journal du Grand-Monde. Fashion, Polite Literature, Beaux-Arts, &c.. English version. [1846–?]

Gallery of Fashion. [1794–1803]

The Gentlewoman. [See especially 1892–1893]

The Girl of the Period Miscellany. [1869]

The Girl's Own Paper. [1880–19 ?]

Harrison's Complete Dressmaker. [Early twentieth century]

Illustrated London News. [See especially 1914–1918]

Knowledge. [1881– ?]

The Ladies Cabinet of Fashion. [1832–1870]

The Ladies' Field. [Early twentieth century]

Ladies' Treasury. [1858–1895]

The Lady. [Early twentieth century]

The Lady's Realm. [See especially 1898–1908]

The Lady's World. [1887– ?]

The London and Paris Ladies' Magazine of Fashion. [Mid–nineteenth century]

London Life. [See especially 1930–1940]

London Society. An Illustrated Magazine of Light and Amusing Literature for the Hours of Relaxation. [See especially 1868–1869]

La Mode Française. [1914–1917]

Modern Society. [1880–1917]

Le Monde Elegant, or The World of Fashion. [? –1882?; prior to November 1878, its title was *The Ladies' Monthly Magazine*]

Myra's Journal of Dress and Fashion or *Myra's Journal of Dress and Needlework.* [1875–1893]

Our Home. [Turn of the century]

Photo Bits. [See especially 1909–1912]

Pictorial Review. [Early twentieth century]

Punch. [1841–the present]

The Queen. The Lady's Newspaper and Court Chronicle. [1861–the present] Now called *Harpers & The Queen*

The Rational Dress Society's Gazette. [1888–1890?]

The Saturday Review. [See especially 1868–1888]

Schild's Monthly Journal. [Late nineteenth century]

The Season. Lady's Illustrated Magazine. English edition of *Die Modenwelt.* [1865–19 ?]

Society. [1879–1900] Originally called *The Mail Budget*

The Suffragette. Edited by Christabel Pankhurst. [ca. 1912–1915]

The Sunday Magazine. Edited by Thomas Guthrie D. D. [ca. 1872]

Sylvia's Home Journal. [1877–1895]

The Times: Woman's Supplement. [See especially 1914–1918]

Townsend's Selection of Parisian Costumes [1823–1888]

Weldon's Ladies Journal. [Late nineteenth century]

The West-End. An Illustrated Weekly. [Turn of the century]

The Woman at Home. [ca. 1907]

Womanhood. The Magazine of Woman's Progress & Interests—Political, Legal, Social, and Intellectual—and of Health and Beauty Culture. Edited by Mrs. Ada S. Ballin. [Early twentieth century]

The Woman's World. [1881–?]

The World of Dress. Edited by Mrs. Aria. [Late nineteenth century]
The World of Fashion. [1824–1891]
The Young Englishwoman. [1865–1877]
The Young Ladies' Journal. [1864–19 ?]

American

The Corset and Underwear Review. New York. [ca. 1916 to 1930s]
The Delineator. New York and London. [Late nineteenth century]
Demorest's Monthly Magazine. New York [1874–1887]
Dress and Vanity Fair. New York. [See especially the years just prior to World
    War I]
Elegance de Paris. New York, Paris, and London. [1916– ?]
Godey's Ladies Book. Philadelphia. [1830–1898]
Harper's Bazar. New York. [1868–the present]. Now spelled *Harper's Bazaar.*
Peterson's Magazine. Philadelphia [1843–1898]
Vogue. New York [1892–the present]; London [1916–the present]; Paris [1921–
    the present]

Other

Le Chic Parisien. Vienna and Paris; various foreign editions. [1899–1938]
Die Dame. Berlin and Vienna. [mid-nineteeth century]

V. Store Catalogs and Advertising Pamphlets

Ainé-Montaille. Paris. *La Parisienne à la Campagne.* n.d. [ca. 1906].
Allen Foster & Co. London. *Autumn and Winter Season.* n.d. [ca. 1910].
Au Bon Marché. Paris. *General Catalogue of Winter Novelties 1910–1911; Cos-
    tumes et Confections.* October, 1911; *Winter 1912; General Catalogue of
    the Novelties of the Summer Season.* March, 1914; *Novelties of the Season
    1914–15; Novelties of the Season.* March, 1915.
Au Printemps. Paris. *Robes.* 1910.
Aux Galeries Lafayette. Paris. *Robes Pour Dames.* 1910; *Toilettes d'Hiver.* Octo-
    ber, 1910; *Summer Fashions.* April, 1911.
Au Trois Quartiers. Paris. *Robes.* 1907; *Les Dentelles, Les Robes de Soirée.* Feb-
    ruary, 1910; *Ombrelles, Modes, Gants.* April, 1910; *Nos Nouveautés d'Hiver.*
    October, 1910; *Bas de Soie, Modes, Gants.* November, 1910.
Bond Street Corset Co. London. [untitled]. n.d. [ca. 1907].
Bradleys. London. *Bradleys Winter Book.* 1914–1915.
Cadolle. Paris. *Corsets Cadolle.* n.d. [ca. 1906].
Debenham & Freebody. London. *The Fashion for Underskirts.* 1916; *Exclusive
    Lingerie at Moderate Prices.* October, 1923; "The Secret of Slenderness."
    The New "Corso" Silhouette. October, 1923.
Dickins & Jones. London. *Half Yearly Sale.* 1897; *Upwards of a Century.* 1909.
Dorothy Perkins. London. *Corsets—Underwear—Hosiery & Millinery.* n.d. [ca.
    1928].
D. H. Evans & Co. London. *The Charm of Twilfit Corsets.* Winter 1926.
The Fashion Review. Newtown, North Wales, May 1907.
H. W. Gossard Co. London. *Gossard Foundation Garments.* n.d. [ca. 1928].

Grands Magasins du Louvre. Paris. [untitled] April, 1909; 1910; 1911; *Nouveaux Agrandissements*. Winter, 1912–1913; *Blanc*. 1914.

Grands Magasins de la Samaritaine. Paris. *Album. Eté 1907; Winter 1909–10; Fourrures*. Winter 1910–11.

Harrods. London. *Fashionable Rendez-vous*. n.d. [1909]; *Harrod's Review of Spring Styles*. 1919.

High-Life Tailor. Paris. *À Travers les Ages*. Winter 1908–09.

Jaeger. London. *Pure Wool*. Detailed Trade List. 1914–1915.

Kalamazoo Corset Co. Kalamazoo, Michigan. *Madame Gria Corsets. Certified Correct Styles of 1915*.

Leroy & Schmid. Paris. *Fourrures, Portraits, Miniatures*. 1912.

Liberty & Co. London. *Dress and Decoration*. n.d. [1905]; *Picturesque Dresses*. Autumn, 1913.

Marshall & Snelgrove. London. *Towards New Liberty. A Comment on Modern Tendencies*. Text by Sidney Mannor. 1914.

Peter Robinson, Ltd. London. *The Curtain is Drawn--The Fashion Line for 1914 is Revealed*. 1914.

Pryce Jones. Newtown, North Wales. *Autumn & Winter 1919*.

Rayne. London. [Untitled Shoe Catalog] n.d. [ca. 1912].

Sandow's Patent Health and Perfect Figure Corset Co. London. *The Fashionable Figure: The Companion of Health*. n.d. [ca. 1911].

W. R. Whalonia. London. *Corsets*. n.d. [ca. 1906].

J. D. Williams & Co. Manchester. *The New Warehouse*. 1906.

Woolland Bros. London. *Early Spring Fashions*. n.d. [ca. 1911/1912].

Worcester Corset Co. Worcester, Massachusetts. *Advance Couriers for 1901*. Royal Worcester, Bonton and Sapphire Corsets. 1900.

Secondary Sources
VI. Books, Articles, and Dissertations

Adburgham, Alison. *A Punch History of Manners and Modes, 1841–1940*. London: Hutchinson, 1961.

————. *Shops and Shopping, 1800–1914*. London: George Allen and Unwin, 1964.

————. *Liberty's. A Biography of a Shop*. London: George Allen and Unwin Ltd., 1975.

Anderson, Nancy F. "Eliza Lynn Linton and the Woman Question in Victorian England." Ph. D. dissertation, Tulane University, 1973.

Anspach, Karlyne. *The Why of Fashion*. Ames, Iowa: Iowa State University, 1967.

Arnold, Janet. *A Handbook of Costume*. New York and London: Macmillan Co., 1973.

Aron, Jean-Paul. *Misérable et glorieuse. La Femme du XIXᵉ siècle*. Paris: Librairie Arthème Fayard, 1980.

Ashdown, Dulcie M. ed. *Over the Teacups*. [Excerpts from *The Housewife, The Mother's Friend, The Woman at Home*, and *The Lady's Realm*, 1890–1899.] London: Cornmarket Press, 1971.

Aslin, Elizabeth. *The Aesthetic Movement: Prelude to Art Nouveau*. London: Elek, 1969.

Baines, Barbara. *Fashion Revivals from the Elizabethan Age to the Present Day*. London: B. T. Batsford, 1981.

Banner, Lois. *American Beauty. A Social History . . . Through Two Centuries . . . Of the American Idea, Ideal, and Image of the Beautiful Woman*. New York: Alfred A. Knopf, 1983.

Barrow, Margaret. *Women 1870–1928: A Select Guide to Printed and Archival Sources in the United Kingdom*. London: Mansell, 1981.

Barthes, Roland. *Système de la mode*. Paris: Éditions du Seuil, 1967.

Barker-Benfield, G. J.. *The Horrors of the Half-Known Life: Male Attitudes Toward Women and Sexuality in Nineteenth-Century America*. New York: Harper & Row, 1976.

Batterberry, Michael and Ariane. *Mirror, Mirror: A Social History of Fashion*. New York: Holt, Rinehart, and Winston, 1977.

Battersby, Martin. *Art Deco Fashion: French Designers 1908–1925*. New York: St. Martin's, 1974.

————. "Diaghilev's Influence on Fashion and Decoration." In Charles Spencer, ed., *The World of Diaghilev*. London: Paul Elek, 1974.

Beazley, Alison. "The 'Heavy' and 'Light' Clothing Industries, 1850–1920," *Costume. The Journal of the Costume Society* 7 (1973).

Behling, Dorothy. "French Couturiers and Artist/Illustrators: Fashion from 1900 to 1925." Ph.D. dissertation, Ohio State University, 1977.

————. "The Russian Influence on Fashion 1909–1925," *Dress. The Journal of the American Costume Society* 5 (1979):1–13.

Bell, Quentin. *On Human Finery*. 1947. Revised edition. New York: Schocken Books, 1976.

Benedict, Ruth. "Dress." In *Encyclopedia of the Social Sciences*. Volume 5. New York: Macmillan, 1931.

Bergler, Edmund. *Fashion and The Unconscious*. New York: Brunner, 1953.

Bertin, Celia. *Paris à la Mode*. Translated by Marjorie Deans. New York: Harper & Bros., 1957.

Bidelman, Patrick Kay. "The Feminist Movement in France: The Formative Years, 1858–1889." Ph.D. dissertation, Michigan State University, 1975.

Bigelow, Marybelle S. *Fashion in History: Apparel in the Western World*. Minneapolis, Minnesota: Burgess Publishing Co., 1970.

Binder, Pearl. *Muffs and Morals*. New York: William Morrow and Co., 1954.

Blum, Stella. *Victorian Fashions and Costumes from Harper's Bazar: 1867–1898*. New York: Dover, 1974.

Blumer, Herbert. "Fashion." In *International Encyclopedia of the Social Sciences*. Volume 5. New York: Macmillan, 1968.

Bogatyrev, Petr G. *The Function of Folk Costume in Moravian Slovakia*. Translated by Richard G. Crum. Approaches to Semiotics 5. The Hague: Mouton, 1971.

W. Born. "Crinoline and Bustle," *Ciba Review*. no. 46 (May, 1943):1658–1692.

Boucher, Francois. *Histoire du costume en Occident, de l'antiquité à nos jours*. Paris: Flammarion, 1967.

Robert Brain. *The Decorated Body*. New York: Harper & Row, 1979.

Branca, Patricia. *Silent Sisterhood: Middle-Class Women in the Victorian Home*. Pittsburgh: Carnegie-Mellon University Press, 1975.

Braudel, Fernand. *Capitalism and Material Life, 1400–1800*. Translated by Miriam Rochan. New York and London: Harper & Row, 1973.

Braun-Ronsdorf, Margarete. *Mirror of Fashion: A History of European Costume 1789–1929*. New York: McGraw-Hill, 1964.

Brenninkmeyer, Ingrid. *The Sociology of Fashion*. Winterthur. P. G. Keller, 1962.

Bristow, Edward J. *Vice and Vigilance: Purity Movements in Britain since 1700*. Dublin: Gill and Macmillan, 1977.

Broby-Johansen, R. *Body and Clothes*. New York: Reinhold, 1968.

Brownmiller, Susan. *Femininity*. New York: Simon & Schuster, 1984.

Buck, Anne. *Victorian Costume and Costume Accessories*. London: Herbert Jenkins, 1961; New York: Thomas Nelson and Sons, 1961.

————. "Clothes in Fact and Fiction 1825–1865," *Costume. The Journal of the Costume Society* 17 (1983).

Bunzel, Ruth. "Ornament." In *Encyclopedia of the Social Sciences*. Vol. 11. New York: Macmillan, 1931.

Burn, W. L. *The Age of Equipoise: A Study of the Mid-Victorian Generation*. London: George Allen & Unwin, 1964.

Butazzi, Grazietta. *La Mode: Art, histoire, et société*. Translated from the Italian by Bernard Guyander. Paris: Hachette, 1983.

Byrde, Penelope. *The Male Image: Men's Fashion in Britain 1300–1970*. London: B. T. Batsford, 1979.

Canter Cremeers van der Does, Eline. *The Agony of Fashion*. Pogle, Dorset: Blandford Press, 1980.

Carter, Ernestine. *The Changing World of Fashion*. New York: G. P. Putnam's Sons, 1977.

Chafe, William. *The American Woman: Her Changing Social, Economic, and Political Roles, 1920–1970*. New York: Oxford University Press, 1972.

Charles-Roux, Edmonde. *Chanel: Her Life, Her World, and The Woman Behind the Legend*. Translated by Nancy Amphoux. New York: Alfred A. Knopf, 1975.

Chevalier, Louis. *Labouring Classes and Dangerous Classes during the First Half of the Nineteenth Century*. Translated by Frank Jellinek. New York: H. Fertig, 1973.

Clark, Kenneth. *The Nude: A Study of Ideal Art*. London: John Murray, 1956.

————. *Feminine Beauty*. London: Weidenfeld & Nicolson, 1980.

Claude-Salvy [Marie-Magdeleine Sauvy, Mme Edouard Poisson]. *Le Monde et la mode*. Paris: Librairie Hachette, 1966.

Clephane, Irene, and Alan Bott. *Our Mothers: A Cavalcade in Pictures, Quotation and Description of Late Victorian Women 1870–1900*. London: Gollancz, 1932.

Clephane, Irene. *Ourselves 1900–1930*. London: John Lane The Bodley Head Ltd., 1933.

Colas, René. *Bibliographie générale du costume et de la mode*. Paris: Librairie René Colas, 1933.

Coleridge, Lady Georgina, ed. *The Lady's Realm. A Selection from the Monthly Issues: November 1904 to April 1905*. London: Arrow Books, 1972.

Colmer, Michael. *Whalebone to See-Through: A History of Body Packaging*. London and Edinburgh: Johnston & Bacon, 1979.

Cominos, Peter T. "Late Victorian Sexual Respectability and the Social System," *International Review of Social History* 8 (1963):18–48, 216–250.

————. "Innocent Femina Sensualis in Unconscious Conflict." In Martha Vicinus, ed., *Suffer and Be Still: Women in the Victorian Age*. Bloomington and London: Indiana Univ. Press, 1973: 155–172.

Cooper, Wendy. *Hair: Sex, Society, Symbolism.* New York: Stein and Day, 1971.

Cordwell, Justine M., and Ronald Schwarz, eds. *The Fabrics of Culture: The Anthropology of Clothing and Adornment.* New York: Mouton Publishers, 1979.

Corson, Richard. *Fashions in Hair.* London: Peter Owen, 1965.

———. *Fashions in Make-Up from Ancient to Modern Times.* New York: University Books, 1972.

Cott, Nancy F. *The Bonds of Womanhood: "Woman's Sphere" in New England, 1780–1835.* New Haven and London: Yale University Press, 1977.

———. "Passionlessness: An Interpretation of Victorian Sexual Ideology, 1790–1850," *Signs: Journal of Woman in Culture and Society* vol. 4, no. 2 (Winter, 1978): 219–236.

Courtois, Georgine de. *Woman's Headdress and Hairstyles in England from AD 600 to the Present Day.* London, B. T. Batsford, 1973.

Crawford, M. D. C., and Elizabeth Guernsey. *The History of Corsets in Pictures.* New York: Fairchild Publications, 1951.

Crawford, T. S. *A History of the Umbrella.* New York: Taplinger, 1970.

Crow, Duncan. *The Victorian Woman.* New York: Stein and Day, 1972.

Cunnington, C. Willett. *Feminine Attitudes in the Nineteenth Century.* London: William Heineman, 1935.

———. *English Women's Clothing in the Nineteenth Century.* London: Faber & Faber, 1937.

———. *Why Women Wear Clothes.* London: Faber & Faber, 1941.

———. *The Perfect Lady.* London: Max Parrish and Co., 1948.

———. *English Women's Clothing in the Present Century.* London: Faber & Faber, 1952.

Cunnington, C. Willett and Phillis. *The History of Underclothes.* London: J. Joseph, 1951. Revised edition by A. D. and Valerie Mansfield. London: Faber & Faber, 1981.

Cunnington, Phillis. *Costume in Pictures.* London: The Herbert Press, 1964.

Daumard, Adeline. *La Bourgeoisie parisienne de 1815 à 1848.* Paris: S.E.V.P.E.N., 1963. Abridged edition, *Les Bourgeois de Paris au XIXᵉ siècle,* 1970.

Davenport, Milia. *Book of Costume.* London and New York: Crown Publishers, 1948.

Davidoff, Leonore. *The Best Circles: Society, Etiquette and the Season.* London: Croom Helm, 1973.

John D. Davies. *Phrenology Fad and Science: A 19th Century American Crusade.* New Haven: Yale University Press, 1955.

Degler, Carl. "What Ought to be and What Was: Women's Sexuality in the Nineteenth Century," *American Historical Review* 79 (December, 1974):1467–1490.

———. *At Odds: Women and the Family in America from the Revolution to the Present.* New York and Oxford: Oxford University Press, 1980.

Delamont, Sara, and Lorna Duffin, eds. *The Nineteenth-Century Woman: Her Cultural and Physical World.* New York: Barnes & Noble Books, 1978.

Delbourg-Delphis, Marylène. *Le Chic et le Look.* Paris: Hachette, 1981.

Descamps, Marc-Alain. *Psychosociologie de la mode.* Paris: Presses universitaires de France, 1979.

Deslandres, Yvonne. *Le Costume, image de l'homme.* Paris: Albin Michel, 1976.

Devlin, Polly. *Vogue Book of Fashion Photography 1919–1979*. New York: Simon and Schuster, 1979.

Dormoy, Marie. *Jacques Doucet*. Abbeville: Les Amis d'Edouard, 1931.

Dorner, Jane. *Fashion in the 20s and 30s*. London: Ian Allan, 1973.

Dulac, Jean. *Les Artistes du livre: Andrew E. Marty*. Paris: Henry Babou, Éditeur, 1930.

Dunbar, Janet. *The Early Victorian Woman: Some Aspects of Her Life (1837–1857)*. London: George G. Harrap, 1953.

Ensor, R. C. K. *England 1870–1914*. Oxford: Oxford University Press, 1936.

Erté. *Things I Remember*. New York: Quadrangle/New York Times Book Co., 1975.

Etienne, M. *Corset-Gaine et soutien-gorge*. Paris: J.-B. Baillière et Fils, 1958.

Evans, Mary. *Costume Throughout the Ages*. Philadelphia and New York: J. B. Lippincott, 1930.

Evans, Richard J. *The Feminists: Women's Emancipation Movements in Europe, America, and Australasia, 1840–1920*. New York: Barnes & Noble, 1977.

Ewing, Elizabeth. *Underwear: A History*. New York: Theatre Arts Books, 1972.

———. *Dress and Undress: A History of Women's Underwear*. New York: Drama Book Specialists, 1978.

———. *History of Twentieth Century Fashion*. London: Batsford, 1979.

———. *Fur in Dress*. London: B. T. Batsford, 1981.

Fairbrother, Trevor. "The Shock of John Singer Sargent's 'Madame Gautreau,'" *Arts Magazine* vol. 55, no. 5 (January, 1981): 90–97.

Fairholt, Frederick W. *Satirical Songs and Poems on Costume: From the 13th to the 19th Century*. London: Printed for the Percy Society, 1949.

Fairservis, Walter A. *Costumes of the East*. Riverside, Connecticut: Chatham Press, 1971.

Fischel, Oskar. *Chronisten der Mode. Mensch und Kleid in Bildern aus Drei Jahrtausenden*. Potsdam: Müller & Co. Verlag, 1923.

Flügel, Dr. J. C. "Clothes Symbolism and Clothes Ambivalence," *International Journal of Psychoanalysis* 10 (Spring 1929):205–217.

———. *The Psychology of Clothes*. London: The Hogarth Press and The Institute for Psycho-Analysis, 1930.

Foote, Shelly. "Bloomers," *Dress. The Journal of the Costume Society of America* 5 (1980).

Forrester, Wendy. *Great Grandmama's Weekly: A Celebration of the Girl's Own Paper*. Guildford and London: Lutterworth Press, 1980.

Fouquet, C., and Y. Kniebiehler. *La Beauté pour quoi faire? Essai sur l'histoire de la beauté féminine*. Paris: Temps Actuels, 1982.

Freeman, Sarah. *Isabella and Sam: The Story of Mrs. Beeton*. London: Victor Gollancz, 1977.

Garland, Madge. *The Changing Face of Beauty*. New York: McBarrows, 1957. London: Weidenfeld & Nicolson, 1957.

———. *The Changing Form of Fashion*. New York: Praeger, 1970.

Garrett, Helen T. "Clothes and Character: The Function of Dress in Balzac." Ph.D. dissertation, University of Pennsylvania, 1941.

Gaudriault, Raymond. *La Gravure de mode féminine en France*. Paris: Les Éditions de l'amateur, 1983.

Gay, Peter. *Art and Act. On Causes in History—Manet, Gropius, Mondrian.* New York: Harper and Row, 1976.

————. "Victorian Sexuality: Old Texts and New Insights," *The American Scholar* 49 (Summer, 1980): 372–378.

————. *The Bourgeois Experience: Victoria to Freud.* Vol. I, *The Education of the Senses.* New York: Oxford University Press, 1984.

Geertz, Clifford. *The Interpretation of Cultures: Selected Essays.* New York: Basic Books, 1973.

Gernsheim, Alison. *Fashion and Reality: 1840–1914.* London; Faber & Faber, 1963.

Giafferri, Paul-Louis de. *The History of French Masculine Costume.* New York: Foreign Publications, 1927.

Gibbs-Smith, Charles H. *The Fashionable Lady in the Nineteenth Century.* London: H. M. S. O., 1960.

Gill, Eric. *Clothes: An Essay Upon the Nature and Significance of the Natural and Artificial Integuments Worn by Men and Women.* London: Jonathan Cape, 1931.

Ginsburg, Madeleine. "Rags to Riches: The Second-Hand Clothes Trade, 1700–1978," *Costume. The Journal of the Costume Society* 14 (1980): 121–135.

————. *An Introduction to Fashion Illustration.* Owings Mills, Maryland: Stemner House Publishers, 1982.

————. *Victorian Dress in Photographs.* New York: Holmes & Meier, 1983.

Girouard, Mark. *The Return to Camelot. Chivalry and the English Gentleman.* New Haven and London: Yale University Press, 1981.

Giustino, David de. *Conquest of Mind: Phrenology and Victorian Social Thought.* Totowa, New Jersey: Roman and Littlefield, 1975. London: Croom Helm, 1975.

Gloag, John. *Victorian Comfort: A Social History of Design from 1830–1900.* London; A. C. Black, 1961.

Glynn, Prudence. *In Fashion: Dress in the Twentieth Century.* London: George Allen and Unwin, 1978.

————. *Skin to Skin: Eroticism in Dress.* New York: Oxford University Press, 1982.

Gombrich, Ernst H. "Style." In *International Encyclopedia of the Social Sciences*, Vol. 15. New York: Macmillan, 1968.

————. "The Logic of Vanity Fair" and "In Search of Cultural History." In *Ideals and Idols: Essays on Values in History and Art.* Oxford: Phaidon Press, 1979.

————. *The Sense of Order: A Study in the Psychology of Decorative Art.* Ithaca, New York: Cornell University Press, 1979.

Gordon, Michael. "From an Unfortunate Necessity to a Cult of Mutual Orgasm: Sex in American Marital Education Literature, 1830–1940," in James M. Henslin, ed., *Studies in the Sociology of Sex.* New York: Appleton-Century-Crofts, 1971.

Gorham, Deborah. *The Victorian Girl and the Feminine Ideal.* Bloomington: Indiana University Press, 1982.

Gosselin, Chris and Glenn Wilson. *Sexual Variations: Fetishism, Sado-Masochism, and Transvestism.* London and Boston: Faber & Faber, 1980.

Gurel, Lois M., and Marianne S. Beeson, eds. *Dimensions of Dress and Adornment: A Book of Readings*. Dubuque, Iowa: Kendall/Hunt Publishing Co., 1975.

Hall, Carrie A. *From Hoopskirts to Nudity: A Review of the Follies and Foibles of Fashion, 1866–1936*. Caldwell, Idaho: Caxton Printers, 1938.

Hall-Duncan, Nancy. *The History of Fashion Photography*. New York: Alpine Book Company, 1979.

Haller, John S. and Robin M. *The Physician and Sexuality in Victorian America*. Urbana, Chicago, and London: University of Illinois Press, 1974.

Halttunen, Karen. *Confidence Men and Painted Women: A Study of Middle-Class Culture in America, 1830–1870*. New Haven and London: Yale University Press, 1982.

Hammond, Paul. *French Undressing: Naughty Postcards from 1900 to 1920*. London: Jupiter Books, 1976.

Harms, Ernst. "The Psychology of Clothes," *The American Journal of Sociology* 44 (September, 1938):239–250.

Harrison, Brian. "Underneath the Victorians," *Victorian Studies* 10 (March, 1967):239–262.

Harrison, Fraser. *The Dark Angel: Aspects of Victorian Sexuality*. New York: Universe Books, 1977.

Hiler, Hilaire and Meyer. *Bibliography of Costume*. New York: H. W. Wilson, 1939.

Hellerstein, Erna Olafson, Leslie Parker Hume, and Karen M. Offen, eds. *Victorian Women: A Documentary Account of Women's Lives in Nineteenth-Century England, France, and the United States*. Stanford: Stanford University Press, 1981.

Hiley, Michael. *Victorian Working Women: Portraits from Life*. London: Gordon Fraser, 1979; Boston: David R. Godine, 1979.

Hill, Margot Hamilton and Peter A. Bicknell. *The Evolution of Fashion: Pattern and Cut from 1066 to 1930*. London: B. T. Batsford, 1967.

Hinding, Andrea. *Women's History Sources, A Guide to the Archives and Manuscript Collections in the United States*. New York: R. P. Bowker Co., 1979.

Holden, Angus. *Elegant Modes in the Nineteenth Century*. London: George Allen and Unwin, 1935.

Holland, Vyvyan. *Hand Coloured Fashion Plates, 1770–1899*. London: B. T. Batsford, 1955.

Hollander, Anne. *Seeing Through Clothes*. New York: Viking Press, 1978.

Horn, Marilyn. *The Second Skin: An Interdisciplinary Study of Clothing*. Boston: Houghton Mifflin, 1968, 1975.

Horn, Pamela. *The Rise and Fall of the Victorian Servant*. New York: St. Martin's Press, 1975.

Houghton, Walter E. *The Victorian Frame of Mind: 1830–1870*. New Haven: Yale University Press, 1957.

Howe, Bea. *Arbiter of Elegance*. London: Harvill Press, 1967.

Hudson, Derek. *Munby: Man of Two Worlds. The Life and Diaries of Arthur J. Munby 1828–1910*. London: John Murray, 1972.

Huizinga, John. *Homo-Ludens: A Study of the Play Element in Culture*. London: Routledge and Kegan, Paul, 1949.

Hynes, Samuel. *The Edwardian Turn of Mind.* Princeton: Princeton University Press, 1968.

Jaher, Frederick Cople. "Nineteenth-Century Elites in Boston and New York." *Journal of Social History* 1 (Fall, 1972): 32–77.

Jenkyns, Richard. *The Victorians and Ancient Greece.* Oxford: Basil Blackwell, 1980.

Kayne, Madame. *The Corset in the Nineteenth and Eighteenth Centuries.* Brighton: Greenfields, n.d. [ca. 1932].

Kern, Stephen. *Anatomy and Destiny: A Cultural History of the Human Body.* New York: Bobbs-Merrill Co., 1975.

Kniebiehler, Yvonne. "Le Discours médical sur la femme: Constantes et ruptures," in *Mythes et représentations de la femme au dix-neuvieme siècle.* Special number of *Romantisme.* Paris: Librairie Honoré Champion, 1976.

Kohler, Carl. *A History of Costume.* New York: Dover, 1928, 1963.

König, Rene. *Macht und Reiz der Mode.* Dusseldorf and Vienna: Econ Verlag GmbH, 1971. Translated by F. Bradley, under the title *A La Mode: On the Social Psychology of Fashion.* New York: Seabury Press, 1973. Also published as *The Restless Image: A Sociology of Fashion.* London: Allen & Unwin, 1973.

König, Rene and Peter Schuppissed, eds. *Die Mode in der Menschlichengesellschaft.* Zurich: Modebuch-Verlagsgesellschaft, 1958.

Kroeber, A. L., and Jane Richardson, "Three Centuries of Women's Dress Fashions: A Quantitative Analysis" (1940). In A. L. Kroeber, ed., *The Nature of Culture.* Chicago: University of Chicago Press, 1955.

Kunzle, David. "The Corset as Erotic Alchemy: From Rococo Galanterie to Montaut's Psysiologies." In Thomas Hess and Linda Nochlin, ed., *Woman as Sex Object: Erotic Art, 1730–1970.* New York: Art News Annual 38, 1972.

———. "Dress Reform as Antifeminism: A Response to Helene E. Roberts's 'The Exquisite Slave'," *Signs: Journal of Woman in Culture and Society* 2 (Spring, 1977):570–579.

———. *Fashion and Fetishism: A Social History of the Corset, Tight-Lacing and Other Forms of Body Sculpture in the West.* Totowa, New Jersey: Rowman and Littlefield, 1980.

Langley Moore, Doris. *E. Nesbit: A Biography.* Philadelphia and New York: Chilton Books, 1966.

———. *The Woman in Fashion.* London: B. T. Batsford, 1949.

———. *Fashion Through Fashion Plates 1770–1970.* London: Ward, Lock, 1971.

Langner, Lawrence. *The Importance of Wearing Clothes.* New York: Hastings House, 1959.

Lartigue, J. H. *Diary of a Century.* London: Weidenfeld and Nicolson, 1970.

Latour, Anny. *Kings of Fashion.* London: Weidenfeld and Nicholson, 1958.

Lauer, Jeanette C. and Robert H. "The Battle of the Sexes: Fashion in 19th Century America," *Journal of Popular Culture* 13 (Spring, 1980): 581–589.

———. *Fashion Power: The Meaning of Fashion in American Society.* Englewood Cliffs, New Jersey: Prentice-Hall, 1981.

Laver, James. *Vulgar Society: The Romantic Career of James Tissot.* London; Constable, 1936.

———. *Taste and Fashion from the French Revolution to Today.* London: George G. Harrap and Co., 1937.

————. *Dress: How and Why Fashions in Men's and Women's Clothes have Changed during the Past Two Hundred Years*. London: John Murray, 1950.

————. *Clothes*. New York: Horizon, 1953.

————. *Edwardian Promenade*. London; Edward Hulton, 1958.

————. *Women's Dress in the Jazz Age*. London: Hamish Hamilton, 1964.

————. *Manners and Morals in the Age of Optimism 1848–1914*. New York: Harper and Row, 1966.

————. "Fashion, Art, and Beauty," in the Metropolitan Museum of Art *Bulletin* 26 (November, 1967):117–128.

————. *Modesty in Dress*. Boston: Houghton Mifflin, 1969.

————. *The Concise History of Costume and Fashion*. New York: Abrams, 1969; London: Thames and Hudson, 1969.

Leach, William. *True Love and Perfect Union: The Feminist Reform of Sex and Society*. London: Routledge & Kegan Paul, 1981.

Lebas, Catherine and Annie Jacques. *La Coiffure en France du Moyen Age à nos jours*. Paris: Delmas International S. S., 1979.

Leloir, Maurice. *Dictionnaire du costume et de ses accessoires, des armes et des étoffes des origines à nos jours*. Paris: Librairie Grund, 1951.

Leprevots, Anne-Francoise. *Memoire de fin d'étude: Bibliographie du costume*. Paris: Techniques de la Documentation, 1965.

Lester, Katherine M. and Oercke, Bess. *Accessories of Dress*. Peoria, Illinois: Manual Arts Press, 1942.

Levy, Howard S. *Chinese Footbinding: The History of a Curious Erotic Custom*. New York: W. Rawls, 1967.

Lougee, Carolyn C. *Le Paradis des Femmes. Women, Salons, and Social Stratification in Seventeenth-Century France*. Princeton: Princeton University Press, 1976.

Louys, Madeleine. *Le Costume pourquoi et comment*. Brussels: La Renaissance du Livre, 1967.

Lubell, Cecil. *Textile Collections of the World*. 3 volumes. New York: Van Nostrand Reinhold, 1976.

Magnus, Sherry. "Feet, Sex & Power ... The Last Erogenous Zone," *Vogue* (April, 1982): 284–285, 384–386.

Marandon, Sylvaine. *L'Image de la France dans l'Angleterre victoriènne 1848–1900*. Paris: Armand Colin, 1967.

Marcus, Stephen. *The Other Victorians: A Study of Sexuality and Pornography in Mid-Nineteenth Century England*. New York: Basic Books, Inc., 1964.

Marly, Diana de. *The History of Haute Couture 1850–1950*. New York: Holmes and Meier, 1980.

————. *Worth: Father of Haute Couture*. London: Elm Tree Books, 1980.

Martin, Peter. *Wasp Waists: A Study of Tight-Lacing in the 19th Century and Its Motives*. London: Published by the author, 1977.

Marwick, Arthur. *The Deluge: British Society and the First World War*. Harmondsworth, Middlesex: Penguin Books, 1967.

McKendrick, Neil. "The Commercialization of Fashion," in Neil McKendrick, John Brewer, and J. H. Plumb, *The Birth of a Consumer Society: The Commercialization of Eighteenth-Century England*. Bloomington: Indiana University Press, 1982.

McMillan, James F. *Housewife or Harlot: The Place of Women in French Society 1870–1940*. Brighton, Sussex: The Harvester Press, 1981.

Miller, Michael B. *The Bon Marché: Bourgeois Culture and the Department Store, 1869–1920*. Princeton, New Jersey: Princeton University Press, 1981.

Minnich, Helen Benton. "Fashion—The Glass of History." *The Bulletin of the Pasadena Art Institute* 4 (April, 1953): 1–19.

Mitchell, Juliet. *Psychoanalysis and Feminism: Freud, Reich, Laing and Women*. New York: Pantheon Books, 1974.

Moers, Ellen. *The Dandy*. New York: Viking Press, 1960; London: Secker and Warburg, 1960.

Morel, Juliette. *Lingerie Parisienne*. London: Academy Editions, 1976.

Morris, Bernadine. "A History of Discomfort; Told by Corsets," *The New York Times* (October 1, 1980).

Murray, Janet H., ed. *Strong-Minded Women and Other Lost Voices from Nineteenth-Century England*. New York: Pantheon Books, 1982.

Nanu, Adina. *Art, Style, Costume*. Bucharest: Meridiane Publishing House, 1981.

Neale, R. S. "'Middle-Class' Morality and the Systematic Colonizers." In *Class and Ideology in the Nineteenth Century*. London: Routledge & Kegan Paul, 1972.

Nevinson, John L. *Origins and Early History of the Fashion Plate*. U. S. National Museum Bulletin 250. Washington D. C.: Smithsonian Institution Press, 1969.

Newton, Stella Mary. *Health, Art, and Reason: Dress Reformers of the Nineteenth Century*. London: John Murray, 1974.

Norgaard, Erik. *When Ladies Acquired Legs*. London: Neville Spearman, 1967.

"Now About These Corsets," *Bizarre* 3 (1953).

Nystrom, Paul H. *Economics of Fashion*. New York: Ronald Press Co., 1928.

Ormond, Leonee. "Female Costume in the Aesthetic Movement of the 1870s and 1880s," *Costume: The Journal of the Costume Society* 2 (1968):33–38.

Ormond, Richard. *John Singer Sargent*. London: Phaidon, 1970; New York: Harper and Row, 1970.

—————, and James Lomax. *John Singer Sargent and the Edwardian Age*. Leeds Art Galleries, The National Portrait Gallery (London), and the Detroit Institute of Arts, 1979.

Osma, Guillermo de. *Mariano Fortuny: His Life and Work*. New York: Rizzoli International Publications, 1980.

Paoletti, Jo Barraclough. "Changes in the Masculine Image in the United States 1880–1910: A Content Analysis of Popular Humor About Dress." Ph.D. dissertation, University of Maryland, 1980.

Parisian Fashion from the "Journal des Dames et des Modes." 2 vols. Introduction by Cristina Nuzzi. New York: Rizzoli International Publications, 1979, 1980.

Pearce, Arthur W. *The Future Out of the Past: An Illustrated History of the Warner Brothers' Company on its 90th Anniversary*. Bridgeport, Conn.: The Warner Brothers Company, 1964.

Pearl, Cyril. *The Girl with the Swansdown Seat*. New York: The Bobbs-Merrill Co., 1956.

Pearsall, Ronald. *The Worm in the Bud: The World of Victorian Sexuality*. London: Weidenfeld and Nicolson, 1969; New York: Macmillan Co., 1969.

Perrot, Philippe. *Les Dessus et les Dessous de la bourgeoisie. Une histoire du vêtement au XIX*ᵉ *siècle*. Paris: Librairie Arthème Fayard, 1981.

Picken, Mary Brooks. *The Fashion Dictionary*. New York: Funk and Wagnalls, 1957.

————, and Dora Loues Miller. *Dressmakers of France*. New York: Harper and Brothers, 1956.

Polhemus, Ted, and Lynn Proctor. *Fashion and Anti-Fashion. An Anthropology of Clothing and Adornment*. London: Cox and Wyman, 1978.

Probert, Christina. *Lingerie in Vogue Since 1910*. New York: Abbeville Press, 1981.

Prown, Jules David. "Mind in Matter: An Introduction to Material Culture Theory and Method," *Winterthur Portfolio* 17 (Spring, 1982):1–19.

Quennell, J. M. "The World of Fashion." In Peter Quennell, ed. *Marcel Proust*. New York: Simon and Schuster, 1971.

Quennell, Peter. *Victorian Panorama. A Survey of Life and Fashion from Contemporary Photographs*. London: B. T. Batsford, 1937.

Richardson, Jane, and A. L. Kroeber, "Three Centuries of Women's Dress Fashions: A Quantitative Analysis," *Anthropological Records* Vol. 5, No. 2 (1940). Reprinted in Gordon Wills and David Midgley, eds., *Fashion Marketing*. London: George Allen & Unwin, Ltd., 1973, pp. 47–105

Richardson, Joanna. *The Courtesans: The Demi-monde in Nineteenth-Century France*. London: Weidenfeld and Nicholson, 1967.

————. *La Vie Parisienne 1852–1870*. New York: Viking Press, 1971.

Riegel, Robert E. "Women's Clothes and Women's Rights," *American Quarterly* 15 (Fall 1963):390–401.

Roach, Mary Ellen, and Joanne Eicher. *Dress, Adornment and the Social Order*. New York: John Wiley and Sons, 1965.

————. *The Visible Self: Perspectives on Dress*. Englewood Cliffs, New Jersey: Prentice-Hall, 1973.

Roberts, Helene E. "Submission, Masochism, Narcissism: Three Aspects of Women's Role as Reflected in Dress." In Virginia Lussier and Joyce Walstedt, ed., *Women's Lives: Perspectives on Progress and Change*. Newark, Delaware: University of Delaware, 1977.

————. "The Exquisite Slave: The Role of Clothes in the Making of the Victorian Woman," *Signs: Journal of Woman in Culture and Society* 2 (Spring, 1977):554–569.

Robertson, Priscilla. *An Experience of Women: Pattern and Change in Nineteenth-Century Europe*. Philadelphia: Temple University Press, 1982.

Robinson, Julian. *The Golden Age of Style*. New York and London: Harcourt Brace Jovanovich, 1976.

Robiquet, M. Jean. *La Femme dans la peinture française XVᵉ–XXᵉ siècle*. Paris: Les Éditions Nationales, 1938.

Romi. *Histoire pittoresque du pantalon féminin*. Paris: Jacques Grancher, 1979.

Roselle, Bruno du. *La Mode*. Paris: Imprimerie Nationale, 1980.

Rosenberg, Charles. "Sexuality, Class, and Role in Nineteenth-Century America," *The American Quarterly* vol. 25, no. 2 (May, 1973): 131–153.

Rosencranz, Mary Lou. *Clothing Concepts: A Social-Psychological Approach*. New York: Macmillan Co., 1972.

Roskill, Mark. "Early Impressionism and the Fashion Print," *Burlington Magazine* 112 (June, 1970): 390–395.

Ross, Noveline. *Manet's Bar at the Folies-Bergère and the Myths of Popular Illustration*. Ann Arbor, Michigan: UMI Research Press, 1982.

Rossi, William A. *The Sex Life of the Foot & Shoe*. London: Routledge and Kegan Paul, 1977.

Rudofsky, Bernard. *Are Clothes Modern?* Chicago: Paul Theobald, 1947.

————. *The Unfashionable Human Body*. Garden City, New York: Doubleday, 1971.

Ryan, Mary P. *Womanhood in America from Colonial Times to the Present*. New York: Franklin Watts, 1983.

Saint-Laurent, Cecil. *A History of Ladies Underwear*. London: Michael Joseph, 1966.

Saisselin, Remy Q. "From Baudelaire to Christian Dior: The Poetics of Fashion," *Journal of Aesthetics and Art Criticism* 18 (September, 1959):109–115.

Sapir, Edward. "Fashion." In *Encyclopedia of the Social Sciences*, Vol. 6. New York: Macmillan, 1931.

Sas, Isabella. *Corset Discipline*. n.p., n.d. (UK, 1970s).

Saunders, Ann, ed. *La Belle Epoch: Costume 1890–1914*. London: Published for the Costume Society, Victoria and Albert Museum, 1968.

————. *Early Victorian Costume 1830–1860*. London: Published for the Costume Society, Victoria and Albert Museum, 1969.

————. *High Victorian Costume, 1860–1890*. London: Published for the Costume Society, Victoria and Albert Museum, 1969.

Saunders, Edith. *The Age of Worth, Courturier to the Empress Eugenie*. London: Longmans, 1954; Bloomington: Indiana University Press, 1955.

Schapiro, Meyer. "Style." In A. L. Kroeber, ed., *Anthropology Today*. Chicago: University of Chicago Press, 1953.

Schwarz, Gerhart S., M.D. "Society, Physicians, and the Corset," *Bulletin of the New York Academy of Medicine* vol. 55 no. 6 (June, 1979): 551–590.

Smith, Bonnie G. *Ladies of the Leisure Class: The Bourgeoises of Northern France in the Nineteenth Century*. Princeton, New Jersey: Princeton University Press, 1981.

Smith, F. Barry. "Sexuality in Britain, 1800–1900: Some Suggested Revisions." In Martha Vicinus, ed. *A Widening Sphere: Changing Roles of Victorian Women*. Bloomington and London: Indiana University Press, 1977.

Spain, Nancy. *The Beeton Story*. London: Ward, Lock, & Co., 1956.

Spencer, Charles. *Erté*. London: Studio Vista, 1970; New York: Clarkson N. Potter, Inc., 1970.

————. *Leon Bakst*. London: Academy Editions, 1973.

Springer, Annemarie. "Women in French *Fin-de-Siècle* Posters." Ph.D. dissertation, Indiana University, 1971.

Squire, Geoffrey. *Dress, Art and Society, 1560–1970*. New York: Viking, 1974.

Stanton, Domna. *The Aristocrat as Art: A Study of the Honnête Homme and the Dandy in Seventeenth and Nineteenth-Century French Literature*. New York: Columbia University Press, 1980.

Stern, Madeleine B. *Heads & Headlines: The Phrenological Fowlers*. Norman: University of Oklahoma Press, 1971.

Stevenson, Pauline. *Edwardian Fashion*. London: Ian Allan, 1980.

Stockar, Jürg. *Zürich Mode durch die Jahrhunderte*. Zürich: Orell Füssli Verlag, 1974.

Thody, Philip. *Roland Barthes: A Conservative Estimate*. Atlantic Highlands, New Jersey: Humanities Press, 1977.

————. "The Semiotician in the Wardrobe," *TLS* (October 16, 1981):1199.

Tilly, Louise, and Joan Scott. *Women, Work, and Family.* New York: Holt, Rinehart, & Winston, 1978.

Toudouze, Georges Gustave. *Le Costume français.* Paris: Larousse, 1945.

Truc, Gonzague. *Histoire illustrée de la femme.* Paris: Librairie Plon, 1940.

Trudgill, Eric. *Madonnas and Magdalens: The Origins and Development of Victorian Sexual Attitudes.* New York: Holmes and Meier, 1976.

Tudesq, Andre-Jean. *Les Grands Notables en France. Étude historique d'une psychologie sociale.* 2 vols. Paris: Presses Universitaire de France, 1964.

Tweedsmuir, Susan. *The Edwardian Lady.* London: Gerald Duckworth and Co., 1966.

Ulrich, Laurel Thatcher. *Good Wives: Images and Reality in the Lives of Women in Northern New England, 1650–1750.* New York: Alfred A. Knopf, 1982.

Valotaire, Marcel. *Les Artistes du livre: Charles Martin.* Paris: Henry Babou, 1928.

Vanier, Henriette. *La Mode et ses métiers: Frivolités et luttes des classes, 1830–1870.* Paris: Armand Colin, 1960.

Vaudoyer, Jean-louis. *Les Artistes du livre: Georges Barbier.* Paris: Henry Babou, 1929.

Vedrés, Nicole. *Un Siècle d'elégance française.* Paris: Les Éditions du Chêne, 1943.

Vicinus, Martha, ed. *Suffer and Be Still: Women in the Victorian Age.* Bloomington and London, University of Indiana Press, 1973.

————. *A Widening Sphere: Changing Roles of Victorian Women.* Bloomington and London: University of Indiana Press, 1977.

Von Whiteman. *Looking Back at Fashion 1901–1939.* East Ardsky, Wakefield, West Yorkshire: E. P. Publishing Limited, 1978.

Vries, Leonard, and James Laver. *Victorian Advertisements.* London: John Murray, 1968.

Walkley, Christina, and Vanda Foster. *Crinolines and Crimping Irons. Victorian Clothes: How They were Cleaned and Cared For.* London: Peter Owen, 1978.

Warner, Deborah Jean. "Fashion, Emancipation, Reform, and the Rational Undergarment," *Dress. Journal of the American Costume Society* 4 (1978):24–29.

Waugh, Norah. *Corsets and Crinolines.* London: B. T. Batsford, 1954.

————. *The Cut of Women's Clothes, 1600–1930.* London: Faber & Faber, 1968.

Weeks, Jeffrey. *Sex, Politics and Society: The Regulation of Sexuality since 1800.* London and New York: Longman Group Limited, 1981.

White, Cynthia L. *Women's Magazines, 1693–1968.* London: Michael Joseph, 1970.

White, Palmer. *Poiret.* New York: Clarkson N. Potter, Inc., 1973.

Williams, Neville. *Powder and Paint: A History of the Englishwoman's Toilet.* London: Longman's, Green, and Co., 1957.

Wilson, Stephen. "Proust's 'A la recherche du temps perdu' as a Document of Social History," *The Journal of European Studies* 1 (1971):213–243.

Wright, Thomas. *The Romance of the Shoe.* London: C. J. Farncombe and Sons, 1922.

Yarwood, Doreen. *The Encyclopedia of World Costume.* New York: Charles Scribner's Sons, 1978.

Yooll, Emily. *The History of the Corset.* London: Gossard Ltd., 1946.

Young, Agnes Brooks. *Recurring Cycles of Fashion 1760–1937.* New York: Harper and Bros., 1937; Reprint. New York: Cooper Square, 1966.

Zelden, Theodore, ed. *Conflicts in French Society: Anticlericalism, Education and Morals in the Nineteenth Century.* London: George Allen and Unwin, 1970.

————. *France: 1848–1945.* Volume 1. *Ambition, Love, and Politics.* Volume 1I. *Intellect, Taste, and Anxiety.* Oxford: Oxford University Press, 1973, 1977.

Zilliacus, Benedict. *The Corset.* Translated by Fred A. Fewster. Helsinki: Frenckellska Try Okeri Ab, 1963.

VII. Exhibition Catalogs

Brooklyn. The Brooklyn Museum. *Two Centuries of French Fashion.* Text by Michelle Murphy. 1949.

————. *The House of Worth.* Text by Robert Riley. 1962.

————. *Changing Fashions 1800–1970.* Text by Elizabeth Ann Coleman. 1972.

Brussels. Musée du Costume et de la Dentelle. *Dentelle de Bruxelles.* Text by A. Smolar-Meynart and A. Vincke. 1982.

Chicago. Chicago Historical Society. *Eight Chicago Women and Their Fashions 1860–1929.* Text by Elizabeth Jachimowicz. 1978.

Cognac. Musée Municipal de Cognac. *La Mode en 1900.* 1966.

Courbevois. Musée Roybet-Fould. *La Mode au temps des dimanches à la Grande Jatte.* Text by Yvonne Deslandres. 1973.

Durham, North Carolina. Duke University Museum of Art. *From Slave to Siren: The Victorian Woman and her Jewelry from Neoclassic to Art Nouveau.* Text by Dora Jane Jansen. 1971.

Edinburgh. Scottish National Portrait Gallery and The National Museum of Antiquities of Scotland. *Van Dyck in Check Trousers: Fancy Dress in Art and Life, 1700–1900.* Text by Sara Stevenson and Helen Bennett. 1978.

Edinburgh and London. Scottish Arts Council and The Victoria and Albert Museum. *Fashion, 1900–1939.* Text by Madge Garland, Madeleine Ginsberg, Martin Battersby, Valerie Lloyd, and Ivor Davies. 1975.

Hanover, New Hampshire. Dartmouth College Museum and Galleries. *Women's Clothing & Accessories 1800–1930.* Text by Margaret E. Spicer. 1979.

Hartford. The Wadsworth Atheneum. *Dress from Three Centuries.* Text by J. Herbert Callister. 1976.

Kyoto. Kyoto Costume Institute and the National Museum of Modern Art. *Rōman Ishō Ten: Evolution of Fashion 1835–1895.* 1980.

Leicester. Leicestershire Museum and Art Gallery. *Foundations of Fashion: The Symington Collection. Corsetry from 1856 to the Present Day.* Text by Christopher Page. 1981.

Liege. Musée de la vie Wallonne. *Parures et métiers de la femme au XIXe siècle.* 1977.

Liverpool. Merseyside County Museum. *High Society. A display of formal dress for fashionable people, 1875–1920.* Text by Anthea Jarvis. 1980.

―――――. *Liverpool Fashion: Its Makers and Wearers. The Dress Making Trade in Liverpool 1830–1940.* Text by Anthea Jarvis. 1981.

London. The Crafts Council. *The Shoe Show: British Shoes since 1790.* Text by Ken and Kate Baynes. 1979.

London. Victorian and Albert Museum. *Liberty's 1875–1975: An Exhibition to Mark the Firm's Centenary.* 1975.

Manchester. Gallery of English Costume. *Women's Costume 1870–1900.* Text by Anne Buck. 1953.

―――――. *Women's Costume 1900–1930.* Text by Anne Buck. 1956.

New York. Fashion Institute of Technology and Kyoto Costume Institute. *The Undercover Story.* Text by Richard McComb and Cora Ginsburg. 1982.

New York. Museum of the City of New York. *The House of Worth: The Gilded Age 1860–1918.* Text by Jo Anne Olian. 1982.

New York. The Metropolitan Museum of Art, The Costume Institute. *Inventive Paris Clothes 1909–1939: A Photographic Essay by Irving Penn.* Text by Diana Vreeland. 1977.

Paris. Galerie de Luxembourg. *Illustrateurs des modes et manières en 1925.* 1973.

Paris. Musée du costume de la Ville de Paris. *Poufs et tournures. Costumes français de femmes et d'enfants 1869–1889.* 1954.

―――――. *Modes de la Belle Epoque. Costumes français 1890–1910 et portraits.* Text by Madeleine Delpierre. 1961.

―――――. *Grands Couturiers parisiens 1910–1939.* Text by Madeleine Delpierre and Henriette Vanier. 1965.

―――――. *Elégantes Parisiennes au temps de Marcel Proust 1890–1916.* Text by Madeleine Delpierre and Henriette Vanier. 1968.

Paris. Musée Jacquemart-Andre. *Poiret le magnifique.* 1974.

Paris. Musée de la Mode et du Costume. *Secrets d'élégance (1750–1950).* Text by Madeleine Delpierre and Fabienne Falluel. 1978.

―――――. *Chapeaux 1750–1960.* Text by Madeleine Delpierre and Fabienne Falluel. 1980.

―――――. *La Mode et ses métiers du XVIIIe siècle à nos jours.* Text by Madeleine Delpierre. 1981.

Paris. Musée Nissim de Camondo. *La Mode au Parc Monceau epoque Napoleon III.* 1981.

Santa Barbara, California. University of California at Santa Barbara Art Museum. *The Cult of Images (Le Cult des Images): Baudelaire and the 19th Century Media Explosion.* Organized by Beatrice Farwell. 1977.

Washington, D.C. The National Museum of American History, The Smithsonian Institution. *Suiting Everyone: The Democratization of Clothing in America.* Text by Claudia Kidwell and Margaret Christman. 1974.

Williamstown, Massachusetts. The Sterling and Francine Clark Art Institute. *The Elegant Academics: Chroniclers of Nineteenth-Century Parisian Life.* Introduction by William Gavin. 1974.

Index

Page numbers in italic refer to illustrations.